# GENDER, PLACE AND MEMORY IN THE MODERN JEWISH EXPERIENCE

# PARKES-WIENER SERIES ON JEWISH STUDIES
Series Editors: David Cesarani and Tony Kushner
ISSN 1368-5449

The field of Jewish Studies is one of the youngest, but fastest growing and most exciting areas of scholarship in the academic world today. Named after James Parkes and Alfred Wiener, this series aims to publish new research in the field and student materials for use in the seminar room, to disseminate the latest work of established scholars and to re-issue classic studies which are currently out of print.

The selection of publications reflects the international character and diversity of Jewish Studies; it ranges over Jewish history from Abraham to modern Zionism, and Jewish culture from Moses to postmodernism. The series also reflects the interdisciplinary approach inherent in Jewish Studies and at the cutting edge of contemporary scholarship, and provides an outlet for innovative work on the interface between Judaism and ethnicity, popular culture, gender, class, space and memory.

## Other Books in the Series

Holocaust Literature: Schulz, Levi, Spiegelman and the Memory of the Offence
*Gillian Banner*

Remembering Cable Street: Fascism and Anti-Fascism in British Society
*Edited by Tony Kushner and Nadia Valman*

Sir Sidney Hamburger and Manchester Jewry: Religion, City and Community
*Bill Williams*

Anglo-Jewry in Changing Times: Studies in Diversity 1840–1914
*Israel Finestein*

Double Jeopardy: Gender and the Holocaust
*Judith Tydor Baumel*

Cultures of Ambivalence and Contempt: Studies in Jewish–Non-Jewish Relations
*Edited by Siân Jones, Tony Kushner and Sarah Pearce*

Alfred Wiener and the Making of the Wiener Library
*Ben Barkow*

The Berlin Haskalah and German Religious Thought: Orphans of Knowledge
*David Sorkin*

Myths in Israeli Culture: Captives of a Dream
*Nurith Gertz*

The Jewish Immigrant in England 1870–1914, Third Edition
*Lloyd P. Gartner*

State and Society in Roman Galilee, AD 132–212, Second Edition
*Martin Goodman*

Disraeli's Jewishness
*Edited by Todd M. Endelman*

Claude Montefiore: His Life and Thought
*Daniel R. Langton*

# Gender, Place and Memory in the Modern Jewish Experience

*Re-placing Ourselves*

Editors

**JUDITH TYDOR BAUMEL
TOVA COHEN**

VALLENTINE MITCHELL
LONDON • PORTLAND, OR

*First published in 2003 in Great Britain by*
VALLENTINE MITCHELL PUBLISHERS
Crown House, 47 Chase Side, Southgate
London N14 5BP

*and in the United States of America by*
VALLENTINE MITCHELL PUBLISHERS
c/o ISBS, 920 NE 58th Avenue, Suite 300
Portland, Oregon, 97213-3786

*Website*: www.vmbooks.com

Copyright collection ©2003 Frank Cass & Co. Ltd
Copyright chapters © 2003 Contributors

British Library Cataloguing in Publication Data

Gender, place and memory in the modern Jewish experience:
 replacing ourselves. – (Parkes-Wiener series on Jewish studies)
 1. Jewish women – History – 20th century 2. Jewish women –
 Europe – History – 20th century 3. Jewish women in the
 Holocaust 4. Jewish women – United States 5. Jewish women –
 Israel 6. Jews – Identity 7. Sex role – History – 20th
 century 8. Identity (Psychology)
 I. Baumel, Judith Tydor II. Cohen, Tova
 305.4'8924

ISBN 0-85303-4885 (cloth)
ISBN 0-85303-4893 (paper)
ISSN 1368-5449

Library of Congress Cataloging-in-Publication Data

Gender, place, and memory in the modern Jewish experience / editors, Judith Tydor
 Baumel and Tova Cohen.
  p. cm. – (Parkes-Wiener series on Jewish studies)
  Includes bibliographical references and index.
  ISBN 0-85303-488-5 (cloth) – ISBN 0-85303-489-3 (pbk.)
   1. Jews – Identity. 2. Jews – Europe – Identity. 3. Jews – United States – Identity.
 4. Jews – Israel – Identity. 5. Gender identity. 6. Jewish women authors – United States.
 7. Jewish women – Social conditions – 20th century. 8. Women – Israel. I. Baumel, Judith
 Tydor, 1959– II. Cohen, Tova. II. Series.

DS143.G36 2003
909'.04924'0082 – dc21

2003051212

*This book was published with the generous assistance of the Fanya Gottesfeld Heller Institute for the Study of Women in Judaism at Bar-Ilan University.*

*All rights reserved. No part of this publication may be reproduced, stored in or introduced into a retrieval system or transmitted in any form or by any means, electronic, mechanical, photocopying, recording or otherwise, without the prior written permission of the publisher of this book.*

Typeset in Janson 11/13pt by Frank Cass Publishers
Printed in Great Britain by MPG Books Ltd, Victoria Square, Bodmin, Cornwall

# Contents

| | | |
|---|---|---|
| List of Figures | | ix |
| Notes on Contributors | | xi |
| Foreword | *Professor Paula E. Hyman* | xvii |
| Introduction | *Judith Tydor Baumel and Tova Cohen* | xix |

## PART I
## PREWAR EUROPE, THE HOLOCAUST AND THE SECOND WORLD WAR

| | | | |
|---|---|---|---|
| 1 | Woman? Youth? Jew? – The Search for Identity of Jewish Young Women in Interwar Poland | *Gershon Bacon* | 3 |
| 2 | Her View Through My Lens: Cecilia Slepak Studies Women in the Warsaw Ghetto | *Dalia Ofer* | 29 |
| 3 | The Forgotten Leadership: Women Leaders of the Hashomer Hatzair Youth Movement at Times of Crisis | *Eli Tzur* | 51 |
| 4 | Family Origins and Political Motivations of Jewish Resistance Fighters in German-Occupied Europe | *Ingrid Strobl* | 67 |

5  Gendered Perceptions and Self-Perceptions
   of Memory and Revenge: Jewish DPs in
   Occupied Postwar Germany as Victims,
   Villains and Survivors           *Atina Grossmann*        78

6  Oblivion Without Guilt: The Holocaust
   and Memories of the Second World War
   in Finland                       *Petri J. Raivo*        108

7  Engendered Oblivion: Commemorating
   Jewish Inmates at the Ravensbrueck
   Memorial 1945–95                 *Insa Eschebach*        126

## PART II
## THE UNITED STATES

8  'The Girl I Was': The Construction of
   Memory in Fiction by American
   Jewish Women                     *Sylvia Barack Fishman*  145

9  The Impact of Gender on the Leading
   American Zionist Organizations   *Mira Katzburg-Yungman*  165

10 Post-Holocaust Memory:
   Some Gendered Reflections        *Debra Kaufman*         187

## PART III
## ZIONISM, THE YISHUV AND THE STATE OF ISRAEL

11 Girls in the Zionist Youth Movements
   in Libya                         *Rachel Simon*          199

12 The West in the East: Patterns of
   Cultural Change as a Personal
   Kibbutz Experience               *Esther Meir-Glitzenstein*  213

13 Women's Names and Place(s):
   Exploring the Map of Israel      *Shulamit Reinharz*     240

14  A Tale of Two Monuments            *Maoz Azaryahu*    252

15  Time, Place, Gender and Memory:
    From the Perspective of an Israeli
    Psychologist                       *Amia Lieblich*    269

Index                                                     287

# *Figures*

| | | |
|---|---|---|
| Figure 6.1 | Area of the Jewish cemetery in Helsinki dedicated to commemoration of those killed in the wars of 1939–44. | 115 |
| Figure 6.2 | The memorial erected in the Jewish war cemetery. | 115 |
| Figure 6.3 | 'Apua hakevat kädet' (Hands seeking for help), a memorial dedicated to the eight Jewish refugees expelled from Finland in 1942 who then died as victims of the Holocaust in the Birkenau concentration camp. | 123 |
| Figure 7.1 | 'Woman, carrying' (Will Lammert), erected at the Ravensbrueck Memorial Site in 1959. | 127 |
| Figure 7.2 | 'Ravensbrueck group of mothers' (Fritz Cremer), erected at the Ravensbrueck Memorial Site in 1965. | 127 |
| Figure 7.3 | 'Buckenwald-Memorial' (Fritz Cremer), erected at the Buchenwald Memorial Site in 1958. | 129 |
| Figure 7.4 | 'The Mother' (Arndt Wittig), erected at the Neubrandenburg Memorial Site in 1976. | 129 |
| Figure 7.5 | 'Mother' (Gerhard Thieme), placed near the city of Schwerin in 1973. | 131 |
| Figure 7.6 | 'Germany, pale Mother' (Fritz Cremer), erected in 1964 at the Mauthausen Memorial site. | 131 |
| Figure 7.7 | 'Mother with dead son' (Käthe Kollwitz), created in 1937. | 132 |
| Figure 7.8 | A swearing-in ceremony for soldiers of the National People's Army at the Ravensbrueck Memorial Site in 1979. | 136 |
| Figure 7.9 | Soviet soldiers carrying members of the Communist Youth League in their arms on the occasion of the 40th anniversary of the concentration camp's liberation on April 20, 1985, Ravensbrueck Memorial Site. | 136 |

| | | |
|---|---|---|
| Figure 7.10 | Memorial stone, placed at the Ravensbrueck Memorial Site in 1988. | 138 |
| Figure 14.1 | Batya Lichansky working on top of the Work and Defense monument, 1937. | 258 |
| Figure 14.2 | Chana Orloff, on top of the ladder, while the Ein Gev monument is being put in place. | 259 |

# Notes on Contributors

*Maoz Azaryahu* is a senior lecturer at the Department of Geography, University of Haifa. His research interests include the geography of national memory in Germany and in Israel, and the cultural history of landscapes and places in Israel.

*Gershon Bacon* is an Associate Professor of Jewish History at Bar-Ilan University, where he holds the Klein Chair for the History of the Rabbinate in Europe during the Modern Period. His areas of research are the social, political and religious history of Polish Jewry in the nineteenth and twentieth centuries. Among his best known works are *The Politics of Tradition: Agudat Yisrael in Poland 1916–1939* (1996) and *The Jews in Poland and Russia: Bibliographical Essays* (1984).

*Judith Tydor Baumel* is an Associate Professor of Jewish History at Bar-Ilan University. She received her PhD from Bar-Ilan University where she teaches in the Department of Jewish History. Her topics of interest are gender, representation, Holocaust, and State of Israel studies. She has written several books on these topics including *Double Jeopardy: Gender and the Holocaust* (Vallentine Mitchell, 1998) and is associate editor (together with Walter Laqueur) of *The Holocaust Encyclopedia* (Yale, 2001).

*Tova Cohen* is a Full Professor of Hebrew Literature at Bar-Ilan University, specializing in nineteenth-century Hebrew literature and Jewish women's writings during the nineteenth and twentieth century. Since 1998 she has been the director of the Fanya Gottesfeld Heller Center for the Study of Women in Judaism at Bar-Ilan University. Her books deal with various aspects of literature of the Jewish Enlightenment during the nineteenth century and her recent publications with topics of gender.

*Insa Eschebach* DPhil, is historian at the memorial site and museum Neuengamme, Hamburg, Germany. She has published on the field of postwar memory and gender images, and is co-editor of the book: *Gedächtnis und Geschlecht. Deutungsmuster in Darstellungen des nationalsozialistischen Genozids* (Frankfurt am Main, 2002).

*Sylvia Barack Fishman* is Associate Professor of Contemporary Jewish Life in the Near Eastern and Judaic Studies Department, and co-director of the Hadassah International Research Institute on Jewish Women, both at Brandeis. Her new book, *Jewish Life and American Culture*, explores the way American Jews negotiate the Jewish and secular pieces of their lives, using both statistics and interview data in this comprehensive sociology of American Jewish communities. Her May 2001 monograph, *Jewish and Something Else: A Study of Mixed Married Families*, is the first systematic interview research on interfaith family life. Professor Fishman's earlier books include *A Breath of Life: Feminism in the American Jewish Community*, which was named a 1994 Honor Book by the National Jewish Book Council, and *Follow My Footprints: Changing Images of Women in American Jewish Fiction*. She has written numerous articles on Jewish families today, American Jewish identity, Jewish education, Jews in fiction and film, and changing roles of Jewish women. She earned her PhD from Washington University in St Louis, where she received a Danforth Fellowship, and did her undergraduate work at Yeshiva University's Stern College for Women, which presented her with the Samuel Belkin Award for Distinguished Professional Achievement.

*Atina Grossmann* is Associate Professor of History at the Cooper Union in New York City where she teaches modern European history and gender studies. Her publications include *Reforming Sex: The German Movement for Birth Control and Abortion Reform, 1920–1950* (New York, 1995, 1997), *A Question of Silence: The Rape of German Women by Occupation Soldiers*, (Ann Arbor, 1997), *Trauma, Memory and Motherhood: Germans and Jewish Displaced Persons in Post-Nazi Germany, 1945–1949* (Archiv für Sozialgeschichte, 1998) and *Crimes of War: Guilt and Denial in the Twentieth Century* (co-editor with Bartov and Nolan, New York, 2002). She is working on *Victims, Victors, and Survivors: Germans, Allies, and Jews in Occupied Postwar Germany, 1945–1949* (forthcoming Princeton, 2003).

*Mira Katzburg-Yungman* is an Israeli who received her education at the

Hebrew University of Jerusalem. She is the author of a forthcoming book on the history of Hadassah (to be published in 2004 by the Littman Library of Jewish Civilization) and of various articles on American and English Zionism, the co-editor of *American Jewry*, an annotated source book on German and eastern European emigration, translated into Hebrew. She is also the editor of *American Jewry, 1914–1950*, a forthcoming bilingual anthology of sources and articles, with introductions and annotations. Mira Katzburg-Yungman is in charge of developing and teaching academic courses on American Jewry by distance education at the Open University of Israel.

*Debra Renee Kaufman* is the Director of Jewish Studies, a Matthews Distinguished Professor and Professor of Sociology at Northeastern University. She was the former Coordinator and founder of the Women's Studies Program there as well. Her most recent visiting professorship was at Oxford University where she was a member of the Centre for Hebrew and Jewish Studies. Her many published articles and chapters range widely across feminist and gender issues in the family, the workplace, religion and feminist theory and methodology. Among her most notable books are *Achievement and Women* (co-authored with Barbara Richardson) which received honorable mention for the C. Wright Mills award for notable contributions to sociological thought, and *Rachel's Daughters: Newly Orthodox Jewish Women*, which was nominated for the Jesse Bernard Sociologists for Women in Society Award and the E. H. Cooley Social Psychology Award, and was a featured book for the Jewish Book Publications. Other publications include a special edited edition of *Contemporary Jewry*, entitled: 'Women, Scholarship and the Holocaust' and several chapters and journal articles on post-Holocaust Jewish identity among young adults between 20 and 30 years of age in the United States, Great Britain and Israel.

*Amia Lieblich* teaches in the Department of Psychology at The Hebrew University, Jerusalem. Born in Israel, Professor Lieblich received her PhD in Psychology from the Hebrew University, where she is now teaching and doing her research. She has been one of the pioneers in teaching the psychology of gender and studying gender in Israel. Her studies focus on psychological aspects of Israeli society – mainly the effects of the war on the lives of Israelis and the life of individuals and the community in the kibbutz – using qualitative methods of research. Together with Ruth Ellen Josselson and Dan McAdams she edits the annual series of 'The Narrative Study of Lives'.

*Esther Meir-Glitzenstein* is a research fellow at the Ben-Gurion Research Center at Sde Boker, and a Lecturer at the History Department, Ben-Gurion University of the Negev. Her recent research deals with Iraqi immigrants in Israel in the political, social and economic fields, including questions of memory and identity. Her book *Zionism and the Jews in Iraq 1941–1950* was published by Am Oved publishers (Tel Aviv, 1993).

*Dalia Ofer* is a Max and Rita Haber Professor of Holocaust and East European Studies, at the Avraham Harman Institute of Contemporary Jewry, Hebrew University of Jerusalem, and the academic head of the Vidal Sassoon International Center for the Study of Antisemitism. She published extensively on the Holocaust in eastern Europe, on immigration to Palestine and Israel and on the memory of the Holocaust in Israel and the development of the patterns of commemoration. She serves as the Hebrew University representative in the academic committee of Yad Vashem and in the board of the International Research Institute of Yad Vashem. She is the Head of the Board of Directors of the Hebrew University High School. Her recent book together with Lenore J. Weitzman, *Women in the Holocaust* (Yale University Press, 1998), was nominated among the three finalists to the Jewish Book Award, 1999 in both Holocaust and Women categories. Her book *Escaping the Holocaust: Illegal Immigration to the land of Israel* (Oxford University Press, 1991) won the Jewish Book Award in 1992 and the Hebrew edition of the book received the Ben Zvi Award of the same year. In 1996 she published together with Hannah Wiener, *The Dead-End Journey: The Tragic Story of the Kladovo-Sabac Group* (Lanham: University Press of America). In 1997 she edited *New Immigrants and Veterans in the Mass Immigration to Israel, 1948–1952* (Jerusalem: Yad Ben Zvi).

*Petri J. Raivo*, PhD, is Docent in Cultural and Landscape Geography at the University of Oulu in Finland. He is currently working as a Research Fellow of the Finnish Academy in a project 'Historical Landscapes and Geographical Memory' (Finnish Academy project 48572), where his research activities are concerned with the nationalistic landscapes of war and conflicts.

*Shulamit Reinharz* is the Jacob Potofsky Professor of Sociology at Brandeis University. Between 1991 and 2001 she was the Director of the Women's Studies program, and created a graduate program which included one of the first MA programs in Jewish Women's Studies. In

1997, she created the Hadassah International Research Institute on Jewish Women (HIRIJW); and in 2001, she opened a building called the Women's Studies Research Center, to house the HIRIJW and other programs she founded. Her last book, *Feminist Methods in Social Research* (Oxford, 1992) won several prizes.

*Rachel Simon*, PhD, is an independent scholar at Princeton, studying Jewish communities in the modern Middle East and North Africa, with special reference to Libya, gender issues, education and Zionism. She has published numerous articles in the field and the book *Change Within Tradition among Jewish Women in Libya* (Seattle: University of Washington Press, 1992).

*Ingrid Strobl*, PhD, born in 1952 in Innsbruck, Austria; studied German Language and Literature and Art History in Innsbruck and Vienna. Doctoral dissertation: Rhetorik im Dritten Reich (Rhetoric in the Third Reich). Lives as a freelance researcher and author in Cologne; doing research work, publishing books and making film documentaries primarily on the topic of Jewish resistance/the resistance of Jewish women against the German occupation and 'Final Solution'. Her latest publication: *Die Angst kam erst danach. Jüdische Frauen im Widerstand in Europa 1933–1945* (Fear Came Later. Jewish Women in Resistance in Europe, 1938–1945) (Frankfurt am Main, 1998).

*Eli Tzur* studied at the London School of Economics and received his PhD from Tel Aviv University. He teaches Jewish History at the Academic College Seminar Hakibbutzim and specializes in the history of the Jewish and Israeli labor movement. He heads the Institute for the History of the Youth Movements at Givat Haviva. He is the author of *The Fields of Illusion: Mapam 1948–1954* and the recently published *Guardian of Israel*, a biography of General David Shaltiel. His forthcoming book deals with the history of the Hashomer Hatzair Movement in Poland during the 1930s.

# *Foreword*

Women's Studies, which focuses on the interpretation of women's experience and of the cultural representation of women, has entered a new phase. This book, in fact, demonstrates the transformation of feminist scholarship in the course of the past decade. When the pioneers in Women's Studies conducted the first research in the field, their goals were largely compensatory. They wanted to discover, and recover, the women whose history and accomplishments had been defined as insignificant, primarily by the historians whose work determined such matters. They wanted to restore women's voices in history. Never asking about women and their roles, not surprisingly, scholars never 'saw' them as historical actors or as members of a group whose status much mattered. They never heard what they had to say.

Even in the earliest years of feminist scholarship, however, there were claims made for the significance of the field of Women's Studies for the general understanding of history and culture. Gerda Lerner, the doyenne of Women's History in the United States, is well known for her comment that investigating the history of women required something more than 'add women and stir'. The inclusion of female voices, female experience, and reflections on the nature and status of women in the writing of history, sociology, and literary criticism, she argued, would challenge the conventional wisdom that a scholarship that considered only the voices, experience, and the nature and status of men had propagated. As the past three decades of feminist scholarship have demonstrated, the earliest hopes for the transformative nature of Women's Studies have been realized. In the case of Jewish Studies, feminist scholarship has not only recovered women's voices and experience, it has questioned the very definition of Judaism itself, as essentially a collection of canonical texts studies and interpreted by male leaders, the rabbis, and has complicated our understanding of such issues in the modern period as assimilation and the nature of Jewish politics.

Most importantly, feminist scholars have introduced the term 'gender' as an analytical tool. The social construction of the differences between the sexes, gender points to the interaction of the sexes and foregrounds the issues of the distribution and deployment of power in society. Because power underlies human experience on both the personal and social level, investigating gender norms and relations provides an insight into the very essence of historical, literary and psychological research. With gender as its primary analytical tool, Women's Studies has become increasingly multi-disciplinary. Moreover, Women's Studies increasingly draws on a body of theoretical, often philosophically based, literature that serves to integrate it within the scholarship in general fields.

This volume on gender, place, and memory is a splendid example of how the focus on gender providesa key to understanding a variety of manifestation of Jewish identity and memory. Moving beyond the often-heard complaint that women's voices and experience have been ignored, it reflects new research that inserts women and gender concerns into the scholarly discourse on the Holocaust and on the historical development of American and Israeli Jews. These sophisticated studies implicitly reveal the consequences of the prior omission of women from historical and literary reflection and challenge all readers to reconsider the dimensions of the Jewish experience in the past century.

*Paula E. Hyman*

# *Introduction*

## JUDITH TYDOR BAUMEL and TOVA COHEN

The challenges of modernity, with its social constructs, political co-ordinates, national aspirations, and issues of class and gender, have made the issue of understanding oneself into a complex task. Yet, who we are, where we come from and how we remember our past remain three of the most central components of human identity. Determining the boundaries of Jewish identity is even more difficult, particularly in the modern era, which has become one of choice. In certain cases, being Jewish is still a pivotal part of a person's self-definition. For others, it is but one of a number of factors of which the personal whole is now composed. For a third group, the 'Jewish' factor in the 'Modern Jewish experience' is little more than a whiff of memory, a recollection of a grandmother lighting Sabbath candles, smells of a Friday night dinner, the nostalgic recalling of a past which may play little part in one's future.

Different memories of different places and different gendered experiences provide the backdrop to understanding the variation of Jewish life and identity. These places and experiences shade Jewish memories in a myriad of shades, forming the rainbow of colors of which modern Jewish life is composed. The starting point of this volume is the juxtaposition of these three factors – gender, place and memory – and the attempt to understand the roles that they played in creating what we know of as the modern Jewish experience. The original impetus for the idea to publish a volume of collected essays on this topic was an interdisciplinary conference held at Bar-Ilan University in Ramat-Gan in January 2001. Bringing together scholars from three continents, the conference created the fertile atmosphere in which this volume began to evolve. The articles appearing in this volume are based, in part, on a number of the conference papers, and we are pleased that their authors have agreed to participate in this project.

Given the importance of place and history in this collection, the articles in this book are divided according to three geographical/historical coordinates. The first is Europe prior to and during the Second World War, the second is the United States, and the third is the Zionist movement, the Yishuv and the State of Israel.

The volume opens with seven articles that deal with the European arena. Several of the articles focus upon the gendered social and political history of European Jewry during the 1920s, 1930s, and 1940s. Other articles in this section deal with issues of memory, commemoration and representation, drawing primarily upon social history and historical geography. Gershon Bacon of Bar-Ilan University explores the search for identity among Jewish young women in interwar Poland, using the Yivo collection of autobiographies as a starting point in an attempt to determine the major components of which such young women's identities were composed. Moving into the Holocaust period, Dalia Ofer of the Hebrew University discusses Cecilia Slepak's studies of women's lives under adversity, conducted in the Warsaw Ghetto during the early 1940s. A member of the *Oneg Shabbat* underground documentation project, Slepak carried out what appears to be the only wartime sociological studies of girls and women in a ghetto during the Holocaust. Eli Tzur of Giv'at Haviva and Seminar Hakibbutzim, analyzes three cases of women's political leadership in the Zionist Hashomer Hatzair movement in wartime, examining their historical roots and asking why in only one instance did the attempt for a complete women's alternative leadership succeed. The concept of gendered social and political history during the Holocaust is continued by Ingrid Strobl of the Chaika Grossman Archives, who combines a series of interviews with historical documentation in order to probe the family history and political motivations of women active as resistance fighters in German-occupied Europe. Atina Grossmann of the Remarque Institute at NYU and Cooper Union, moves us into the postwar period, with an article that examines the lives of the Jewish Displaced Persons from a gendered viewpoint, and focuses on the dual issues of memory and revenge. Two articles dealing with memory and plastic commemoration conclude this section. Petri J. Raivo of Oulu University explores the memories of the Holocaust and the Second World War in Finland. Examining written and figurative memorials throughout Finland, he probes the issue of war and memory in a country which lost only eight of its Jews by deportation during the Second World War. Insa Eschebach of the Humboldt University examines half a century of commemoration of Jewish Inmates at the Ravensbrueck Memorial, erected by the German government after the war on the site of the women's concentration camp of the same name.

## Introduction

The volume's second geographical locus is the United States. The articles included in this section examine the issues of gender and memory from the vantage point of three disciplines: literature, history and sociology. Sylvia Barack Fishman of Brandeis University probes the construction of memory in fiction by American Jewish women writers. Focusing upon texts by Tillie Olsen and Rebecca Goldstein, she shows how the 30 years separating the texts create a new construct of Jewish women's identity and memory. Mira Katzburg-Yungman of the Open University in Israel explores the role played by the gender issue in the history of Hadassah, the leading American Zionist women's organization asking whether the organization indeed exhibited 'female' characteristics. Closing this section, Debra Kaufman of Northeastern University discusses her sociological study of post-Holocaust memory among young American-Jewish males and females.

The final section of the book is composed of five essays, focusing on Zionism, the Yishuv and the State of Israel. Articles in this section examine gendered issues of history and memory from the vantage points of history, sociology, historical geography and psychology. Rachel Simon of Princeton University discusses the lives of girls in Libya and the roles they played in the Zionist Youth Movements in that country during the 1940s. Among the topics she explores are the special problems arising from the creation of a mixed-sex Zionist youth movement in a traditional North-African society. Esther Meir-Glitzenstein of Ben-Gurion University at Sde Boker re-creates the experiences of young Oriental Jewish women on kibbutzim during the 1940s and 1950s, utilizing their letters and diaries in order to present readers with undiluted first person experiences. In a gendered re-reading of geography and topography from the sociological viewpoint, Shulamit Reinharz of Brandeis University explores the map of Israel, noting the number of settlements named for women and examining their significance in a geographical and sociological context. Maoz Azaryahu of the University of Haifa delineates the history of two monuments in Israel fashioned by famous women sculptors – the fighters' memory at Hulda created by Batya Lichansky and the memorial of a mother and child at Ein Gev, created by Chana Orloff – comparing their motifs from a gendered perspective. The volume closes with a reflective essay by Amia Lieblich of the Hebrew University, who re-examines the coordinates of this volume – time, place, gender and memory – from the perspective of an Israeli psychologist.

Many people have assisted in creating this volume of essays and bringing this project to completion and it is our pleasure to thank them for their efforts. The Fanya Gottesfeld-Heller Center for the Study of Women in Judaism was the pivotal center of both the conference and of this volume. Nicole Ben-Baruch of the Fanya Gottesfeld-Heller Center for the Study of Women in Judaism was instrumental in carrying out all the administrative activities connected with the volume and she was assisted by Sandra Latoucha. The Faculty of Jewish Studies at Bar-Ilan University provided the academic home for the original conference which gave birth to this volume. The Aron and Rachel Dahan Center for Society, Culture and Education in the Spanish Jewish Heritage at Bar-Ilan University supported the publication of this volume. Professor Shulamit Reinharz, Director of the Hadassah International Research Institute on Jewish Women at Brandeis, was greatly supportive of the project. Professors Shmuel Sandler, Stuart Cohen, Susan Handelman and Shmuel Feiner of Bar-Ilan University assisted with important advice and direction. Our thanks to Frank Cass Publishers and to their capable staff who worked on the publication of this book.

We would like to close on a personal note. During these troubled times, there are those who have begun to question the significance of purely academic investigations, stating that the intellectual and practical challenges of the twenty-first century will have to be faced on a very different battlefield. However, we believe that the issues of 'who we are', 'where we are' and 'what we remember' – in other words, gender, place and memory – are the very questions that remain at the basis of our identity, in this case, our Jewish identity, and that their answers guide us towards a better understanding of ourselves. It is our fervent hope that this volume will contribute to this understanding, and that the knowledge gained from its contents will strengthen us as we prepare to face the challenges of the future.

Judith Tydor Baumel and Tova Cohen  
Ramat-Gan, May 2002

# PART I

## PREWAR EUROPE, THE HOLOCAUST AND THE SECOND WORLD WAR

# 1

# *Woman? Youth? Jew? – The Search for Identity of Jewish Young Women in Interwar Poland*

GERSHON BACON

INTRODUCTION

Any study of interwar Polish Jewry must run up against the obstacle of the ultimate 'what if?' question. As we examine the many social, economic, political and cultural trends within that community, we can only speculate regarding their eventual direction, due to the tragic destruction of almost all of Poland's over 3 million Jews in the Nazi Holocaust. The impossibility of knowing how the 'story' might have turned out does not free us from making the attempt to understand the events and trends of the two interwar decades, since in this relatively short period we are witness to numerous changes that left their imprint on Polish Jewry. With a few exceptions, however, the historical literature on Polish Jewry, does not reflect this social dynamism, focusing instead on issues of Jewish politics or Polish anti-Semitism. Even those studies based on the mass of demographic data on Jews from the Polish censuses of 1921 and 1931 as well as local, regional or organizational surveys do not go beyond some general indications of social change. Until recently, the regnant historiography presented a picture of Polish Jewry as a national or nationalizing community frozen in time.[1] When we consider the larger picture of interwar Poland and interwar Polish Jewry, we discover that along with the acknowledged power and influence of Jewish nationalism on the 'Jewish street', other trends and influences existed, such as the Polish public school, which worked toward the eventual acculturation of Polish Jews, even in the face of acknowledged discrimination and anti-Semitism.

How did these conflicting trends play out in the lives of the younger generation of Polish Jews, those who grew up in the new conditions of the reborn Polish state? The picture is complex, and even at this writing has not been completely freed from the ideological debates of previous generations of historians, the products of that community. Lately, the growth of research in Poland itself on topics related to Polish Jewry has added new voices and new approaches to the ongoing historiographical debate. Thus, we find ourselves in the midst of the process of developing a new historical narrative for interwar Polish Jewry.

In the case of young Jewish women, the issue is even more clouded, since for the most part their particular experience was never examined separately from that of Jewish males. In the eyes of contemporary commentators and even of historians, the operative categories of Jew vs. Gentile, of middle class vs. working class or of parents vs. children seemed of primary importance, and not the category of male vs. female.[2] As Paula Hyman noted, in the Jewish communal debate 'the problems that communal leaders identified as deserving of immediate attention ... tended not to be issues of assimilation but questions of securing economic and political equality for their vulnerable constituents, of solving the "Jewish Problem" through nationalism, socialist revolution or emigration. Such matters fell in the domain of public policy, from which both Jewish and general society tended to exclude women and their particular concerns. Insofar as assimilation was itself a secondary issue, the question of women remained marginal.'[3]

We should recall in this context that in the interwar period itself, there were serious pioneering attempts at sociological, cultural, historical and psychological work on Polish Jewry. One area worthy of note was the study of Jewish youth, but here too the issue of women's concerns did not receive separate treatment. In his path-breaking work, *The Way to Our Youth*,[4] Max Weinreich analyzed the nature, aspirations and problems of Jewish youth in Poland from every possible angle except that of young women vs. young men, which does not figure as a separate category for analysis.

However, the raw material upon which Weinreich built much of his presentation, namely the collection of youth autobiographies gathered by Yivo (the Jewish Scientific Institute) in Vilna, does offer the researcher interested in gender issues a unique window into the lives of young people in interwar Poland. The collection derives from competitions organized by Yivo in 1932, 1934 and 1939; the institute also collected and copied some older autobiographies and diaries. In this way it managed to collect about 900 autobiographies, of which 300 survived the Second World War and are found in the Yivo archive in

New York. Over half of the autobiographies are in Yiddish, 71 in Polish, nearly 60 in Hebrew and a few in other languages such as German and Spanish. Note that for the purposes of the contest, youths between the ages of 15 and 24 were eligible, a definition of youth that does not exactly fit our contemporary notions of youth and adolescence.[5]

For the most part, these autobiographies, although mentioned and even quoted selectively by such historians as Ezra Mendelsohn,[6] Celia Heller[7] and Alina Cała, have not been subjected to any systematic analysis, except for the recent pioneering efforts of Ido Basok, and have never been exploited for an examination of gender issues (with the lone exception of a recent unpublished conference paper by Cała).[8] The excellent article of Marcus Moseley discusses the Yivo autobiographies from the viewpoint of literary development and also the history of reading.[9] The goal of the present paper is to present a necessarily small, but representative sample of women's autobiographies from this collection with respect to language (Hebrew, Yiddish), social class (working class, middle class) and ideological orientation (Zionist, socialist, orthodox). Using the techniques developed by both historians and literature scholars for dealing with autobiographies, a gendered analysis of these materials, problematic though they may be, yields some interesting findings about the search for identity of Jewish young women in interwar Poland. That process parallels the experiences of their male contemporaries, but also differs from them in a number of significant ways.

Although this was perhaps unconscious at first, as I worked on the paper I realized that the 'search' in the title of the article had a double meaning. First of all, there was the search of the women at that time for identity, but second, and no less important, there was a search on the part of historians in our own time. For the latter, the challenge was to raise gender issues in the first place, even if they may not have been on the explicit agenda of the writers or collectors of the material at hand. I found myself engaged in a search for women's stories, for women as subjects.

## THE YIVO AUTOBIOGRAPHIES – ADVANTAGES AND METHODOLOGICAL CHALLENGES

If our goal is to penetrate the minds of young Jewish women in the interwar period, the Yivo material has the clear advantage of transmitting to us the views of these young people in 'real time', some as late as the summer of 1939, where the writers did not know of the horrific events to come in the war years. This stands in stark contrast to the many memoirs composed after the Holocaust, some even in very recent times, which often include a chapter about the prewar years, but this picture is usually 'tainted' (for understandable reasons) by being filtered through the prism of the experiences that befell the writers during the Holocaust years.

On the other hand, expectations regarding the potential readers may have had their effect on the form and content of the autobiography. To take but one blatant example, the young woman from Grójec (of whom we will speak at length below) notes in her autobiography that her usual language was Polish, even to the point that she wrote poetry in that language. Nevertheless, considering the public image of Yivo as the center for Yiddish culture, she felt constrained to write her autobiography in Yiddish, despite the numerous spelling mistakes in her manuscript. Another example of anticipated (or perhaps feared) readership led to a certain amount of self-censorship. Many of the young people relate their involvement or the involvement of their friends in leftist and Communist activities, which were illegal at the time, hence the use of pseudonyms and a certain circumspection in relating the events of their lives. With all that, the autobiographies are explicit enough and relatively candid about this aspect of the young people's lives.

In approaching this material, we have the advantage of being able to call on the insights of the voluminous literature on autobiography in general, and the well-developed sub-specialty of analysis of women's autobiography. In her essay 'The Lives of the Obscure', Virginia Woolf expressed an interest, shared by many readers then and since, in autobiography as a source of information about certain sorts of people who might otherwise remain unknown.[10] The written testimonies of these otherwise anonymous (and in many cases, still pseudonymous) young people in Poland, most of whom certainly did not survive the Holocaust, offer us a unique channel to their inner world and their perceptions of the surrounding society.

As voluminous as the theoretical literature on autobiography may be, the Yivo youth autobiographies do not easily fit into any major existing category of analysis. Most discussions of autobiography work from the assumption that we are dealing with the work of an adult who has 'lived' most of his or her life. When it comes to youth autobiography, we have the obvious difference that this is clearly a 'work in progress', and neither author nor reader know how the 'story' will turn out. This crucial lack of knowledge has to have affected the ways that the writer tried to tell his or her own story. Among the various types of autobiography, the closest type would appear to be the working-class autobiography. On this type, Regenia Gagnier notes that unlike middle-class autobiography, most working-class autobiographies do not end with success, but rather in media res (in the middle of the story).[11] Nor does marriage or thoughts of marriage play a role in the autobiographies of Jewish young women here under scrutiny, and thus they deviate from the classic patterns of middle-class women's autobiography which wrote of 'early life with fathers and afterlife with husbands'.[12] Even though some of these women were already in their twenties, at most there are some memories of first love or first infatuation, but little else. As Shaul Stampfer has shown, in the interwar period marriage age for Jewish men and women kept rising, to the point that in 1931 only about half of Jewish women aged 25–29 and only 44 per cent of urban Jewish males in that age group were married.[13] The reasons for the delay in marriage appear to have been mostly economic. In this respect, then, the women's lives here under scrutiny are fairly typical.

The open nature of the autobiography competitions sponsored by Yivo may also have helped to overcome some of the barriers noted by scholars which prevented women's voices from being heard or published. Suzanne Bunkers stated regarding nineteenth-century women's diaries and journals: 'a Midwestern woman's class played a central role in determining not only whether she wrote diaries and journals but also whether her autobiographical writings were considered worth saving and donating to historical society archives'.[14] The Yivo project managed to short circuit some of the stumbling blocks, so that at least the most motivated young people of all classes could gain public expression and an accepted place in the archives. In this respect, the Yivo autobiography competition resembled other projects from that era both in form and in its findings. Thus in 1930 a union of women textile workers in Germany sponsored an essay contest entitled 'My Workday, My Weekend' which chronicled, among other things, the family tensions encountered by young women workers still living at home with parents and siblings, a situation replicated in the Yivo material.[15]

The youth autobiographies offer much to the historian. Our sample of three such autobiographies of young women aims at showing the more general usefulness of this material for understanding the lives of the younger generation, and will then proceed to issues more closely related to gender. In both areas, we gain valuable insights on many aspects of Jewish life in interwar Poland.

## THREE SAMPLE AUTOBIOGRAPHIES: SUMMARIES

*Autobiography #3708*

R. Goldberg (pseudonym Rega), age 22 in 1939, from Łódź.

This is the story of a young woman from a working class family in Łódź. Her parents separated, then reconciled. She tells of attending a kinder heim, a kind of day care center, from a young age, then a Yiddish elementary school. The autobiography stresses the constant financial problems of the family, with one or the other parent out of work, and the experiences of the young girl in school and the Skif socialist youth group. Exposed to Communist literature by a cousin, she eventually becomes an activist in the Communist youth group, engaged in circulating literature. Arrested by the police, she spends a hair-raising two nights in jail in the company of 'ganevtehs and prostitutkes' (female thieves and prostitutes), witnesses the severe beating of a young man for suspected Communist activity, but she herself reveals nothing and is released for lack of evidence. Nevertheless, her political activity led to her being thrown out of school at the end of the seventh grade. A short spell of work in a textile factory is put to an end when Polish workers in the plant go on strike until the 'Jewess' was removed from the shop floor. At this point, she tells of her first love interest, a fellow activist in political organizational work, but she eventually gives him up as part of her decision to make financial independence and leaving her parents' home her first priority. She decides to take up corset-making, taking lessons with a master, which she attempts to pay for by giving private lessons. Her income, however, is insufficient, and she reaches the brink of suicide when she is forced to borrow money from her father to pay for the master's lessons. She tries living away from home for a while, but is brought back by her mother's begging. Conditions at home, however, have not changed, and the young woman searches for another alternative. She hits on the idea of moving to Paris, living with relatives, working in her trade and resuming her schooling. To her dismay, she learns that she cannot get a passport due to her political past.

*Autobiography #3618*

Rabinowicz (no first name given, pseudonym Hanzi), age 17 in 1934, from small shtetl near Vilna (not identified).

# The Search for Identity in Interwar Poland

This is the only autobiography by a woman written in Hebrew in the entire Yivo collection. The young woman's father is from lower-class origin but well educated. Her mother, on the other hand, is from a middle-class background but with little education. The father, who is a wife beater, a drunk, a womanizer and gambler, often leaves the family to take teaching jobs in other towns, sending little money home, and returning home to impregnate his wife yet another time. The subject was raised by her grandmother, and describes a tortured relationship with her father. The turning point and dominating factor in her life was a bout of scarlet fever that almost killed her and left her blind in one eye. For her, the way to escape her present circumstances is to attend the Tarbut gymnasium in Vilna, and in the course of her narrative we learn how she literally begs, borrows and steals to achieve her goal. In her gymnasium years, we hear of her religious feelings and their dissipation, her activities in Betar and then her subsequent attraction to Hashomer Hatzair and to socialist ideals (even while she recounts stealing from her grandmother and from other people on occasion). The young woman tells of her first love interests, including her crush on a lecturer who came to Vilna from Palestine. As with the first example, the autobiography ends with no resolution of her outstanding issues.

*Autobiography #3559*

No name given (pseudonym Esther), age 19 in 1939, from Grójec.

This is the story of a young woman from a strict Hasidic home. She attends the local Bet Yaakov school and also the local Polish public school. There are conflicts with her father over what she should read and which books she should borrow from the library. Besides school and reading, she is active in the Bnot Agudat Yisrael youth movement. She does well in public school and her teachers encourage her to go on to the gymnasium. Her father will not hear of this and promises to send her to the Bet Yaakov seminary in Kraków. Financial reserves make this impossible, and 'Esther' began to give private lessons. After her father's sudden death, she and her mother and sister had no means of support. The young woman is hired as the teacher of an unlicensed Bet Yaakov school in a small shtetl. Despite her growing religious doubts, she takes the job and finds that she has to organize the school from top to bottom, constantly in fear that the police would close down the unlicensed facility. Her source of stability all through this period is her first and only close friend, who has left the orthodox way of life, and with whom she had to meet and correspond in secret. 'Esther' finally had to close down the school and move back home, where she again took up giving private lessons. Her close friend had become drawn to socialism and shared her socialist literature with 'Esther'. While remaining a member of Bnot Aguda, 'Esther' became a believer in socialism. All through her youth, this young woman had taken to writing, and even composed novels, poetry and other writing in Polish. She saw the Yivo autobiography contest as an opportunity to set down some of her most intimate thoughts in Yiddish, while preserving her anonymity. Once again, the end of the autobiography leaves the writer and the reader with no resolution of outstanding issues and conflicts.

On the basis of these three samples, we now proceed to examine some of the general and gender issues that emerge from a close reading of such texts.

## THE YIVO YOUTH AUTOBIOGRAPHIES – RECURRENT GENERAL THEMES

### *Poverty*

For the most part, the Yivo youth autobiographies tell the tales of sad families in difficult circumstances. One theme that emerges clearly is the overwhelming and grinding poverty that was the lot of so many Jews in interwar Poland. Moshe Kligsberg, who composed an 'analytical topical guide' to these autobiographies, put it thus:

> The great majority of the families of our group belonged to the poor section of the population, since adequate food – according to the habits of the given social environment – was constantly lacking. … In many of the documents hunger occupies a considerable space in the narrative; in some it is dealt with at great length. A still stronger factor than actual hunger was the constant process of pauperization which affected all social strata of the Jewish population in Poland since the beginning of Poland's independence in 1918. … The process of pauperization had a more profound effect on the minds and moods of the young people than a more or less constant status of poverty. The experience of having less food day after day, less and worse clothing, of moving constantly to smaller living quarters, increasing lack of means to

pay tuition, etc. – all this influenced mightily the attitude of the young people toward the problems of their future and left a lasting impression upon their personalities.[16]

The most superficial perusal of the Yivo material brings the reader in contact with descriptions of a literal struggle for survival, with the protagonists and their families going for days with little more than bread for sustenance. Under such conditions, how much room remained for contemplation of the 'self'? To these young people, such discussions at length may have seemed a luxury or even frivolous. Nevertheless, even in the midst of the descriptions of their dreary lives, we can on occasion read of what brings them some happiness, their attitudes to nature, to the soul etc.

## Schooling as central, formative experience

For the Jewish young people of interwar Poland, the school, of whatever type, held major significance. For some, school was a place of escape, from the poverty and tensions of the family, from the shtetl to the big city, or even abroad. The young woman from Grójec mentions that the very word school had a sense of magic for her.[17] Those writers who idolized and idealized their contemporaries who were workers and wage-earners still did not wish to give up on their aspirations for continuing their education if circumstances would permit.

The autobiographies confirm what I called elsewhere the 'victory of schooling'. In the course of one generation, Polish Jews underwent a literal revolution in this crucial area in the life of the individual and the community. The compulsory education law of the reborn Polish Republic succeeded in changing the nature of Jews' education where generations of prodding by tsarist officialdom as well as the preaching by Jewish Maskilim and assimilationists had failed. Whether in the public schools or in the various Jewish school networks, Jewish children were educated according to curricula that deviated in almost every aspect from that of traditional Jewish education. Even the Yesodei ha'Torah schools, sponsored by the orthodox party Agudat Yisrael and which maintained the dominant role of religious studies in their curriculum, had to introduce significant elements of secular education in Polish as the price of government recognition. Parental wishes and changed values among Jewish youth played as significant a role in this transition as the external pressures of Polish legislation or bureaucratic harassment of Jewish schools. For parents and children, the aforementioned 'victory of schooling' was an investment in the future. Even in the 1930s, in the face of economic depression and growing anti-Semitism (and the emigration of young people to Palestine and other destinations), Jews attended secondary schools in relatively large numbers.[18]

All the writers here under scrutiny attest to the influence of teachers, whether for the subject matter they transmitted, but especially as role models looked to for their attitudes on life and the world. The young woman from Łódź ('Rega'), for example, spoke of the influence of her teacher, whom she characterized as a cynical man who laughed at everything, but who was willing to discuss any subject with his female charges. He taught his students to look at all problems in a fundamental manner, and under his influence she decided that, whatever she would do further on in her life, she would make an effort to find ways to continue learning.[19] The values imparted by teachers, school peers and in the youth movements often clashed with the values of home and parents. The teachers of the young woman from Grójec ('Esther') urged her to go on to the gymnasium, even arranging a scholarship for her, but her father objected strenuously to this possibility.

Added to the formal influence of teacher and school was the no less important influence of the world of books and reading, oftentimes against parents' wishes and, in the case of the young woman from the small town near Vilna ('Hanzi'), at the risk to her personal health.[20] The autobiographies give us a glimpse of the 'bookshelf' of these young people, what they were reading, what made an impression on them, whether they were popular works of literature of the time, perhaps by now long forgotten, or political pamphlet literature distributed by young people at the risk of arrest and imprisonment. 'Hanzi', for example, mentions that the first book she read was a Hebrew biography of Herzl. In her gymnasium years, she recalls the lasting effect on her of the book *Man Is Good*, written in German by Leonhard Frank and translated into Hebrew in 1920, a work which criticized all aspects of present-day society, but expressed hope for a fraternal future for all mankind. On what could be termed one of her first encounters with a young man, in this case the son of the cantor of her shtetl, a studious young man also studying in the city, she recalls that she had with her a copy of Anton Vitalievich Nemilov's *The Biological Tragedy of Woman*, a work of popular science translated into many languages at that time, including English, Yiddish and Hebrew. 'Hanzi' tells how they read some selections together and afterward discussed each selection in

*The Search for Identity in Interwar Poland* 13

turn. For the pseudonymous 'Esther' of Grójec, the library of her Polish public school had as much magic as the school itself: 'what a treasure lay behind the glass doors of the library's bookcase'. When she informed her parents that the teachers allowed the students to sign up for the library, her father stated outright that he did not want her reading Polish books. Her tears were of no avail. Here her mother came to the rescue and instructed her to sign up for the library without her father's knowledge. Thus began a period of intensive reading, which the young lady had to keep secret from her father. When, despite her best efforts, her father discovered her disobedience, he suggested a compromise whereby the local Bet Yaakov teacher would supervise her Polish reading books.[21] This young lady also engaged in composing her own writings in Polish. She writes in her autobiography that her diaries, poems and two novels in Polish gave her an outlet for the melancholy she felt during her tour of duty as a lonely young teacher in an unregistered Bet Yaakov school in a small shtetl. One novel, entitled 'Why?', dealt with the cruel fate of the weak and defenseless of the world, while the second, entitled 'Blood Sacrifice', told the tale of a Hasidic young man who left his religious lifestyle, but in a moment of crisis, a fire in the bet midrash (study house), sacrifices his life for his earlier convictions.[22]

*Youth movement activity as key experience*

In addition to the school, the focus of the experience of the three young women was in the local branch of one or another Jewish youth movement. The clubhouse served as more than a meeting place. It was the locus for political debate and indoctrination, the place for meeting the opposite sex (with the obvious exception of the young woman from the Bnot Agudat Yisrael movement), a kind of separate 'youth world', at least emotionally distant from the often oppressive atmosphere of the home, with its own way of life.[23] 'Rega' tells of joining the Jewish socialist children's association SKIF in the sixth grade, where she listened with interest to the various discussions in the clubhouse, but did not take an active part 'due to my shyness. I never had the courage to express my own opinion.' A cousin of hers who was a Communist took it upon himself to complete her political education: 'He got me to understand that the only correct theory which can save the proletariat in the entire world is the Bolshevist.' He had an infectious enthusiasm and impressed her with his descriptions of the heroic fight and martyrdom of the illegal Communist fighters, and gave her to read illegal Communist brochures. The young woman heard one version of social justice and freedom in the SKIF meetings and another from her cousin. She tried to resolve for herself which was the right path, who was really fighting for the best ideals. Though at this point she could not come to a definite conclusion, her sympathies lay with the Communist party, 'which impressed me with its illegality'.[24]

Participation in the youth movements also provided opportunities for the development of leadership skills. 'Hanzi' spent time both in Betar and later in Hashomer Hatzair. In her autobiography, she recalls the time she returned from Vilna to her shtetl and on that occasion gave a lecture to the local Betar branch. About 120 people attended, and 'when I began I forgot that I was among people, and it seemed to me that I was reciting in front of a book out loud. I lectured for over an hour and a half, and everyone listened; apparently this was an interesting lecture. The first attempt succeeded, and I felt that I have strong powers.' Only when she left the building did she realize that her mother and grandmother had been standing watching her performance through the window. Their faces expressed satisfaction, but she was embarrassed, since she evidently wanted this whole episode to be part of her world only.[25]

### Polish–Jewish relations

Throughout the texts under consideration, issues of the relations between Jews and Poles emerge in many different forms. On occasion, the young people see themselves as the 'other' in Polish society. The young 'Esther' was strongly influenced by her years in the Polish public school and fancied herself a Polish patriot. Her teachers chose her to read a poem at the public celebration of Marshal Piłsudski's name day. As she witnessed the growth of anti-Semitism in Polish society, though, she became pessimistic regarding the ultimate prospects of Polish–Jewish relations:

> I had been so devoted to Poland, had been bound to her with the threads of my soul. Now I had to give up the glorious dream of Polish–Jewish coexistence. ... Daily the newspapers brought fresh, gruesome news regarding persecution of Jews. My belief in Poland's 'heart' became eclipsed. I no longer saw a people with brotherly feelings for all its citizens, as it had been in her prewar dreams.[26]

The autobiography of 'Hanzi' includes an incident from the time of her convalescence after the severe bout of scarlet fever that left her scarred for life. One Shabbat morning she saw a starving cat in the street and stole some bread from the pantry to give it to the cat. From behind a Polish shoemaker approached her, gave her a kiss on the forehead and said that Poland was not worthy of a girl like her. The young woman reports that she did not understand his meaning. Besides that, there was a lot of talk in the shtetl concerning this man, of whom it was said that he had come from Russia to organize the local workers, and that he had been involved in an act of arson that had caused a major fire in the town.[27]

For me, the most surprising example was in the autobiography of 'Rega', who recounts the hostile reception she encountered on the factory floor, as her Polish co-workers immediately went out on strike to protest her presence:

> in the factory, all the workers were Christians. When they saw me (I look like a typical Jewess), they called a meeting and decided unanimously that they would strike until the Jewess would leave the factory ... What caused me chagrin was not that I would not get any work, even if I wanted it so much. What bothered me was the fact that the workers struck because of me, and this was only because I am Jewish. Earlier I had heard a lot and read regarding anti-Semitism, *but until then I had never encountered it directly*.[28]

Her last comment is especially striking in the light of numerous testimonies concerning the all-pervasive nature of Polish anti-Semitism and raises some interesting questions.

### *Issues of class status/class relations in the Jewish community*

Given the exposure of our autobiographers to socialist and even Communist ideas, it is not at all surprising that issues of class and the relations between the various strata in the Jewish community feature in their writing. Some of these women were tortured by this subject, asking themselves if they measured up to their contemporaries who sacrificed for the cause. 'Rega' recounts how her school was purged of 'political agitators', as the left-leaning girls were called by the authorities. For her part, she feigned ignorance of political matters. The principal summoned her father to school to urge her to keep away from undesirable organizations, and when that didn't help, the father kept her at home, allowing her to go out only when he could accompany her. The young woman promised her father to be 'good and frum [pious]' and stay away from the organization, but she had no intention to keep that promise: 'the most important thing for me was work in the organization. All else was nonsense.'[29]

Of the three autobiographies under consideration here, that of 'Hanzi' has some of the most biting comments on class issues, as she shares her observations on her various social frameworks and her fellow students or youth movement members, assigning 'grades', as it were, for class consciousness. Much of the vitriol in her remarks stems from the comparison between her difficult situation and theirs, such as in her comments on the members of Betar:

> most of them were products of government gymnasia, bourgeois, their dress was nice, and as 'intelligents' they speak Polish. I hated them with an absolute hatred. I always had one dress, which I had to launder every two days. In general the dress was dirty or torn in several places. The Revisionist academics made an even worse impression on me; they only could march in Polish processions with the banner of Betar. I never walked with them and I despised them and mocked them.[30]

Regarding her shtetl, she presents the following breakdown of the population:

> in the shtetl people young and old were divided into two camps: 1) the children of the rich who have all the books and a nice school bag, who dress nicely, never walk barefoot, go out walking with their parents on Shabbat afternoon toward evening and not with friends, and were not pious; 2) children of the poor, who were more pious, downtrodden, and who always submitted to the wishes of the wealthy.[31]

More than once, she reveals her feelings of crisis as she was torn between the nationalist Zionism of Betar and the socialism of Hashomer Hatzair:

> on one hand I felt national egoism, and on the other hand great sympathy for the world proletariat, for Russia and her revolutionary actions. I felt respect for those who marched on the First of May with the red flag, the flag of labor, in their hand. I wanted to be the same as they, and to unite my voice with their song of rebellion.[32]

## WOMEN'S ISSUES, WOMEN'S VOICES, GENDER ISSUES

The discussion above illustrates the potential richness of the youth autobiographies as historical sources for Jewish life in interwar Poland, especially the lives of young people in that turbulent era. The question remains, however, whether the autobiographies of women offer a special or different perspective, and whether they testify to a different set of reactions or experiences to the same situation. To take but one example, was the experience of 'Rega', who remarked that although she had heard and read of anti-Semitism, she had until that time never personally encountered it, reflective of a qualitative difference between the experiences of men and women in Poland? 'Esther' tells of the encouragement she received from her teachers in the Polish public school, most particularly of her being chosen to perform in school events in honor of Marshal Piłsudski. Compare this to the shame suffered by the young Norman Salsitz, chosen by his teacher to sing a song in a similar celebration in his town, only to find out at the last moment that he, the traditionally garbed young Jew with sidelocks, had to perform hidden from the audience by a screen.[33] The gender issue in Polish anti-Semitism has not, to the best of my knowledge, been explored in scholarly literature. Did there exist, for example, some sort of perverted 'chivalry' that left Jewish female students unharmed during violent outbreaks against Jewish students on university campuses? Were relations among Jewish and Polish female pupils in elementary schools less tense than those of their male counterparts? The material under consideration here, and by extension the entire corpus of youth autobiographies, offers us a chance to look at these questions and others.

In looking at the youth autobiographies, we ask ourselves where is the woman, as opposed to the young person, in this material? As part of our search, we should first clarify for ourselves what exactly we seek – a female voice? a gendered voice? a feminist voice? From the sample here under scrutiny, as well as from a more general perusal of the contents of the Yivo material, it emerges that there exist some materials related to the first two categories, but it would probably be too much to expect to discover examples of the third. If the sensitivity to gender, whether on the part of young women or young men, is not prominent, the problem lay not just in the authors, but also in the lack of available narratives for women's lives. In their absence, it was easy to slide into conventional categories of Jew/Gentile, youth/older generation or privileged/underprivileged. In making these comments, I am in no way trying to give 'grades' to these autobiographies according to the standards of our own day, which would be neither fair nor particularly helpful in historical analysis. On the other hand, judicious use of the tools of analysis developed in recent years in the field of women's autobiographies does yield some important results when we apply them to the material at hand.

*Issues of style and self-expression: relations with father*

Though acknowledging notable exceptions to such generalizations, scholars who have dealt with autobiography as a genre have noted differences between men's and women's autobiographies. In men's writings, we find patterns established by the two prototypical male autobiographies, those of Augustine and Rousseau. Augustine built his life story around the dramatic structure of conversion, where the self is presented as the stage for a battle of opposing forces, and the climactic victory of one force completes the drama of the self. Rousseau's autobiography, more secular in nature, presents characters and events as little more than aspects of the author's evolving consciousness. Neither of these approaches find echoes in women's writing about their lives. Mary Mason asserts that, on the contrary, the discovery of female identity

> seems to acknowledge the real presence and recognition of another consciousness, and the disclosure of female self is linked to the identification of some 'other'. This recognition of another consciousness – ... rather than deference – this grounding of identity through relation to the chosen other, seems ... to enable women to write openly about themselves.[34]

This other need not be a male or males, whether father, husband or peers, but often is.

In the Yivo material here under discussion, the form of writing and the structure of the narratives fit the 'female' style, where relations with others, whether parents, schoolmates or others loom large, as opposed to 'male' style, which is characterized by a more clearly focused discussion of ideological awakening and moving toward some loosely or more carefully defined goal. Ideological awakening does make a significant appearance in these women's autobiographies, but even here the young women are constantly measuring themselves against friends and comrades, or speaking about how they fit in with the group.

Much of the self-definition of the protagonists emerges through conflicts with the father, which dominate in these narratives. This stems in part from the function of the father as decision maker in the patriarchal family, the typical pattern among Polish Jews of the period. For 'Esther', this meant battles over her education, her reading, her friends, where her father intervened, mainly for religious reasons. 'Rega' found herself in a battle of wits with her father who forbade her to continue her political activities, while she was determined to continue them. At one point, he reminded her that his own (presumably unlicensed) commercial activities were not completely legal, and therefore an audit of the entire family in the wake of her political activities could bring disaster on the household.[35] The young woman refused to listen to her father's screaming. Only when he told her in a calm voice that as long as she lived in his home and was dependent on him, he had the right to demand that she obey him and stop her illegal work. 'Rega' recounts that until then she had not considered that her father might be suffering because of her behavior. If she had to obey her father as long as she was dependent on him, then she had to find a way to become economically independent, even at the cost of temporarily suspending the political work that meant so much to her.[36] The decision to take up corset-making as a trade led directly to the crisis in relations with her father that brought her to the brink of suicide. This occurred when she found herself forced to ask her father for a temporary loan to pay the master giving her lessons. Her father reacted first with anger that in such an important decision he had not been consulted, and then by commenting that she was willing to take from her father, but not to help the family. She felt defeated as her lack of independence stared her in the face: 'I came to the conclusion that I was a terrible shlimazl. I was 20 years old and still had to come to my father.' During a sleepless night she contemplated various ways to end her life, 'but the instinct to live was stronger and triumphed'. She awoke the next day with new resolve.[37]

The nature of the struggle with the father in the search for identity certainly involved dealing with the tyrannical aspects of the patriarchal family as far as women were concerned, but it also had to do with the image of the father and how the protagonist measured up, or not, to that image. This type of struggle finds most poignant expression in the autobiography of 'Hanzi', which shows the complex relationship with her abusive, drunken and generally irresponsible father, who nonetheless aroused her respect due to his intellectual talents and to the similar spiritual struggles that both he and she underwent. Even as she declared her disgust at her father's behavior, she sought validation from him. This found its clearest expression in her account of a rare visit that her father paid her in Vilna:

> I felt at once that he is shaping plans how to free himself of us. Then the image of Mother would arise in my thoughts, as she held the little one to her chest and around her the rest of the children demanding food. More than black bread, occasionally some beet soup or onions they never saw: we are all miserable and my fate was the worst. I feared to raise the issue of home with my father lest he get angry. On the one hand I felt tense in his presence and distant from him, since he was so closed and an iron wall separated us, and since he understood so much more than me. On the other hand, I felt for him an unmediated and instinctive closeness, in that both of us suffered, in his heart there was an internal war, and in my heart that same fire burned always. And many other excuses were found while comparing him and me. Before he departed he said 'good-bye' and nothing more. On the evening before his traveling he kissed me several times. *Then he revealed the secret with a shining face, that I have many of his spiritual characteristics.*[38]

As we scrutinize this material in the search for women's consciousness, even in those places where it is not mentioned explicitly, the very necessity of reckoning with the man (usually the father) seems to be an integral part of that consciousness.

*Love and sex*

In his survey of the autobiographies, Kligsberg noted a significant difference between males and females on this subject:

> The great majority of the girls scarcely touch this subject, whereas boys are very frank and often relate their sexual experiences at length. Not one of the girls tells anything about her early sexual observations or knowledge. ... Many of the boys speak about their masturbation and sometimes in great detail. ... In a few cases boys relate about collective masturbation of groups of boys that they observed. ... As far as love in the period of later adolescence is concerned, girls discuss it more often and more frankly. ... The boys relate their love affairs in great detail; they enumerate all the girls they were going out with, tell about intimate relations, including intercourse.[39]

Two of our three autobiographers do provide us with some details about their first encounters with the opposite sex. For 'Rega', this occurred during her illegal organizational work for the Communist youth movement. At a literary evening she made the acquaintance of a comrade whom she found attractive, but she doubted she would ever see him again and nothing would come of this chance meeting. Still, she thought of him a great deal. A few weeks later, they met once again and started working together in the youth organization, often on a daily basis. This went on for about a year. Despite their close contact, she had doubts that he could be interested in her. After all, she thought, even though they were both 19 years old, he had been an activist for years, had organized strikes, had spent time in jail. She, on the other hand, had until recently been in school, dealing with abstract problems, and saw herself as politically immature.[40] The depth of her feelings for this young man came to the fore only after she made the decision to suspend her political work and devote herself to learning a trade:

> my comrades regarded me with contempt ... I made an effort to avoid them. Also my [boy] friend I avoided; as often as he tried to approach me, I would not let him. Often, against my will, I thought: oh, if I could meet him now! When that happened, I held myself strong ... The most important thing for me was: how does one become independent?[41]

The autobiography of 'Hanzi' has a number of frank discussions of her views of relations with boys. We already mentioned her being attracted to the son of the local cantor, with whom she discussed the book *The Biological Tragedy of Woman*. She tells us that she was attracted to him more for his talent than for his looks. She evidently sought his company on other occasions, but unsuccessfully, to which she remarks that 'I was so low in my own eyes that I couldn't imagine the love of someone else for me'.[42] Of course, the fact of her being maimed by scarlet fever runs as a major thread all the way through her narrative. A report of one of her earliest discussions with her grandmother seems a chilling premonition. At that time, her mother gave birth to her third daughter. 'Hanzi' was the first, the grandmother informed her, and a second daughter had died. The girl who died was very beautiful, and God took her because of her beauty. God hates beauty, she asserted, because beauty leads to sin. 'Thus explained Grandma, and I argued that in no way did I want to be beautiful.'[43]

In a long account of a discussion with her father, the subject of boys also came up. The situation in the Tarbut gymnasium, where boys and girls learned together, was new for her after the school in the shtetl. She told her father of the flirting that went on in the classroom and during breaks, but as for her:

> the boys never accosted me and never touched me. I didn't wonder about this. I knew I was ugly because of the eye. The apathetic feeling of boys toward me also repelled me from any thoughts of love. While other girls sat together and told anecdotes, I sat at the other end deep in thought, almost always serious. On the one hand I felt myself depressed and downtrodden; on the other hand energetic and independent. This specific situation brought it about that I never liked one boy. When I couldn't stop feelings of the heart, I felt love for boys in general, as the other sex; as a collective and not as individuals.[44]

As she became aware of sexuality through her reading and through what she observed among her peers, 'Hanzi' also noticed the relations between her parents. On those rare occasions when her father was home, he spoke with her mother but little during the day, but in the night he would draw near to her, which the daughter realized even if she was sleeping in another room. Her conclusion: 'this was without doubt sex without love. From what I have read in books about sex and biology, I learned that from such a coupling are born children who are not completely normal. *I drew conclusions regarding all the Jewish masses.*'[45]

Of all the men that she mentions in her autobiography, the lecturer from Palestine, Nathan Bistritski,[46] aroused the strongest feelings:

> I cannot describe my feelings toward him. Could this be love? Perhaps? But no! This was something more than love. I saw him as the man of tomorrow; a man who blended his efforts into the project of human liberation (national chauvinism had grown weaker). This was perhaps a synthesis of love, respect and something more, a successful synthesis. After I found out about his lecture that was going to take place, entitled 'Moscow and Jerusalem', I sold my only Latin book and bought a ticket.[47]

The thoughts and feelings of 'Rega' and 'Hanzi' demonstrate the complex interaction between emotions, political and personal aspirations, and family conflicts that these young women had to deal with.

## Personality of the individual woman

In this material, there may be some conscious suppression, and it may be necessary sometimes to 'read' the silences no less than the articulated thoughts. Nevertheless, there is a clear woman's voice heard in this material, a voice that has not always found its way into the historical narrative of Polish Jewry. Once again, the autobiography of 'Hanzi' brings out this point most clearly. This could be in her often-expressed desire for acknowledgment of her father's love for her – 'It seemed to me that he hated me with a complete hatred, and I for my part loved him with heart and soul, a love not out of acquaintance perhaps, but of emotion and the heart.'[48]

Especially powerful and unusual are 'Hanzi's' writings on her religious feelings on the one hand and on their gradual fading on the other. How often do we encounter a woman as a religious personality in her own right? In her youngest years, she notes with pride her success in school, particularly in math. On market days she would walk around the whole day and do figures for poor women in the market for sales of potatoes, carrots, beets and the like. The women would bless her by God, and she felt that this blessing touched her soul:

> Indeed, I dreamed about God a great deal. Sometimes, father would sit me on his knee and tell me something. Even though my father was not pious and without doubt did not believe in God, nevertheless he would try to explain to me the most important things without touching upon the holy hidden things. He always knew how to arouse in me hopes and not disappointments.[49]

This young woman saw herself as different from all the others in her class in school because of her fanatical religiosity. Her belief gave her the strength to live in such terrible conditions, since she hoped for better times. When she would read a chapter of Psalms (this happened very often), she felt complete spiritual satisfaction, and paid no heed to the fact that others made fun of her. Her religious feelings increased in intensity after her severe illness, since it was in religion that she found her only consolation. Almost every day she would pray and read psalms. At this time, she notes, her mother took her to the next village where there lived the famous saint and sage Rabbi Yisrael Meir Hacohen, known after the title of his most famous book as the 'Hafetz Hayyim'. The blessing of the tzaddik made her even more fanatical in her religiosity.[50] In the wake of her illness, she found special comfort in the Bible: 'what was I to do? I read and looked a great deal in the Bible. It was my only friend that did not disgust me. The Bible rested always at the head of the bed, and I would read it, especially early in the morning. At nights, Grandma did not allow me, fearing for my eye.'[51]

As strong as these childhood religious feelings were, for 'Hanzi' there came a time of crisis: 'I fought with myself with regard to religion a quixotic war; the same war that Lilienblum fought in his time.'[52] Historians often refer to the effect that Lilienblum's autobiography *The Sins of Youth* had on generations of Jewish young people who saw his inner struggle as their own, but the subject is always considered to be male. Here a young woman saw that story as at least in part her own as well. Although her doubts chipped away at her faith, she still saw herself as at an advantage compared to her father:

> I turned to God with all the troubles of my soul. Even in moments of doubt, there still remained that grain that was so dear. That same grain, without which one could burst at times of disaster. The fact is that faith in that exalted and stable one helped me with spiritual support. Life had taken away from him that last spark![53]

Further on in her narrative, she notes that the religious feelings slowly died, until only some distant memories of God remained. Her spiritual odyssey, intertwined with her slow discovery of the personality of her father, is a precious document.

No less intriguing is the autobiography of 'Esther', torn between her attraction to socialism and her activity in the orthodox Bnot Agudat Yisrael youth movement. Her autobiography includes a fascinating description of her doubts, coupled with her strong identification with Jewish tradition, with what she saw as the great contributions of the Jewish people to mankind, yet her refusal to accept the negative attitude to secular culture she encountered in the youth movement. In a lyrical passage, she consigns these doubts to the pages of her diary:

> I loved my organization, despite the fact that I saw its faults. I did not wish to lose the opportunity to learn. I was silent. I was silent only in front of people. For myself I wrote. No one knew what the leaves of my notebook contained. Regarding that only perhaps the trees could describe, and they were silent witnesses. I loved them, in their gentle, motherly shade I poured out my heart, my feelings and thoughts.[54]

These voices and others waiting to be transcribed and published bring us back to the complex reality of the individual woman or man, and by extension the complex reality of Polish Jewry. No neat ideological, political or religious definitions do justice to the young women's lives that we have examined here.

## CONCLUSION

The sample material from the Yivo youth autobiographies has opened for us a window into the lives of young Jewish women in interwar Poland. We can see the nature of the patriarchal society then extant, although the young women here described do not directly challenge that society. The world of young people that we encounter here, whether in the gymnasium or in the youth movements, gave young women and men a temporary escape from the dreary existence that was their lot at home. We can even posit some important connections between this youth world and the underground and resistance movements that would spring up in the ghettos of Poland during the Holocaust. The separate youth world would then become even more important in the struggle for survival as family units disintegrated under the stresses of ghetto life, of starvation and illness, and eventually deportations to unknown destinations. We should note also the connections with radical politics of whatever stripe, and as a consequence the willingness to flout standards of legality, even finding that illegality attractive. Those attitudes would be crucial in the formation of the resistance groups. In short, for at least a nucleus of Jewish young men and women, we find that already in the interwar period they had assimilated some of the crucial techniques that would serve them well in the war years.

The stories we have examined are sad stories with no relief at their conclusion. Such is the case with the youth autobiographies in general, of which our three stories are but typical examples. In her study of women's writing, Carolyn Heilbrun observed that 'above all prohibitions, what has been forbidden women is anger, together with the open admission of the desire for power and control over one's life'.[55] Coincidentally or not, the young women who contributed their autobiographies to the Yivo competition were born around the same time as the generation of women poets in America which Heilbrun contends changed the nature of women's writing. These young American poets lifted the constraints on women's writing, finding a way to express their anger; harder still, she contends, they managed to bear, for a time at least, the anger in men that their work aroused.[56] The young women of Poland may not have expressed the anger that Heilbrun saw as so crucial, except perhaps toward socially acceptable targets of the time (e.g. bourgeois values), but the desire for independence and control over their lives features prominently. We will never know if they would have reached the conclusions that their American counterparts reached decades later. Even so, telling their stories may enable us to revise the historical narrative of the 3 million strong community to which they belonged. The recently published anthology in English translation of materials from the Yivo youth autobiographies, entitled *Awakening Lives* (edited by Jeffrey Shandler), will enable a much larger readership to appreciate this unique and very special source material.

## NOTES

Special thanks to Marek Web, chief archivist of the Yivo Institute, and to his staff for their help in locating and reproducing materials that served as the basis for this research project.

1. For the beginnings of a more balanced view, see e.g., Ezra Mendelsohn, 'Ha'umnam hayeta yada shel ha'Tziyyonut be'Polin al ha'elyonah?', in Haim Avni and Gideon Shimoni (eds) *Ha'Tziyyonut u'Mitnagdeha ba'Am ha'Yehudi* (Jerusalem: Ha'Sifriya Ha'Tziyyonit, 1990), pp. 241–6.
2. See Gershon Bacon, 'The missing 52%: the state of research on Jewish women in interwar Poland', in Dalia Ofer and Lenore Weitzman (eds) *Women in the Holocaust* (New Haven: Yale University Press, 1998), pp. 55–67.
3. Paula E. Hyman, *Gender and Assimilation in Modern Jewish History: The Roles and Representation of Women* (Seattle and London: University of Washington Press, 1995), pp. 91–2.
4. Max Weinreich, *Der Veg tzu undzer yugnt: yesoides, metoden, problemen fun yiddisher yugnt-forshung* (Vilna: Yivo Institute, 1935).
5. Alina Cała, 'The Social Consciousness of Young Jews in Interwar Poland', *Polin* 8 (1994): 42.
6. Ezra Mendelsohn, *Ha'Tenua Ha'Tziyyonit be'Polin: Shenot Hithavut, 1915–1926* (Jerusalem: Ha'Sifriya Ha'Tziyyonit, 1986), pp. 304–5.
7. Celia Heller, *On the Edge of Destruction: Jews of Poland Between the Two World Wars* (New York: Columbia University Press, 1977), pp. 225–6, 242–3, 268 and passim.
8. See Ido Basok, 'Maamadot u'tefisa maamadit etzel yeladim u'vnei noar yehudim be'Polin bein ha'milhamot', *Gal-Ed* 18 (2002): 225–44; 'Neurim ve'erkhei neurim be'tenuot ha'noar be'Polin she'bein ha'milhamot', in Yisrael Bartal and Yisrael Gutman (eds) *Kiyyum va'Shever: Yehudei Polin le'Dorotehem* (Jerusalem: Merkaz Zalman Shazar, 2001), vol. 2, pp. 591–601; Alina Cała, 'Gender, Jewish Tradition and the Reality of the 2nd Republic of Poland', unpublished conference paper,

conference on interwar Poland held at Simon Dubnow Institute, Leipzig, December 1999.
9. Marcus Moseley, 'Life, Literature: Autobiographies of Jewish Youth in Interwar Poland', *Jewish Social Studies*, 7(3) (2001), pp. 1–51. The author notes that an abridged and altered version of the article appears as part of the introduction to an anthology of the youth autobiographies, entitled *Awakening Lives: Autobiographies of Jewish Youth in Poland before the Holocaust* (New Haven: Yale University Press, 2002), under the general editorship of Jeffrey Shandler and with introductions by Barbara Kirshenblatt-Gimblett, Marcus Moseley and Michael Stanislawski.
10. *The Dial* 78 (1925): 381–90, cited in William C. Spengemann, *The Forms of Autobiography: Episodes in the History of a Literary Genre* (New Haven, CT and London: Yale University Press, 1980), p. 205.
11. Regenia Gagnier, *Subjectivities: A History of Self-Representation in Britain, 1832–1920* (New York and Oxford: Oxford University Press, 1991), p. 43.
12. Ibid., p. 44.
13. Shaul Stampfer, 'Marital Patterns in Interwar Poland', in Yisrael Gutman, Ezra Mendelsohn, Jehuda Reinharz and Chone Shmeruk (eds) *The Jews of Poland Between Two World Wars* (Hanover and London: University Press of New England, 1989), pp. 186–7.
14. Suzanne L. Bunkers, 'Midwestern Diaries and Journals: What Women Were (Not) Saying in the Late 1800s', in James Olney (ed.) *Studies in Autobiography* (New York and Oxford: Oxford University Press, 1988), p. 193.
15. Atina Grossmann, '*Girlkultur* or Thoroughly Rationalized Female: A New Woman in Weimar Germany?', in Judith Friedlander and the New Family and New Woman Research Planning Group (eds) *Women in Culture and Politics: A Century of Change* (Bloomington: Indiana University Press, 1986), pp. 68, 70. My thanks to Atina Grossmann for this reference.
16. Moshe Kligsberg, *Child and Adolescent Behavior Under Stress: An Analytical Topical Guide to a Collection of Autobiographies of Jewish Young Men and Women in Poland (1932–1939) in the Possession of the YIVO Institute for Jewish Research* (New York, 1965), p. 21, cited by Moseley, 'Life, Literature', footnote 42.
17. Yivo youth autobiography #3559, p. 132802.
18. Gershon Bacon, 'National Revival, Ongoing Acculturation – Jewish Education in Interwar Poland', *Yearbook of the Simon Dubnow Institute* 1 (2002): 71–92.
19. Yivo youth autobiography #3708, p. 141516.
20. For an extensive discussion of this subject, see Moseley, 'Life, Literature', passim.
21. Yivo youth autobiography #3559, pp. 132807–8.
22. Ibid., pp. 132845–6.
23. On the influence and nature of the youth movement local branch, see Moshe Kligsberg, 'Di Yiddishe Yugnt-bavegung in Poiln tsvishn beide velt-milkhomes (a sotsiologishe shtudie)', in Joshua Fishman (ed.) *Studies on Polish Jewry 1919–1939* (New York: Yivo Institute for Jewish Research, 1974), Yiddish section, pp. 172–9. Kligsberg quotes extensively from the youth autobiographies, but he too avoids any discussion of gender issues.
24. Yivo youth autobiography #3708, p. 141513.
25. Yivo youth autobiography #3618, p. 136456. Full translation can be found in *Awakening Lives* (see n.9, above), pp. 197–225.
26. Yivo youth autobiography #3559, pp. 132822–3. Full translation can be found in *Awakening Lives* (see n.9, above), pp. 321–43.

27. Yivo youth autobiography #3618, p. 136440.
28. Yivo youth autobiography #3708, p. 141518; emphasis added.
29. Ibid., p. 141515.
30. Yivo youth autobiography #3618, pp. 135453–4.
31. Ibid., p. 136432.
32. Ibid., p. 136461.
33. Norman Salsitz, *A Jewish Boyhood in Poland: Remembering Kolbuszowa* (Syracuse: Syracuse University Press, 1992), pp. 249–50.
34. Mary G. Mason, 'The Other Voice: Autobiographies of Women Writers', in James Olney (ed.) *Autobiography: Essays Theoretical and Critical* (Princeton, NJ: Princeton University Press, 1980), p. 210.
35. Yivo youth autobiography #3708, p. 141520.
36. Ibid., pp. 141521–2.
37. Ibid., pp. 141524–5.
38. Yivo youth autobiography #3618, p. 136457; emphasis added.
39. Moshe Kligsberg, *Child and Adolescent Behavior*, p. 25, cited by Moseley, 'Life, Literature', footnote 117.
40. Yivo youth autobiography #3708, pp. 141519–20.
41. Ibid., p. 141523.
42. Yivo youth autobiography #3618, p. 136459.
43. Ibid., p. 136427.
44. Ibid., p. 136448.
45. Ibid., p. 136458; emphasis added.
46. On Nathan Bistritski (Agmon), see *Encyclopedia Judaica* (Jerusalem: Keter, 1971), vol. 2., col. 367.
47. Yivo youth autobiography #3618, p. 136468.
48. Ibid., p. 136430.
49. Ibid., p. 136431.
50. Ibid., p. 136439.
51. Ibid., p. 136442.
52. Ibid., p. 136445.
53. Ibid., p. 136458.
54. Yivo youth autobiography #3559, pp. 132826–7.
55. Carolyn G. Heilbrun, *Writing a Woman's Life* (New York: Ballantine Books, 1988), p. 13.
56. Ibid., p. 60.

# 2

# *Her View Through My Lens: Cecilia Slepak Studies Women in the Warsaw Ghetto*

## DALIA OFER

The document studied in this paper is a report based on interviews of women conducted in the Warsaw ghetto between December 1941 and the spring of 1942 by the journalist Cecilia Slepak.[1] Following her introduction, she presents several brief life stories of women from different social classes. Her work was part of a wider initiative to document life in the Warsaw ghetto a year after its establishment and to evaluate its impact on both individuals and the public.[2]

Writing in the midst of the extraordinary situation in the Warsaw ghetto, Slepak juxtaposed women with formerly unacceptable occupations such as thief, a woman who used her sex to make a living, and beggar alongside traditional 'women's work' and new occupations for women. She describes the lives of 16 women, among them housewives; a cleaning woman; one who worked in the food storage centers, public kitchens and orphanages; and a woman who served on the house committees. She also wrote about women in the performing arts – a dancer, an actor and a musician – as well as small vendors and smugglers and professional women such as agronomist, translator and librarian.[3]

Slepak did not hesitate to describe the dark sides of women's life, and the reality that emerges from their life stories may be interpreted in different ways. Today we look at the history of the ghetto residents with a clear image of the ghetto's ultimate destruction, whereas for Slepak, the ghetto is a reality to be accepted and criticized. She empathized with the women and their plight; she does not pass judgment on their choices, but views their activities as part of their effort to live.

Before the war, Slepak had been part of an intellectual elite immersed in secular Jewish culture as well as integrated into Polish culture. These individuals took a realistic and critical view of the Jewish community and the conduct of individual Jews. Thus, including a woman that used sex to make a living in the sample of ghetto women was no outrage for Slepak. Prostitutes had been part of Jewish life before the crisis of the war and the formation of the ghetto, and there was no reason to think that such professions would be abolished in the ghetto. Moreover, in the context of ghetto life, it was merely one more way to get by. None of the post-Holocaust terminology referring to the Jews as martyrs or saints appears in her report. She was viewing the rhythm of life around her with an open mind and with great respect to her interviewees, aware of their femininity. Nevertheless her own biases come through her descriptions.

I will examine Slepak's representation in the context of the ghetto and its meaning for me as a woman historian. I read her text with the awareness that my view is colored by the construction of the memory of the Holocaust in today's culture, particularly in Israel, and with a gender perspective that was not formulated then as it is today. I will therefore move back and forth from the year 2000 to the 1930s and 1940s, hoping to establish a dialogue that will enrich my understanding of the women in the ghetto and yet will not violate Slepak's authenticity.

In my discussion I will describe the women and how they functioned in the environment of the ghetto: at work, in the family and in their social lives. I will reflect on how they understood their role as women and their own attempts to foresee their future. I will study the impact of Nazi policy on their inner world – their approach to universal and Jewish values – after two and a half years of German occupation and a few months before the mass deportation to Treblinka. I will ask if there is a gender differentiation in both their understanding and representation of the reality.

My methodology will be mostly narrative analysis including content and style, active and passive voice, and terminology. I will be looking for conflict and resolutions suggested by the text, and will examine their outlook on the future of Slepak and the women she spoke with. I will engage in a dialogue with the text in which I will try to 'link' myself with the mindset of the women and create an interconnection despite the distance of time, space and mentality between us.[4] I am aware that my conclusions and observations are more tentative than certain.

I begin my dialogue with Slepak by turning first to her table of contents in which she lists women's functions, work and professions.

*Studies of Women in Warsaw Ghetto* 31

[Dialogue]

I imagine myself interviewing Cecilia Slepak about her work, and I ask her: I want to understand your view on the metamorphosis of the women from the time of the initial storm of the war and occupation to the confinement in the ghetto. You interviewed the women after one year of ghetto life, during which thousands in the ghetto died of typhus, starvation and cold, and daily life was no longer 'normal'. In the months preceding the establishment of the ghetto, what was the impact of the war and occupation on the women's point of view? In the ghetto itself, how did they view their present lives, and what was their perspective on the future? Ghetto conditions allowed for little privacy, and the public sphere continually penetrated the private sphere. Individual and community were bound together by the orders of the occupier, and the relationship often proved to be contentious. What were the roles of women at home, in the workplace and in public activities, and how did they accommodate to the situation? Today we know that regardless of any heroic or fearful efforts to make a living, regardless of success or failure to save the dear ones, the fatal end had already been decided and scheduled, even as you and your friends initiated the research project on ghetto life. Is this knowledge an obstacle or an advantage for understanding this particular human endeavor in the ghetto?

From the list of women's workplaces I learned of educational institutions, orphanages, illegal activities and places of detention. I read of women working in restaurants and dance halls, of women who died in the hospital, and one who established a library. I read about mothers left alone after their husbands were deported or arrested, and about a woman who separated from her husband because of a family disagreement and was then left alone to provide for the children. Women were involved in the petty economy of small commerce, exchanging household's goods for food, and smuggling. There were women who were able to obtain daily credit in order to be able to trade, repaying the loans by the evening. Your narrative, Cecilia, presents the contradictions of living in a society that functions with great difficulties and ample suffering, with great feelings of loss and mourning. And yet the voices of the women epitomized the vitality of living, the desire to overcome the tragedies, alongside great weariness. In addition, women's voices expressed the legitimacy of enjoying pastimes, such as a card game during the long evening curfew, a session at the hairdresser and to listen to a whisper of love.

You gave little space to accounts of ghetto institutions like the Judenrat, but told of a woman who begged for a job in its employment office. You commended the women who established public kitchens, a source of professional and social satisfaction, while also giving a voice to those who depended upon the kitchens and expressed great reservation about them.

You were not the only one who viewed ghetto life with an open and critical eye, with neither hatred nor heroic acclaim. This attitude was shared by most of the participants in the research project on 'A year in the life of the ghetto – two and a half years of nazi occupation'. Unlike others who dealt with a single major theme, such as education, hunger, medicine, religion or armed resistance, you presented multidimensional life stories of women.[5] The dominant theme of your report is living, perseverance and resistance, providing a broad description that touched almost all of these other themes and included all aspects of being.

I wish to understand your narrative, which is about daily life in the midst of an extreme political and social crisis. All routines had been transformed and people had to reinvent their daily reality. Is it right to speak about every day life in the ghetto? Your narrative opened with a portrait of a sunny day in the Warsaw ghetto at 10 o'clock:

> The Jewish streets are hustling with an apprehensive rhythm of their uprooted life. People [like] trees, walk, almost with no movement, they stand bound to the wall. Faces, voices, smiles mingled with each other.[6]

Your phrase, 'the rhythm of uprooted life' follows the description of the people as almost paralyzed, motionless like trees facing the ghetto's wall. Yet voices rather than silence is ruling the air. Were they waiting for a smuggler with whom they planned to meet? Passively waiting for an associate to rescue them from the isolation of their previous life? Or perhaps this is their form of protest and quest for liberation?

The description goes on and makes us listen to the voices and imagine the scenes:

> 'Fresh roll, good, white, cheap!'
> '*Warsawer Zeitung*' [Warsaw newspaper]
> ...
> 'The best cigarettes, cheap cigarettes'
> 'For potatoes, ... carrots'
> 'Good people have mercy on a mother of three orphans!'
> 'Sweets – Oi gewald! A thief! Catch her!'
> 'I am hurrying to the hairdresser. ... I have an appointment in the afternoon.'

'Thank G-d I made some money this week.'
'At the office, the payments are late.'
'I have nothing more to sell, how can I provide for the family?'
'Yes, the appeal for the children had good results.'
'How expensive! I do not know how and on what to save.'
'Spring, what a beautiful sun. We want so much to live. We must endure.'

Your own voice concludes: 'At 10 in the morning the Jewish streets are already vibrating with the multitude of voices of the destitute and the light of hope of the day.'[7]

Jealousy and hatred, love affairs, family feuds, professional satisfaction – are you merely turning the tragedy of these women and the ghetto into a series of detailed, but banal, stories? I wonder if such stories could be termed banal at all in the face of the Nazi oppression and the goals of their anti-Jewish policy. You, Cecilia, never forgot the political dimension; you were preoccupied with the Nazi rule, the tragedy of the Jews and the suffering of the Poles. For me, the political aspect already includes the 'Final Solution' and the attempted annihilation of the Jews. I step back to the winter of 1942, and erase from my mind the knowledge that two months after you completed your draft – a copy of which I read today – you and probably all the women you interviewed were sent to Treblinka. I cannot help thinking about the life stories you recount, your comments, and I ask myself: what would you have written had you been aware of the inexorable doom?
[End dialogue]

The dialogue between Slepak and myself is tricky, for I must provide both questions and answers. My tentative responses will employ a number of concepts: identity and self-understanding in relation to the family; activities in the domestic and public sphere; the responsibility of earning one's living; external and inner conflicts and their resolution; the means of survival, the need for flexibility and other behavioral characteristics.

## Ms KR's life story

I'll start with your story of Ms KR, a vegetable seller, in the spring of 1942.[8] (I ask, when in May?: before the night of the killings on the 18th, or afterward, when nightly killings became routine?)[9] She was sitting on a small bench leaning against a wall, praising the low prices and the freshness of her vegetables in her tired voice. She looked much older than her age, her thin face and blinking eyes reflect her hunger.

Selling vegetables was not a new trade for Ms KR. Before the war she had a large stand in the market, and together with her husband, who manufactured women's coats, they provided for their family of two children, a 10-year-old daughter and a 7-year-old boy. They lived well in a three-room apartment and kept extra food supplies at home in case of hard times. When the war broke out in September 1939, she continued to go to the marketplace every day, unafraid of the shells and bombs that hit the city. Her sister-in-law convinced her and her husband to leave their apartment, since a fire brigade was located in their courtyard, and they feared that this made the building more vulnerable to bombardments. She agreed reluctantly to move in with her sister-in-law and continued to go to her own apartment daily and take belongings and food. In the heavy bombardment of the city on September 25, her building was hit and burned and the family lost all it had. Ms KR was shocked at the loss, and regretted that on the previous day, despite her wish to go there to remove food and valuables, she had not done so. Instead, she had listened to her sister-in-law's fatalistic approach that one never knew what was safe, and therefore one should let things happen. Ms KR, by contrast, had always believed that she should consider various options and be flexible to meet the new challenges. Thus, one period of Ms KR's life ended. She had to begin anew, without her belongings and all that she had achieved over the decade of her married life.

The family was unable to rent a new apartment and they moved into the kitchen of her brother's one-room apartment. Conditions were very difficult, but the couple tried to recover their businesses. Her husband lost his small workshop and turned to trade, but as Ms KR said 'he had no talent for trading'. Afraid of the Nazi raids in the streets, he stayed home with the children and tried to replace his wife in doing domestic chores. 'Yet no one can escape his fate', said Ms KR. One day the Nazis came to the building and took all the men for work. Mr KR was physically weak and was hurt badly by the Germans, who were unhappy with his slow pace of work.

Ms KR returned to her vegetable stand in the market, but the scarcity of produce led her to try a new venture together with her two sisters who sold fish. They worked hard from early morning to the curfew hour and managed well. She was happy that she was able to provide for the family and they were not hungry, although their cramped living conditions were still her major problem. In June 1940, she decided to move in with her sisters. Her husband, who didn't get along with the sisters, stayed behind and thus, some nine months after the loss of her home and possessions, Ms KR's family was dismembered despite the recovery of her business. She began a new period in her life as head of her family and sole provider. As we know very little about Ms KR's relationship with her husband before the war, we cannot know the reasons for their separation. It is clear, however, that the decision was not easy for Ms KR. Despite being an independent woman and the support she received from her sisters, she had to 'regain her self-confidence and cure herself from the shock of the separation'. Still, we see that she conducted her life according to her own preferences and was making choices.

The five months between June and November 1940 are not presented in detail, although they conclude a dramatic time in her life, beginning with the German occupation in October, the economic venture established with her sisters and her emergence as sole provider for her children.

The establishment of the ghetto in November 1940 cut her and her sisters off from the marketplace, which was outside the demarcation lines. This was devastating, and their economic conditions worsened every day. Selling vegetables was not profitable because of the limited supply and high prices. Most Jews could not afford vegetables; only bread was in demand. After learning the new situation Ms KR and her sisters decided that 'their way to an economic recovery' would be by selling bread.

Thus began the third period in Ms KR's life. Together with her sisters, they organized a stand, carrying the loaves from the bakery a few times a day, watching carefully to keep thieves off their backs as well as at the stand itself, since the starving people kept trying to grab a loaf and quickly eat it up. The three sisters and their children divided the tasks and all were involved in the business in one way or another. Yet they barely made a living, and could only have made a profit by expanding the business. But they had no resources to invest and each day they depended on a credit of 100 Zl from the baker. The three families together earned 20–25 Zl per day, barely enough to live (a loaf of bread at the time cost 3–3.5 Zl), but 'they were happy because the bread sufficed for all of them'.

The three sisters displayed great energy during the worst months of the ghetto economic and social situation. Being able to provide for the three adults and six children was quite an achievement under those conditions. Thousands died of starvation and typhus in the winter and summer of 1941. Many records documented the unburied corpses on the ghetto streets, and the constant noise of beggars and children singing and begging for food. Slepak's appreciation for the efforts of Ms KR and her sisters is summed up by her statement: 'these were the last days of no hunger for Ms KR and her family'.

This period in Ms KR's life ended abruptly in September 1941 when she came down with typhus. The chain of events ended with the tragedy of the death of her two sisters. Unable to afford medicines, she and her sisters were forced to borrow money from neighbors in order to provide better food for those who were ill. One of the sisters died at home, and the other, although receiving somewhat better care in the hospital, also died. Ms KR was left with six sick children (four of them the children of her sisters), a number of debts to repay, and she no longer had the bread stand. She sold her remaining possessions to provide medicine and food for the children, who recovered.

But she had no rest, for she had to find work. She washed laundry and cleaned homes – jobs that were physically demanding, yet she was happy when she had work. She also received a meal in the homes where she worked and often got leftovers to take home. The children's situation was very difficult, for they lay in bed during the long winter days, without clothing and heat, and ate a meal only after she returned home with food. Yet they were not dying or swollen with hunger. She sold her food rations to buy a larger amount of grains, which was their main source of nutrition. Despite the dire conditions, Ms KR maintained a positive attitude and did not despair. She was grateful that she was still alive, and that the children endured as well, which she considered a miracle.

Ms KR shared with Slepak a shocking experience she had during the winter. One evening on her way home, she stared at the window of a sweet store and asked the saleswoman the prices. The saleswoman scolded her and drove her away: 'no sweets, no price, we know you, get out of here you thief'. She was painfully hurt; this was not the only time that people rejected her because of her appearance.

During the spring of 1942 she was unable to carry on with cleaning and washing and so went back to selling vegetables. Her story is telling. A neighbor lent her some money in the morning, which she must repay in the evening. With this loan, she bought produce from a smuggler. Since she got her goods through a middleman she paid a higher price, but she was unwilling to risk going to the *matta* – the place by the wall where smugglers passed the produce for a cheaper price. Her daughter replaced her at the stand when she went to fetch the produce, with her son to help protect her from thieves along the way. Once again, everyone cooperated in order to provide food for the family, but it remained very difficult. She made only 5–6 Zl a day at a time when the price of a loaf of bread was 11–12 Zl.

'I learned to compromise', Ms KR told Slepak. 'I was once an observant woman and would not eat *treif* [non-kosher food]; now I do not ask what is in the soup. I am happy that I have a bowl of soup for me and for the children.' And Slepak added, 'The war did not corrupt her morality, her honesty and self-respect. Even in the most difficult moments, even when she confronted the death of her dear ones, she did not go out to beg and did not send the children to do it.' And to make sure that the reader would be convinced Slepak added in parenthesis, 'as a neighbor acknowledged'.

This was the final period of Ms KR's life story in both senses. Slepak's interview was ended, but a more tragic ending emerged a few weeks later with the mass deportation to Treblinka. Ms KR and her children were probably among the first to be deported. Apart from this painful knowledge, we see that in this final period, she continued to struggle and did not collapse despite the unimaginable calamities. If her life moved steadily downhill, it was not because she failed to try to invent a new reality and create new options, but rather due to the political system that doomed her. Although aware that things were getting worse and worse, she was not fatalistic; she continued to make decisions and to exercise what options remained to her. When interviewed in the late spring of 1942, she thought she could somehow endure and that she could try some new venture and make an easier path for herself.

[Dialogue]
Cecilia, you end Ms KR's story with her hope for a better future. She planned to emigrate to the United States to be with her sister. Twice, her American sister had sent food parcels, which Ms KR sold in order to buy basic nutrition, keeping only a small part of the package for her own family. The prospect of emigration was an anchor of hope and an assurance of her self-respect. You also emphasized that Ms KR was too proud to reveal her full distress even to her sister; she was ashamed of her situation, and felt that its full disclosure would have stripped her of human dignity. You thought that this explained why she never walked into the self-help institutions, and only lately had she received free vouchers for her children to receive meals in the public kitchen, and three free food rations. You expressed admiration for her fortitude.

Only two of her inner conflicts were presented in your narrative. The first was her dismay over having listened to her sister-in-law and consequently failing to remove food and valuables from her apartment, and the second, her decision to move away from her brother's apartment to live with her sisters and separate from her husband. Ms KR had revealed that she was religiously observant and I can understand that separating from her husband was unconventional. However, once she made the decision, she did not keep troubling herself about it, and she and her former husband remained on good terms, although neither supported the other financially. Her husband then disappeared from the narrative and was not mentioned in her account of the months in the ghetto.

Your narrative brought to light your respect for Ms KR, and your appreciation of her choices She preferred to obtain daily credit, sell vegetables and live on 5–7 Zl a day rather than beg or apply for assistance from the self-help organizations. Her independence and flexibility were evident in her efforts to try new jobs and open new ventures as an entrepreneur in the petty business of the ghetto. She did not lose her core belief in the humanity of her neighbors and those around her and believed strongly in human dignity, seeking to maintain her own as well. Beyond your terrifying image of the old-looking, poor, thin, ragged woman, you found expectation and hope.
[End of dialogue]

*Guta's life story*

Another woman described offers a more perplexing and no less fascinating portrait. Slepak left us two versions of this life story. I will first tell her story combining the information of both versions and then try to understand the difference between them and what I learn about Slepak's account from the different narratives.[10]

Guta was an attractive 19-year-old when the war began – only one week after her happy marriage. She had grown up in a family who owned a restaurant where much alcohol was served and the environment was quite brutal. While helping her parents, she had learned how to charm and calm drunken patrons. Her husband, a dental technician, fled to Vilna a few days after the war broke out, and promised to send for her shortly after the violence would cease. She was very fearful during the three weeks of the shelling and bombing of Warsaw, but was able to control herself and help her parents in the restaurant, which remained open during that time. Soldiers came to the restaurant and consumed a lot of alcohol. Since her parents had stored flour and other supplies, they did not suffer from shortages during these difficult weeks.

In October, after the battles were over, her husband sent for her. A person who would help her cross over to Vilna, which was not under

German occupation at that time, contacted her. She was happy at the prospect of joining her husband, but she returned to Warsaw after nearly being hit by the shooting of the Soviet's border guards. Witnessing people being injured, killed or barely escaping with their lives when confronting the Soviet border guards shocked her. In Warsaw, she found her parents dazed after the Nazis had confiscated their restaurant stores. Unable to maintain the restaurant, their economic situation deteriorated.

Guta however, did not lose courage. She engaged in trade in order to recover her parents' restaurant. Success did not come easily, but after a while she was able to establish some fine business contacts as a broker of gold and jewels, and thus assisted her parents to reopen the restaurant, which provided a base for her trading contacts. The place attracted many suspicious people – Jews, who worked with the Germans, as well as Germans, Poles and others, an adventurous company that posed some risk to the family.

At the same time, Guta developed a romantic relationship with a Volksdeutsche (ethnic German) who had rented a room in her parents' flat. Her parents hoped that their tenant's presence would shield them from further Nazi confiscation. Thus, they kept much of their valuables and items not allowed to Jews, such as furs and foreign exchange, in his room. The intimate connection with the Volksdeutsche led to a broader trading business. The Volksdeutsche was able to cross the border from Poland to the Reich where he exchanged gold and jewelry for goods demanded in the Polish market.

Guta and her lover went out to dance halls and other public places, she without her armband. Their intimate relationship was well known to others living in the apartment house. Perhaps because of informants, the restaurant and their apartment saw a number of visits by police and Gestapo agents, who seized some of their possessions each time. Guta and her Volksdeutsche friend were arrested by the Gestapo and interrogated for Rassenschande, but they managed to keep from revealing their relationship, even though Guta as a Jew received harsh treatment. This stormy period of her life lasted more than ten months, until the family was driven into the ghetto in November 1940.

Despite the loss of capital her parents suffered with the move to the ghetto, they were able to find a place and reopen a restaurant. As long as Guta's lover was able to visit her in the ghetto, the family managed to retain their new business. He supplied the restaurant with food and alcohol at prices that allowed them a good profit. With his help, Guta was also able to obtain passage permits to the Aryan side, and so she was able to continue her trade. She was also a vivacious and charming spirit in the new restaurant and the patrons loved her. All this lasted for a few months until her romantic relationship began to cool. Her lover came less often, and then his visits stopped altogether. After a period in which Guta and her parents labored hard to maintain the restaurant, they finally had to close. The family, which included her father, mother, brother and sister-in-law, reached the brink of hunger, and Guta felt a responsibility to pull them out.

Guta had to start all over again. As a new beginning, she found a job as a waitress in a café and dance hall. Yet despite her long hours, she found she could not provide for the family. Determined to succeed, she once again took up her trade and smuggling, as well as continuing her job. Her activities caused much pain to her father, but her mother tolerated them, since they were a valuable contribution to the survival of the family.

Taking advantage of the location of their apartment building close to the ghetto wall, she contacted a Polish acquaintance – a shoemaker who lived across from them on the Aryan side. She telephoned her order for fruit, cigarettes, tobacco and other goods, and after midnight they signaled each other to begin the transfer of the merchandise. She was quick and knew her way around, and the operation proved very successful. She also developed a friendly relationship with her partner, who often crossed the wall assumedly for business, but actually as part of their intimate relationship.

One night, this new venture almost cost Guta her life. A German policeman caught her by the wall, but she managed to run away, and the dark night saved her from his deadly bullet. However, in December 1941, at the peak of her new success the ghetto borders were redrawn. Guta's family moved to a single room in another family's apartment, away from the passage out of the ghetto walls.

Guta did not give in to despair and her adventures did not end at that point. In July 1941, she had been offered a job in a new café-bar. She had a great reputation as an attractive, intelligent and interesting young woman who liked to enjoy herself with her clients in the bar. Here, her chances to make better money were higher. The place was notorious for its guests, mostly non-Jews and Jews who worked with Germans. After a while, she developed a relationship with Bolek, a Polish police inspector who became very fond of her and wanted her to be his mistress only.

Guta enjoyed this relationship, which offered many advantages to herself and her family. She also tried to help others who were in trouble or caught by the Polish police. Among them people who were confined for crossing to the Aryan side and people picked up in street raids to be deported to forced labor camps. Slepak hinted that Guta and her parents did not refuse payment for such services. Unfortunately, when her brother was picked up she was unable to save him despite elaborate efforts. He was sent to an unknown destination.

Slepak's talks with Guta ended in May 1942. Saddened by her brother's deportation, she took some time off work, but maintained her relationship with Bolek the police inspector. What was her fate in the critical months from July to September 1942? We do not know. Was she able to get false documents and pass to the Aryan side? Perhaps; in any event, her chances were better than those of Ms KR, although still very limited.

[Dialogue]
Guta's story reveals a number of peaks and ebbs, although exact dates are uncertain:

> September – November 1939
> December 1939 – November 1940
> December 1940 – summer 1941
> Summer 1941 – December 1941
> January 1942 to the date of the interview (probably after May 16, the last date named in the interview, but before June 1942).

I learn that Guta showed consistent effort to deal with the crises that followed the arbitrary rule of the Nazi occupiers. She was daring, courageous and creative, knew how to maneuver people, and was ready to engage in illegal activity and make use of conditions in her favor. Although she expressed her terror of the violence of the war, she continued to work with her parents in their restaurant during the siege of Warsaw. She seems to have been free from hypocrisy, self-righteousness and self-pity. Can I read in her story a moral deterioration – for she was not faithful to her husband, and was willing to sell her body in order to maintain a good life? I don't think this was the intent of your narrative, despite the unease often expressed in your subtext. Your own embarrassment was reflected in your two versions of Guta's life story; as you elaborated the ups and downs of her tale, I read two distinct narratives.

While in your first version you labored on the 14 months before the move to the ghetto, you concluded the last period of the ghetto in a few lines. You only mentioned that she was ready to sell her body.

Moreover, before you reached this stage you explained why she had to take this job that pushed her to the ebb. In this context, your selection rendered a favorable explanation of Guta's conduct.

In the second version Guta and her parents were depicted as very instrumental people. Their relationship with the Volksdeutsche was motivated only by their interest to safeguard their economic situation. You hardly mentioned her effort to cross the border to her husband. However, the last stage of Guta's life story was central in your narrative of this version. The description was long and detailed and it offered a behavioral pattern – a chain of relationships from the Volksdeutsche to the Polish shoemaker and to Bolek. Moreover, we were told that she received the job as a bar-café girl because she had a reputation as an attractive young woman that received the favor of clients.

Why did you write two versions of Guta's story? Which one did you prefer? I sense your empathy for her, and your appreciation for her irresistibly clinging to life, her devotion to her parents and those with whom she worked. You detailed the interrogation by the Germans after they discovered the photo of her Volksdeutsche lover in her pocket, and you stressed that despite the harsh treatment she received, she kept silent, knowing what a grave sin he had committed in their eyes.

You sought an explanation for her future development by looking at the environment of Guta's childhood – in the restaurant, surrounded by alcoholics and low class people. Yet you did not portray as inevitable the path she took – indeed, that path was chosen by her, and not altogether rejected by her family. Though you mention the criticism of the neighbors, you qualified this by stressing the moral atmosphere of the ghetto. The permissiveness came out of a general spirit that accepted unconventional manners. You wrote this judgment in relation to Jewish women in the ghetto, but added in brackets that such conduct was typical for women in the war years.

When such interpretations entered your straightforward narrative, your attitude to Guta became more respectful, disclosing your own conflict over this manner of survival. Unable either to condemn or praise Guta, you were not, however, a neutral observer of Guta in the ghetto. You, too, were part of the ghetto environment and felt its pain and fears. Therefore your voice was ambivalent – you reverberated sympathy to Guta beyond the intellectual empathy of the researcher. Was it the woman in you that in these tragic days reasoned out how difficult it was for a young attractive girl like Guta to avoid using her femininity and sex to make a living? I think that it follows what you wrote in your introduction concerning the means and strategies that Jewish women employed from their cultural and social resources to 'become victorious in the struggle for life'. Therefore, the part of you that might denounce Guta in normal times was not allowed to speak up. You related to her temperament as a cause for her romantic involvement, but also to her readiness to confront challengescourageously.

Did Guta herself suffer from any inner conflict? You never voiced it directly, but you related to the fact that her association with men did not satisfy her own feelings, she was looking for affection and connections, in particular after her first relationship with the Volksdeutsche. You also described her long working days and the pace that ate up the energy demanded to accommodate clients. Was she losing control, you asked? You demonstrated how limited was her freedom to decide when and how much to be engaged in the business. By putting her situation in these terms you alluded to the fact that the pleasures of wine and other drinks and her own safety were shaky, more than could have been imagined otherwise.
[End of dialogue]

*Bathia Temkin's life story*

The final story that I have chosen is that of librarian Bathia Temkin – the only woman named in Slepak's report that survived the war by passing as an Aryan. Temkin was also mentioned in Ringelblum's notes.[11]

Temkin at that time was 30 years old, married and a certified librarian with a university education. She had continued to work in a public library – even during the siege of Warsaw – until December 1939, when a Nazi order was issued that prohibited Jews from working in a non-Jewish institution. She had enjoyed her work and her coworkers maintained friendly relationships with her even after she was forced to leave her job.

In January 1940, she obtained a job in the clothing department of CENTOS, the refugee aid committee. Tens of thousands of refugees poured into the city following the deportations of Jews from smaller towns and villages and from the western parts of Poland. In the cold winter of 1940, the need for clothing for the refugees (who often arrived with nothing) was very acute. Temkin demonstrated her devotion and skill in organization and distribution, making use of every garment that was contributed to CENTOS. Although she was helping many people, she had her own dream. Among the contributions were also toys and books; and she set aside the books, hoping to establish a children's library. This was a courageous unlawful enterprise, since the Nazis had closed the Jewish schools and other educational institutions, including libraries.

However, with great zeal she gathered all the books and toys and hid them in the garment storage. After her work hours, she would select those suitable for the future library and distributed the others to children's homes, refugee assembly centers (punkts) and the 'children's corners' established by the house committees.

In May 1940, CENTOS was reorganized, and she was dismissed, since her husband, who was one of the directors of CENTOS, provided for the family. She continued to work as a volunteer, however, as a means of concealing her true goal of collecting and hiding the children's books for the future library. November 1940 approached, and the rumors about the formation of the ghetto became a reality. Bathia Temkin felt that now she had to find a suitable place for her books, otherwise she would lose them. When she discovered that the hall of one of the city libraries would be in the ghetto area, she began to lobby to keep it as a library. It had to be hidden from the Nazi authorities, however, and she managed to convince the CENTOS directors to place their plaque at the entrance.

Once she had an 'official' place and the tacit cooperation of CENTOS for her work, she became even more energetic in collecting books from former libraries and private collections all over town. She lobbied the Judenrat to obtain permission from the Nazis to allow the library to operate openly. Despite two refusals in the fall of 1940 and in April 1941, the desired permit finally arrived after the library had functioned illegally for nearly half a year. The library – open for only a few hours each day – was located in the unheated and poorly lit basement of the building. Only one 13-year-old girl from one of the children's homes assisted Temkin.

After half a year of operation the use of the library was extended. Children were allowed to borrow two books each time, one in Yiddish and one in Polish. Temkin encouraged them to read Yiddish literature and was even ready to teach Yiddish. Once a week she read aloud to the children at story time. Some of the young patrons told her their fathers would read the books they had checked out to the family on Fridays. She also opened a reading room for journals and reference books, and adults also came to read. Temkin was happy. It was a dream come true. Children from the orphanages and children's homes came along with the happier children who lived with their families to find comfort with the books. Payment was set similar to regular public libraries, with the poor children being exempt.

From November 1941, Temkin was nominated director of the library and received payment for her work, which she needed in order to support her mother and refugee sister. She felt embarrassed to be paid, since she knew how little CENTOS had, and she appreciated her own satisfaction:

> I work with love; I live because of my work, and emotionally it was healing me. I believed that I am promising a future for these children. When I was working in better conditions in the garment department of CENTOS, I was often sick and missed work. Today I am working in worse conditions and more intensively yet I am healthy; my good feelings about my work is strengthening me and made me immune.

[Dialogue]
When I read Bathia Temkin's account, I feel your great admiration for her. She was a woman of vision who was able to integrate public service with her own need for personal satisfaction in her work. Her dedication to her work shows her selfless concern for something greater than personal survival. Yet I feel this portrait is only partial: you have told us nothing of her personal life, and the circle of her family. In this 'clean' account, we find no personal hungers and wants, no fear or violence experienced during the siege or under the oppressive Nazi occupation. It is an intellectual account of responsibility, her enthusiasm and dedication to her work, and her love of books are the only emotions revealed. You wrote about her feelings of satisfaction, and recorded that she herself felt that such feelings were at odds with the reality of the ghetto environment.

Temkin possessed a clear sense of self-identity; she was a professional woman with educational and cultural goals. She established the library because it was an important part of her understanding of what it was to be human. Like all children, those in the ghetto deserved to have access to the treasures of reading; it held out the promise for their future and their human qualities. You described Temkin's inner voice that called her to her mission and left her restless until it was accomplished. You wrote, 'A person called by his mission believes in it against all odds. Temkin believed as strongly as a belief could be that in the final analysis she would accomplish her goal.' This leaves me with troubling thoughts. In regular times perhaps this is true, but what about the period of destruction? So many dedicated people with beautiful goals were starving to death, were being deported to forced labor camps or were sick with no hope of getting well. Because she and her husband worked with CENTOS, Temkin was among those able to sustain their dreams. She was not among the newly wealthy who 'lived well' in the ghetto. The dividing line between craving for food and being full was very thin, and yet she was among the privileged for whom destitution did not ruin their ability to dream of a cause, activate their capacities to serve it, and find satisfaction in doing so. This, in turn helped them overcome the physical hardship and scarcity, as Temkin herself indicated in the quote given above.

You described her as self-confident, active and creative. Your narrative however, does not leave room for pride, since you emphasize her apologetic tone for being paid as director of the library. Her subtext: I should have done it for free since I get so much out of it, but I need the money.
[End of dialogue]

## CONCLUSION

I have reconstructed three of Slepak's biographies and introduced an imaginary dialogue between us, emerging from the text. I can name this process 'to imagine the real'.[12] This is basically the task of historians. In this I am following Collingwood's *Idea of History* in which he called upon the historian to walk in the footsteps of his historical protagonist, assuming that the common human capacities can bridge between present and past. But I also follow Sam Weinburg's opinion that the historian must appreciate the differences between herself and the historical hero.[13] The gap in time, mentality and culture, that divides past and present calls upon the historian to view history as the study of the 'other'. Only then, said Weinburg, can a historian establish the historical empathy called for by Collingwood. I am also aware of the tension between the reconstruction of the historical past and collective memory. I am approaching the past not only with my own personality, values and ideology, but also with the images and myths assimilated as a member of a community. I am myself both consumer and contributor to the collective memory. Therefore 'to imagine the real' is a difficult task.

My first task was to study Slepak herself, but little information was available. Thus her representations of other women becomes the major source from which to understand Slepak. I view her as a cultural and social feminist. She was an educated, liberated woman who thought that every woman (and probably all human beings) should be autonomous to fulfill her vision. She placed a high value on education, for she thought that tradition and society prevented women from developing and kept them in the domestic sphere. In her sample six women were professionals, a higher proportion than was to be found in general Jewish community. She pointed out that despite the trying conditions in the ghetto, these women gained great satisfaction from their work. Ms Temkin the librarian was presented in this paper, however, in the full document Slepak is describing an agronomist who worked with TOPOROL, the society for agricultural training. In the ghetto TOPOROL initiated the cultivation of small plots of land to grow vegetables and enrich the diet of the ghetto inhabitants.[14] She presented the story of Ms BT, a dietitian, who worked in organizing the public kitchens, was highly professional and extremely absorbed in her work. She was therefore able to overcome tensions encountered in her crowded dwelling.[15] These professional women were able to develop their potentials and were flexible to adapt to the new conditions. She commented for example that although Jewish women were not respected for being efficient workers, in the crisis of war and ghetto they demonstrated an intuition that enabled them to perform in the most efficient manner.[16]

She also respected the traditional attitude of housewives and working-class women to their husbands, and appreciated their responsibility to their families.[17] She describes the risks they were willing to take upon themselves in order to protect their men and children. She found courage in women's readiness to give up a working place they found for themselves to their husbands, in the hope that the working permit would avoid deportation to a forced labor camp.[18]

Thus, despite the ugliness of the war, the crises and tragedies of life in the ghetto, the situation nevertheless brought forth the potential of many women. Only in this context can we understand what she meant when she wrote that women were victorious on the battlefront of life. Therefore she appreciated using femininity to receive contributions for the needy and approved card games to collect money for the refugee children.[19]

Slepak thought that human life must be inspired by an engagement between the individual and the collective. She thought that even in the most difficult times the individual must be responsible for the well-being of the community. Therefore, she expressed most appreciation for those working at the refugee assemblies, helping in the public kitchens, educating children and doing volunteer work.[20] She was critical of women who took on 'high-status' tasks, such as Ms Chairperson of a house committee; and she expressed her reservations about the upper bourgeoisie.[21] She admired the working women who found the energy to pay attention to the poor and needy.[22] In Slepak's value system, it was those who showed self-respect, did their utmost to find work and refrained from begging who won her admiration. She evidently felt that those who could be inspired by and dedicated to a cause were the ones best able to endure life in the ghetto and preserve their humanity.[23]

Activism was important in Slepak's ideology. The abnormal conditions of the war and occupation demanded that women become active in promoting the survival of their families in non-conventional ways. Slepak rarely used the word 'love' but refers to the relationships of couples and other relatives, mothers and children, and between friends. In the face of many dangers, especially the possibility that men would be conscripted abruptly for forced labor, women assumed they were in less danger, and were able to move about more freely. They also did not hesitate to make use of 'women's mannerisms' to distract Polish and German police and thereby save lives.[24]

In the wartime situation, and in particular under ghetto conditions, choices were very limited. However, the women Slepak described did make choices; they were constantly thinking of alternatives. Some choices that she noted were those of the decision to work and not to beg in the streets, to engage in smuggling, to cross to the Aryan side despite the danger or to become a prostitute. Choices emerged as an outcome of both general and specific conditions, a woman's particular personality and her standards. Making choices reflected a sense of autonomy and activism, but one also finds resentment toward the enforced situation. In addition, women made deliberate decisions such as to cross the border to Vilna, to establish a library or to look for a particular job.[25]

Slepak wrote as if there was a future for the women she interviewed. They believed that they would survive the war, emigrate, create a new life for themselves, perhaps acquire new professions. Despite the obvious hardships, hunger, death and misery, her narrative is one of hope. Her heroines were dedicated to life, to overcoming, to enduring and to survival.

Slepak offered many philosophical comments in her descriptions either interfering with the life story of the women or when she came to conclude an individual story. In each case she was connecting the nuanced stories with her values and how she viewed the women's values. Even in the spring of 1942, she did not hesitate to suggest practical advice about the value of vocations, the importance of work and self respect, and how honesty and devotion was important. Were we writing these biographies, would our narrative be quite different, as we know the end?

## NOTES

This paper is dedicated to the late Israel Shaham who introduced me to Slepak's work and helped to translate it.

1. Cecilia Slepak's research is to be found in the Ringelblum Archive (ARI/49), divided into a number of bands. Her subjects are identified only by an initial. I use the Yad Vashem Archives copy (YVA) JM/217/4 and JM/215/3 (henceforth Slepak, followed by a band number). We have very little information of Slepak. Ringelblum writes that she received her reputation from the translation of Shimon Dubnor's 12 volumes of *History of the Jews* into Polish and she was asked to write on the women in the ghetto. He mentions that she was deported to Treblinka in the first great deportation, summer 1994. See Emmanuel Ringelblum, *Ketavim aharonim*, Vol. 2 (Jerusalem: Yad Vahsem, 1994), pp. 223–5. Ringelblum's notes were published in English as *Notes from the Warsaw Ghetto*, ed. and trans. Jacob Sloan (New York: 1958). The Hebrew version, however, offers the full original Yiddish text.
2. For further information on this research initiative in the ghetto see, Joseph Kermish, (ed.) *To Live wih Honor and Die with Honor: Selected Documents from the Ghetto Underground Archives 'O.S' (Oneg Shabbath)* (Jerusalem: Yad Vashem, 1986); Raya Choen, 'Emmnuel Ringelblum: Between Historiographical Tradition and Unprecedented History', *Gal-Ed on the History of the Jews in Poland*, Vol. XV–XVI (1997): 105–17.
3. Slepak, band 1 table of content. See also the plan of the research 'prospect of the research', YVA JM 3489.
4. I was assisted greatly from the methodology presented in the following works: Jerom Bruner, 'The Narrative Construction of Reality', *Critical Inquiry*, Vol. 18 (1991): 1–21; June Price, 'Acknowledgment: A Review and Critique of Qualitative Research Texts', *Making Meaning of Narratives in The Narrative Study of Lives*, Vol. 6 (1999): 1–24; Shula Reinharz, 'Who am I?' in Ruth Hertz (ed.) *Reflexivity and Voices* (Thousand Oaks: Sage), pp. 3–20; Paul John Eakin, 'Autobiography and Value Structures of Ordinary Experience', *The Narrative Study of Lives*, Vol. 6 (1999): 25–43; Gabriele Rosenthal, 'National Identity or Multicultural Autobiography: Theoretical Concepts of Biographical Construction Grounded in Case Reconstruction', *The Narrative Study of Lives*, Vol. 5 (1997): 21–39; Janelle L. Wilson, 'Lost in the Fifties: A study of Collected Memories, ibid., pp. 147–81; Ruthellen Josselson, 'Imagining the Real: Empathy, Narrative, and the Dialogic Self', *The Narrative Study of Lives*, Vol. 3 (1996): 27–44.
5. See Kermish, *To Live with Honor*.
6. Slepak, band 1.
7. Ibid.
8. Slepak, band 3.
9. On the night of Friday May 18, a small group of SS men walked into the ghetto

and entered specific houses according to a list of names they had. They dragged the men out and shot them in the streets. Their bodies were left to be collected in the morning. There was no explanation why these 52 men were shot (there were 60 names on the list) and it created great terror in the ghetto. The night was named the Night of Barthelomei or the Bloody night. Since then and until the great deportation from the ghetto, starting on July 21, 1942, the terror reigned in the ghetto and almost every night killing of Jews was taking place. For details see, Yisrael Gutman, *The Jews of Warsaw 1939–1943: Ghetto, Underground, Revolt* (Bloomington: Indiana Press, 1982).
10. Slepak, band 3.
11. Ringelblum, *Ketavim aharonim*.
12. I borrowed this expression from the title of Ruthellen Josselson's article, see note 4.
13. Robin George Collingwood, *The Idea of History* (Oxford: Clarendon Press, 1993); Sam Weinburg, 'Making Historical Sense', in Peter Seixax and Sam Weinburg (eds) *Teaching and Learning History in a National and International Context* (New York: New York University Press, 2000), pp. 14–18. Sam Weinburg, 'Historical Thinking and Other Unnatural Acts', www.pdkintl.org/kwin,9003.htn.
14. Slepak, band 1, Ms KR.
15. Slepak, band 2.
16. Ibid.
17. Slepak, band 3. Ms G, aged 31, a housewife and mother of a 13-year-old girl, who is described as a nouveau riche. However, she described her initiatives when her husband lost his business and her parents and her sister's family were unable to make a living. She was ready to be engaged in all kinds of trades to support the families.
18. Slepak, band 1, Ms H, aged 30, described as very pretty and Aryan looking from the lower middle class, who worked in the stocking department of a large export enterprise before the war and lost her job when the war broke out. She was ready to try all trades in order to help her husband who was a painter. In her case too, Slepak is demonstrating the use of femininity to gain advantage in commerce and in finding a working place.
19. Slepak, band 3, Ms G.
20. Slepak, band 2, in the description of the public sense of responsibility of Ms BT, the dietitian.
21. Slepak, band 3, Ms G, see note 17.
22. Slepak, band 1, Ms H. In the ghetto despite her difficulties helped refugees.
23. See her comments on Ms C, the corset maker, and Ms F, the wife of the shoemaker; both band 1.
24. Slepak, band 1, Ms. H, and the story of Ms F, the wife of the shoemaker. For a longer description of this woman see, Dalia Ofer, 'Between Rupture and Cohesion: The Jewish Family in East European Ghettos During the Holocaust', *Studies in Contemporary Jewry*, Vol. XIV (1998): 143–65.
25. See also Dalia Ofer, 'Gender Issues in Ghetto Diaries and Interviews: The Case of Warsaw', in Dalia Ofer and Lenore L. Weizman (eds) *Women in the Holocaust* (New Haven, CT: Yale University Press, 1998): 143–67.

# 3

# The Forgotten Leadership: Women Leaders of the Hashomer Hatzair Youth Movement at Times of Crisis

## ELI TZUR

### INTRODUCTION

This paper is dedicated to the much-neglected issue of female participation in the leadership of left-wing organizations as reflected both in ideology and praxis. It focuses on similarities and differences between the general socialist movements and the Jewish-Zionist youth movements, and particularly the oldest movement in this category – Hashomer Hatzair. Although the study concentrates upon a particular organization, working within an anomalous society of east-European Jewry during a specific historical period that stretched between the emergence of nation-states and the Holocaust, the question it raises is of a general nature. Every radical movement, whose aim is the destruction of old norms and the restructuring of the existing society is doomed to be cut off not only from the power framework, but also from the social structures and their values. Confined within its social and cultural bubble the revolutionary movement develops its counter-culture which sustains it during the periods of isolation and persecution, supplies the *espirit de corps*, and justifies its acts. This counterculture is tested when the movement takes power. On those unfortunate occasions when movements have tried to compel the general society to accept its values in the purest form the results can be demonstrated by the examples of Khmer Rouge in Cambodia or the Taliban in Afghanistan. Those are extraordinary examples and usually short lived. But after a short period almost all the winning movements succumb to the old values and the cultural norms reassert themselves. One can follow the triumph and the demise of the 'proletarian culture' after the Bolshevik revolution to be replaced by the traditional style, although still connected to the party propaganda. The purpose of this paper is to explore whether the above-described generalization fits the field of gender and is reflected in the territory of female leadership. The Hashomer Hatzair youth movement which is the chosen area of my investigation was deeply influenced during the given period by the international socialist movement and especially by its Soviet variation. Therefore one should start with Russia, on whose outskirts Hashomer Hatzair crystallized.

## THE REVOLUTIONARY WOMAN IN RUSSIA

It is generally accepted that until the beginning of the twentieth century women did not participate in the leadership of political organizations. This situation changed at the *fin de siécle*, when women, studying for the first time in formal school systems, used this as a stepping stone to various groups. While academic attention has been paid to the activities of western suffragettes, the much more crucial contribution of women to the underground movements in eastern Europe has been totally forgotten.

Surprisingly it was in reactionary and backward Russia that women appeared in the forefront of political movements. The reactionary character of Russian society, which prevented any avenue of feminine expression, pushed many young women toward the revolutionary movements which were essentially an antithesis to the regime and created a milieu of counterculture. In this environment, women, who were according to a contemporary source 'more ruthless and more dedicated to the cause' than the male revolutionaries, flourished. Among the tiny 'brotherhood' of Tsar Alexander II's assassins, Sofia Perovskaya was prominent. Later, women such as Vera Zasulitch, who tried to assassinate the military governor of the capital, and became one of the founders of the Russian Social Democracy, and Yekaterina Breshko-Breshkovskaya, the figurehead of the Social Revolutionary Party, the largest Russian party on the eve of the Bolshevik revolution, were accepted political leaders. It was at this time that a Polish Jew from Zamosc, Rosa Luxemburg, became world famous as one of the most prominent theoreticians of the Russian and German social democracy.

The socialist founding fathers, Marx and Engels, stated in their *Communist Manifesto*, that one of their movement's aims is the annihilation of women's status as chattel, and the desire to turn them into equal human beings. In spite of this view, both of them adhered to a traditional bourgeois attitude, which locked women within the homestead walls. When toward the end of the nineteenth century, women emerged, as stated, in the socialist political leadership, it happened by negation of their gender, by the party becoming gender-blind. When in 1913, at the International Women's Day, the Bolshevik *Pravda* called for female workers' meetings, it was made obvious that this was not 'a concession to female separatism'. This approach is very clear in the letters exchanged between Lenin and his close personal friend and a prominent socialist feminist, Inessa Armand. While Armand wanted the gender issue to receive special attention, Lenin claimed that after the revolution the issue would resolve itself and that there was no need for any special treatment of the gender issue. In regard to 'the demand for freedom of love', an important issue for the socialist feminists at the beginning of the twentieth century, he stated 'that what mattered was the objective, class relations and not ... subjective wishes'.[1]

The Bolshevik victory, in spite of the declarations of gender equality, signaled the end to the short period of female participation in the leadership. As they became Russia's rulers, the Bolsheviks reverted to the normative Russian culture which pushed women back into their traditional role. The traditional outlook of the Bolsheviks when dealing with the social-cultural issues, compared with the macro-engineering of Russian society, becomes apparent when investigating the leading strata of the emerging society. During the Soviet period the sign of belonging to the ruling elite was participation in the Communist Party conferences and congresses. During the first decade of the Soviet state the representation of women in these events remained stable, although fluctuating. Table 3.1 illustrates this picture.[2]

TABLE 3.1
ATTENDANCE AT SOVIET COMMUNIST PARTY
CONFERENCES/CONGRESSES, 1917–29

| Conference/congress | Date | All participants | Women |
| --- | --- | --- | --- |
| 7th Conference | April 1917 | 152 | 10 |
| 8th Congress | March 1919 | 305 | 9 |
| 9th Congress | March 1920 | 530 | 28 |
| 10th Congress | March 1921 | 690 | 19 |
| 11th Congress | March 1922 | 522 | 9 |
| 13th Congress | May 1924 | 748 | 20 |
| 16th Conference | April 1929 | 254 | 2 |

In comparing the pre-revolutionary period with the years when the Bolsheviks were in power, it becomes apparent that the female leadership was mainly the result of the revolutionary movements' social and cultural isolation and the declarative attitude of the socialist movement, which proclaimed general equality, including equality between the sexes. As ideology became praxis, the new leaders retreated from the counterculture *Weltanschauung* to a traditional set of values.

The Bolsheviks realized their promises of equality as soon as they came to power. A western researcher of the Soviet attitudes to gender stated that

> the Russian revolution was intended to remove all limits to women's equality. Collective organizations were to take over the kinds of tasks ... that had traditionally restricted women and limited their full participation in economic life. ... Accompanying those changes was a 'sexual revolution' ... that encouraged equality in love and sex as well as in economics and politics.[3]

In order to change women's status and role in the emerging Soviet society, the Bolsheviks had not only to promulgate new laws, but to build a new leadership supported by a cadre of feminist activists. They therefore included 'women and their interests as an integral part of an insurgent coalition. Women not only participated actively but, for the first time, they organized themselves to advance a program for their own liberation.'[4]

Aware of the underrepresentation of women in the Party organs, the active feminists in the Party leadership organized a special section of the Party Secretariat dedicated both to activity among women and to promoting their particular interests – the *Zhenotdel*. But as the new regime stabilized, it quickly reverted to the traditional values (similarly in culture and the arts). American historian Wendy Goldman described this process by stating that 'the party officially and explicitly jettisoned its commitment to a revolutionary vision of women's liberation. One of the victims of this process was the *Zhenotdel*. The transformation of this vision into reality barely survived the first decade of the Soviet Union and moved into oblivion.'[5]

Ten years after the Bolshevik revolution many of women's social achievements had become an accepted feature of Soviet society. However, in two main issues the Soviets reverted to pre-revolutionary standards: gender relations within the family and in connection with the subject of this paper – its female leaders. The statistics of the Party conventions and the liquidation of the very organ in charge of developing this leadership shows the extent of the retreat in the gender politics, a retreat into traditional values.

## THE GENDER POLICIES OF HASHOMER HATZAIR

The Jewish youth movement Hashomer Hatzair which appeared in the Polish and Galician arena on the eve of the First World War absorbed many of the messages of the Russian revolutionary counter-culture, including its approach to the female leadership. The young people belonging to Hashomer Hatzair were influenced by its messages either directly or indirectly (through German linguistic filters) and colored them with a romantic gloss. The most widely read book, read by all its members, was Brzozowski's *Flames* which described a group of young revolutionaries in Tsarist Russia. One could describe its impact as producing a radical and romantic mood, and not one of rational thought. Demanding the unity of ideology and praxis, the members of Hashomer Hatzair viewed any gap between ideological promises and their limited realization in politics with disdain. This general attitude was also applied to gender. In parallel to this over-arching approach, typical to the *jugendkultur* of a youth movement, the first generation of Hashomer Hatzair members which grew up in traditional families, with their defined framework of women's activities, mainly confined to the household chores and communal philanthropy, was molded by its social milieu. This overall picture was colored by regional differences, which had a great impact on the role of female members as leaders.

Here I shall discuss female participation in three different historical events that were characterized by two main features: all were periods of acute external crisis and in all, female leadership played an unusual role. The three events were the Russo–Polish war of 1920, the German–Polish war of 1939 and the mobilization census that took place in Palestine during 1940.

## THE RUSSO–POLISH WAR

The Russo–Polish war erupted in 1920 as a result of the aspirations of the newly emerged Polish state to restore the historical borders of the eighteenth-century Polish Commonwealth. This war was the second round of the military conflict on the eastern Polish border, where the Poles prevented the establishment of the Ukrainian state in eastern Galicia in 1919. The first conflict was characterized by hectic Polish anti-Jewish activity, culminating in the Lwow pogrom, carried out by the Polish military units, a feature repeated in the 1920 war in the Pinsk area. As a result of the war conditions in Fall 1919 the Galician (i.e. the part of Poland which prior to the First World War had been part of the Habsburg empire) Hashomer Hatzair's leadership decided to flee the Lwow area and renew its activities away from the frontline, in Łódź. There were personnel changes and two men were nominated as movement leaders for the duration. One of them, Sam Spiegel, later became famous as a Hollywood tycoon. One young woman was affiliated with the movement's central apparatus, but only in a technical secretarial capacity and on a temporary basis, until the Łódź facilities would become fully operative.[6]

In the area known as 'Congress Poland', the situation during the 1920 war was different. In the clashes that took place during 1919, the brunt of the fighting fell on various volunteer units, such as the Haller formation, which conquered Lwow. As a rule the Jews remained outside the ranks, but in 1920 there was a general call up. Although the Jewish youth was recruited, it was considered an unreliable political element, and many of the Jewish soldiers were interned in the camp in Jablonia. When youth group leaders were drafted into the army, the existing leadership of Hashomer Hatzair was taken over by a group of feminist activists. This change was especially sweeping in the capital city of Warsaw. Here a group of girls organized and ran the local chapter of Hashomer Hatzair, which was the biggest and most influential branch of the movement. Their success was undeniable. But as the military tension eased after a few months, and the mobilized soldiers returned home, the sense of emergency passed and the female leadership returned its posts to the demobilized male leaders. This transformation occurred naturally, as both sexes viewed the female rule as a temporary stage during the emergency and the male leadership as the usual state of affairs. There were no signs of protest among the demoted feminist leadership.[7]

These two short episodes illustrate the role of female leadership in the Jewish youth movement in Poland in the early 1920s. The Galician Hashomer Hatzair, although more accustomed to the liberal practices of the Habsburg empire and therefore versed in the praxis of independent youth movement, accepted the conservative view in terms of its female members. The Polish movement, one of the first Jewish organizations which became legal after the German conquest of Poland during the First World War, was deeply influenced by the Russian underground counterculture, which accepted its female members as equal participants in its activities. At the same time it limited the exceptional role of female leaders to times of emergency, eliminating them as the crisis passed. Although the alternative female executive existed for only a few months and was limited mainly to Warsaw, it created a feminist myth which had its impact on future generations of Hashomer Hatzair female members. The comparison between the female role in Galicia and Warsaw emphasizes the differences between the social atmosphere in those places: the Galicians acted in the traditional eastern-European ways, as they did not develop radical gender policy. In Warsaw the movement was able to formulate radical gender policies fitting the radical counterculture, but being connected to their families and to the surrounding society, the movement reverted to the traditional set-up as soon as the emergency passed.

## THE VRUTKY DISCUSSION REGARDING THE ROLE OF WOMEN IN HASHOMER HATZAIR

Ten years after the events described above, the Hashomer Hatzair movement convened for the first time to discuss the role of women in the youth movement. The gathering occurred during the Hashomer Hatzair third world conference in Vrutky, Slovakia which was held in September 1930. For the most part, the participants described the state of socialist literature dealing with women's liberation, while avoiding any discussion of the existing conditions both in the youth movement and its kibbutzim. The chief referent of the kibbutz movement, Shulamit Bat-Dori, claimed that the women in the kibbutzim had passed the stage of external struggle for their rights and moved on to the process of self-improvement in the ideological, cultural and professional spheres. She did not mention the matter of female leaderships.[8]

The movement's main ideologue and leader, Meir Yaari, was more ready to admit the kibbutz's failure to grant the female kibbutz members full equality. He tied this failure in with the problems of absorption in Palestine and proclaimed that full gender equality would be achieved by unceasing feminist struggle, or in his terms – auto-emancipation.[9] His attitude pointed to the accepted view within left-wing Zionism – those sectors that wish to improve their status could do it by their own efforts without the establishment's assistance. This approach liberated the leaders from responsibility to the weaker sectors of the movement, while keeping the hope alive that the situation would improve at some time in the future. Only one speaker, a young girl from the Polish provincial town of Kalish, reminded the movement's dignitaries that in emergency conditions, 'the number of boys dwindles, and then the girls, naturally, take the reins of the local organizations'.[10]

While these conditions are extraordinary, the women leaders must be groomed and prepared. She therefore agitated for a special female movement within the youth organization, a proposal rejected by the movement. In her presentation she relied on the collective memories of the female rule in Warsaw in 1920, which proved that in an emergency the girls could save the movement. Ironically, the gathering was organized by Gola Mire, one of the Galician movement leaders, who later led the rebellion against the Hashomer Hatzair leadership and became one of the genuine resistance leaders and heroines during the Holocaust era. But in Vrutky she preferred to lecture about girls' education in the movement, while accepting the benevolent negligence of the kibbutz leadership.[11]

The Vrutky discussion showed that the leadership preferred to bury the question of female leadership under a mountain of platitudes, without any change, even when the girls were a majority in the youth movement. The problem was postponed for another decade and for a real crisis.

## THE GERMAN–POLISH WAR OF 1939

In the summer of 1939 it become obvious that a clash between Poland and Nazi Germany was unavoidable. On the eve of the German invasion of Poland the Hashomer Hatzair leadership, aware that the emergency conditions would lead to a mass mobilization which would include its upper echelons, decided to form an alternative leadership, based on boys under the call-up age and girls. Members of this group were elected on the basis of their educational and organizational prowess. As one team member, Hajka Grossman, recollected in 2000:

> I received a telegram from Warsaw to come there immediately. I took a train and arrived at the movement's headquarters. And I was only 19. I had been told that, as the war is unavoidable, and the boys would be called up, the movement is organizing an alter-

native leadership composed of girls and under-age youngsters. I was selected as one of its members. I was shocked and confused ... Here my youth ended.[12]

In spite of these preparations, when the war began all the premeditated plans dissolved. The older groups of the movement joined the stream of refugees fleeing to the East and all the prepared command structures, either established or alternative, were defunct. Eventually the movement's senior groups and most of its leadership gravitated to Vilna, the only major city of Poland occupied neither by the Germans nor by the Soviets, and viewed by the Zionists as the escape route to Palestine. This gathering of the political elite of Polish Jewry is known as 'the Vilna concentration'. While the leaders concentrated in Vilna, the rank and file remained in the occupied parts of Poland and this circumstance required reconnecting the dismembered body into one entity. This task was put on the shoulders of the alternative movement's leadership, and it became an ultimate test of one's loyalty and courage. The story of one of the alternative leaders is illuminating. Mira Epstein remained in Warsaw throughout its blockade, and after Poland's capitulation, as the movement began to reorganize itself, the Vilna group believed that it would resurrect the Warsaw organization. But Epstein was exhausted, tired and scared by her war experiences, and decided to return to her family home in Baranowicze, leaving both the movement and its written history forever.[13]

On the other hand, other members of the alternative leadership were sent from the relative security of Vilna, back to Nazi-occupied Warsaw. The first member to be sent back was Tosia Altmann, a veteran movement activist, who later became a symbol of Hashomer Hatzair in the German-occupied territory. After returning to German-occupied Poland, she almost single-handedly resurrected the youth movement, which had been paralyzed by the war events. For the youngsters in the ghettos she became 'the movement', as she described it herself in a clandestine publication. In all correspondence between Hashomer Hatzair in Poland and in Palestine, Poland was called 'Tosia's land', similar to the code used in the 'Hechalutz' organization, where Poland was dubbed 'Tzivia's land' after Tzivia Lubetkin, another prominent woman leader in the underground. Altmann took part in the now famous New Year meeting in Vilna, where she read the manifesto, calling the Jewish youth 'not to go like lambs to the slaughter', but to fight. She died in the aftermath of the Warsaw ghetto uprising, wounded in the battle in the Mila 18th hideout. Altmann was not alone in this status of female movement leaders. In the underground Zionist youth movements in the ghettos there were a large number of women leaders. It is interesting to read their description by the Warsaw ghetto historian, Emmanuel Ringelblum:

> The heroic girls, Chajke and Frumke – they are a theme that calls for the pen of a great writer. Boldly they travel back and forth through cities and towns of Poland. They carry 'Aryan' papers identifying them as Poles or Ukrainians. One of them even wears a cross, which she never parts with except when in the ghetto. They are in mortal danger every day ... Without a murmur, without a second's hesitation, they accept and carry out the most dangerous missions ... The girls volunteer as though it were the most natural thing in the world ... Nothing stands in their way, nothing deters them ... The story of the Jewish woman will be a glorious page in the history of Jewry during the present war. And the Chajkes and Frumkes will be the leading figures in this story.[14]

In his eulogy Ringelblum mixed up the courier girls who connected isolated ghettos with leaders who arrived there in order to organize the local organizations and present the ideological or educational lines, as they emerged in Warsaw. All of them were symbols of bravery, loyalty and dedication, but the level of their activity was different. While he mentions these two names, he does not differentiate between Hajka Grossman of the Hashomer Hatzair alternative leadership mentioned above, Frumke Plotnicka of the Hechalutz and the heroic girl-couriers who fulfilled their orders. Tosia, Tzivia, Frumke and Hajka were educational, organizational and political leaders, whose main arena of activity was the youth movement. As the movements' branches became sections of the underground, their status as leaders changed, and their place was taken by men who intended to lead their followers into a battle.

This process was not limited to the Jewish youth movements, but was an accepted mode of operation also in the non-Jewish Polish left. Until her death, Hanka Sawicka was a leader of the Communist Youth. Wanda Wasilewska was a figurehead of the Union of the Polish Patriots in USSR. Only a few of the female leaders retained their position after the underground was created. Hina Borowska and Sonya Madajsker became the *éminence grise* of the Communist organization in the Vilna ghetto, even deciding that the commander of the United Partisan Organization, Itzik Wittenberg should commit suicide as he surrendered to the Nazi authorities. Gola Mire became an accepted authority in Kraków, both in the Polish Communist and the Jewish undergrounds, dying during the attempted escape from the Gestapo prison. In the Jewish youth movements and particularly in Hashomer Hatzair the transformation from educational entity to fighting organization was smooth and the female leaders became not commanders but spiritual leaders. Few, like Hajka Grossman, who since 1943 was a chief of reconnaissance unit in a partisan brigade, became field commanders.

Even taking into account the large number of fighting women in the Jewish underground, the importance of female leaders in the Jewish underground, as it evolved from the Jewish youth movements is surprising and in comparison with any similar underground movements elsewhere. This spectacular feature of the Jewish underground was marked both by the participants of the events and biographers, who wrote the biographies of many, although not all, of these leaders. Their faces, when taken by the SS men after an arduous battle, were portrayed in the von Stroop report as those of 'Halutz fighting girls'. Placing the story of the female leaders in the ghettos in the general thesis of this paper, one can point to the decisive difference between them and all other revolutionary women leaders: the Hashomer Hatzair movement could not revert to the traditional social ways as the Jewish society did not survive and the counterculture as it grew before the war and especially during it remained the only existing culture, including its gender attitudes.

## THE 1940 MOBILIZATION CENSUS IN PALESTINE

In order to understand the singularity of this phenomenon, one can compare it with the situation in the kibbutz movement composed of the Hashomer Hatzair graduates.

In March 1940 (approximately the date of Altmann's arrival in Warsaw) the first general conference of female kibbutz members was convened, whose organizers had to apologize 'that although we always opposed particular meetings on gender base, as we believed in solving all our problems together, the new situation compelled us to do so'.[15] Even then the discussion was not focused on problems of women within the kibbutzim. A few months later, after the French defeat, and with the Italian navy roaming the Mediterranean, the Yishuv authorities decided to call for a general census of the male population in the possibility of an eventual mobilization. In preparation for the census the kibbutz organizations answered special questionnaires dealing with their female members' occupations and status. From these one can learn that the majority worked in traditional women's roles: cooking, childcare and so on. Thus, after a generation of declarations about gender equality, women still ended up where they had begun. In public activities as well, their participation was limited mainly to the internal social sphere, with underrepresentation in the central organs and economic institutions.[16]

On the basis of that data the female kibbutz activists demanded an equal chance in the professions, reserved until now for male members, the right to be nominated to work in central organs, when their mate would take care of the household chores and care for their children. For the first time they required a fixed quota of female members in the movement's central institutions.[17] What women achieved in the western countries as a result of war economy conditions, female kibbutz members demanded to be enshrined in regulations. However, these demands were not fulfilled, and the only result of these demands was a book entitled *Women-kibbutz members*, edited in 1944 by one of the leading feminists in the kibbutz movement, Lilia Basevitz.[18]

Although the editors stated in the introduction that this was to be the first volume of the collection, publication was never continued. The introduction to the book presented the *Weltanschauung* of its creators as follows:

> This book of Women-Members does not concentrate on questions particular to them only. It reflects the life of a generation ... In the Hebrew Liberation Movement a man and a woman had taken a path, being driven by common ideas, founded on two bases: Zionism and Socialism. Both of them had been ordered to strive for personal and material independence, for equality in the inter-personal relations and to building the new society without the oppression of the weak by the strong in any category; national, sexual or social. In the kibbutz life those imperatives were translated into a language of reality. The experience of the first generation proved that not always was the female kibbutz member understood by a male member and supported by him.[19]

The introduction pointed to the main issue of the book: the price paid by women and the meager results of a generation's endeavors. One can assume that the mood of the feminist kibbutz members was of contrition and disappointment. Surprisingly, a copy of this book was found in a cache of material buried in Slovakia by Haviva Reik, a Hashomer Hatzair member and one of the paratroopers sent from Palestine to Slovakia during the Second World War and executed there by the SS, who was throughout her life a willful, strong and independent woman. The gender relations in the kibbutz movement remained static for another generation and until the 1970s the central kibbutz institutions remained a male-dominated domain.

## CONCLUSION

Although they belong to the same movement with unchanged ideology and rank and file of similar cultural and social profile, we can discern clear differences between the three episodes described above. In 1920 the female leadership was a short episode limited to the capital city of Poland. In the 1940 draft preparations in Palestine, the female activists acknowledged their failure to participate in the leading ranks of the kibbutz movement and concentrated mainly in professional equality. The only place where women became effective leaders was in German-occupied eastern Europe. Although later historiography diminished their role by merging them with the liaison women who were in charge of transferring orders and directives from the center to the provincial ghettos, the outstanding role of Tosia, Tzivia and Hajka cannot be denied. A question arises: why did female leaders fully realize their potential only there? In my opinion two main reasons elevated the women to their outstanding role during this period. The first was the uniqueness of this historical period; the second was the cultural gap between this period and the other aforementioned periods.

Already during the war one of the few women who reached Palestine from Poland stated that 'the unique reality of the ghetto has raised women's importance. She became brave, searching and finding new ways of keeping her family alive, wandering in search of food in trains using false documents.'[20] In his diaries, the Nazi ruler of the General Gouvernement, Hans Frank, claimed that the Jewish women were more resilient than the men and therefore more dangerous. Besides the obvious advantages of female physiology, in the special conditions of Jewish existence, an important factor was the Jewish women's mental ability, honed through generations to survive and ensure the survival of her family. But this general description does not explain why the fully-fledged female leadership appeared only in one sector of Jewish society and only then during one brief period. In spite of the abilities of the Jewish female leaders, Jewish traditional society limited the scope of their activities to domestic affairs. During the crisis the women broke their shackles, but this act was influenced by the longevity of the crisis. Both in 1920 and in 1940 the crises were short episodes. In 1919 the Hashomer Hatzair movement's decision-makers, living within the walls of their homes, were still a part of the Jewish traditional society, captives of its norms and values. In 1940 the kibbutz society revived the Jewish eastern European family values and viewed the question of female leadership from that perspective. The view that the kibbutz movement revives the traditional values was already accepted by the editors of the book *Women-kibbutz members*. In the Polish movement, confined within the ghetto walls, the leaders lived in communal housing, fully detached from their families as well as from normative society, creating a subculture of their own. In this artificial environment two developments took place: the personal growth in stature of the new cadre and a change in attitude. On a personal level one can accept the description of one of the participants of those events, written during the war:

> those girls weren't outstanding and specialized in their duties. They were young girls. They weren't outstanding, because all the girls were likewise. We saw how a person grew and loomed larger above himself in his everyday job. You should know that often the everyday work is harder and more demanding than an act of heroism which takes only few moments.[21]

Those qualities could flourish only when the reality broke the confinements of the tradition. In these conditions the movement's declared ideology became a reality, not dependent upon Jewish sociology or political considerations. Separated from Jewish traditional society, from the directives sent from the kibbutz movements in Palestine, the youth movements in the ghettos could fully develop their unique culture, of which one of its major tenets was a realization of women's leadership.

At the beginning of this paper I presented a general thesis that on the second day of the revolution the revolutionary movement sheds its *avant-garde* counterculture and reverts back to traditional values, which it had hoped to overturn. The main reasons for this upheaval were the pressures of reality and moving from a small group of brothers in arms to the masses of the ordinary people. The case of the Hashomer Hatzair female leaders seems to prove this generalization. Only the uniqueness of the situation combined with the counterculture tradition of youth movement transformed into an underground organization enabled the emergence of women leaders for a prolonged period of time, leaders who were able to cope with the demands put upon them at the most tragic era in the long history of the Jewish people.

## NOTES

1. V.I. Lenin, *Collected Works*, Vol. 35 (Moscow: Progress, 1966), p. 182.
2. 7th (April) All-Russian Conference of RSDRP (bolsheviks) (in Russian), the Protocols (Moscow: GIPL, 1958); 8th Congress of RKP/b/ (in Russian), Protocols (Moscow: GIPL, 1959), p. 451; 9th Congress of RKP/b/ (in Russian), Protocols (Moscow: GIPL, 1960), p. 480; 10th Congress of RKP/b/ (in Russian), Stenographic Report (Moscow: GIPL, 1963), p. 760; 11th Congress of RKP/b/ (in Russian), Stenographic Report (Moscow: GIPL, 1961), p. 716; 13th Congress of RKP/b/ (in Russian), Stenographic Report (Moscow: GIPL, 1963), p. 711; 16th Conference of RKP/b/ (in Russian), Stenographic Report (Moscow: GIPL, 1962), p. 761.
3. Anne E. Gorsuch, '"A Woman is not a Man": The Culture of Gender and Generation in Soviet Union, 1921–1928', *Slavic Review*, 55: 3 (Fall 1996): 636.
4. Wendy Goldman, 'Industrial Politics, Peasant Rebellion and the Death of the Proletarian Women's Movement in the USSR', *Slavic Review*, 55: 1 (Spring 1996): 47.
5. Ibid., p. 77.
6. A Circular to all the movement's branches, n.d., Central Archives of Hashomer Hatzair (henceforth CAHH), (2)71.1–2.
7. Sprawozdanie Komendy Okregu i Gniazda Warszawskiego za rok 5681, CAHH (1)2.1–2.
8. *Hashomer Hatzair, Organ of Hashomer Hatzair Organization's Graduates*, Vol. 4, No. 23–24, December 15, 1930, pp. 16–20.
9. Ibid., pp. 4–5.
10. Ibid., Sarah Zajfe, 'Thoughts', p. 21.
11. Ibid., pp. 6–9.
12. Hajka Grossman, 'Almost a Confession' (Hebrew), *Yalkut Moreshet*, 69 (May 2000): 108–9.
13. Zelig Gajer to the Hakibbutz Haartzi executive, September 11, 1939, CAHH. (2)28.3–h.
14. Emmanuel Ringelblum, *Notes from the Warsaw Ghetto* (New York: Schocken Books, 1958), pp. 273–4.
15. R. Lev, 'The Tasks' (Hebrew), *Hashomer Hatzair, An Organ of the Hakibbutz Haartzi*, 9: 12 (March 21, 1940): 12.
16. Yona Ben-Yaakov, 'Women in Kibbutz' (Hebrew), *Hashomer Hatzair*, 9: 47 (November 20, 1940): 8.
17. Rifka Gebelder, 'About the Women's Status' (Hebrew), ibid., p. 9.

18. *Haverot baKibbutz* (Hebrew) (Ein Harod: Hakibbutz Hameuchad, 1944).
19. Ibid.
20. Rozka Korczak-Marle, A Lecture delivered to a Labour Women Council, February 1945 (Tel Aviv: Moreshet), p. 104.
21. Ibid.

# 4

# Family Origins and Political Motivations of Jewish Resistance Fighters in German-Occupied Europe

## INGRID STROBL

Materially speaking, my childhood was very poor. We had very little to eat, and sometimes we didn't even have any shoes. But we had lots of love from our parents, and fairness, honesty. And learning, culture. We couldn't go to the university and had no books. But my older sister wrote down an entire poem by Peretz for me, on a roll of paper. That was my book; I took it to school with me. Only there was a problem if somebody asked me to read a certain page, because it didn't have any pages.[1]

This statement by the former Jewish resistance fighter Guta Rozencwajg about her childhood in Poland of the 1920s is characteristic in several ways: many of the women who later joined the resistance had similar experiences and were brought up in like manner. Not all of them were poor, but almost all speak of loving parents who conveyed to them high moral values from their earliest years on, and who placed a strong emphasis on education.

For my comparative study on the participation of Jewish women in the resistance in German-occupied Europe, I interviewed some 60 women from different European countries.[2] This group is, of course, not representative; however, it gives quite a good impression of the conditions under which the Jewish women resistance fighters grew up and became politicized.

The women I interviewed are of the age group born between 1909 and 1927; most of them were born between 1920 and 1925. Since the majority of the Jewish resistance fighters were on the whole young, these age groups may be considered as representative for the average activists of both sexes.

One striking thing that the former resistance fighters in western Europe interviewed by me had in common was the fact that 90 per cent of them were immigrants or immigrants' children, most of whom came from eastern European countries. On the whole, immigrants of both genders made up a large majority of the Jewish or Jewish-influenced resistance in France and Belgium. This explains the similarities between the childhood memories of eastern and western European resistance fighters. Differences are evident between the generations rather than geographically. Symptoms of change, as for instance the tendency away from the orthodoxy and toward political constellations are to be observed in France as well as in Poland.

The 1931 census listed 3,136,000 Jewish residents in Poland; this was about 10 per cent of the total population.[3] Poverty and anti-Semitism forced generations of Polish Jews (of both sexes) to emigrate. From the last quarter of the nineteenth century on, a migration from the countryside into the cities was also taking place.[4]

Traditional historical studies provide hardly any information on the lives, work and daily life of Jewish women in Poland between the wars.[5] The poverty of the housing, the lack of electricity and sanitary facilities strongly suggest that the housework was hard and troublesome and that it occupied a lot of time. In the majority of households the dietary laws were observed, which added to the workload. Many wives and daughters helped out in the workshops or business or supported the family by work done at home.

In the first third of the twentieth century, a distinct change took place in the self-image and conduct of Jewish women in Poland. Contributive to this change were the revolutions of 1905 and 1917, the general atmosphere of rejuvenation on which they were based, the vital role played by women in them as well as the increasing urbanization of the Jewish population. The image of the wig-wearing, pious Jewess, devoted/subservient to God and her husband, had for the most part already become anachronistic in the 1920s. The working women in the big cities especially developed a new consciousness which was often socially and politically oriented.[6]

The Polish–Jewish mothers of the first decade of the century in France and Belgium brought the virulent transformation of the traditional image of womanhood with them into the country of migration, whereas the migrant situation demanded of them additional mobility, flexibility and independence. In an unfamiliar environment, unable to speak the language, they had to make a home for their families and often help support them. This led to a good deal of insecurity, but at the same time to women's new significance as the source of warmth and security within the family in an environment that was experienced as foreign and incomprehensible.[7]

The fact that the daughters grew up as children of immigrants led to an often striking transformation: those who, according to traditional ideas of the times, were supposed to stay at home now served as mediators between the family and the outside world; they usually learned the language more quickly than their parents did, they formed contacts with the local population faster, and were often sent out to gather information, resolve conflicts and investigate the possibilities. Many girls took advantage of what this situation offered them: like their brothers, they joined youth movements or political groups, developing a sense of responsibility which enabled them later, under the German occupation, to care for their parents and siblings who, in their hiding places, had to rely on them.[8]

Many of the former resistance fighters I interviewed who had lived in Poland or grew up as the children of Polish immigrants in western Europe, described their mothers – no matter what their social standing was – as sensible, politically and culturally interested persons who encouraged their daughters to get an education and to become self-sufficient human beings. Frequently, the mother is described as the one who, like the father, was pious, but not too severely so – whether it was that she herself wore no *sheitl*, or whether she allowed the children to break rules. The religious life at home as determined by their mothers, is described by most of the women – even when they themselves had long since discarded or given up their own beliefs – as both enjoyable and festive.[9]

Of the Jews who lived in France in the 1930s, two-thirds were immigrants, most of whom were from the countries of eastern Europe. The majority lived in Paris and worked in the 'classic' branches of employment – the textile and ready-made clothing, fur and leather industries. They had close connections to the members of the family that had stayed in Poland; a photo of the Polish grandparents hung in almost every living room (if and when there was a living room). Some of them remained pious or at least traditional, and some relaxed their religious bindings in a France tending toward laicization and assimilation.[10]

The women interviewed by me come from families of all social strata. Most of them are from the lower middle class, their fathers being small shop owners, travelling salesmen and pharmacists. Several women are daughters of craftsmen or workers. The fathers of the middle class women were factory owners, merchants and members of the professions. Their mothers were to a large extent housewives who, however, often helped out in their husband's businesses. Some also were occupied in their own independent vocations or had at least learned a vocation. Three mothers of the resistance fighters I interviewed had graduated from secondary school, one mother worked as a restaurant owner and cook, one as a printer, one as a worker in an automobile factory and seven contributed to the family income as seamstresses.[11]

In Belgium, immigrants made up 90 per cent of the Jewish population. As in France, most of them came from eastern Europe and brought their language and culture with them to Brussels, Antwerp and Liège.[12] Hélène Waxman remembers:

> My mother had a very hard time in her first years in Belgium. She didn't speak the language, the housework was too much for her and she also had two small children to care for. And she didn't know a soul. So she said to father, listen, if you want to stay in Belgium, then you will have to work at home, because I just can't deal with it all by myself. So father set up a workshop at home. My mother then learned French in night school, which she could only do because father was at home. From that point on, things went better for her.[13]

More than half of the women interviewed come from a family with two or three children; five women are 'only children', and the rest come from families with four or five siblings. This is the same for western and eastern Europe, the average family size in Poland being the same as in France or Belgium. Neither are there any great differences in the number of children from orthodox or assimilated families. The decline in the birth rate in the 1920s and 1930s in Poland that was so lamented by Jewish demographs and reform politicians was due not least of all to the changes in role and self-image of Jewish women.[14]

No matter what the social class and place where they grew up, most of the women I spoke to described their childhood as happy and their parents as loving – who to be sure were in some cases quite strict and demanded that their children obey the rules, but who never practiced any physical or mental cruelty toward them. Even women who describe their childhood as unhappy or who refer to themselves as rebellious children were, according to their own statements, never struck. This is unusual for the disciplinary methods in that era, but it tallies with the results of Marion Kaplan's study on the Jewish middle class during the German Empire.[15] Apparently, Jewish parents subscribed much less than did non-Jewish parents to the idea that one must physically discipline children if one loved them.

Education, to which girls were also entitled, played a central role in almost all of the families. In workers' families as well as elsewhere, books and newspapers were read, theatrical performances attended or musical entertainment engaged in at home. Although there were definite class differences, it becomes clear from the childhood memories of the women interviewed that literature, culture, education and languages occupied an important place in all social strata.[16]

Hélène Waxman remembers:

> I had a very clear-sighted, gifted father. On Saturdays, he worked 'till noon. In the afternoon he read to us, in Yiddish, the works of Scholem Alechem. The only gifts we were given as children were books. My mother learned many languages, due to the circumstances of the times. At school she spoke Russian, Poland having been under Russian rule up to 1918. Then came the Germans, during the First World War, so she learned German. Then Poland became independent and she learned Polish. And in Belgium, finally, she learned French. She knew Yiddish anyway. So we were a working-class family, but a family, so to speak, of educated workers.[17]

More than two-thirds of the women interviewed come from traditionally religious or pious families; almost a third refer to their parents as assimilated. However, the definitions that the women make use of seldom correspond to the 'pure form'. What the women refer to as 'pious', 'traditional' or 'assimilated' often proves to be a rather individual mixture. Thus for example Mirjam Ohringer, daughter of Polish immigrants in Holland, remembers that in her socialist home on the one hand the holidays were not observed, but that on the other her mother kept a kosher household 'so that my pious grandmother would have no excuse not to come visit us'.[18] Virginia Cohen, daughter of Dutch Jews, remembers: 'We kept the Sabbath, with Kiddush and a white tablecloth and everything. After the meal, Father read to us from the Ilias and the Odyssee; he read the original and then translated it for us into Dutch.'[19] Chasia Bielicka-Bornstein, who grew up in the eastern Polish town of Grodno, reports, that her mother was pious, but that she accepted that the children increasingly distanced themselves from religion. In exchange, the children respected their mother's beliefs and tried not to hurt her feelings: for instance, at home, they would never have used a meat knife to spread butter on the bread.[20]

The majority of the former resistance fighters I interviewed had, no matter what their social origins, attended a secondary or a vocational school. And those whose parents could not afford to send them to a secondary school or university also grew up, with few exceptions, with the conviction that as girls they had a right to education and to good vocational training. At the time of the German invasion, many of the women were schoolgirls, some of them college students. Those who were already employed were working as seamstresses, nurses, office personnel, factory workers, social workers, Kindergarten teachers, photographers, pharmacists, midwife, hatmaker, journalist and attorney. Some helped out in their fathers' businesses.

For most women as well as men, the way into the resistance movement was through a social or political group. Whoever was not already organized or was not at least close to an organization had difficulty in finding access to resistance groups, which had to cover their tracks in order to protect themselves from infiltration and discovery.

The women who participated in the resistance in German-occupied Europe belonged to the Bund, the Youth Association of the Communist Party or the Party itself, they were members of the left-wing Zionist movements Hashomer Hatzair and Dror, the liberal Zionist youth movement Akiba or – though only a few – in the revisionistic, right-wing Zionist youth movement Betar. Some came from a home in which the father or the mother and sometimes both parents were Zionists, Bundists or Communists.[21]

The Spanish Civil War was for many of the young women who were Communists or who sympathized with the leftists, a decisive politicizing factor. The 15-year-old Sarah Goldberg sold buttons for the Spanish Republic in her school in Brussels. The dedication to Spain was Sarah Goldberg's initiation: 'Step by step, I then became engaged in the leftist organizations.'[22] Ida Rubinstein, who was in the Workers' Sports Club YASK in Antwerp, stresses the significance of the workers' sports clubs for the political development of Jewish immigrant children: 'The YASK was open to everyone. We didn't feel like we were a party or part of a party back then, at 15. We didn't join the party 'till later. We led a scouts' life, with songs and excursions. Then came the Spanish War, which had a strong influence on me.'[23]

The young men and women who were members of the left-Zionist youth movement Hashomer Hatzair played quantitatively as well as qualitatively a large role in the Jewish resistance. In France they contributed, together with the Jewish scouts, to saving Jewish children and youths; in Poland they played an important part in the establishment and operations of the underground groups in the ghettos.

Hashomer Hatzair was organized coeducatively and, at least theoretically, stood for the equality of the sexes. Its moral principles were very strict. Members were not allowed to smoke, drink alcohol or have sexual relationships with one another. 'We were very pure and very rigorous', Chasia Bielicka-Bornstein remembers.[24] 'We were terribly strict with ourselves', says Chaika Grossman.[25] But this rigorous strictness apparently corresponds to a great tenderness and comradeship among them which is expressed in conversations and reminiscences.

Yet not all members of a political or social organization joined the resistance. Why some did and others did not is difficult to reconstruct today. The memories of the women are, as far as the question of their motives is concerned, influenced by the emotions and experiences of the decades lying between their youth and the present day. In addition, the question as to the motives of the former Jewish resistance fighters poses itself differently with regard to each country, organization and point of time.

Ida Rubinstein, who fought as a Jewish Communist partisan in Toulouse, says: 'I joined the Resistance for purely political reasons. But since I am Jewish, I most certainly had a double motivation.'[26] Fanny Rozencwajg joined the Jewish partisans in Belgium after her mother was deported, 'and, to be sure, because my mother was deported.'[27] Survivors of the Jewish Communist resistance in France refer to the fact that many young men and women who could escape from the first big police-raid in Paris in July 1942, but whose parents and brothers and sisters were seized and deported, joined the resistance as a consequence of this experience.[28]

Women who worked for a social or educational institution, as for example the Jewish Children's Relief OSE (Oevre de secours aux enfants), in France, found themselves through their vocation in a situation in which social work or childcare turned into resistance. Their resistance was based not on a consciously made decision, but rather – slowly but surely and without at first being so defined – it became part of their work. In a given case, it was not so much the necessity to fight the Germans that moved these women to action. It was their concern to help and ultimately to save the lives of the children and young people for whose wellbeing they were responsible.

The young women who were active in the Hashomer Hatzair or the Jewish Scouts in western Europe, also became used to their work in the resistance without further ado. Denise Lévy, one of the leaders of the Jewish Scouts, was informed one day that a police-raid among the foreigners under her protection was imminent, so that she had to find hiding places for them at once. The hiding places, however, could not exist for long without false identification papers, so she began to produce these. Questioned as to her motives, Denise Lévy said: 'We couldn't let the children be arrested. To be arrested meant to be deported. At that time we didn't know exactly what happened to the deportees, but being deported was bad enough. We wanted to prevent it in any case.'[29]

If one asks Zionist activists who fought in Poland about their motives, they usually answer that they had not wanted to end up in the gas chamber, that they had wanted to do something, to defend themselves, to avenge the dead, to do honor to the name of the Jewish people. However, all these were the reasons that moved them after the first large liquidations, after it became clear to them that the Germans really would destroy the entire Jewish people. But before this lies the period of time between the invasion of the Germans, the ghettoization and the liquidation of the first ghettos. The foundation stones for the construction of an underground movement were laid within this period; the young women who fought in the ghetto uprisings and later with the partisans had already decided at this time to work illegally. Today they are no longer aware of the reasons for this, or these are simply no longer important. For them there is an 'ante' and a 'post' chronology: the inferno in which they lived and acted after the 'Final Solution' had begun, covers up almost everything that existed before.[30]

The calls to armed resistance in the ghettos in Poland were legitimatized from the first moment on with the motive of 'honor'.[31] 'Even if we are too weak to defend our lives', wrote Mordechai Tennenbaum, commander of the Bialystok ghetto uprising, 'we are nevertheless strong enough to defend Jewish honor and our honor as human beings.'[32] Almost all of the former Jewish resistance fighters from Poland whom I interviewed assign first place to motives like 'honor' and 'dignity'.

One strong motive for the Jewish resistance in western as well as in eastern Europe was the need for revenge. Israel Gutman defines the ghetto uprisings as the only act of revenge that could be carried out under the prevailing circumstances.[33] Chaika Grossman remembers the following: 'In the ruins of the synagogues, into which they drove all the people before burning them down, there was inscribed on the walls: "Revenge us!"'[34] Pierre Broder, editor of *Unzer Wort*, the illegal newspaper of the Belgian left-wing Poalei Zion, wrote in June, 1942: 'The annihilation of the Polish Jewry must ... touch off in us the fire of battle, the fire of revenge.'[35]

Looking back, the question arises as to whether the dramatic appeals in newspapers and the calls to arms of the underground served primarily propaganda and mobilization purposes, or whether they also reflect the feelings of the participants. Did the Jewish resistance fighters long for revenge? I asked all the women I interviewed this question, and the majority of them answered 'Yes' without hesitation. Some former Communists answered 'No', asserting that their motives were political in nature and that revenge had thus played no role for them. Rachel Cheigham, who fought in the Zionist Armée Juive, rejects this as a rationalization: 'I am quite sure that most people are lying when they say that revenge was unknown to them. The need for revenge was, after all that the Germans had done, simply human.'[36]

Thus the motives of the former Jewish resistance fighters in joining the resistance or in organizing it themselves were highly differentiated and interwoven. A political mindset and organization, the identification with the Jewish people and/or a Jewish nation which was to be created, the pedagogical and/or social responsibility for children and young people, the desire to help, and a personal anger and despair: these form the individual components from which a different picture emerges for each of the women. In addition, the youthful age of the women bestowed upon them a high degree of willingness to run risks. The fact that there was no way out of the real situation of the Polish Jews in the last phase of the 'Final Solution', the awareness that neither survival nor an effective military success was possible, called forth the wish to at least go down in history. Representative for many of her comrades in the resistance, Gusta Draenger from Kraków wrote in her prison diary: 'Let us leave behind something to be remembered by, which someday someone will show due respect for.'[37]

## NOTES

1. Interview with Guta Rozencwajg (Holon, 1996).
2. Ingrid Strobl, *Die Angst kam erst danach. Juedische Frauen im Widerstand 1939–1945* (Frankfurt am Main, 1998).
3. See Reuben Ainsztein, *Jewish Resistance in Nazi-Occupied Eastern Europe* (London, 1974), pp. 183 ff.
4. See Marcus Joseph, *Social and Political History of the Jews in Poland 1918–1939* (Berlin, New York, Amsterdam, 1983), p. 18.
5. According to information from Professor Dalia Ofer of the Hebrew University,

Jerusalem, studies have been made in Hebrew in the meantime. Unfortunately, due to the language barrier, I have no access to these and could not make use of them here.

6. Interviews with: Chaika Grossman (Kibbutz Evron, 1991, 1992, 1993); Chasia Bielicka-Bornstein (Kibbutz Lehavot Habaschan, 1995, 1996); Anja Rud (Tel Aviv, 1992, 1996); Hela Szyper-Rufeisen (Bustan Hagalil, 1996); Elsa Lustgarten (Haifa, 1996); Masza Putermilch (Tel Aviv, 1996). See also Ester Kreitmann, *Deborah – Narren tanzen im Ghetto* (Frankfurt, 1984).

7. See Annette Wieviorka's presentation of Polish-Jewish immigrant families in Paris in Annette Wieviorka: *Ils étaient juifs, résistants, communistes* (Paris, 1986). On the role of the Jewish woman as creator and preserver of the sheltered inner family as a refuge in the midst of potentially inimical surroundings, see Marion Kaplan, *The Making of the Jewish Middle Class* (Oxford, 1991). The women I interviewed often described their mothers as having this role. The men I asked as a supplement also remember their mothers as dominant women who mastered the difficult life in immigration and were at the same time loving, 'maternal' and tolerant. Interviews with: Henri Krischer (Nancy, 1987, 1992); Jacquot Szmulewicz (Nancy, 1987, 1992); Abraham Neiszaten (Cologne, 1992, 1994, 1996); Albert Rozencwajg (Rischon Lezion, 1996).

8. See Strobl, *Die Angst kam erst danach*, p. 342 ff.

9. Interviews with: Mirjam Ohringer (Amsterdam, 1996); Virginia Cohen (Amsterdam, 1996); Chasia Bielicka-Bornstein, Sarah Goldberg (Brussels, 1992); Rachel Cheigham (Paris, 1996); Denise Lévy (Paris, 1996); Fanny Rozencwajg (Rischon Lezion, 1996).

10. See René Poznanski, *Etre Juif en France pendant la seconde guerre mondiale* (Paris, 1994), p. 32 ff; Wieviorka, *Ils étaient juifs, résistants, communistes*, p. 55; interview with Jacquot Szmulewicz (Nancy, 1987).

11. See Strobl, *Die Angst kam erst danach*, p. 303 ff.

12. See op.cit., p. 137 ff.

13. Interview with Hélène Waxman (Brussels, 1996).

14. See Strobl, *Die Angst kam erst danach*, p. 303 ff.

15. See Kaplan, *The Making of the Jewish Middle Class*.

16. These are not universally valid statements about Jewish families in Poland and western Europe in the 1920s and 1930s. They only reflect the circumstances in which the women whom I interviewed grew up. Surely there was also violence in the family and households as well as lack of education and culture among Polish Jews and Jewish immigrants. Nevertheless, it is striking that, with a gradation of differences, for almost all 60 of the former women resistance fighters it is rather the opposite that is the case.

17. Interview with Hélène Waxman.

18. Interview with Mirjam Ohringer (Amsterdam, 1996).

19. Interview with Virginia Cohen (Amsterdam, 1996).

20. Interview with Chasia Bielicka-Bornstein.

21. See Strobl, *Die Angst kam erst danach*, p. 317 ff.

22. Interview with Sarah Goldberg (Brussels, 1992, 1994, 1996).

23. Interview with Ida Rubinstein (Brussels, 1996).

24. Interview with Chasia Bielicka-Bornstein.

25. Interview with Chaika Grossman.

26. Interview with Ida Rubinstein.

27. Interview with Fanny Rozencwajg (Rischon Lezion, 1996).
28. See Wieviorka, *Ils étaient juifs, résistants, communistes*; Rayski Adam, *Le choix des juifs sous Vichy* (Paris, 1992); Rayski Adam, 'Diversité et unité de la résistance juive', in *Les Juifs dans la Résistance et la Libération* (Paris, 1995); Krischer Henri, 'Les barricades de la MOI', in *Les juifs dans la Résistance et la Libération* (Paris, 1995).
29. Interview with Denise Lévy (Paris, 1996).
30. See Strobl, *Die Angst kam erst danach*, pp. 231 ff.
31. See Yehoyakim Cochavi, 'The motif of "honor" in the Call to Rebellion in the Ghetto', in A. Cohen and Y. Cochavi (eds) *Zionist Youth Movements During the Shoa* (New York, 1995), pp. 245–53.
32. Ibid., p. 246.
33. See Israel Gutman, 'The Youth Movement as an Alternative Leadership', in A. Cohen and Y. Cochavi, *Zionist Youth Movements*, p. 16.
34. Interview with Chaika Grossman.
35. Unzer Kampf, Juin 1942, quoted from Maxime Steinberg, *La Traque des Juifs 1942–1944*, vol. 2 (Brussels, 1986), p. 2.
36. Interview with Rachel Cheigham (Paris, 1996).
37. Gusta Draenger-Dawidson, 'Tagebuch der Justyna', in *Im Feuer vergangen. Tagebuecher aus dem Ghetto* (Berlin, 1962), pp. 216 ff.

# 5

# *Gendered Perceptions and Self-Perceptions of Memory and Revenge: Jewish DPs in Occupied Postwar Germany as Victims, Villains and Survivors*

ATINA GROSSMANN

As we write the history of the post-1945 years, we are only now rediscovering what was amply obvious to contemporaries: that occupied Germany in the immediate postwar period was the unlikely, unloved and reluctant host to hundreds of thousands of its former victims, housed in refugee camps in the US and British zones and in the American sector of Berlin. Of course, at war's end, millions of people, including ethnic Germans expelled from eastern Europe as well as former soldiers, forced laborers, and survivors of death and work camps, were on the move. The available statistics, both those cited by historians and those collected at the time, are stunningly variable and surely inaccurate, itself a sign of the chaos that accompanied peace and the speed with which conditions changed. Anywhere between 10 and 20 million people clogged the roads, struggling from East to West and West to East. Astonishingly, between May and September 1945, the victors had managed to repatriate about 6 of the 7 million persons defined as 'displaced' and eligible for return to their homelands (hence not including the German *Vertriebene*, expellees) whom they had initially faced in the occupied areas.

A significant number of those who remained uprooted and on western Allied territory as DPs (displaced persons) were Jewish survivors of Nazi genocide and involuntary migration (primarily to the Soviet Union from Poland); precisely the people both the Allies and the Germans had least expected to have to deal with in the aftermath of National Socialism's genocidal war.[1] It is, I think, particularly difficult for historians to chronicle adequately the Jewish DP experience, and not only because of the obvious problems raised by having to confront the planned extinction of an entire people and its consequences. This is a topic for which there are vastly more contemporary sources than good current work. Moreover, some of the best and most comprehensive recent studies are in Hebrew.[2] Most confusingly, the history of the Jewish DPs, like perhaps that of any community which had endured overwhelming losses and lived in transit, is not only their own but that of many other interested (and more or less powerful) parties. It involves: Allied occupation policy and its trajectory from unconditional surrender and denazification to Cold War anti-Communism and cooperative reconstruction in western Germany; British policy toward Palestine; US policy on immigration in general and American–Jewish pressures in particular; Zionist demands and actions to deliver Jews to Palestine for the establishment of a Jewish state; the politics of the Soviet Union and the newly Communist East European nations from which many of the survivors came; the emerging mandates of the United Nations and the international relief organizations; and finally the varied experience of the by no means monolithic Jewish survivor community itself. In my previous work, I have juxtaposed German and Jewish postwar history, insisting (as I would still, despite some highly skeptical responses) that the story of the Jewish DPs (and other survivors) needed to be firmly inserted into our ever more sophisticated narrative of postwar German history.[3]

In this chapter, I want to jettison for the moment the relative safety net of a more familiar German history approach and focus on a few aspects of the specifically Jewish experience. Particularly, I want to discuss three linked points: first, the highly contradictory and ambivalent perceptions and self-perceptions of Jewish DPs as survivors, victims and indeed, villains, and (more cursorily) how those perceptions changed over time and entered into our present debates about trauma, memory and memorialization; second, the remarkable baby boom among Jewish survivors, which, while duly noted, has until very recently escaped the serious attention of current researchers; and third, some ways of thinking about notions of revenge and memory in relation to sexuality and reproduction.

## PERCEPTIONS: *MIR SZEINEN DOH* (YIDDISH FOR 'WE ARE HERE')

It seemed, at times, that as difficult as it was to comprehend that European Jewry had been subjected to systematic extermination, and that the 'Final Solution' had indeed been put into operation, it was almost more difficult to grasp that there were in fact survivors – several hundred thousand – who required recognition and care. American officer Saul Padover's early description of the 'veritable Völkerwanderung of refugees' is telling in its assumption that the Jews had all been murdered:

> Thousands, tens of thousands, finally millions of liberated slaves were coming out of the farms and the factories and the mines and pouring onto the highways. ... They were all there, all except the Jews. The Jews, 6 million of them, the children and the women and the old men, were ashes in the incinerators and bones in the charnel houses.[4]

But, in fact, not all European Jews had turned to ashes. Between 1945 and 1948, the US and British zones of occupied Germany became a temporary home for approximately – and again, the numbers are rough and constantly changing – a quarter of a million Jewish survivors (some recent estimates are higher, up to 330,000). Some were German Jews who had emerged from hiding or returned from exile or the camps; most were east European survivors who had been liberated by the Allies on German soil (some 90,000 were liberated alive, many died within three weeks, leaving about 60,000 or 70,000). Their ranks were soon swelled by tens of thousands of Jews who poured in from eastern Europe. These mostly Polish Jews comprised three distinct groups; concentration and labor camp and death march survivors who had been freed in Germany but initially returned to their home towns hoping to find lost family members or repossess property, Jews who had survived among the partisans or in hiding, and finally a large cohort who had been repatriated to Poland from their difficult but life-saving refuge in the Soviet Union and then fled again, this time in a western direction, when convinced that there was no future for Jews in Communist-occupied eastern Europe.[5]

In August 1945, Earl G. Harrison, dean of the University of Pennsylvania Law School and a former United States Immigration Commissioner, submitted to President Truman a report on his fact-finding tour of DP camps in the US zone. It declared that:

> We appear to be treating the Jews as the Nazis treated them except that we do not exterminate them. They are in concentration camps in large numbers under military guard, instead of the

SS troops. One is led to wonder whether the German people, seeing this, are not supposing that we are following or at least condoning Nazi policy.[6]

The passionate outrage of the highly publicized report was hyperbolic and unfair to the substantial efforts that had been made by the US military, but it did push the American occupiers and especially General Eisenhower to appoint an advisor on Jewish affairs and meet Jewish demands for separate camps with improved conditions and rations and recognition as a collective entity with some internal autonomy. As a result, American controlled DP camps in Germany, Austria and Italy became by 1946 magnets for Jewish survivors fleeing renewed persecution in the homelands to which they had briefly returned, and for Zionist organizers seeking to prepare them for *Aliyah* to Palestine, especially after the pogrom in Kielce, Poland on July 4, 1946.[7]

It seemed therefore, both to Germans and Allied Military Government, that Jews in Germany were more present than ever before, increasing in numbers and demands daily. Military Government and local German officials as well as overwhelmed American-Jewish and UNRRA (the United Nations Relief and Rehabilitation Administration which had originally been established in 1943 to organize the repatriation of the millions expected to be displaced by the war) relief workers in the camps, Zionist Palestinian emissaries, and DP teachers and leaders themselves, often saw the DPs as 'beaten spiritually and physically', hopeless, depressive, afflicted with 'inertia', and 'an air of resignation', unsuited to any kind of normal life. Both sympathetic and hostile witnesses regularly and graphically bemoaned the 'uncivilized' state of the survivors. They seemed oblivious to the most elementary rules of hygiene, uninhibited in regard to the opposite sex, unwilling to work or take any sort of active initiative. At the same time they were labeled 'jittery, excitable, anxiety prone'.[8] All these reports cited symptoms that today are clearly associated with 'post-traumatic stress disorders'. Already in 1946, social workers and psychiatrists were defining pathologies that the psychiatrist William Niederland, himself a refugee from Nazi Germany, would later explain as a particular 'survivor syndrome' – which, painfully, would become both a stigmatizing label for people who, in most ways, eventually became ultra-functional citizens of their new homelands, and a necessary diagnosis for claiming restitution from the future West German government.[9]

Given our own late-twentieth-century inflationary romance with the language and theory of trauma and memory, and its corollary valorization, one might even say sacralization, of Holocaust survivors, it is salutory to recall how very unromantic, unappealing and alien the DP survivors appeared, even to those who meant to aid them.[10] In his autobiographical novel, Hanoch Bartov recalled the reaction of tough Jewish Brigade soldiers from Palestine who entered Germany determined to 'Hate the butchers of your people – unto all generations!' and fulfill their mission of 'The rescue of the Jews, immigration to a free homeland', with 'dedication, loyalty and love for the remnants of the sword and the camps'. But despite these 'Commandments for a Hebrew soldier on German soil', the Brigade men were not prepared for what they found once they actually encountered the remnants they had pledged to avenge and rescue: 'I kept telling myself that these were the people we had spoken of for so many years – But I was so far removed from them that electric wire might have separated us.'[11]

The Israeli historian Idith Zertal has characterized the painful shocking encounter of the Yishuv with the survivors, 'between the Jews of Europe and the reborn Israel', as a kind of 'return of the repressed', which provoked the fear and anxiety Freud diagnosed when something that had once been *'heimlich'*, familiar and homelike, becomes *'unheimlich'*, frightening and inexplicable.[12] Today, immersed in our highly politicized memorial cultures, we have mostly repressed the powerful contemporary consensus among Allies, Germans, Zionists and Jewish observers: that the survivors were 'human debris', at best to be rehabilitated and resocialized into good citizens (and soldiers) of a future Jewish state, at worst to be marked as 'asocial' and beyond human redemption.[13] I.F. Stone, the American Jewish leftist journalist who covered as a 'participant observer' the underground route to Palestine, noted briskly about his first impression of the DPs in the camps, 'They were an unattractive lot.'[14] As one survivor ruefully stated, 'the concentration camp experience is nothing that endears you to people'.[15]

Paradoxically, however, the flip side to the stigmatization of Jewish DPs as both incorrigible and pathetic, was a kind of romantic vision, heavily influenced by the Zionist ethos that dominated DP life, of the tough survivor who had emerged like a phoenix from unimaginable devastation. Kathryn Hulme, an adventurous young American war welder turned UNRRA worker, described her reaction to the Jewish DPs assigned to her camp. They were hardly the 'ashes of a people' announced by so many reporters; on the contrary they were indeed survivors, 'charged with the intensest life force I had ever experienced'. They were – at least their toughened leaders – entirely unlike either the docile well behaved defeated Germans or the 'professional' non-Jewish Polish and Baltic DPs with whom she had previously worked; rather they were 'contrary, critical and demanding'. Resorting to nonetheless admiring stereotypes, she described, 'their wiry bodies ... smoldering eyes ... voices unmusical and hoarse ... their hands moved continuously'. In fact, she concluded, 'They didn't seem like DPs at all'.[16]

Hulme vividly recorded the indignities of the 'Strange half world of the DP camps', 'a small planet adrift from earth like a raft in space' where the war's uprooted lived, 'bracketed between the two liberations', first from the Nazis in 1945 and then finally from the DP camps after 1947 and into the 1950s. She worried that DPs had nothing else 'to do than sit around and produce babies at such a frightful pace that soon the per capita birth rate of DP land would exceed that of any other country except possibly China'. Jews, she explained were less than one-fifth of the US zone's DP population but 'they were such an articulate minority that if you only read the newspapers to learn about occupation affairs, you gained the impression that they were the whole of the DP problem'. Jews made headlines with arrests for black market activities and not infrequent violent confrontations with local Germans and American GIs; they staged angry demonstrations and dramatic hunger strikes denouncing anti-Semitic acts by occupation authorities and local Germans and demanding emigration to Palestine. They were treated to high level inspection tours by US officials and journalists, who, Hulme thought, handled them with 'kid gloves'.[17]

Eleanor Roosevelt dramatized her efforts to draft an International Declaration of Human Rights with her 1945 tour of Zeilsheim camp near Frankfurt. In September 1946, at a ceremony conducted in the War Room of the US headquarters in the IG Farben Building in Frankfurt, General McNarney extended full recognition to the Central Committee of Liberated Jews as official representatives – at least on matters of social welfare and self-governance – of Jewish Displaced Persons. Indeed, while survivors who had expected to be treated as allies by the occupiers bitterly protested the lack of attention to their plight – especially the devastating fact that their German victimizers were running around free in their own country while Jews sat in camps waiting for emigration permits – it was also true that 'The Jewish DPs were on exhibit to visitors from the moment of their liberation'. Moreover, the DP leadership knew very well how to manipulate these displays and stage their calls for better treatment and entry to Eretz Yisrael.[18] To their sullen and resentful German neighbors, the DP camps appeared as a kind of *Schlaraffenland* of 'sugar and spam, margarine and jam, plus cigarettes and vitamized chocolate bars', as well as centers of black market activity fed by privileged access to the cigarette and food supplies of the occupiers. Yet, as Hulme conceded, 'They sounded like the prima donnas of the DP world, but I thought that perhaps they deserved the rating'.[19]

Despite the overcrowding, the unappetizing rations, the lack of privacy, the smells, the sheer hopelessness of idle waiting, the sometimes humiliating and uncomprehending treatment by military and relief workers who 'looked down on us ... as if we were some kind of vermin or pests',[20] the DP camps and the new families they housed provided a makeshift therapeutic community for survivors who had 'been liberated from death' but not yet 'been freed for life'.[21] The Americans, in cooperation with UNRRA had indeed, made the commitment, that 'reasonable care be taken of these unfortunate people'.[22] But they did so with reluctance and often resentment; as Irving Heymont, the American (and, as he later revealed, Jewish) commander of Landsberg DP camp, confessed in his memoir, 'When I raised my right hand and took the oath as an officer, I never dreamed that there were jobs of this sort'.[23] In the characteristic rapid turnaround of sentiment in the postwar years, it was the victims of Nazism, still displaced and unruly, who soon came to be seen, even by the victors, as the disreputable villains, while the Germans, – with their 'clean German homes and pretty, accommodating German girls' – came to be viewed as victims, pathetic but appealing, and later with the Airlift in Berlin, even heroic.[24] As the impact of the Harrison Report faded into Cold War politics, it seemed to many that 'The guilt of the Germans was forgotten', and that, as a depressed Jewish relief official, Zorach Wahrhaftig, put it:

> ... eighteen months after liberation ... the war is not yet over for European Jewry. They are impossible to repatriate and almost as difficult to resettle. No one wants them now just as no one wanted them before and during the war.[25]

When it came to the Jewish DPs, disgust and fear was mingled with, and often outweighed, admiration and sheer awe at the fact of their survival. Moreover, support for the Jewish DPs, sympathy for their Zionist vision and outrage at their treatment, was often linked to left-wing sentiments; anger at weakening denazification, and the turn away from the politics of vengeance and justice to reconciliation with the former enemy in the service of the Cold War, a process daily reinforced by the omnipresent fraternization with German *Fräuleins*.[26] Only a day before the moving ceremony at the IG Farben headquarters, Secretary of State Byrne's conciliatory speech to the Germans in Stuttgart on September 6, 1946 signaled these shifts in policy and the upcoming end of the brief relative 'golden age' for the Jewish DPs under US occupation, after the Harrison Report and before the intensification of the Cold War.

By 1948, DP leader Samuel Gringauz stated sourly in the American-Jewish journal *Commentary* that, 'Jewish survivors in German DP camps are an obstacle to Cold War reconciliation with Germany ... they are still in acute conflict with the nation which Allied occupation policy wants to make into an ally'.[27] For antifascists involved in postwar reconstruction and relief efforts, such as Bartley Crum of the Anglo-American Committee of Inquiry on Palestine which investigated conditions in the DP camps and Ira Hirschmann, Fiorello La Guardia's personal UNRRA representative, who distrusted the Germans and mourned the demise of the alliance with the Soviet Union, the poor treatment of the DPs and denial of immigration to Palestine and elsewhere were just another aspect of a dangerous policy that coddled the Germans and corrupted the occupiers. Especially liberal and leftist Americans, including a significant number of former German-Jews now stationed in Germany, saw the turn toward reconciliation and recovery for Germany as a source of future fascism. The new agenda of 'business before democracy' persecuted former resisters and punished the victims by keeping them locked away in DP camps, rather than supporting their desire to begin a new life in Palestine, which many officials had discovered on official tours as a 'miracle of orange groves and olive trees'.[28] Anger at the treatment of Jewish DPs and pro-Zionism was thus frequently linked to bitterness over the Cold War and the sacrifice of denazification and real democracy in the name of anti-Communism and rebuilding Germany.

Clearly also, these perceptions shifted over time; from the initial sympathetic shock of liberation, to frantic irritation at the mass influx in 1946 combined with enthusiastic or reluctant admiration, especially for Zionist commitments (which not incidentally relieved the Americans of having to worry about large-scale Jewish immigration) in 1947/48, and finally, the well-known disdain for the 'hard-core' of DPs who had either integrated into German economic life (generally via the black or grey market) or were simply too sick or exhausted to move, and therefore remained in Germany after 1948. In any case, at least between 1945 and 1949, Jewish DP life in occupied Germany, centered around the large camps near Munich and Frankfurt, had generated a unique transitory society; simultaneously a final efflorescence of a destroyed East European Jewish culture, a preparation for an imagined future in Eretz Yisrael, and a 'waiting room' in which new lives were indeed – against all odds – begun.

## *MASCHIACHSKINDER*: THE BABY BOOM

In some kind of supreme historical irony, Jewish DPs in occupied Germany, after the war and the *Shoah*, were producing a record number of babies. In 1946, occupied Germany, far from being *judenrein*, counted the highest Jewish (some, pointing to the unusually skewed young and fertile population of survivors, say, the highest overall) birth rate in the world.[29] The 'steady rush of weddings'[30] in the DP camps came, sometimes within days, to neighbors in the next barrack or to distant kin or friends from what had once been home, whom one did not necessarily know or love very well. There were, as a young woman survivor recalled, 'so many marriages, sometimes really strange marriages that never would have happened before the war'.[31] Certainly they did not, could not, produce 'normal' domestic life. Particularly the young mothers in the DP camps were in many ways utterly unsuited for motherhood and domesticity (in any case limited in the camps). They had come into Nazi ghettos and death camps, partisan groups or hiding as teenagers, and had been given no time in which to grow up. Their own mothers were generally dead (often killed or selected for death before the survivors' eyes), or they had once had children, now lost and murdered, sometimes hidden with Christians and very hard to repossess.[32] Reading postwar accounts, it seems that so many young survivors told their interviewers, 'The hardest moment was when they took my mama away'.[33] As a shocked US Army rabbi reported back to Jewish agencies in New York: 'Almost without exception each is the last remaining member of his entire family ... Their stories are like terrible nightmares which makes one's brain reel and one's heart bleed.'[34] No one knew how to respond to people who had survived the unimaginable. When Saul Padover did finally encounter the Jewish survivors he had thought no longer existed, he wrote, 'I never knew what to say to these people. What sense did words make?'[35]

The veritable baby boom of 1946–47 was, however, a phenomenon much more complicated and remarkable than the 'manic defense' against catastrophic experience and overwhelming loss diagnosed by contemporary psychoanalytically oriented psychiatrists and social workers.[36] And the perceptions of this drive for marriage and children, by both DPs and those who dealt with them, were multilayered, strongly felt and contradictory. 'In the midst of the depressed desert life', (the recurring exodus metaphors were of course not accidental) of the DP camps, one male survivor wrote in a memoir titled *Risen from the Ashes*, 'a noticeable change occurred: people who had survived singly in all age groups were struck with a strong desire to be married'.[37] The American-Jewish journalist Meyer Levin also sensed that, for all the Jews' immediate preoccupation with the barest necessities of survival, their primary need was 'to seek some link on earth ... This came before food and shelter.'[38]

The rapid appearance of babies and baby carriages in the dusty streets of DP camps throughout the American and British zones served as a conscious and highly ideologized reminder that '*mir szeinen doh*', (Yiddish for 'we are here'). Despite everything, women who only weeks or months earlier had been emaciated, amenorrheic 'living corpses' became pregnant and bore children.[39] A *She'erit Hapleitah* (surviving remnant, or more literally, left-over remnant of a remnant) had survived the Nazis' genocide and seemed determined to replace the dead at an astonishingly rapid rate.[40] Attempting to dramatize survivors' desperate determination to emigrate to Palestine, Bartley Crum of the Anglo-American Committee claimed that, 'In many camps I was told that Jewish women had deliberately suffered abortions rather than bear a child on German soil.'[41] Remarkably, however, the opposite was more common. Survivors were not deterred even by the knowledge that for purposes of *Aliyah* to Palestine and emigration elsewhere, pregnancy and young children were only an obstacle.[42] David P. Boder, the American psychologist whose interviews with survivors conducted shortly after liberation, have recently been edited and published by Donald L. Niewyck, described a young woman who had lost her entire family. Now, 'Recently married and visibly pregnant, she eagerly awaited her turn to emigrate to Palestine', and 'Was perhaps the most cheerful and open of the survivors.'[43] The dominant US relief agency, the American Joint Distribution Committee, found itself having to scramble to build Jewish ritual baths for brides (*Mikveh*), and to produce gold wedding rings, as well as wigs for Orthodox wives.[44] Major Heymont noticed in Landsberg:

that the use of contraceptives is highly frowned upon by the camp people. They believe it is everyone's duty to have as many children as possible in order to increase the numbers of the Jewish community.[45]

Whatever the surely highly variable nature of individual experiences, there is no doubt that for the DPs themselves and for those who managed and observed them, the rash of marriages, pregnancies and babies collectively represented a conscious affirmation of Jewish life. This was true for both men and women. But women especially were determined to claim domestic reproductive roles which they had once been promised in some long ago and now fantastic past. Women survivors of the death camps, sometimes of medical experiments, were anxious to reassure themselves of their fertility, as well as prove male potency (which, it was widely rumored, had been subjected to emasculating potions and experiments in the camps). Pregnancy and childbirth served as definitive material evidence that they had indeed survived.[46]

Observers were shocked by a kind of 'hypersexuality' among the mostly youthful inhabitants of the DP camps who had been denied the usual processes of adolescent sexual and romantic experimentation. They noted with a certain astonishment, both impressed and appalled, that, 'The appearance of numbers of newborn babies has become a novel feature of the Jewish DP camps.'[47] Abraham S. Hyman, a legal affairs officer attached to the US Jewish Advisor's Office, observed unsentimentally, as did virtually everyone, that, 'The overpowering desire to end the loneliness and to establish or reestablish family life led to marriages of men and women who patently had nothing else in common and were acknowledged as "marriages of desperation" by the people themselves.' He cited a by now much quoted explanation by a Zeilsheim DP to a member of the Anglo-American Committee of Inquiry: 'I was lonely; she was lonely. Perhaps together we will be half as lonely.' At the same time however, Hyman – again, like virtually everyone who came into contact with the DP survivors, – was moved and impressed by their 'amazing recuperative powers' and apparently irrepressible 'zest for life'.[48] As many survivors have articulated, they were young and finally freed from constant fear; they wanted to live, to taste the pleasures of youth long denied: 'our young bodies and souls yearned to live'.[49] Yet, sexual longing mixed with a painful sense of inexperience, of having missed out on some crucial youthful socialization and pleasures. The quick marriages promised some sense of comfort and stability to people who possessed neither, but were often also cause for more anxiety and insecurity. Buried deeply were stories of rape and sexual assault, at the hands of Soviet liberators and other protectors, as well as Germans and local fascists (and also in the forest partisan encampments, where women were subject to sexual coercion and assault by both Red Army soliders and Jewish partisans).[50] It is worth noting in this context that the experience of liberation (and the prospect of future heterosexual relations) may have been profoundly different for women and men precisely because so many women found themselves having to fear, or indeed undergo, renewed attack, this time from those whom they had welcomed as liberators.[51]

Nonetheless, over and over again, relief workers and interviewers heard the same message: 'All I wanted right away was a baby. This was the only hope for me.'[52] By the winter of 1946, reports claimed that 'a thousand [Jewish] babies were born each month' in the American zone.[53] A 1946 AJDC survey recorded 750 babies born every month just in the official US zone DP camps and perhaps even more dramatically that, 'nearly one third of the Jewish women in the zone between 18 and 45 were either expectant mothers or had newborn babies'.[54] The recorded Jewish birth rate in Germany for 1948, right before the proclamation of the state of Israel on May 16, 1948 and the easing of US immigration regulations eventually reduced the Jewish DP 'problem' to small but highly visible proportions, was a whopping 35.8/1000.[55] All of these striking demographic markers can, of course, be related to empirical data such as the 60/40 (or even two to one) male/female sex ratio among Jewish survivors, the youthfulness of Jewish survivors,[56] the higher rations (up to 2,500 calories a day) and guaranteed (if primitive) housing for Jews. Having sex and making babies was also a way to deal with the frustration and loneliness of leading a waiting life – *auf dem Weg* – in the transit camps, and the disappointment at the reality of the long yearned for liberation.

Still: the high birth statistics require further attention. For Jewish survivors, fertility and maternity worked as a mode of reidentifying and reconstructing. It provided a means, both of claiming personal agency and an intact individual body, and of constructing a viable new community – after extraordinary trauma and even in transit. Let me be clear: the baby boom among the *She'erit Hapleitah* could not offer any redemptive meaning to the catastrophe (*Churban*) that had been experienced.[57] But it did perhaps, offer a possible means to 'redeem the future'[58] or at least to begin the regenerative work of making and imagining one. We can draw here on Dominick LaCapra's insistence that 'one be attentive as well to the efforts of victims to rebuild a life and to make use of counterforces that enable them to be other than victims, that is, to survive and to engage in social and political practices related to the renewal of interest in life (for example, having children)'.[59] Having babies – the most normal of human activities under normal circumstances – and indeed precisely what would have been expected by East European Jewish religious and social tradition – now became both miraculous and an entry into 'normal' humanity, even if it often seemed to offer only a kind of make-believe normality, a 'parallel life' to the memories of the preceding trauma. New babies and families provided a means of bridging the 'radical discontinuity' of life cycle that the survivors had endured. If, as many psychologists and psychiatrists have now argued, Holocaust survivors' loss of 'basic trust' had fundamentally and permanently damaged their faith in themselves and the outside world, caring for an infant could perhaps initially offer the most direct and primal means of reaffirming the self.[60]

## REVENGE AND MEMORY

In that sense, the quick construction of new families could also be interpreted as a kind of genealogical and biological revenge in a situation where the possibilities (and indeed the motivation) for direct vengeance were very limited.[61] Jewish infants, born on territory that had been declared *judenrein* to women who had been slated for extermination, were literally dubbed *Maschiachskinder* ('children of the Messiah').[62] Marriage, pregnancy and childbirth clearly represented a possible reconstruction of collective or national, as well as individual, identity. The baby boom was the counterpart, indeed was closely linked, although in ambivalent ways, to the passionate political Zionism that gripped (in one form or another) virtually all survivors. It offered a means of establishing a new order and a symbolic sense of 'home', even and especially in the refugee camps.[63]

It is also crucial to keep in mind that this Jewish baby boom did not simply go on behind the gates of the DP camps, and unnoticed by Germans. Jewish interaction with Germans was certainly not limited to the oft-cited arenas of black (or grey) marketeering or bar ownership. Jews gave birth in German hospitals where they were treated by German physicians and nurses; Jews hired German women as housekeepers and nannies, they sometimes, especially given the surplus of men, dated, had sex with, and even (in a much stigmatized minority of cases) married German women (by 1950, 1,000 such marriages had been registered, and surely there were many more relationships).[64] DP mothers crisscrossed the streets of German towns with their baby carriages; the many Jewish marriages and births in the DP camps were registered in the German *Standesämter* (marriage bureaus).[65]

Indeed, the much photographed parades of baby carriages proudly steered by DP parents were intended as conscious displays of self-assertion, for themselves and also for others. They clearly communicated the politics of 'we are here' to politicians debating Palestine and immigration policy, relief organizers adjudicating rations and housing and German citizens confronted with their discomfiting former victims. Just as historians have expanded their definitions of resistance during the war and Holocaust to encompass actions that did not rely on weapons, so too perhaps we should think about broadening our notions of 'revenge' when analyzing DP experience. Jewish survivors in Germany, it should be stressed, did not see their presence on that 'cursed soil' only – as we tend to do today – as a perverse historical 'irony' but also as a kind of justice and 'payback'. The Germans, Jews contended, owed them their space, their former barracks and estates, their rations, and their services. There was a kind of 'in your face' quality to Jewish mothers brandishing their babies, just as there was to the banners flying from former German official buildings, or the posters carried in processions and parades through German towns; a pleasure in rousing a village baker and insisting that he bake *challah* for *Shabbes*, or ordering a grocer to supply pounds of herring for a holiday feast.[66]

Significantly, there is very little record of what might be construed as the most obvious form of bodily 'revenge', namely rape or sexual possession of German women by Jewish survivors or soldiers. The Red Army had engaged in mass rape as it fought its way west into Nazi Germany; the Soviet Jewish writer Ilya Ehrenburg was widely believed to have incited Red Army soldiers to 'Take the flaxen-haired women, they are your prey', an accusation never proven and which he vigorously denied.[67] Those assaults had been interpreted – and anticipated – as acts of revenge, but they had in fact been relatively indiscriminate. Jewish survivors relate multiple stories of having to flee rape by their Soviet liberators, even as others (or sometimes the same women) talk of the Russians' kindness.[68] Certainly Germans complained about rapes and pillage by DPs, but the villains are generally identified as non-Jewish eastern European former slave laborers. In the early Yiddish edition of his memoir, Elie Wiesel referred to nights of rape and plunder by liberated Buchenwald survivors: 'Early the next day Jewish boys ran off to Weimar to steal clothing and potatoes. And to rape German girls' (*un tsu fargvaldikn daytshe shikses*), but the passage is not central to his account and is revised and then expurgated in later editions.[69] Hanoch Bartov's autobiographical novel contains a riveting description of his Palestine Brigade unit's efforts to contain and come to terms with the rapacious actions of some of their comrades, while also insisting on understanding and protecting the violators. The protagonist recognizes that even the 'unwritten law of the Red Army', granting a 24-hour free zone for acts of vengeance could not 'help my sick heart. I could not shed innocent blood, I would never know peace.'[70] The American-Jewish journalist Meyer Levin included in his account of his journeys across devastated liberated Europe a tormented analysis of his own fantasies about raping 'blond German' women and how they wilted in the face of the women's abject surrender. He and a buddy steered their US Army jeep, imagining their revenge; 'the only thing to do was to throw them down, tear them apart', on ' … a wooded stretch of road' with 'little traffic, and a lone girl on foot or on a bicycle'. But when they finally encountered the perfect victim, alone on a bike who asked to go along with them, 'young, good looking and sullen … her presence was a definitive challenge', they finally realized that while her fear was 'exciting', 'It wasn't in us.'[71] There was little sympathy to be found among survivors for the women victimized by the Red Army, but also little appetite for joining in. Larry Orbach, a young Jewish survivor recalled with bitter satisfaction his trip home to Berlin from Auschwitz and Buchenwald after a three week quarantine for typhus:

> I wore the dark blue Eisenhower jacket the Americans had given me on which I had sewn my number, B.9761, and my yellow prison triangle on the lapel pocket so that any Nazis I might meet could appreciate the dramatic reversal in our relationship. The other travelers tried to avert their eyes from me, but they could not. Beyond the trauma, they were now compelled to confront the living reminder of the monstrous horror they had so long ignored, or from which they had at least managed to blind themselves … As the train chugged on under the night sky, a drunken Russian soldier raped a young German girl in full view of everyone. No one raised a hand to help her; there was no sound but her screams. So much for the Master Race, who, in Auschwitz, I had watched slam the head of a Jewish baby into the wall of a shower room.

The baby had died instantly, his brain protruding and his blood spurting; they had laughed, full of triumph and swagger. Now they were too meek even to protect one of their own children. Nor did I intervene; these were people who had set me apart, told me I could not be one of them.[72]

Revenge took other forms. One of the most striking features of the DPs' presence was the calculated appropriation of former Nazi 'shrines' and German terrain for their own symbolic purposes. Representatives from the first DP conference at St Ottilien in July 1945 chose to announce their demand for open emigration to Palestine in the Munich Brau Keller, from which Adolf Hitler had once launched his 1923 attempted putsch. When the Central Committee of Liberated Jews of Bavaria moved into a 'bombed out floor' of the Deutsches Museum in Munich, it was pointed out with a certain amount of glee that, 'Hitler once prophesied that the time would come when a person would have to go to a museum to find a Jew'. In January 1946, the congress of the Central Committee of Liberated Jews met in the Munich City Hall, center of the former *Hauptstadt der Bewegung*, and festooned for the occasion with a banner that read 'So long as a Jewish heart beats in the world, it beats for the Land of Israel.' The Council of the Central Committee convened its September 12, 1946 meeting in Berchtesgarten, right near Hitler's Eagles Nest redoubt, already richly adorned with the autographs of many GIs and survivors. Examples of such resignifying abound; perhaps the most famous was the *Streicherhof*, a socialist Zionist kibbutz on the former estate of the notorious Bavarian *Gauleiter*. It 'became a prime attraction for journalists and others', where '[A]ll the visitors were treated to the experience of seeing the dogs on the farm respond to Hebrew names that the trainees had taught them, as their salute to Streicher.'[73]

Historians who have recognized such public actions as 'symbolic revenge' have, however, generally not also problematized the 'baby boom' in those terms, situating it rather as a 'personal' response on an individual or familial level, naturally linked to the effort to restore a sort of normality to traumatized disrupted lives.[74] I would suggest however, that Jews – very clearly in the published record and in political representations – perceived pregnancy and maternity as another form of this resignifying, indeed of a certain kind of revenge, marking that they were more than just 'victims' and precisely did not dwell obsessively on the traumatic past. DP culture did place a premium on collecting personal histories, on bearing witness for the future. Almost immediately after liberation, the first memorials were raised and a day of remembrance was proposed; the latter was set for the anniversary of liberation as a deliberate representation of the inescapable link between mourning the catastrophe and hope for renewal.

The DPs quickly set up their own Central Historical Commission headquartered in Munich and charged it with collecting eyewitness accounts of persecution as well as any cultural artifacts such as art and songs which could be recuperated from camp and partisan life; in fact the very first DP Congress in St Ottilien, Bavaria in July 1945 had called on survivors to collect the names of all the exterminated. At the same time, with the help of the legendary rogue US Army chaplain Abraham Klausner, lists of survivors were quickly published. By summer 1945, five volumes with over 25,000 names had already been published; in December the Army printed the sixth volume of this *She'erit Hapleitah*. Theater, music, cabaret and press in the refugee camps directly addressed the horrors of the war years, to the point that Jewish relief workers were both shocked by the matter-of-fact treatment of extreme horror in DP culture and irritated by what they deemed obsessive remembering. The DP orchestra in the US zone performed its premiere in striped pajamas, with a piece of 'barbed wire fence' marking the stage.[75] Koppel S. Pinson, the educational director of the Joint (American Jewish Distribution Committee) in Germany, complained that:

> The DP is preoccupied almost to a point of morbidity with his past. His historical interest has become enormously heightened and intensified. He is always ready to account in minutest detail the events of his past or the past of his relatives.[76]

But in its preoccupation with the mundane everydayness of camp life and political association, with all its customary factionalism and bickering, daily life in the DP camps also fostered a kind of productive forgetting. Especially the young Zionist survivors were too consumed with planning their future to spend time recording a painful past. As Israel Kaplan, the Riga historian who headed the Commission, noted with some chagrin, 'In such a period of instability and living out of suitcases, and given the background of dramatic events, it is possible to make history, but not to write history.'[77] In another example of the paradoxical expectations and images attached to Jewish survivors, they were simultaneously berated for remembering too much and not enough.

Let me interject at this point that, along with noticing how our perceptions of survivors have radically changed, it is also useful to note how much our current obsession with memorializing, is a product of our own very late twentieth century and turn of the millennium preoccupations. It is perhaps our own panic about the loss of individual and collective memory that shapes our conviction that memory is crucial for recovery and reconstruction.[78] Directly after the war, both for survivors and those who worked with them (albeit in different ways), remembering was not necessarily considered the optimal way to deal with trauma. Indeed, one of the most powerful forces driving the quick marriages among survivors was surely the need to be with someone who required no explanation or rehearsal of the traumatic recent past, who recognized the many references that were invoked, and who understood, at least on some level, the lack of words, or the inadequate words that were available.

At the same time, it is clear that the conventional impression of 'silence', of inability to speak, constituting the very essence of trauma, as formulated by current psychoanalytic and literary theory, has to be relativized. Memorialization and commemoration commenced, as we have seen, virtually immediately. Buffeted between their assigned roles as embodiments of Jewish victimization and survival, bearers of new life, and asocial self-pitying wrecks, survivors were keenly aware of their role as guardians of memory and eyewitness to the indescribable as well as the obligation, often repeated, to ' find revenge in existence'. In a sermon on September 17, 1945, the first Yom Kippur after liberation, DP leader Samuel Gringauz exhorted especially the young, 'the carriers of our revenge',: 'You must show the world that we live. You must create and build, dance and sing, be happy and live, live and work.'[79]

The most powerful metaphor for 'life reborn' of course was the dream of a new Jewish state, physically and emotionally cut off from the traumatic history of European Jewry. In the powerful film *Lang ist der Weg*, filmed in the DP camps, the young heroine tries to tell her handsome partisan veteran lover about how damaged she is; he cuts her off, telling her that he doesn't want to know, she must not remember. He pledges to spirit her away to Eretz Yisrael because she will not be able to forget as long as she remains on bloodied and cursed German, indeed, European soil. In the final scene of the film, the young couple have resolved the problem: while they have not yet reached Palestine, they are lounging on the grass of a kibbutz (*Hachschar*, agricultural settlement) in Bavaria, preparing for their *Aliyah*, and playing with a newborn child – the most eloquent statement of survival and ability to start anew.[80]

Bearing children worked to mediate the continuous tension between remembering and forgetting. Babies, in their names and in their features, bore the traces of the past, of those who were dead and lost. Indeed, in some significant ways, the bearing of new life was not only a signal of survival and hope, but also an acknowledgment of the losses that had gone before. Jewish DPs were continually accused of manically 'acting out' rather than 'working through' their mourning. Since the Jewish religion (in Ashkenazi practice) prohibits naming children after the living, survivors did, in their naming practices, recognize the death of loved ones, whom they had, for the most part, not been able to bury, or even to confirm as dead. Certainly, however, imaginatively, and in their ever-present demandingness, children also represented futurity. As the first issue of the DP newsletter *Unzre Hoffnung* stated, employing the language of health and hygiene that remained dominant after the war: 'We must turn to today and prepare a better tomorrow, a beautiful and a healthy tomorrow.'[81]

Jewish women survivors, living in a kind of extraterritoriality on both German and Allied soil, were prefiguring on their pregnant bodies a kind of imaginary nation which they hoped – at least that was the public message – to realize in Palestine/Eretz Yisrael. Their babies had 'red hot' political valence, not only for the Allies, but also for the Zionists who dominated political and cultural life in the DP camps. The DP press and political actions demanding open emigration from Germany to Palestine invariably foregrounded images of babies and baby carriages.[82] The DP camp newsletters drove their message home with pages of marriage and birth announcements, always juxtaposed to ads searching for lost relatives or details on their death, business and death announcements, and emigration notices. Problematizing the place of motherhood in DP women's lives on the one hand, and in DP politics in general on the other, is especially important because in sharp contrast to women's often prominent (and heroized) roles in the anti-Nazi resistance, women did not fill important public positions in the DP camps and were not part of the DP leadership. Indeed, when David Ben Gurion attended the first Congress of Liberated Jews in Bavaria, convened at the Munich *Rathaus* in January 1946, he asked with some bewilderment and genuine 'censure' why there were no women delegates. Contrasting this glaring absence with the resistance heroines celebrated in Palestine, he demanded (according to at least one observer):

> Don't the women ... who endured so much and showed so much courage have anything to say here? In Palestine I met women who fought in the ghettos? They are our greatest pride. Isn't it sad enough that you lack children? Must you in addition artificially eliminate the women and create a population of men only?[83]

Ben Gurion's early admonition about the lack of children contained of course at least part of the answer to his own question about women's apparent non-participation in the active and often rancorous political life of the DP camps; very soon most women survivors would be preoccupied with the bearing and raising of new families.[84]

## CONCLUSION

For the Jewish DPs, the personal and the political of survival were linked: in the birthing of babies and the social glue of fervent Zionism. Current critical, especially Israeli, historiography has decried the cynical instrumentalization of Jewish survivors (the 'seventh million' in Segev's terms) by the Yishuv, the contempt that Zionist leaders felt, more or less openly, for the many traumatized survivors, the manipulation of media and officials to create the impression that every Jew was desperate to go to Palestine, and the harsh determination with which the 'reservoir' of 'human material' in the DP camps was recruited by Zionists to populate the land and man its military.[85] Still, it seems to me that the dream and the passionate commitment was genuine and intense. Especially young people who had lost their entire families (the majority, except for families who had survived in Soviet Central Asia) found in the Zionist peer culture, self-affirmation and community, and perhaps, the utopian vision that sustained survival; indeed, for some of their leaders, had already done so, in the ghettos, partisan groups and camps.[86] As one impressed American-Jewish Zionist GI noted admiringly about the young survivors he encountered at Kibbutz Buchenwald, 'the recuperative powers of the average human being, physical and mental, are remarkable, provided only that there is something to recuperate for'.[87]

And so, to continue the theme of paradoxical perceptions: the same observers who were horrified by the depressing culture of a remnant community in waiting, and angered by its 'villains', the idle and the criminal, the 'bedraggled' and 'abject', caught in 'a continuation of the war – not the destructive war of mortars, but the despairing war of morale' – were also deeply impressed by its dynamism and stubborn survival. As Ira Hirschmann, La Guardia's personal representative to UNRRA, reported, DPs' dignity was continually assaulted, by the 'insufficient tasteless food, … broken-sized shoes and clothing, their self-respect crushed, with no prospect of a normal life ahead of them'. Wondering that they did not 'tear them limb from limb', he was both impressed and aghast at the 'incredible self-restraint' Jews observed toward German POWs in a nearby camp and the surrounding placid German farmers who were better treated by the American victors. Clearly, as has been indicated, revenge is an important theme to follow and took multiple forms. But despite some dramatic stories, actual plans and actions of violence were few. The evidence is actually quite contradictory; on the one hand, many Jews, one senses, did not even want to engage with Germans enough to violate them, and on the other hand, Military Government officials groused that 'they love getting into fights with Germans'.[88] Revenge operated on complicated (surely also gendered) levels, in everyday interactions with Germans and most importantly, internally. It meant proving that there was a future, both in terms of Zionism and the establishment of a Jewish state where Jews would no longer be a vulnerable minority, and in the birth of babies and the formation of new families. Indeed, 'revenge' may very well be an insufficiently pliant term to convey the excruciatingly complicated mix of overwhelming loss, satisfaction at surviving against all odds, urgent desire to reclaim 'normality' and finally determination to demonstrate – to Germans, Allies and other Jews – that 'we are here', expressed by Jewish DPs. Angered at the denial of free immigration to Palestine and the United States, Hirschmann suggested that the Jewish DPs should properly be called not DPs, but BPs, 'Betrayed Persons'. Nonetheless, he insisted, 'These people who had cheated the death chambers had emerged physically scarred and beaten, but spiritually triumphant.'[89] Today, we might argue differently, understanding the baby boom and DP culture as expressions of a parallel life, a living on, when one had in a sense, as the philosopher Susan Brison has put it, outlived oneself; surviving in a life that did not replace or displace the horrors that had been experienced, but existed alongside and with it, in a highly vibrant form.[90]

DP experience suggests important questions about the intersection of the personal and the political, and definitions of mourning, trauma and revenge. It poses questions about the place of sexuality, pregnancy, childbirth and motherhood in defining survival and victimization, as well as furnishing possible reconstructions of ethnic or national identity in the wake of Nazism and the Second World War (or other violent trauma, either individual or collective). It raises issues about how to recognize the centrality of maternity without reproducing in our analysis conventional gender assignments.[91] We are confronted with the 'stubborn question' of how, as Denise Riley has memorably put it, 'to assert a category without becoming trapped within it'. The baby boom in particular challenges us to conceptualize historically the entangled levels of individual and personal, familial and cultural, and collective or national, experience and representation of the body, gender and sexuality. It points finally to the simultaneous human 'normality' of the survivors – even as they were categorized by others as victims, villains or survivors – and to the tragic mystery that still shadows and blocks our understanding of what they endured and how they continued to live.

NOTES

A revised version of this article appears in the *Journal of the History of Sexuality*, 11: 1–2 (January–April, 2002), pp. 291–318.

1. As examples of the range of figures cited, depending on who is counting whom when and how they are defined: Zorach Wahrhaftig, *Uprooted: Jewish Refugees and Displaced Persons After Liberation, From War to Peace* Nr. 5, Institute of Jewish Affairs for the American Jewish Congress and World Jewish Congress, New York, November 1946, estimated that the Allied Armies had to cope with over 7 million DPs in occupied territories, plus some 12 million ethnic German expellees. Robert G. Moeller, in *Protecting Motherhood: Women and the Family in the Politics of Postwar West Germany* (Berkeley: University of California Press, 1993), p. 21, refers to 10 million ethnic German expellees plus 'another 8 to 10 million "displaced persons" – foreigners forced to come to Germany as workers during the war and others removed from their homelands by the Nazis for racial, religious or political reasons, including survivors of concentration camps'. Most recently, Donald L. Niewylk, *Fresh Wounds: Early Narratives of Holocaust Survival* (Chapel Hill: University of North Carolina Press, 1998), p. 21, notes that in 1945 Jews were 'less than one per cent of the 14 million refugees from Hitler's War, although by 1947, they made up a far larger proportion – perhaps as much as one third – of the approximately 700,000 unrepatriated displaced persons in Europe'.
2. See the archives of the UNRRA (United Nations Relief and Rehabilitation Administration), the AJDC (American JOINT Distribution Committee relief organization), and YIVO (East European Jewish Historical Archive) in New York, and Yad Vashem, and the Central Zionist Archives in Israel (to name just a few of the most prominent), allied government and military reports, American Jewish organizational records, local German records, the DP press and institutional papers, memoirs and diaries, and oral history collections. Two surveys, on which I have relied, are unpublished German theses; Nicholas Yantian, 'Studien zum

Selbstverstaendnis der Jüdischen "Displaced Persons" in Deutschland nach dem Zweiten Weltkrieg', MA essay, History, Technical University Berlin, 1994; and Jacqueline Dewell Giere, 'Wir sind Unterwegs, Aber Nicht in der Wüste: Erziehung und Kultur in den Jüdischen Displaced Persons-Lagern der amerikanischen Zone im Nachkriegsdeutschland, 1945–1949', PhD dissertation, Education, Goethe Universität, Frankfurt, 1993. Unfortunately for me, much of the extensive and ever growing Hebrew language literature on the topic has not (yet, one hopes) been translated into English. Indeed, the liveliest discussions about Jewish DPs have been conducted in the context of Israeli debates about the revision of the Zionist historiographical narrative. See for example, Yosef Grodzinsky, *Chomer enoshi tov* ('Human Material of good quality – Jews vs. Zionists in the DP camps, Germany, 1945–1951'), Tel Aviv: Hed Artzi, 1988; study by Ze'ev Mankowitz, in English, 'The Formation of *She'erit Hapleitan*: November 1944–July 1945', *Yad Vashem Studies* 20 (1990): 337–70; 'The Affirmation of Life in *She'erit Hapleitan*', *Holocaust and Genocide Studies* 5 (1990): 13–21; Judith Tydor Baumel, 'DPs, Mothers and Pioneers. Women in the *She'erit Hapleitan*, *Jewish History* 11:2 (1997); in Hebrew (among others) also studies by Keynan, Kochavi and students of Yehudah Bauer. A translation into English from Hebrew of Mankowitz's important comprehensive study *Life Between Memory and Hope: The Survivors of the Holocaust in Occupied Germany 1945–1946* (Cambridge: Cambridge University Press, 2002).

3. See Atina Grossmann, 'Trauma, Memory and Motherhood: Germans and Jewish Displaced Persons in Post-Nazi Germany, 1945–1949', *Archiv für Sozialgeschichte* 38 (1988): 215–39.
4. Saul K. Padover, *Experiment in Germany: The Story of an American Intelligence Officer* (New York: Duell, Sloan, Pearce, 1946), p. 343. Many survivors recount their problems in convincing Soviet soldiers that they were Jews and not Germans; 'Ivrey kaputt', they were frequently told.
5. There is to my knowledge, remarkably little published material about the tens of thousands of mostly Polish Jews who had fled to the Soviet Union, and often ended up in Soviet Central Asia. One compelling unpublished (so far) memoir: Regina Kesler, MD, *A Pediatrician's Odyssey From Suwalki to Harvard*, edited by Irving Letiner and Michael Kesler. Statistical data is inexact and bewildering, largely because of change over time, inconsistencies in categorizations among those collecting data and the difficulties of counting a highly mobile and sometimes illegal population. Giere, 'Wir sind Unterwegs', p. 102 cites Joint Distribution Committee figures of 145,735 Jewish DPs officially registered in the American zone (alone) in November 1946, with 101,614 in DP camps, 35,950 living in German towns and cities, 4,313 in children's homes and 3,858 in *Hachscharah* (agricultural Kibbutzim). Yosef Grodzinsky, in his English translation of a Hebrew text, *Human Material of Good Quality – Jews vs. Zionists in the DP camps, Germany 1945–1951* (Tel Aviv: Hed Aertz, 1998) lists figures which now seem to be commonly accepted: an estimated 70,000 in late summer 1945, 220–260,000 Jewish DPs altogether at the height of Jewish flight west in late 1946, and 245,000 in summer 1947. However, by looking at migration patterns to target countries (rather than trying to establish figures in Europe) he comes to a remarkably high total of 330,000 Jewish DPs altogether between 1945 and 1951.
6. Among many sources: Michael Brenner, *Nach dem Holocaust: Juden in Deutschland 1945–1950* (Munich 1995) (now also in English from Yale University Press), p. 18.
7. In May 1947, the US zone housed 60 assembly centers, 14 children's centers, 38

*Hachsharot*, 17 hospitals, 1 convalescent home, 3 rest centers, 3 sanitoria, 1 transit camp, 1 staging area, 139 recognized groups of DPs living in German communities. Additionally, there were two assembly centers in the American sector of Berlin and 18 camps in the US zone of Austria. By comparison, there were only 2 assembly centers and 2 children's centers in the British zone and 1 children's center in the French sector of Berlin. There were also camps and *Hachscharot* in Italy. See Abraham S. Hyman, *The Undefeated* (Jerusalem: Gefen, 1993), pp. 146–7.

8. Quoted in Alex Grobman, *Rekindling the Flame: American Jewish Chaplains and the Survivors of European Jewry, 1944–1948* (Detroit: Wayne State University Press, 1993), p. 57. See also Leonard Dinnerstein, *America and the Survivors of the Holocaust* (New York: Columbia University Press, 1982). For examples of such basically sympathetic but highly unsentimental and critical views of survivors, see the remarkable letters home to wives in the United States by two American Jewish officials, one military and the other from the American Joint Distribution Committee; Jacob Rader Marcus and Abraham J. Peck (eds) *Among the Survivors of the Holocaust 1945: The Landsberg DP Camp Letters of Major Irving Heymont* (Cincinnati: Monographs of the American Jewish Archives, Vol. 10, 1982) and Oscar A. Mintzer, editing by Alex Grobman, *In Defense of the Survivors: The Letters and Documents of Oscar A. Mintzer, AJDC Legal Advisor, Germany, 1945–46* (Berkeley: Judah L. Magnes Museum, 1999).

9. See William G. Niederland, *Folgen der Verfolgung: das Überlebens-Syndrom Seelenmord* (Frankfurt am Main: Suhrkamp, 1980), based on his pioneering article in *Hillside Hospital Journal*, 1961. On the trauma and trauma diagnoses of Jewish survivors, see, among many other sources, Aaron Haas, *The Aftermath: Living with the Holocaust* (Cambridge: Cambridge University Press, 1995); and Israel W. Charny, *Holding on to Humanity. The Message of Holocaust Survivors: The Shamai Davidson Papers* (New York: New York University Press, 1992).

10. For a smart critique, see Michael André Bernstein, 'Homage to the extreme: The Shoah and the rhetoric of catastrophe', *Times Literary Supplement*, March 6, 1998: 6–8.

11. Hanoch Bartov, *The Brigade*, translated by David S. Segal (New York: Holt, Rinehart and Winston, 1968, orig. Hebrew 1965), pp. 56, 148.

12. Idith Zertal, *From Catastrophe to Power: Holocaust Survivors and the Emergence of Israel* (Berkeley: University of California Press, 1998), pp. 8–9.

13. Phrases such as 'human debris' or 'living corpses' were ubiquitous in contemporary reports (indeed, there is a remarkably consistent and repetitive language in most documents describing Jewish DPs). For one example, see the accounts in Karen Gershon, *Postscript: A Collective Account of the Lives of Jews in West Germany since the Second World War* (London: Victor Gollancz, 1969).

14. I.F. Stone, *Underground to Palestine and Reflections 30 Years Later* (New York: Pantheon, 1978), p. 24. In general, see Yehudah Bauer, *Out of the Ashes* (Oxford: Pergamon, 1989) and *Flight and Rescue: Bricha* (New York: Random House, 1970).

15. Haas, *Aftermath*, p.18.

16. Kathryn Hulme, *The Wild Place* (Boston: Atlantic Monthly Book, Beacon Press, 1953), pp. 71, 212–13.

17. Ibid., p. 124.

18. Abraham S. Hyman, *The Undefeated* (Jerusalem: Gefen, 1993), pp. 250 ff.

19. Hulme, *The Wild Place*, pp. 211–12.

20. Jacob Biber, *Risen from the Ashes* (San Bernardino, CA: Borgo Press, 1990), p. 14.

21. Wahrhaftig, *Uprooted*, p. 86.
22. Lt. Col. Mercer (US Army), February 5, 1946, OMGUS 4/20–1/10. See also Wahrhaftig, *Uprooted*, p.39.
23. Heymont, *Among the Survivors*, p. 38.
24. Samuel Gringauz, 'Our New German Policy and the DPs. Why Immediate Resettlement is Imperative', *Commentary* 5 (1948), p. 510. In general, see also Dinnerstein, *America and the Survivors*.
25. Report by Zorach Wahrhaftig, November 27, 1945 on 'Life in camps six months after liberation', *Archives of the Holocaust*, Vol. 9, p. 134; Wahrhaftig, *Uprooted*, p. 39. For case studies of relations between Jewish DPs and a local German population in Landsberg, see Angelika Eder, 'Jüdische Displaced Persons im deutschen Alltag: Eine Regionalstudie 1945–1950', *Fritz Bauer Jahrbuch* 1997, pp. 163–87, and D. Kohlmannslehner, 'Das Verhältnis von Deutschen und Jüdischen Displaced Persons in Lager Lampertheim 1945–1949', unpublished paper, Fritz Bauer Institut archives.
26. Contemporary critics regularly blamed American GI and officer contact with German women for the conciliatory policies and antipathy toward Jewish DPs. This is a complicated theme that deserves much more analysis; German women did exercise real influence in the early postwar years, not only through their sexual relationships with the occupiers, but also in their positions as translators and clerical workers.
27. Samuel Gringauz, 'Our New German Policy and the DPs. Why Immediate Resettlement is Imperative', *Commentary* 5 (1948): 508–14, p. 508. He sees the period from fall 1945 until summer 1947 as a 'golden age', p. 509.
28. Ira A. Hirschmann, La Guardia's Inspector General for the UNRRA, in his passionate book, *The Embers Still Burn: An Eyewitness' View of the Postwar Ferment in Europe and the Middle East and our Disastrous Get Soft with Germany Policy* (New York: Simon and Schuster, 1949), pp. 45, 149.
29. See among numerous sources, Abraham J. Peck, 'Jewish Survivors of the Holocaust in Germany: Revolutionary Vanguard or Remnants of a Destroyed People?' *Tel Aviver Jahrbuch fuer deutsche Geschichte* 19 (1990): 38; Michael Brenner, *Nach dem Holocaust*, p. 36 and Margarete L. Myers, 'Jewish Displaced Persons Reconstructing Individual and Community in the US Zone of Occupied Germany', *Leo Baeck Institute Yearbook* 42 (1997), pp. 306–8.
30. Jacob Biber, *Risen from the Ashes*, p. 49.
31. Edith Horowitz in Brana Gurewitsch, *Mothers, Sisters, Resisters: Oral Histories of Women Who Survived the Holocaust* (Tuscaloosa: University of Alabama Press, 1998), p. 73.
32. See Deborah Dwork on the contest over hidden children in postwar Netherlands, *Lessons and Legacies* (1998) and paper by Marion P. Pritchard on Jewish DP children, paper for 'Lessons and Legacies: The Meaning of the Holocaust in a Changing World', Dartmouth College, 1994, revised 1997 (thank you to Marion Pritchard).
33. Edith Z in Donald L. Niewylk, *Fresh Wounds: Early Narratives of Holocaust Survival*, (Chapel Hill: University of North Carolina Press, 1998), p. 171.
34. Letter to Stephen S. Wise, June 22, 1945, in Abraham J. Peck (ed.) *The Papers of the World Jewish Congress 1945–1950: Liberation and the Saving Remnant, Archives of the Holocaust*, Vol. 9, American Jewish Archives, Cincinnati, New York, 1990, p. 30. On the important role of US military rabbis in dealing with Jewish DPs, see Grobman, *Rekindling the Flame* (1993), and Louis Barish, *Rabbis in Uniform* (New York: J. David, 1962).

35. Padover, *Experiment*, p. 359.
36. For a fine analysis of this literature, see Isidor J. Kaminer, '"On razors edge" – Vom Weiterleben nach dem Überleben', *Fritz Bauer Institut Jahrbuch 1996*, pp. 146–7, 157.
37. Biber, *Risen*, p. 37.
38. Meyer Levin, *In Search* (New York: Horizon Press, 1950), pp. 183–4.
39. See Zalman Grinberg, 'We are Living Corpses', in *Aufbau*, August 24, 1945. For a strong argument against the view of survivors as 'living corpses' and for the agency, and what Peck has called 'the revolutionary ideology', of the She'erit Hapleitan (which focuses on political organization rather than reproduction), see Ze'ev Mankowitz, 'The Formation of *She'erit Hapleitan*: November 1944–July 1945', *Yad Vashem Studies* 20 (1990): 337–70, and 'The Affirmation of Life in *She'erit Hapleitan*', *Holocaust and Genocide Studies* 5:1 (1990): 13–21.
40. See Juliane Wetzel, 'Mir szeinen doh. München und Umgebung als Zuflucht von Überlebenden des Holocaust 1945–1948', in Martin Broszat (ed.) *Von Stalingrad zur Währungsreform. Zur Sozialgeschichte des Umbruchs in Deutschland* (Munich: R. Oldenbourg, 1988). See also Angelica Koenigseder and Juliane Wetzel, *Lebensmut im Wartesaal. Die Jüdischen DPs (Displaced Persons) in Nachkriegsdeutschland* (Frankfurt am Main: Fischer, 1994), pp. 104–105, 187, and *Peck*, 'Jewish Survivors', pp. 35–8. The term *She'erit Hapleitah* derives from reworkings of Biblical references to the survivors of the Assyrian conquest.
41. Bartley C. Crum, *Behind the Silken Curtain: A Personal Account of Anglo-American Diplomacy in Palestine and the Middle East* (Jerusalem: Milah Press, 1996; orig. New York, 1947), p. 90. There is, not surprisingly, little information on the number and experience of Jewish women DPs who considered, sought, and/or underwent abortions (at a time when they were widespread among German women). This is a topic where careful research with memoirs and oral histories is particularly important.
42. 'And the urge to arrive in time for the birth of the child in *Eretz* was real on every vessel that left for Palestine with its host of pregnant women, some of whom were smuggled on to the ships in their ninth month despite the *Haganah* regulation making the seventh month the limit.' Levin, *In Search* p. 360. See also Wahrhaftig, *Uprooted*, pp. 52–4.
43. Niewylk (ed.) *Fresh Wounds*, p. 94.
44. Judith Tydor Baumel, 'DPs, Mothers and Pioneers: Women in the *She'erit Hapleitah*', *Jewish History* 11:2 (Fall, 1997), p. 103. See also her *Kibbutz Buchenwald: Survivors and Pioneers* (New Brunswick, NJ: Rutgers University Press, 1997).
45. Heymont, *Among the Survivors*, p. 44.
46. An American relief worker reported that a Belsen survivor describing medical experiments, 'believes that well over the majority of Jews alive – certainly 90 per cent of those the Nazis could get at, will not have children – including himself and his wife'. Oscar A. Mintzer, *In Defense of the Survivors: The Letters and Documents of Oscar A. Mintzer AJDC Legal Advisor, Germany 1945–46*, edited by Alex Grobman (Berkeley: Judah L. Magnes Museum, 1999), letter to his wife dated February 17, 1946, p. 166. It is worth noting how many 'Holocaust memoirs' actually include (or conclude with) time in the DP camps and experiences of marriage, pregnancy and childbearing. See, among many, memoirs, Sonja Milner, *Survival in War and Peace* (New York, 1984) and Sala Pawlowicz, with Kevin Klose, *I Will Survive* (London, 1947). In general, see Lenore Weitzman and Dalia Ofer (eds) *Women in the*

*Holocaust* (New Haven, CT: Yale University Press, 1998); also Sybil Milton, 'Gender and Holocaust – ein offenes Forschungsfeld', Sara R. Horowitz, 'Geschlechtsspezifische Erinnerungen an den Holocaust', and Atina Grossmann, 'Zwei Erfahrungen im Kontext des Themas "Gender und Holocaust"', in Sigrid Jacobeit and Grit Philipp (eds) *Forschungsschwerpunkt Ravensbrück: Beiträge zur Geschichte des Frauen-Konzentrationslagers* (Berlin: Hentrich, 1997), pp. 124–46.

47. Wahrhaftig, *Uprooted*, p. 54. Occupation and relief officials, as well as Germans, were often caught between disbelief at the horror and magnitude of the extermination and incomprehension of the fact that there remained, after all, hundreds of thousands of survivors who resisted repatriation and for whom there had to be found not just 'relief' but a new life (what was still called 'a final solution') outside of Europe. Report by Wahrhaftig, *Life in camps six months after liberation*, p. 130.
48. Hyman, *The Undefeated*, pp. 17, 246, 270.
49. Biber, *Risen*, p. 46.
50. See especially Nechama Tec's treatment in *Defiance. The Bielski Partisans: The Story of the Largest Armed Rescue of Jews by Jews During World War II* (New York: Oxford University Press, 1993), pp.126–70; also her more recent presentations on women and the resistance.
51. Haas, *Aftermath*, pp. 98–99. I am indebted to Michael Brenner for formulating this point about the particular experience of female survivors; based on his mother, Henny Brenner's unpublished memoirs. In fact, if one re-reads Holocaust memoirs, the fear of rape by Red Army liberators comes up frequently. Brana Gurewitsch, editor of *Mothers, Sisters, Registers*, notes in her introduction, p. xviii, 'After liberation, when chaos reigned and all women were considered fair game by Soviet liberators, women survivors took extraordinary measures to avoid rape.'
52. Haas, *Aftermath* p. 102. See also the numerous examples in the testimonies collected by the American psychologist David P. Boder, right after war's end, in Niewylk (ed.) *Fresh Wounds*.
53. Grobman, *Rekindling the Flame*, p. 17. This baby boom is well-portrayed in the American documentary film, *The Long Journey Home*, Simon Wiesenthal Center, Los Angeles, 1997.
54. Cited in Hyman, *The Undefeated*, p. 247. In January 1946, the AJDC (Joint) counted 120 children aged between 1 and 5 years old; in December 1946, 4,431. Not all these babies had been conceived in the DP camps; the high birth and young child numbers also reflected the many new arrivals from Poland who had survived with their families in the Soviet Union. (Given the current state of historiographical debate about [neo] totalitarianism, it may be not incidental to point out, that this too was a major difference between Nazism and Stalinism; Jews survived in Stalin's Soviet Union, albeit under difficult conditions.)
55. Jacobmeyer, 'Jüdische Ueberlebende', p. 437. See also Brenner, *Nach dem Shoah*, p. 36. For comparative purposes: the German birth rate in 1933 stood at 14.7 (9.9 in Berlin); in the aftermath of the First World War it had reached 25.9 in 1920. Two-thirds of Jewish DPs eventually ended up in Israel; altogether about 100,000 went to the United States and 250,000 to Israel. On the reaction in Israel, see Tom Segev, *The Seventh Million: The Israelis and the Holocaust* (New York: Henry Holt, 1993) and Hanna Yablouka, *Survivors of the Holocaust* (London: Macmillan, 1999).
56. Wahrhaftig, *Uprooted*, p. 54 (and in numerous other sources). By comparison, in Berlin at war's end, approximately the opposite (over 60 per cent female) ratio applied.

57. The most insistent critic of any attempts to lend 'meaning' to the Holocaust has been Lawrence L. Langer. See his most recent book, *Admitting the Holocaust: Collected Essays* (New York: Oxford University Press, 1995). On this theme also, there is a huge literature, ranging from the theological to the psychoanalytic and political.
58. Mankowitz, 'The Formation of *She'erit Hapleitan*', p. 351.
59. LaCapra, *History and Memory* (Ithaca, NY: Cornell University Press, 1998), pp. 204–5.
60. On the problem of destroyed trust, and the influence of psychiatric work done with Holocaust survivors on later treatment of refugee trauma, see the essays in E. Valentine Daniel and John Chr. Knudsen (eds) *Mistrusting refugees* (Berkeley: University of California Press, 1995), especially introduction, p. 4. On the relationship between survivors and their children, see among many studies, Martin S. Bergmann and Milton E. Jucovy (eds) *Generations of the Holocaust* (New York: Basic Books, 1982); also the pioneering work of Judith Kestenberg and Henry Krystal.
61. We might consider this gendered view of 'revenge' in light of current discussions about the relative lack of vengeful actions by survivors, and a newer focus on a few dramatic actions (such as the poisoning of German wells scheme). See John Sack, *An Eye for an Eye* (New York: Basic Books, 1993), among other texts.
62. I am grateful to Samuel Kassow, History Department, Trinity College, for this reference.
63. Comparative anthropological literature is useful in this context. See especially Lisa Malkii's analysis of the ways in which refugee camp settings encourage 'construction and reconstruction of [their] history "as a people"' and the importance of children in that process, in *Purity and Exile: Violence, Memory and National Cosmology Among Hutu Refugees in Tanzania* (Chicago: University of Chicago Press, 1995), p. 3.
64. Figure from Yantian, 'Studien zum Selbstverstaendnis', p. 43.
65. See Eder, 'Regionalstudie'.
66. Interestingly, Theodor W. Adorno makes a point of discussing in his *Soziologische Schriften II* (Suhrkamp: Frankfurt am Main, 1975), pp. 258–60, the 'Rachesucht' (lust for revenge) attributed to DPs and Jews by Germans after the *Zusammenbruch*.
67. Ilya Ehrenburg, in his memoir *The War: 1914–1945. Volume 5 of Men, Years – Life* (Cleveland: The World Publishing Company, 1964), translated by Tatiana Shebunina in collaboration with Yvonne Kapp, p. 32, explicitly denied longstanding accusations that he, a Soviet Jew in the Red Army, had been 'urging the Asiatic peoples to drink the blood of German women. Ilya Ehrenburg insists that Asiatics should enjoy our women. "Take the flaxen-haired women, they are your prey".' Ehrenburg, however, insisted, p. 175, that, despite 'isolated cases of excesses committed in East Prussian towns that had aroused our general indignation ... The Soviet soldier will not molest a German woman ... It is not for booty, not for loot, not for women that he has come to Germany.'
68. See for example, the accounts by women survivors in Gurewitsch (ed.) *Mothers, Sisters, Resisters*. On rape of German women by Red Army soldiers, see Atina Grossmann, 'A Question of Silence: The Rape of German Women by Occupation Soldiers', in Robert G. Moeller (ed.) *West Germany under Construction: Politics, Society and Culture in the Adenauer Era* (Ann Arbor: University of Michigan Press, 1997), pp. 33–52; and Norman Naimark, *The Russians in Germany: A History of the Soviet Zone of Occupation, 1945–1949*, (Cambridge, MA: Harvard University Press, 1995), pp. 69–140.

69. See Naomi Seidman's careful study of Wiesel and the various versions of *Night*, 'Elie Wiesel and the Scandal of Jewish Rage', *Jewish Social Studies* 3:1 (Fall, 1996): 1–19, esp. p.6.
70. Bartov, *The Brigade*, pp. 117, 245; see also pp. 46–7, 224–9.
71. Levin, *In Search*, pp. 278–80.
72. Larry Orbach and Vivien Orbach-Smith, *Soaring Underground: A Young Fugitive's Life in Nazi Berlin* (Washington DC: Compass Press, 1996), pp. 330–1.
73. Hyman, *Undefeated*, pp. 35, 39.
74. For example, Ze'ev Mankowitz, *Life Between Memory and Hope: The Survivors of the Holocaust in Occupied Germany 1945–46* (Cambridge: Cambridge University Press, 2002). Personal conversation, Jerusalem, Israel, January 2001.
75. Hyman, *Undefeated*, p. 252. Hyman is especially eloquent on this issue of memorialization as a 'step into the land of the living', and on the occupation of Nazi sites.
76. Koppel S. Pinson, 'Jewish Life in Liberated Germany', *Jewish Social Studies* 9:2 (January 1947), p. 108. Similarly, the British were highly irritated by the insistence of Jewish DPs in their zone – a conscious maneuver by their leader Josef Rosensaft – on still calling their DP camp in Hohne near Bergen Belsen concentration camp, Bergen Belsen. See Hyman, *Undefeated*, p. 78.
77. Interestingly the DP proposed Day of Remembrance, on the date of liberation, the 14th day of the Hebrew month of *Ijar*, was never accepted either in the Diaspora or in Palestine. The state of Israel declared *Yom HaShoah* for the 27th *Nissan* because it fell right between the remembrance of the Warsaw Ghetto uprising and the establishment of the state of Israel, thus safely bracketing Holocaust remembrance between two markers of resistance and rebirth. For a fine analysis of the debates about remembering see the excellent MA Thesis by Nicholas Yantian, 'Studien zum Selbstverstaendnis', pp. 27–42.
78. The literature on trauma and memory is, by now, enormous. Among many examples, see LaCapra, *History and Memory after Auschwitz* and Cathy Caruth (ed.) *Trauma: Explorations in Memory* (Baltimore, MD: Johns Hopkins University Press, 1995). On the relationship between our memory panic and memory boom, see Andreas Huyssen, *Twilight Memories: Marking Time in a Culture of Amnesia* (New York: Routledge, 1995); on the 'fetishizing' of memory, see Marita Sturken, 'The Remembering of Forgetting', *Social Text*, 16:4 (Winter 1998): 102–25; for a critique of our fascination with (and confusion of) individual and collective trauma, see Pamela Ballinger, 'The Culture of Survivors: Post-Traumatic Stress Disorder and Traumatic Memory', *History and Memory* 10:1 (Spring 1988): 99–131.
79. Dr Samuel Gringauz in his Yom Kippur sermon at Landsberg DP camp on September 17, 1945. Cited in Hyman, *Undefeated*, pp. 16–17.
80. *Lang ist der Weg*, German/Polish co-production (1949). Available from National Jewish Film Center, Brandeis University.
81. Dieter E. Kesper, *Unsere Hoffnung. Die Zeitung Überlebender des Holocaust im Eschweger Lager 1946* (Eschwege, 1996). Newspaper of UNRRA camp in Eschwege, discovered in Heimatarchiv, Nr.1. June 4, 1946. The published text is a translation of the original Yiddish.
82. Major John J. Maginnis referred to the DP influx in Berlin as a 'red hot' political crisis in his *Military Government Journal: Normandy to Berlin* (Amherst: University of Massachusetts Press), p. 326. For the ubiquitous babies and baby carriages, see for example the extraordinary photo collection in *Ein Leben Aufs Neu: Das Robinson Album. DP Lager, Juden auf deutschen Boden 1945–1948* (Vienna: Christian

Brandstatter, 1995). See also the photographs in the 2001 calendar of the United States Holocaust Memorial Museum, culled from the recent exhibition, 'Life Reborn: Jewish Displaced Persons 1945–1951' and the accompanying volume, *Life Reborn: Jewish Displaced Persons 1945–1951. Conference Proceedings*, Menachem Z. Rosensaft (ed.) (Washington DC: United States Holocaust Memorial Museum, 2000).

83. Quoted by Leo W. Schwarz in *The Redeemers: A Saga of the Years 1945–1952* (New York: Farrar, Straus and Young, 1953), p. 87.
84. On the image of women in the resistance and their valorization in Palestine and early Israeli society, see Judith Tydor Baumel's essays in *Double Jeopardy: Gender and the Holocaust* (London: Valentine Mitchell, 1998). On women's roles in the DP camps see especially Margarete L. Myers, 'Jewish Displaced Persons Reconstructing Individual and Community', and her excellent paper, 'Domestic Life in Transit: Jewish DPs', delivered at Workshop on Birth of a Refugee Nation, Remarque Institute, New York University, April 2001 (under name Margarete Myers Feinstein).
85. See for example, Tom Segev, *The Seventh Million*, Idith Zertal, *From Catastrophe to Power*, and Grodzinsky, *Human Material*.
86. It is important to keep in mind that many of the Zionist groups in the DP camps had arrived together via the *Bricha* and traced their origins back to the ghettos and camps. In fact, much of the early DP leadership in Bavaria came from the same workcamp, Dachau Kauffering, which had received many Jews as they arrived on death marches from the East.
87. Kieve Skiddel, unpublished letter, Ober Peissen, June 21, 1945.
88. Mintzer, *In Defense of the Survivors*, p. 301.
89. Hirschmann, *Embers*, pp. 72, 75, 81, 101.
90. See Susan Brison, 'Outliving Oneself: Trauma, Memory, and Personal Identity', in Diana T. Meyers (ed.) *Feminists Rethink the Self* (Boulder, CO: Westview Press, 1997), pp. 12–39.
91. Denise Riley, 'Some Peculiarities of Social Policy Concerning Women in Wartime and Postwar Britain', in *Behind the Lines; Gender and the Two World Wars*, Margaret Higgonnet *et al.* (eds) (New Haven: Yale University Press, 1987), p. 269. On 'the fantasy of maternal love' as a force in feminist theory and women's activism, see most recently, Joan W. Scott, 'Fantasy Echo: History and the Construction of Identity', *Critical Inquiry* (Winter 2001): 284–304, esp. 303–4.

# 6

# Oblivion Without Guilt: The Holocaust and Memories of the Second World War in Finland

## PETRI J. RAIVO

Captain Salomon Klass was sitting in his command tent when two high-ranked German officers came and saluted 'Heil Hitler'. They were carrying an iron cross to present to Klass for his heroic deeds in rescuing a troop of German soldiers cut off by the Russians in Eastern Karelia. Klass did not respond to the salute but told the officers that he was a Jew serving in the Finnish Army and did not want anything from the Germans. The two officers turned pale and, with blank looks on their faces, turned about and left. (Aron Livson, chairman of the Finnish Jewish Veterans' Organization, in an interview with *Verkkouutiset*, December 5, 1997)

### INTRODUCTION: THE DIVIDED MEMORIES OF THE JEWS AND THE SECOND WORLD WAR IN FINLAND

Finland was the only country that fought on the side of Germany during the Second World War that did not discriminate between its Jews and other citizens and never participated officially in the Nazi's final solution for annihilating the Jewish population from Europe. Even during the war, Finnish Jews enjoyed exactly the same civil rights and duties as other Finns. The fact that Jewish officers and men were serving in the Finnish army during the years 1941–44, sometimes even physically side by side with German soldiers, is a unique quirk of fate in the history of the Second World War, for simultaneously millions of people were being annihilated in territories elsewhere that had been occupied by the Third Reich or its allies. This lack of anti-Semitism or racial hatred has been seen as a logical part of the national heritage of the war and as evidence that the nation's participation should be looked on as a separate military effort to defend its independence and sovereignty and the civil rights of its people without any troublesome links with the Nazi ideology.

The Finns' relationship with their German brothers-in-arms was not only a practical one however, and there is still a dark shadow of the Holocaust lurking in the darkness: the memory of eight Jewish refugees extradited from Finland to Germany, and to eventual incarceration in death camps, by the local police authorities and with the approval of the Finnish government. This has been a sad stain on the Finnish history of the Second World War, so sad that efforts have been made either to repress it as a regrettable but isolated episode or to use it for political purposes, as evidence of certain National Socialist sympathies and anti-Semitic attitudes among the wartime authorities.

Both of these memories – that of the Jewish soldiers and their sense of duty and that of the civilian refugees as helpless victims of the Holocaust – are thus commemorated, but in different contexts and different tones of voice. This chapter will discuss how the processes of remembering and commemoration of the Jews and the Holocaust have taken their place as a part of national narrative related to the memory of the Second World War. It will analyze how and why these two different, conflicting memories have come to be maintained in two separate categories, and in doing so, it will argue that they are in a sense negotiating with the national war heritage and the narratives associated with the war experience.

## 'WIR HABEN KEINE JUDEN FRAGE': THE JEWS IN FINLAND UP TO THE END OF THE SECOND WORLD WAR

The Jews have been a small minority in Finland, but their role and significance in society has been more considerable than their actual number would lead one to presume. The history of a permanent Jewish population dates back less than 200 years. It started after Finland became an autonomous Grand Duchy within the Russian Empire in 1809. The original Jews who came to Finland were soldiers, as a result of the extension of military service in the Imperial Army to the Jewish population in 1827 (Harviainen, 1999: 335), under a cantonment system in which Jewish boys were taken from their parents to be brought up in military barracks for service in different parts of the empire. The system was subsequently abolished by Tsar Alexander II in 1855 (Rautkallio, 1987: 3), as a consequence of which the couple of hundred Jewish conscripts serving in Finland had the opportunity to take up permanent residence in the Grand Duchy with their families. Most of them remained to live in their former garrison towns at the end of their term of duty, earning their living as pedlars, merchants and craftsmen. By the early 1880s there were something less than a thousand Jews in Finland, out of a total population of just over 2 million (Rautkallio, 1987: 8).

The great Slavophile movement in Russia emerged immediately after the accession of Alexander III to the throne in 1881, in the shape of an aggressive campaign to Russify all minority nationalities. The Jews were special targets of these hostile attempts at oppression. By the turn of the century, anti-Semitism had spread throughout Russia and blood was shed in pogroms in southern Russia, the Ukraine and Poland in particular (Rautkallio, 1987: 9). New regulations imposed tighter residential and economic restrictions on the Russian Jews than ever before. The Grand Duchy of Finland remained beyond the range of these measures, which meant that the Jews resident there managed to remain fairly well untouched by the pitiless policies implemented in other parts of the Russian Empire. There were nevertheless certain marks of the adoption of a stricter Jewish policy by the Finnish authorities as well; for example, the civil rights of the Jews were limited in that they were only allowed to apply for temporary residence permits, which led to a feeling of uncertainty regarding the future. Despite these limitations, however, the Jews in Finland enjoyed an exceptional status relative to those in other parts of the Russian Empire (Rautkallio, 1987: 11–16). Full and equal civil rights with freedom to apply for all state posts, except for those in the church, of course, were achieved only when Finland gained independence in 1917 (Harviainen, 1999: 336–9). By the 1930s there were some 2,000 Jews who were Finnish citizens living in the southern cities of Helsinki, Turku and Viipuri (Rautkallio, 1989: 35).

Even though it took them so long to achieve civil rights, the Jews were generally in quite a tolerable position, although there were some signs of anti-Semitism in prewar Finnish society, too. Prejudices came to the fore every now and then in articles and cartoons in some right-wing newspapers (Harviainen, 1999: 339) and there was a certain amount of institutional discrimination. In his investigations into the status of the Jewish soldiers in the Second World War, for instance, the historian Hannu Rautkallio (1989: 40) finds certain evidence that the

Finnish army, and especially the training school for officers in the reserves, consciously rejected most of the Jewish candidates for conscription. But even in this matter, attitudes were becoming more tolerant by the late 1930s.

The anti-Semitic movement in Finland has always been a very marginal one in general terms. There are certain historical reasons for this, one of which is related to the bitter experiences of racial questions that the Finns themselves had had. Since the eighteenth century they had been treated as a people whose racial and physical characteristics were related to those of the Lapps or the Mongols rather than Europeans. In other words, they were seen as people of a different origin and with different racial characteristics, who were inferior to their Scandinavian neighbors (Jakobson, 1999: 143). From that point of view it is no wonder that most Finnish politicians and intellectuals of the 1930s and 1940s regarded the German racial discourse as repulsive and incomprehensible. The memories of the same discourse targeted at Finns themselves and maintained loudly by German scholars and media, and even more so by the Swedish equivalents, were too immediate.

The Lutheran Church also adopted a tolerant attitude toward the Jews, although Luther himself has achieved a questionable reputation because of his strong anti-Semitic attitudes. The majority of the Finnish Lutheran pastors saw the Jews as a people mentioned in the Bible as a chosen people of God and the people from among whom Jesus had emerged (Harviainen, 1999: 339). The Jews were also out of the focus of political racial hatred, which was mostly targeted at the Russians. Particularly during the 1920s and 1930s, the most hated arch-enemy for the right-wing Finns – the sub-racial, atheistic and even sub-human Bolshevik – was seen primarily as a Russian, not as a Jew (Luostarinen, 1986).

There were also some important factors emanating from inside the Jewish community that helped with their integration into Finnish society. One of them was education. The Jewish School, established in 1893, became an official part of the Finnish school system in 1918 (Harviainen, 1999: 339), and this had from the outset assumed an important role in establishing the Jews as a community in Finnish society as well as in maintaining and transmitting the Jewish traditions and heritage. To help this integration, the Finnish Jews usually spoke both Finnish and Swedish. The synagogue congregations in Helsinki and Turku were officially Swedish-speaking, while the language of the congregation in Viipuri was Finnish.

When the Winter War broke out between Finland and the Soviet Union in November 1939, it was self-evident for the Finnish Jews that those men in the community who were liable to military service would join the ranks of the army to defend their country. Thus 260 men from the Jewish community in Finland served in the Finnish army during the Winter War, 200 of them in the frontline forces (Rautkallio, 1989: 55).

When the Winter War ended in March 1941, the Second World War was in its early stages. The Soviet Union continued to exert pressure on its tiny neighbor, whose fears grew when the Baltic States were forcibly incorporated into the USSR in August 1940. Isolated from the West and with Sweden staunchly neutral, Finland turned toward Germany. This former silent supporter of the Soviet Union during the Winter War became interested in Finland as a support area and useful ally in a possible war with Russia. Germany was also interested in the nickel resources of the Finnish mines. For the Finns it now seemed that the country's independence had been saved. There were even possibilities of regaining the ceded areas and gaining revenge over Russia for all the bitter defeats of the Winter War.

When Germany invaded the Soviet Union in the summer of 1941, Finland, now better prepared and equipped than in the Winter War, entered the fray as a co-belligerent. Despite the fact that Finland was now fighting on the side of Nazi Germany, the Finnish Jews again served in its army, both as officers and as rank-and-file soldiers. Because of their good knowledge of Yiddish and thus their frequent ability to speak fluent German, some of them came into physical contact with German troops in Northern Finland. Occasionally this gave rise to some confusing or even comical situations, but the encounters were kept businesslike, as befitted professional soldiers, and there were no refusals of cooperation on either side during the war. It even happened twice that the German troops offered an iron cross for bravery to a Jewish soldier on the Finnish side (and once to a Jewish nurse), but all of those nominated refused to accept this decoration of honor. According to oral history collected from Jewish war veterans in Finland, it also often happened that Finnish soldiers let the Germans know that they were Jewish, and in most cases the knowledge did not affect the relationships between them (Rautkallio, 1989: 96–7).

The position of the Jewish community as an acceptable part of Finnish wartime society is well illustrated by a discussion that took place between the Finnish prime minister, Johan Wilhelm Rangell, and the German SS leader Heinrich Himler in summer 1942. When

Himler made inquiries about the Finnish Jews, Rangell answered firmly that his country did not have a Jewish question, because: 'In Finland there are a couple of thousand Jews, decent families and individuals whose sons are fighting in our army like other Finns and who are as respected citizens as all the rest' (quotation from Jakobson, 1999: 372).

## SACRIFICE, UNITY AND VICTORY: THE JEWS AND THE NATIONAL NARRATIVE OF THE WAR

For the Finns, the Second World War meant five years of fighting in three separate wars. The first of these was the Winter War against the Soviet Union in 1939–40, the second the Continuation War, once more against the Soviet Union, in 1941–44, as a co-belligerent with Germany, and the third the Lapland War of 1944–45 against Germany, to drive the Wehrmacht troops out of Lapland. These wars are usually looked on in Finland as parts of a constant, logically coherent effort to defend the country's independence. As a part of the Finnish nationalistic narrative, the Second World War is usually seen purely as a defense of the country's independence, a separate war into which the nation was driven against its will and which it survived only through its own will-power. This epic narrative is visible in both the memory and the memorials, through metaphors or themes of *sacrifice*, *unity* and *victory* associated with the war experience and heritage (Raivo, 2000a, 2000b). The Jewish soldiers who participated in these wars between 1939 and 1945 in the ranks of the Finnish army are naturally included in this national memory.

The first and oldest of these metaphors is the theme of sacrifice. The Second World War was a great tragedy, and thus a great sacrifice for Finland. Out of a population of less than 5 million people, some 93,000 Finnish soldiers were killed in action and a further 200,000 or so wounded (Raivo 2000b: 149). Finland had to cede some of its northern and eastern territories to the Soviet Union, amounting to about 10 per cent of its total area, and 423,000 refugees, representing 11 per cent of the country's population, had to be evacuated and resettled in the remaining parts of Finland (Laitinen, 1995). Among these refugees were some 300 Finnish Jews evacuated from the Karelian city of Viipuri (Vyborg), who were mostly resettled in Helsinki (Rautkallio, 1989: 54). All in all, some 25 per cent of the Finnish Jews had to leave their home areas due to the war.

The most typical Finnish memorial alluding to the Second World War is a cemetery for the fallen in a local churchyard. Each of these acts as a national icon and symbol of the war (Raivo, 2000a: 141). The burying of soldiers killed in action in the cemeteries of their home parishes was a particularly Finnish phenomenon and institution during the war, and about 83,000 soldiers are buried in 622 such graveyards all over the country (Tuomisto, 1998: 276). The erecting of memorials and building of sites of commemoration was a central part of the local mourning process. Even the smallest and poorest local authorities insisted on erecting a monument to their local war dead as a matter of honor, and monuments and memorials of this kind employed Finnish sculptors almost entirely for the first two postwar decades (Reitala, 1994: 113–14).

One of these memorials is situated in the Jewish cemetery of Helsinki, where 13 fallen soldiers who had been members of the Helsinki congregation were buried and seven who were lost in action are named. The sacrifices that the Jewish soldiers had to make were extremely precious to the Helsinki synagogue, for the number of victims was so high that in practice all the local families lost a son, brother, husband or father. The loss of lives among Jews of Helsinki in the Russo-Finnish Winter War was among the greatest suffered by any religious community in the whole of Finland (Rautkallio, 1989: 55).

The area dedicated to the memory of those who fell in the wars of 1939–44 is part of the larger civilian Jewish cemetery, where one section has been marked off for war graves. It is typical of Finnish war cemeteries that they are situated in conjunction with local civilian graveyards in this way. In the Jewish cemetery of Helsinki, as in all the other 621 Finnish cemeteries for those killed in the war, the graves are arranged in straight lines and regular rows (Figure 6.1). Each carries a small headstone with the name of the person, date of birth, date of death and place of death marked. It is a graveyard of both military uniformity and brotherhood: all those buried or named there are equal. This idea of brotherhood-in-arms, and of equality, is an essential part of the commemoration of the Second World War in Finland; and the rows of graves in the cemeteries are a physical manifestation of this (Raivo, 2000b: 152).

Just as the majority of Finnish war cemeteries have a large stone memorial decorated with a relief or statue, the Jewish cemetery has a stone decorated with a combination of the Star of David and a hand holding a sword – a symbol of Judaism linked with the emblem of the Finnish war veterans (Figure 6.2). It is a modest but strong metaphor

*The Second World War in Finland* 115

FIGURE 6.1

Area of the Jewish cemetery in Helsinki dedicated to commemoration of those killed in the wars of 1939–44. Thirteen members of the Helsinki Jewish community are buried here and six who were lost in action are listed by name. This section is marked off from the general civilian Jewish cemetery. Photo: Petri J. Raivo.

FIGURE 6.2

The memorial erected in the Jewish war cemetery is a stone decorated with a combination of the Star of David and a hand holding a sword – the symbol of Judaism linked with the emblem of the Finnish war veterans. Photo: Petri J. Raivo.

telling of the commitment and sacrifices of the Jewish community in Helsinki and all over Finland during the difficult years of the war.

Altogether these five years of fighting resulted in the deaths of 23 men from the Jewish community – nearly 8 per cent of the total number of some 300 Jewish soldiers who participated in the wars (Harviainen, 1999: 341). If there were doubts at all on the part of the Finns or the Jews, these must have concerned the Winter War and its sacrifices, which finally gave the Jewish community the feeling of being accepted as an equal and fully respected part of Finnish society. This contribution and sacrifice by a small minority – some 2,000 inhabitants – was far in excess of their number within the population, as was noted by the Finnish establishment even during the war. On Finnish Independence Day, December 6, 1944, Marshal Mannerheim, then President of Finland and wartime Commander-in-Chief, visited the synagogue in Helsinki to pay tribute to the fallen heroes of the Jewish community (Harviainen, 1999: 341). Finland had survived, and so had its Jewish population, but not without sacrifices.

In addition to sacrifice, there is an evident theme of unity in the Finnish war memories and memorials (Raivo, 2000a, 2000b). This spirit of the Winter War, the unification of the nation and the beginning of the healing process following the Civil War of 1918, is probably the most important theme of the national narrative. This narrative maintains that Finland survived the Winter War and the other wars that followed because of the unity of its people. There are many reasonable arguments to support this narrative of unity. The Molotov-Ribbentrop non-aggression pact signed by the Soviet Union and Germany and the reckless bullying of tiny Finland by Stalin were events that shocked the left-wing Finns into forgetting their previous disputes and taking up arms to defend their country. All this had taken place some 20 years after the bitter and cruel Civil War that had so deeply divided the Finns.

National unity is thus a central message of the narrative and monuments of the war of 1939–44, but it was not only unity between the White and the Reds. It can also be seen as a celebration of a common consensus between the Finnish and Swedish linguistic groups, between Lutheran and Orthodox Christianity and with all the minorities – Jews, Lapps, Tartars or Russians – who participated in the war effort as full and respected citizens.

The Finns themselves see no real differences between the three wars that they had to fight in 1939–45, because the image of the enemy was always the same, the Soviet Union and the Red Army, and the threat was always the same, the loss of independence and sovereignty. The 1941–44 war is known in Finland as the 'Continuation War' because it is understood as an extension of the Winter War and an attempt to make up the losses suffered in it. Even the Lapland War against the Germans can be included in the same category because it was fought against a background of the harsh terms of peace dictated by the Soviet Union and the continual fear of occupation if Finland did not fulfill these terms.

Thus the participation of the Finnish Jews in the war of 1941–44 was a self-evident fact, because it was seen as the second act in the struggle to retain independence that had started in the Winter War. For the Finns, including the Jewish community, the Second World War started in November 1939 and not in July 1941. That is the key to understanding why Finland's Jews did not see any contradiction in the idea of defending Finland as an ally of Germany, nor was it as impossible for them as later commentators outside Finland were apt to think. For the Finnish Jews, the Continuation War was above all a means of defending Finland and not of fighting for the master race represented by Germany.

Another important aspect of the ethos of unity was the spirit of comradeship that prevailed among the Finnish soldiers and former war veterans, which overshadowed ideological differences, and thus also ethnic differences. This strong sense of togetherness in spite of different backgrounds and ideologies created by the common experiences of frontline soldiers is always mentioned whenever the war is remembered. The Jewish veterans are no exception to this, and their interviews and memoirs always stress the good spirit, equal treatment and strong feeling of togetherness that prevailed in relations with their fellow Finnish soldiers. Thus the stories of the Jewish soldiers are very much a part of the male-dominant narrative of the war (Rautkallio, 1989; Jakobson, 1999).

> I felt that discrimination ended the very moment that I entered Light Anti-Aircraft Battery 17 at Rukajärvi. Since then I have not felt any discrimination, not during the war, nor later as a student, as a research assistant, as a young scientist, as a docent, or as a university professor. The change was brought about by the battery commander, Lt. Aarne Westerlund, who became a major after the war. He wisely set out to create a spirit of solidarity among our incoherent troop of reservists, in which I was one of the youngest members. (voice of an anonymous veteran in Tuuri, 1991: 285)

Apart from the area in the Jewish cemetery in Helsinki dedicated to those who fell in the war, there were no special military detachments or arrangements for the Finnish Jews. They were in principle dispersed, fighting in different units all over the front, although because most of them were living in the same areas and because the Finnish conscription system was territorially organized, many of them, especially those from Helsinki, were in practice serving in the same detachment. This was not because of their ethnicity but because of their place of residence. During the Winter War that detachment was the 10th Infantry Regiment, which mostly consisted of Swedish-speaking men from the Helsinki region. There were some 60 Jewish soldiers, mainly from the Helsinki area, serving in the third company of the third battalion of that regiment, accounting for one third of the total number of Jewish soldiers in Finland (Rautkallio, 1989: 56). The corresponding detachment in the Continuation War of 1941–44 was the 24th Infantry Regiment (Rautkallio, 1989: 130), in which attempts were also made to attend to the religious needs of the Jewish soldiers by erecting a temporary field synagogue 'Scholkas shul' at the front on the River Svir (Syväri), which must have been utterly unique in the military annals of Germany and its allies. An organization of Jewish war veterans in Finland (Suomen Juutalaisten Sotaveteraanien Veljespiiri) was established in 1981 (Harviainen, 1999: 341).

The theme of victory is also a vital part of the collective memory and heritage of the war. According to the national narrative, the Finns did not lose the war, even though they were on the side of the losers and had to cede territories. For most of the Finns, the outcome of the war was a successful defense, in that their troops were able to frustrate the strategic aims of the Red Army to conquer and occupy the territory of Finland and overthrow the country's way of life and traditions of democracy (Raivo, 2000b: 155). The status of the Finnish Jews as fully authorized citizens with equal rights and demands alongside other Finns is a logical part of this narrative of victory, as it demonstrates that even in the pressure of war Finland was a functioning democracy that secured and guaranteed the civil rights and equal treatment of its citizens. The treatment accorded to the Finnish Jews was not grounded in any special agreement made during the war, it happened because Finland was able to continue acting as a constitutional democracy (Jakobson, 1999: 377). Thus the example of the Finnish Jews carries a strong message of victory for the spirit of democracy, in that it is seen to have worked even during the difficult and hard times of war.

## BEYOND THE NATIONAL MEMORY: FINLAND AND THE VICTIMS OF THE HOLOCAUST

The Holocaust or 'shoah' – the systematic extermination of the Jewish population in countries occupied by Germany or its European allies – is without doubt the most painful, dismal and distinctive memory related to the Nazi regime and to the Second World War. The memory of the victims of the Holocaust has also been one of the most visible modes of commemoration of that war. It has also been one of the most difficult themes to commemorate appropriately, especially in countries that participated in the war on the Axis side. Germany itself, for example, has had to perform a constant balancing act in its recollections and commemorations of the war and the Holocaust. As pointed out by Young (1993), there has been such an enormous feeling of disgrace and guilt that it has been almost impossible to deal with certain processes, occurrences and places related to the memories of Nazism, anti-Semitism and the Holocaust.

On the other hand, the memory of the Holocaust, or actually its interpretation, has been a part of the national memory in many countries, and thus a part of the national mythology. The manner in which Poland, for example, has commemorated the Holocaust as it took place there is closely tied to the sufferings of the Polish nation, more so than to the extermination of the Jewish population. In other words, according to the Polish national narrative the victims were first and foremost Poles, and not particularly Jews, despite the fact that some 3.2 million out of the 3.6 million Polish Jews were victims of the Holocaust. The explanation partly lies in the fact that the postwar communist regime paid special attention to preserving the memory of political victims (Young, 1993: 122–3).

The nationalistic narrative is also clearly visible in the way the Holocaust is remembered and commemorated in countries like the USA, and especially in Israel, where the memory of the shoah has become a central part of the national narrative. Here the Holocaust is remembered both on account of the sufferings of the victims and through the ideals and myths of the nation, stressing the role of resistance, ghetto uprisings, heroism and the fight for survival. The uprising in the Warsaw ghetto and the fighting that followed have received considerable attention as a part of the recollection of the Holocaust, for example (Young, 1993: 210).

In Finland the Holocaust is mostly remembered as a brutal and criminal act of genocide that exterminated 6 million European Jews, an event which took place somewhere else and was perpetrated by other people. It does not belong to the national memory of the war, and has in a sense been consigned to an 'oblivion without guilt'. Finland was the only country fighting on the side of Germany during the Second World War that never participated officially in the Nazi plans for a final solution to annihilate the Jews in Europe. Finnish Jews were mentioned in the death lists maintained by Adolf Eichmann and in the papers of the Wannsee meeting, and when Hitler made his visit to Finland in 1942, for example, there were rumors of demands and lists put forward by the Germans, but no official request was ever made (Jakobson, 1999: 372). This is mainly because the Germans already knew that Finland would not accept any demands regarding the Finnish Jews. Especially from 1942 onward, Finland was too important an ally and co-belligerent for Germany to consider putting pressure on its government over this ideological matter. The upholding of a spirit of comradeship-in-arms and the binding of the fate of Finland ever more closely to that of the Third Reich were far too important to be jeopardized by raising the 'Jewish Question' (Jakobson, 1999: 372; Rautkallio, 1987).

This state of affairs implied a kind of dual morality as far as the Jewish question in wartime Finland was concerned. As no action was demanded or needed against the Jews, the Finnish authorities could imagine or pretend that there was nothing wrong in this respect in the other Axis countries either. For the Finns, the question or suspicion of any harassment of European Jews, not to mention genocide, was a distant and theoretical matter. The pieces of information that the authorities had collected were buried under other issues of war or were simply passed over in silence.

People in Finland were nevertheless well aware of the Nazi attitudes toward the Jews and the harassment of their communities elsewhere in Europe. The Finnish press, for example, had become alert to anti-Semitic developments before the war, especially in the course of 1938. There were numerous news dispatches and special articles in various Finnish newspapers reporting on Nazi policies and actions aimed against Jews, and most of the main newspapers commented on the oppressive measures especially after the pogrom of the infamous *Kristallnacht* (Rautkallio, 1987: 49). Not only the persecution of Jews but also the racial policy of the Third Reich in general received attention in the Finnish press, and international reactions to the situation relating to German Jewry were also covered. Later in the war the official censorship forced the press to remain silent over Jewish issues.

After the outbreak of the war, especially after 1941, the fate of the Jewish population in Europe was overshadowed by the question of Finland's own struggle for existence, although the maltreatment of Jews in neighboring countries occasionally aroused audible criticism. This happened in summer 1943, for example, when Professor Eino Kaila launched a public appeal in protest against the harassment of the Jews in Denmark, especially the treatment of Professor Niels Bohr there (Rautkallio, 1987: 42), but generally, and officially, the harassment of Jews became one of those matters about which Finland kept silent (Jakobson, 1999: 119).

The public audience did not receive adequate information on these matters during the war itself, but the authorities did. In fall 1941, for example, the State Police were informed of the fate of the Estonian Jews at the hands of the local Gestapo and the Estonian political police (Rautkallio, 1989: 74). The mass transportations of Jews taking place in German-occupied territories were also quite well known to politicians and higher officials, and in fall 1942 at the latest the Finnish diplomatic and military representatives stationed in Germany saw conspicuous signs of the persecution of Jews there (Rautkallio, 1987: 173). The scale of the genocide may have been unknown to the Finnish authorities, but information had filtered through about the existence of concentration camps and even death camps at least by 1942. Various recollections and interviews published after war also made it clear that many of the Finnish Jews already had information of that kind, or at least some presentiment of such a situation, by 1942. The pieces of information that they received were undoubtedly enough to give a picture of the systematic terrorization of Jewish civilians in occupied territories – not just spontaneous acts of cruelty – even though the real scale of the operation, its final goal and the brutality of it all was not understood or appreciated (Rautkallio, 1989: 96–7).

But there is more to the Jewish question in Finland than just the silence over German racial policy. Not all the Jews present there during the war were Finnish citizens. Refugees had already begun to appear before the war, especially after the German-Austrian *anschluss*. Finland was one of the few European countries that received Jewish refugees from Austria. By the beginning of the Continuation War in 1941 there were some 150 Jewish refugees from Germany and other countries controlled by the Third Reich (Rautkallio, 1985: 82), and also some 500 Jewish soldiers from the Red Army being held as prisoners of war (Harviainen, 1999: 341). Most of the refugees were staying in Helsinki, but once war broke out again in 1941 the State Police evacuated them to the countryside to keep them out of the Germans' sight and thus to avoid any problems that might have occurred (Rautkallio, 1987: 108).

The situation became a critical one for some of the Jewish refugees in fall 1942, when Finnish State Police (VALPO) arrested ten of them, probably at the request of the Gestapo in Estonia or in response to a hint from that direction. These arrests did not remain secret, and the leaders of the Helsinki synagogue contacted the government in an appeal for the release of the people concerned. The Finnish government took action, and mass deportations of refugees were prohibited, but it could not achieve a consensus of opinion for the release of all the prisoners, and finally it was decided to return five Jews together with 24 other foreign prisoners to Germany because of their criminal records (Rautkallio, 1987: 203). Technically it was not a question of ethnicity or race but of criminal justice. In reality there was something more behind it, however, as according to the archives of the Finnish State Police only two of those deported had a criminal record of any kind (Jakobson, 1999: 375). Finally, there were eight Jews among those who left instead of five, the number being increased by a wife and two children who followed the deportees. Altogether 27 people were expelled from Finland on the same ship, of whom 19 were non-Jewish citizens of Estonia or the Soviet Union (Rautkallio, 1985: 191). This sad episode marks the only occasion during the war when the Finnish authorities deported Jews, although other foreign prisoners were handed over to the Gestapo later (Rautkallio, 1985: 201). Altogether some 70 civilians were deported during the war, but still only eight of them were Jews. The fate of these eight people was nevertheless horrible enough to stain Finland's reputation. Their final destination was the Birkenau death camp, and only one of them survived, Georg Kollman from Austria, whose wife and son followed him to Germany.

It has been a symptomatic part of this attitude of oblivion without guilt that virtually nothing has been done until recently to commemorate these victims of the Holocaust in any visible fashion. It was almost 59 years before Finland produced a public memorial dedicated to its own victims of the Holocaust. This sculpture, named 'Apua hakevat kädet' (Hands seeking for help), designed by Professor Rafael Wardi and the sculptor Niels Haukeland, was unveiled in November 2000 (Figure 6.3). It stands in the park on the hill of Tähtitorninmäki near the South Harbour in Helsinki, near the place from which the SS *Hohenbör* set sail in November 1942.

FIGURE 6.3

'Apua hakevat kädet' (Hands seeking for help), a memorial dedicated to the eight Jewish refugees expelled from Finland in 1942 who then died as victims of the Holocaust in the Birkenau concentration camp. The monument stands in a park on the hill of Tähtitorninmäki overlooking the South Harbour in Helsinki, near the place from which the SS *Hohenhör*, carrying the deportees, left in November 1942. Photo: Petri J. Raivo.

The memorial is constructed of grey granite trimmed with two plates of steel, one of which is embossed with hands as a symbol of civilian refugees begging for help and protection. The granite stone carries the inscription in Finnish and Swedish: 'From the South Harbour that opens out in front of you, the Finnish State Police sent eight Jewish refugees to Tallinn to surrender to the German authorities, and thereby consigned them to the Holocaust, on the sixth of November, 1942.' The other side of the stone bears the names of the victims and their dates and places of birth and death, together with a verse from the Old Testament (Isaiah 56:5) 'They shall receive from me something better than sons and daughters, a memorial and a name in my own house and within my walls; I will give them an everlasting name, a name imperishable for all time', quoted in Finnish and Hebrew.

All the Finnish Jews and almost all the Jewish refugees from Central Europe resident in Finland during the war were spared the horrors of the Holocaust. Recognition of this was received after the war from the World Jewish Congress, which praised the Finns for the fact that no persecution of Jews had taken place in their country during the war, even though the country had been subjected to severe pressure while fighting on the side of the Third Reich (Rautkallio, 1987: 260). It is pointless to deny that the deportation of the eight refugees was and still is a disgraceful embarrassment to the Finns, because the authorities must have known enough about German racial policy to understand what fate awaited these people. The cancellation of these particular deportations could hardly have damaged the nation's vital interests. It is also pointless to deny that there was no anti-Semitism in Finland during the war. There certainly was some such feeling, and the deportations were a sad example of it. As the writer Johannes Salminen has stated in the leading Finnish newspaper, *Helsingin Sanomat*: 'eight lives are not much on the scale of Auschwitz, but enough to make Finland a participant in the Holocaust' (Salminen, 2000).

## CONCLUSION

It has been argued that the memory and memorization of the Second World War has differed from the traditions attached to previous wars, and in many ways the war itself differed from its predecessors. The most significant distinction was that it did not involve only soldiers but also impinged on the civil populations to a greater extent than hitherto. This change in the nature of war also altered the nature of its memory. In other words, following the experiences of Auschwitz, Dresden and Hiroshima, it was no longer possible to remember the war in strong nationalistic terms.

Despite these arguments, however, the elastic nature of national heritage – the interpretation of the past from the present and in accordance with present needs – has shown that it is even possible to bend these horrors to support the nationalistic narrative. In Finland, for example, the Second World War is still a vital part of the collective memory. The national will and need to remember these difficult times has not come to an end, but rather the process is continuing and taking on new forms. The years 1939–44 and the three wars that Finland was forced into are mostly seen as an ultimate test of survival as an independent and sovereign nation. According to this heritage, constructed, manifested and represented through sites of commemoration, a nationalistic narrative of sacrifice, unity and victory has been told.

At the national level the story of the Finnish Jews has fitted in well with this narrative. Regardless of the fact that Finland was a cobelligerent and important ally of Nazi Germany in 1941–44, it managed to keep its citizens apart from the ethnic discrimination, and most important of all, to save them from the horrors of the Holocaust. The Holocaust itself was seen as something that did not take place in Finland and was in no way brought about by the Finns, and thus it is something that is related to a more general context of commemoration than to the national memory. There has been a certain sense of 'oblivion without guilt'. Thus the memorial erected to the eight Jewish refugees arrested and handed over to the German Gestapo is important to refresh the public memory, not so much because it is dedicated to victims of the Holocaust as such, but because it is dedicated to that part of the Holocaust in which the Finnish authorities, and thus Finland as a nation, were indirectly implicated. The situation of oblivion without guilt has now been contested with the names of five men, one woman and two children inscribed in steel and stone.

## REFERENCES

Harviainen, Tapani (1999) 'Suomen Juutalaiset', in Markku Löytönen and Laura Kolbe (eds) *Suomi. Maa, kansa ja kulttuurit*. Helsinki: Suomen Kirjallisuuden Seura (pp. 333–43).

Jakobson, Max (1999) *Väkivallan vuodet: 20. Vuosisadan tilinpäätös I*. Helsinki: Otava.

Laitinen, E. (1995) 'Vuoden 1945 Maanhankintalain synty, sisältö ja toteutus', in E. Laitinen (ed.) *Rintamalta raiviolle: sodanjälkeinen asutustoiminta 50 vuotta*. Jyväskylä: Atena (pp. 52–138).

Luostarinen, Heikki (1986) *Perivihollinen. Suomen oikeistolehdistön Neuvostoliittoa koskeva vihollisuva sodassa 1941–44: tausta ja sisältö*. Tampere: Vastapaino.

Raivo, Petri (2000a) 'Landscaping the Patriotic Past: Finnish War Landscapes as a National Heritage', *Fennia*, 178 (1): 139–50.

Raivo, Petri (2000b) '"This is where they fought" – Finnish War Landscapes as a National Heritage', in Graham Davison, Mike Roper and Timothy Ashplant (eds) *The Politics of War Memory and Commemoration*. London: Routledge (pp. 145–64).

Rautkallio, Hannu (1985) *Ne kahdeksan ja Suomen omatunto*. Espoo: Weilin+Göös.

Rautkallio, Hannu (1987) *Finland and the Holocaust. The Rescue of Finland's Jews*. New York: Holocaust Library.

Rautkallio, Hannu (1989) *Suomen juutalaisten aseveljeys*. Helsinki: Tammi.

Reitala, A. (1994) 'Sodan jäljet Suomen taiteessa', in L. Haataja (ed.) *Ja Kuitenkin Me Voitimme: Sodan Muisto ja Perintö*. Helsinki: Kirjayhtymä (pp. 103–20).

Salminen, Johannes (2000) 'Suomen juutalaisten masentava kujanjuoksu', *Helsingin Sanomat* September 17, 2000.

Tuomisto, A. (1998) *Suomalaiset sotamuistomerkit*. Jyväskylä: Suomen Sotilas.

Tuuri, Antti (1991) *Rukajärven aika*. Helsinki: Otava.

Verkkouutiset (1997) http://www.verkkouutiset.fi/arkisto/Arkisto_1997/5.joulukuu/JUUTSOTA.HTM

Young, James E. (1993) *The Texture of Memory: Holocaust Memorials and Meaning*. New Haven, CT and London: Yale University Press.

# 7

# *Engendered Oblivion: Commemorating Jewish Inmates at the Ravensbrueck Memorial 1945–95*

## INSA ESCHEBACH

'Forgetting on a collective scale can itself assume the guise of a memory', writes Geoffrey H. Hartman. That which appears in the guise of a memory is a 'counter-memory', that is, a 'highly selective story, focused on what is basic for the community and turning away from everything else'.[1]

At the Ravensbrueck Memorial Site there are two monuments which could be described as manifestations of such a counter-memory. Ravensbrueck is located to the north of Berlin and was the central women's camp in the concentration camp system. The camp was liberated by the Red Army in April 1945. In 1959, the German Democratic Republic inaugurated a 'Nationale Mahn- und Gedenkstaette' or National Memorial site.[2] A sculpture known as 'Tragende' or 'Woman, carrying', was created by Will Lammert for the occasion. This is a giant bronze figure of a woman on a pedestal about 7m high; she is carrying another woman, gaunt and sunken (see Figure 7.1). As the central monument at the memorial site, it has served as a topographical focus for many official commemoration ceremonies.

The second monument at Ravensbrueck is placed in the outer area of the memorial site and was sculpted by Fritz Cremer. Erected in 1965, it shows a group of figures known as the 'Ravensbrueck group of mothers'. The three women are carrying a dead child on a stretcher. Another child simultaneously grasps and hides within the skirts of the advancing woman (see Figure 7.2).

Now, what do these two sculptures have in common? As Kathrin Hoffmann-Curtius has pointed out, both are depictions of women engaged in stereotypically female activities: nursing, care-taking or mourning the dead.[3] In stark contrast, Fritz Cremer's 1958

FIGURE 7.1

'Woman, carrying' (Will Lammert), erected at the Ravensbrueck Memorial Site in 1959.

FIGURE 7.2

'Ravensbrueck group of mothers' (Fritz Cremer), erected at the Ravensbrueck Memorial Site in 1965. Photo: I. Eschebach

Buchenwald memorial consists of 11 different, multifaceted male figures representing various 'types of consciousness and attitude'[4]: he who calls out; he who fights; he who pledges; he who discusses; etc. Also, weapons and a flag are part of the sculpture. While the 'Ravensbrueck group of mothers' has a dead child at its centre, the little boy at the Buchenwald Memorial is shown alive. He is standing on his own two feet and belongs to the emphatically vital masculine cohort (see Figure 7.3). It becomes apparent that the sculptural visualizations of concentration camp history, seen at the Buchenwald and Ravensbrueck Memorial Sites, are based on a binary construction of gender imagery. According to Claudia Koonz: 'In the historical iconography of GDR sculptures, heroic males resist and women persevere. Jews are absent.'[5]

Why is this so? I would like to suggest that gender categories structure not only memorializations of national socialism, but also the strategies of forgetting. Put strongly, one might say that the use of gender images at Ravensbrueck (and other memorial sites in the GDR) served the specific purpose of forgetting. These monuments illustrate a process of 'ex-nominating', of 'disnaming' that has been described by Roland Barthes and Silke Wenk. In the transfer 'from that which is real – to its representation' historical phenomena are blanked out and forgotten in favour of principles claiming general validity.[6] This displacement of history has two goals: in conveying a specific interpretation of historical events, these monuments simultaneously manifest norms according to which one should act in the future – norms and principles that assume 'the guise of a memory'. Given this thesis as a backdrop, I should like first to discuss the function of the images of maternalism at the Ravensbrueck Memorial Site. Second – and connected to that – I will address the reasons why Ravensbrueck's Jewish inmates had fallen into oblivion, and why they have only been commemorated in Ravensbrueck since 1988.

In her survey of Shoah Memorials, Judith Baumel came to the conclusion that 'the mother' is the most common image of women in Israeli Holocaust iconography and that this gender representation stems from a pre-existing stereotype.[7] This is also true for Ravensbrueck and for East German sculpture in general. One example of a maternal figure may be seen in Gustav Seitz's sculpture, erected in 1946 at the site of the former Weisswasser concentration camp, a satellite camp of Gross-Rosen. A sculpture by Arndt Wittig, known as 'The Mother', has stood at the Neubrandenburg Memorial Site since 1976 (see Figure 7.4). 'Mother' is also the name given to a sculpture created

FIGURE 7.3

'Buchenwald-Memorial' (Fritz Cremer), erected at the Buchenwald Memorial Site in 1958.

FIGURE 7.4

'The Mother' (Arndt Wittig), erected at the Neubrandenburg Memorial Site in 1976. Photo: M. Moebius

by Gerhard Thieme, which was placed near the city of Schwerin in 1973 (see Figure 7.5). 'O Deutschland, bleiche Mutter' (Germany, pale mother) is a sculpture, crafted in bronze by Fritz Cremer. The artist had created the monument, named after a poem by Bertolt Brecht, in 1964 for the Mauthausen Memorial Site. A replica was erected in Berlin's city center in 1987 (see Figure 7.6).

To address Germany as 'pale Mother' is revealing and points to the historical context in which women became appropriate subjects for monuments: as female allegories representing the nation or national virtues; as Victoria, Athena or Minerva; as Germania, Borussia, Marianne or as 'Motherland'/'Mother Russia' etc. These gender representations, then, are not of specific historical women, but rather of idealized principles intended to guarantee cohesion for an imagined community of equals – not to say brothers.[8] After 1945, the victorious national allegories came to be replaced by 'allegories of the people'.[9] The continuity of the nation was visualized – particularly in socialist commemorative art – through representations of women as mourners, as plaintiffs, as wounded, as care-takers, that is to say as 'Germany's pale mothers'. The 1993 placement of an enlarged replica of Kollwitz's 'Mother with dead son' should be understood in this context. The sculpture, placed in the Central Memorial for the Victims of War and Tyranny in Berlin, shows how the 'mother' becomes a central symbol of the suffering of Germany's population (see Figure 7.7).

Yet, the prominence of women and mothers in German commemorative sculpture does not only point to and imply an assertion of national continuity. A second discourse is superimposed on it – the Christian tradition of martyrdom and salvation. Since the eighteenth century, mourning in Christian cemeteries has been almost exclusively represented through figures and images of women. Relatedly, Weimar war memorials increasingly utilized female figures in mourning, holding the dead in their laps. They are generally referred to as Pieta.[10]

The sculpture mentioned above, 'Woman, carrying', has frequently been referred to as the 'Pieta of Ravensbrueck'. Unlike traditional Pieta representations, however, the foot of the 'Woman, carrying' appears to be stepping over the edge of the pedestal. Her gesture evokes thoughts of overcoming death, of a new beginning[11] – something, the GDR claimed to have achieved. The lamentation of Mary is transformed into an act of compassionate solidarity.[12]

Sarah Horowitz has pointed out that it is not only in literary Holocaust representations that maternalism has played a pre-eminent role, but also in popular culture. Maternalism is the very essence of

FIGURE 7.5

'Mother' (Gerhard Thieme), placed near the city of Schwerin in 1973. Photo: M. Moebius

FIGURE 7.6

'Germany, pale Mother' (Fritz Cremer), erected in 1964 at the Mauthausen Memorial Site. A replica was placed in Berlin's city center in 1987. Photo: I. Eschebach

FIGURE 7.7

'Mother with dead son' (Kaethe Kollwitz), created in 1937. An enlarged replica was placed in the Central Memorial for the Victims of War and Tyranny ('Neue Wache'), Berlin in 1993. Photo: I. Eschebach

goodness and altruism – this perspective would allow access to events which lie far beyond most people's experiences. Maternalism unites the extraordinary with the ordinary, and, for Horowitz, 'tames the Holocaust'.[13] Could one say that maternalism as represented at Ravensbrueck 'tames the Holocaust'? Does the 'Woman, carrying' really refer to the Shoah? Can this sculpture be seen as a Holocaust memorial at all?

The intentions behind both the memorial site, and the monument at the time it was erected, may be discerned in a book which was published in four languages and 10,000 copies shortly after the memorial site opened. It was presented to groups of visitors and school classes right up to the end of the GDR in 1989. The first sentence of the book, defining Ravensbrueck in Christian terms as 'Golgotha', is followed by the dedication of the memorial site: 'It is a memorial to the women of strong will, to the women with knowledge, who held firmly together and who supported and sustained their weaker comrades, the defenseless victims; it is a monument, built here to the everlasting glory of the heroines, who fought here to the very last breath.'[14]

It becomes evident that the memorial site is dedicated to the 'heroines who fought' – the 'defenseless victims' are mentioned only because they were supported and sustained. The heroines, it is said, were 'the antifascist prisoners of all nations', whereby German inmates are given a special role: 'The great ideal of solidarity ... came to Ravensbrueck with the first German antifascists.'[15] Acts of solidarity and compassion are presented as a particular characteristic of German antifascists. The genocide of the Jewish people is not mentioned once – indeed, Jewish inmates occur only twice in this book. At one point, it is stated that 'Jewish women had to unload bricks'. The second mention reads as follows: 'When the Jewish prisoners were punished by the complete stop of rations for several days, the comrades from the other parts of the camp ... smuggled food to them.'[16] Jewish inmates are thus described as those who required help, non-Jewish inmates as those who gave help.[17] Within the narrative, Jewish inmates function as a dark background against which the actions of political prisoners appear all the more glowing.

As a memorial site in honor of the 'heroines who fought' Ravensbrueck was thus in no way intended to commemorate the role the concentration camp had played in the extermination of European Jews. Solidarity and maternalism are depicted as characteristics of the antifascist, and in particular of German antifascist inmates. In the entrance area to the memorial site, they are addressed as 'our mothers and sisters', as socialist founding mothers of the nation, whose legacy the GDR proclaimed itself to have fulfilled.[18]

Now, while the GDR still existed, Ravensbrueck – along with many other national memorial sites – was intended to legitimate the existence and meaning of the state. As John R. Gillis writes, since the French Revolution 'national commemoration in Europe' has celebrated 'a cult of new beginnings'.[19] This observation fits the commemoration ceremonies held at Ravensbrueck in those years. At the opening ceremony in 1959, one of the permitted international speeches was given by an Israeli: once again, neither the genocide, nor the Jewish inmates were the subject of his speech, but rather the GDR:

> The working people of Israel greet most heartily the German Democratic Republic, which, by its very existence, gives a guarantee that racial hatred and anti-Semitism shall never return, and which shows the way to a peaceful and democratic Germany.[20]

The wording suggests not, that it is Israel which 'by its very existence' prevents a return of racial hatred and anti-Semitism; instead, this characterization is identified as a primary attribute of the GDR. Given that, from the early 1950s on, the GDR had branded Israel as an agent of US imperialism, it is perhaps surprising that an Israeli was permitted to be present at all – this was indeed not only the first occasion, but until the demise of the GDR also the last. By 1985 Ravensbrueck's Jewish inmates had become forgotten to such an extent that, for example, when the GDR government representative Kurt Hager gave a speech on the 40th anniversary of the liberation, he failed to mention them once.[21]

In the immediate postwar period, the position of the Holocaust within communist public memory had not yet been firmly defined. In 1945, there were about 4,500 Jewish survivors living in the Soviet Zone of occupation. Until 1948, lively debates took place as to how the annihilation of European Jewry should be established in public memory. Jeffrey Herf refers to a 'competition of the grieving for the limited resource of recognition'[22] in those early years. During the years following liberation, the Soviet Zone and later the GDR still appeared to be the 'natural home' for victims of national socialism. Seen from the early postwar years, the suppression of Jewish themes, which later took place, appears as an 'unexpected paradox'.[23] Nevertheless, the marginalization of Jewish victims is consistent with the theory popularized by the Communist Party in the Weimar Republic. According to this theory, anti-Semitism was above all an instrument used by the capitalist class in order to confuse, weaken and divide the working class.[24] Perhaps this understanding was one of the reasons for rejecting the notion that the genocide could have been carried out for its own sake.

As is well known, in the following years and decades, the Jewish community of the GDR was subject to political control. When at the beginning of the 1950s 'Zionism' and 'cosmopolitanism' were demonized in accordance with Soviet policy, virtually all 'citizens of Jewish origin' – to use the official GDR term – came under suspicion as Zionist spies. Hundreds fled to West Berlin.[25] According to Erica Burgauer, those who remained had usually grown up in Germany, were often from families more or less assimilated long before persecution began and who hardly practiced their faith. In 1989, the communities throughout the GDR had only about 380 members.[26]

Throughout these years, the commemoration ceremonies at Ravensbrueck organized by the state were dominated by communist public memory, with the 'Woman, carrying' as a visual focus. Swearing-in ceremonies for soldiers of the National People's Army took place at the feet of the 'Woman, carrying' (see Figure 7.8). The sculpture, raised on a pedestal, appears as the very model of the 'loving and suffering, caring and grieving woman' on whom 'the army as a brotherhood' depends.[27] According to this reading, her willingness to bear sacrifices legitimates the men's military activities; they are directed toward her defense.

Both German and Soviet military were also present at the ceremonies held annually at Ravensbrueck: government representatives, the invited group of former political prisoners, the population, members of the Communist Youth League and the Soviet and German 'fraternal armies' formed a familial gathering. The pictures of these public events clearly show the staging of the ideal type of a society in which government, the mothers of Ravensbrueck, the 'fraternal armies' and the children are a happily united community (see Figure 7.9). Books such as Primo Levi's autobiographical account *If This is a Man* (1947) could not be published in the GDR because even the slightest criticism of political prisoners' conduct was regarded as insult to the 'heroic antifascist struggle', in particular to that of the German political prisoners.[28] Margarete Buber-Neumann, a former prisoner at Ravensbrueck expressed the following thought: 'Christianity claims that man is purified and ennobled by suffering. I believe the concentration camp proved the contrary. I believe there is nothing more dangerous than suffering, than a surfeit of suffering.'[29] Such insights went against the idealization and glorification of the antifascist prisoners which the state needed as role models. For this reason, Buber-Neumann's work was not published in the GDR either.

The extent to which public memory of Ravensbrueck was shaped by political interest emerges in a letter from the year 1985 which for the first time raises the issue of the non-commemoration of Jewish inmates. The author, Werner Haendler, visited the USA on behalf of the League for International Understanding and summarized his impressions for the Politburo as follows:

> I found confirmed, that in reaction to Nazi extermination policies and influenced by the State of Israel, a broad current of identification with Jewry has developed over the past ten years, particularly in the USA. People who are not religious regard themselves as Jews, indeed they wish to emphasize this. This is an ongoing emotional process which should be taken into account, in particular in our relations with Americans. Visits to memorial sites at the former concentration camps are also often evaluated in

FIGURE 7.8

A swearing-in ceremony for soldiers of the National People's Army at the Ravensbrueck Memorial Site in 1979. Photo: StBG/MGR

FIGURE 7.9

Soviet soldiers carrying members of the Communist Youth League in their arms on the occasion of the 40th anniversary of the concentration camp's liberation on April 20, 1985, Ravensbrueck Memorial Site. Photo: StBG/MGR

terms of whether the Jewish victims are commemorated in an appropriate manner. ... As ... despite numerous indications, no alterations could be achieved at Ravensbrueck, the GDR-USA Friendship Committee has ever since escorted visitors only to Buchenwald and Sachsenhausen where there are no problems, and avoided Ravensbrueck.

Haendler recommended that 'the problems and aspects mentioned should be considered, so as not to expose us to possible further attacks by the US media'.[30]

Haendler's concern over US media attacks came at a time when the government of the GDR was beginning to aim at improving relations with the USA for economic reasons. In 1986 General Secretary Honecker received a delegation from the US Congress for the first time. In the hope of benefiting from American economic aid, the government decided to play the so-called Jewish card.[31] When in January 1986 the World Jewish Congress met in Jerusalem, the GDR government allowed representatives of the East German communities to attend for the first time. A further result of the new policy was the political decision to demonstratively commemorate the 50th anniversary of the November 1938 pogrom.[32] The events commenced with a ceremony held by the Youth League at the Ravensbrueck Memorial Site with a performance by the Leipzig Synagogue Choir. The members of this choir, founded in 1963, were exclusively Christian.[33] They performed Hebrew temple chants and psalms before an audience of 3,500 young people from the surrounding area. This was the first official commemoration of Jewish victims to be held at Ravensbrueck.

Also in 1988, a memorial stone was placed in the ground as a lasting sign (see Figure 7.10). The inscription is in honor and memory 'of the countless Jewish and other victims of fascist racial-madness'. The vague expression 'other victims' refers to a group not regarded as worthy of a name in 1988, the Sinti and Roma. It was only six years later, that they were honored with a separate plaque.

Since the beginning of the 1990s, Ravensbrueck has undergone a process of democratization. In addition to various ceremonies commemorating the history of Jewish women prisoners, other, until now forgotten groups of inmates, have become the focus of attention. On the occasion of the 50th anniversary of the camp's liberation over 1,300 survivors attended, including about 200 men and women from Israel who returned to their place of suffering for the first time in 50 years.[34] In 1997, a still ongoing research project was inaugurated by the

FIGURE 7.10

Memorial stone, placed at the Ravensbrueck Memorial site in 1988. The inscription is in honor and memory 'of the countless Jewish and other victims of fascist racial-madness'. Photo: M. Moebius

German-Israeli Foundation to investigate the forgotten history of Jewish prisoners at Ravensbrueck.[35] Very little had been known before: according to rough estimates, there were about 20,000 Jewish prisoners at Ravensbrueck and its satellite camps; figures which require further investigation, as do the numbers and fate of the Jewish survivors.

To sum up: motherhood or rather maternalism is a widespread motif in socialist commemorative art – a motif that stems from pre-existing stereotypes. Ever since national states emerged, women have been used to represent national virtues and the mother nation. While figurative representations of men have tended to be individualized and to refer to specifics of historical situations, commemorative representations of women have usually stood for principles. Women could be used in memorials – not because they represented women, but because they represented a non-antagonistic community.

After 1945, 'Germany's pale mothers' – grieving and broken but upstanding women – can be found in both the socialist commemorative sculpture of East Germany and in West Germany's Christian commemorative art. As monuments in public space, the German population could read them as symbols of suffering. In this manner, they contribute to the displacement of the question who was responsible for this suffering and for national socialist's atrocities in the first place.

Will Lammert's 'Woman, carrying' is an example of this type of monument. However, situated as she is at the site of the former women's concentration camp, the sculpture represents more than just a principle – it also points to something particular, to the actual, historical context of the site. In this setting, the 'Woman, carrying' represents a general principle and inmates of Ravensbrueck at the same time; she combines the principle of the ultimate good with an interpretation of concentration camp history. What the 'Woman, carrying' says and how she is understood becomes: This is, what has happened here. We have realized maternalism and mutual assistance in our community of prisoners. This interpretation becomes more clear in the written source material of the work's reception. Maternalism and solidarity were characteristics of those women who fought, i.e. of the political prisoners and, more precisely, of the German political prisoners. German women antifascists played a central role in the genealogical narrative of the GDR. They were the founding mothers of the German socialist nation. In honoring them, East German society honored itself.

Geoffrey Hartman has described genealogical narratives, which aimed at providing cohesion for a national community, as modern constructs, as counter-memories, invented 'in order to achieve a national consensus by appealing to one single heroic past'.[36] Seen as part of the GDR's genealogical narrative, the maternal heroines can be identified as such counter-memory: that the non-Jewish German political prisoners were the most privileged group of inmates is thereby forgotten; that there were others outside this group is also forgotten: Jews, Jehovah's Witnesses, Sinti and Roma, so-called 'anti-social elements' to name but a few. Also forgotten is the dramatic difference between those persecuted for political reasons and those persecuted for racist reasons; as a result the Shoah is pushed into oblivion.

That is what the source material indicates and confirms. Nonetheless, the question remains, whether, for instance, the 'Woman, carrying' is more than just the national icon of socialist Germany, she has long been regarded. Is she perhaps more than a female cipher for forgetting? Today still, she is the central monument at the Ravensbrueck Memorial Site. We shall have to wait and see which memories she will pass to future visitors.

## NOTES

This text summarizes some results of a research project conducted by the author at the Institute for Cultural Studies, Humboldt-Universitaet, Berlin; the research project was made possible by the German Research Foundation (DFG).

1. Geoffrey H. Hartman, 'Introduction: Darkness Visible', in G.H. Hartman (ed.) *Holocaust Remembrance. The Shapes of Memory* (Cambridge, MA: Blackwell, 1994), p. 15.
2. See Insa Eschebach, Sigrid Jacobeit and Susanne Lanwerd (eds) *Die Sprache des Gedenkens. Zur Geschichte der Gedenkstaette Ravensbrueck 1945 bis 1995* (Berlin: Schriftenreihe der Stiftung Brandenburgische Gedenkstaetten, Bd. 11, 1999).
3. See Kathrin Hoffmann-Curtius, 'Caritas und Kampf: die Mahnmale in Ravensbrueck', in Eschebach *et al.*, *Die Sprache des Gedenkens*, pp. 55–68.
4. Volkhard Knigge, 'Buchenwald', in Detlef Hoffmann (ed.) *Das Gedaechtnis der Dinge. KZ-Relikte und KZ-Denkmaeler 1945–1995* (New York: Frankfurt am Main, 1998), p. 140.
5. Claudia Koonz, 'Between Memory and Oblivion: Concentration Camps in German Memory', in John R. Gillis (ed.) *Commemorations. The Politics of National Identity* (Princeton University Press, 1994), p. 267.
6. See Roland Barthes, *Mythen des Alltags* (Frankfurt am Main, 1996), p. 124 ff. The concept was opened up for use in the analysis of gender imagery in commemorative sculpture by Silke Wenk, *Versteinerte Weiblichkeit. Allegorien in der Skulptur der Moderne* (Cologne, Weimar, Wien, 1996), p. 37.
7. Judith Tydor Baumel, '"Rachel Laments her Children" – Representation of Women in Israeli Holocaust Memorials', *Israel Studies* 1 (1996): 100–26.
8. See Silke Wenk, *Versteinerte*, p. 95 ff.
9. See Diether Schmidt's interpretation of Fritz Cremer's bronze 'O Deutschland, bleiche Mutter': 'If, in his poem on Germany, Brecht had replaced the imperialist state allegory of Germania by using the realist allegory of the people, then, based on this, Cremer supplied the plastic representation.' Diether Schmidt, *Fritz Cremer. Leben, Werke, Schriften, Meinungen* (Dresden, 1973), p. 50.
10. See Kathrin Hoffmann-Curtius, 'Sieg ohne Trauer – Trauer ohne Sieg. Totenklage auf Kriegerdenkmaelern des Ersten Weltkrieges', in Gisela Ecker (ed.) *Trauer tragen – Trauer zeigen. Inszenierungen der Geschlechter* (Munich, 1999): 259–86.
11. See Susanne Lanwerd, 'Skulpturales Gedenken. Die "Tragende" von Will Lammert', in Eschebach *et al.*, *Die Sprache des Gedenkens*, pp. 39–54.
12. See Hoffmann-Curtius, 'Caritas und Kampf', p. 63.
13. Sarah R. Horowitz, 'Geschlechtsspezifische Erinnerungen an den Holocaust', in Sigrid Jacobeit, Grit Philipp (eds) *Forschungsschwerpunkt Ravensbrueck. Beitraege zur Geschichte des Frauen-Konzentrationslagers* (Berlin: Schriftenreihe der Stiftung Brandenburgische Gedenkstaetten, Bd. 9. 1997), pp. 131–5.
14. Komitee der Antifaschistischen Widerstandskaempfer in der Deutschen Demokratischen Republik (ed.) *Ravensbrueck* (Berlin (Ost), 1960), p. 7 (German version), p. 45 (English version).
15. Ibid., pp. 11, 48.
16. Ibid., pp.11, 49.
17. In her study of literature on Olga Benario, Linde Apel makes a similar observation concerning stereotyped portrayal of Jewish inmates at Ravensbrueck: Linde Apel,

'Olga Benario – Kommunistin, Juedin, Heldin', in Eschebach *et al.*, *Die Sprache des Gedenkens*, p. 198. It would appear that a similar pattern of interpretation lies behind the thematization of 'Resistance and suffering of the Jewish People' in a museum of that name at the Sachsenhausen memorial site. After an appeal by Professor F. Bergmann, Israel and the Israeli 'Union of Antifascist Resistance Fighters' in 1961, that the Sachsenhausen memorial site should commemorate the murdered Jews as well, a museum based on this theme was hastily designed and installed at the site, opened in 1961. Susanne zur Nieden writes, 'A section in the international museum devoted to the Jewish resistance struggle appeared unworthy of consideration, as it would have been equivalent to a recognition of Israel'. The focus of Sachsenhausen's 'Jewish museum' was not the history of the camp's Jewish inmates but rather an idealized portrait of the solidarity between antifascists, represented as proletarian, and the group of Jewish inmates, a portrait not free from anti-Semitic ascriptions. See Susanne zur Nieden, 'Das Museum des Widerstandskampfes und der Leiden des juedischen Volkes', in Guenter Morsch (ed.) *Von der Erinnerung zum Monument. Die Entstehungsgeschichte der Nationalen Mahn- und Gedenkstaette Sachsenhausen* (Berlin: Schriftenreihe der Stiftung Brandenburgische Gedenkstaetten, Bd. 8, 1996): 272–8.
18. See Insa Eschebach, 'Zur Formensprache der Totenehrung. Ravensbrueck in der fruhen Nachkriegszeit', in Eschebach *et al.*, *Die Sprache des Gedenkens*, p. 31.
19. John R. Gillis, 'Memory and Identity: The History of a Relationship', in Gillis, *Commemorations*, p. 8.
20. Komitee der Antifaschistischen Widerstandskaempfer, *Ravensbrueck*, pp. 129, 143.
21. See Komitee der Antifaschistischen Widerstandskaempfer der Deutschen Demokratischen Republik (ed.) *Die Geschichte lehrt: Alles fur den Frieden. 30. April 1985: 40. Jahrestag der Befreiung des Faschistischen Konzentrationslagers Ravensbrueck* (Berlin, 1985), pp. 7–19.
22. Jeffrey Herf, *Zweierlei Erinnerung. Die NS-Vergangenheit im geteilten Deutschland* (Berlin, 1998), p. 88; see Olaf Groehler, 'Der Holocaust in der Geschichtsschreibung der DDR', in Olaf Groehler and Ulrich Herbert (eds) *Zweierlei Bewaeltigung. Vier Beitraege ueber den Umgang mit der NS-Vergangenheit in den beiden deutschen Staaten* (Hamburg, 1992): 41–66.
23. Herf, *Zweierlei Erinnerung*, p. 11.
24. Ibid., p. 26.
25. See Erica Burgauer, *Zwischen Erinnerung und Verdraengung – Juden in Deutschland nach 1945* (Reinbek bei Hamburg, 1993), p. 180 ff.
26. Ibid., p. 145.
27. Karen Hagemann, 'Heldenmuetter, Kriegerbraeute und Amazonen. Entwuerfe "patriotischer" Weiblichkeit zur Zeit der Befreiungskriege', in Ute Frevert (ed.) *Militaer und Gesellschaft im 19. und 20. Jahrhundert* (Stuttgart, 1997): 174–200; see Insa Eschebach, 'Geschlechtsspezifische Symbolisierungen im Gedenken. Zur Geschichte der Mahn- und Gedenkstaette Ravensbrueck, *Metis. Zeitschrift fuer historische Frauenforschung*, 15 (1999): 12–27.
28. See Joachim Meinert, 'Geschichte eines Verbots. Warum Primo Levi's Hauptwerk in der DDR nicht erscheinen durfte', *Sinn und Form*, 2 (2000): 149–94.
29. Margarete Buber-Neumann, *Als Gefangene bei Stalin und Hitler: Eine Welt im Dunkel* (Berlin: Frankfurt am Main, 1993), p. 243 f.
30. Letter from Werner Haendler to Hermann Axen, Member of the Politburo of the Central Commitee of the SED of July 25, 1985. See Insa Eschebach, 'Jahrestage.

Zu den Formen und Funktionen von Gedenkveranstaltungen in Ravensbrueck, 1946–1995', in Eschebach *et al.*, *Die Sprache des Gedenkens*, p. 92.
31. Erica Burgauer, *Zwischen Erinnerung*. p. 223.
32. Ibid., p. 226.
33. Ibid., p. 161.
34. See Eschebach, 'Jahrestage', p. 98 ff.
35. Victims and Survivors: Jewish women prisoners in the Ravensbrueck concentration camp during and after the Second World War. Historical, sociological and political research, German Israeli Foundation Research Project 1997–99; 'Victims, Victimizers and Survivors: a multidisciplinary research on Jewish women in the concentration camp of Ravensbrueck and their environment', German Israeli Foundation Research Project 2001–03.
36. Geoffrey H. Hartman, *Der laengste Schatten. Erinnerung und Vergessen nach dem Holocaust* (Berlin, 1999), p. 164.

# PART II

## THE UNITED STATES

# 8

# 'The Girl I Was':
# The Construction of Memory in Fiction by American Jewish Women

### SYLVIA BARACK FISHMAN

Fiction by American Jewish female writers in the second half of the twentieth century often depicts women remembering their past. Stories and novels by writers such as Tillie Olsen, Grace Paley, Rebecca Goldstein, Daphne Merkin, Cynthia Ozick and Lynne Sharon Schwartz frequently feature protagonists who reconstruct the images of the girls they were, as they attempt to untangle the riddle of their adult lives.

These texts suggest that recapturing one's girlhood is an elusive enterprise, because the past is always reinterpreted. What one 'remembers' blends fragments of actual occurrences with the colors of conflicting emotions evoked by the remembered event, washed by images from literature, music and other cultural influences. The hybrid 'memory', augmented by cultural grafts, is then viewed through the lens of adult experience. As Schwartz's articulate protagonist, Audrey, concludes in her haunting 1989 novel, *Leaving Brooklyn*, even unfulfilled goals can suffuse and distort one's memories of a younger self:

> Perhaps I haven't succeeded in finding the girl I was, but only in fabricating the girl I might have been, would have liked to be, looking backward from the woman I have become. ... And maybe I am this way because she never was, couldn't be. And yet it feels so real. If it wasn't a memory to begin with, it has become one now.[1]

Thus, the creature memory constructs takes on a vivid life of her own in the mind of the remembering woman, independent of 'objective' truth or falsehood.

These texts by and about Jewish women, focusing on the slippery nature of memory, show how narratives interpret and mediate reality as they order their account of the 'facts'. Cultural historians assert that putatively factual texts, such as diary and memoir descriptions of quotidian experience, are mediated by language, as perceptions of remembered daily life emerge in narratives and counter-narratives. Even more so in fiction the gap between 'memory' and 'facts' is an extraordinarily fertile subject for exploration, because 'the genre of the novel' can 'advertise memory's fictional nature more ardently than any autobiography', as Liliane Weissberg points out. In the novel, memory is celebrated but in constant crisis, and thus often becomes part of the action, or performance of the literary text. When the protagonist's thoughts in the text travel backward in time in the attempt to reclaim memory,

> such travel could never be fully successful, and melancholy and a sense of loss were inscribed in all of these objects and their narratives. Memory was desired, but could never fully recover what had been lost. A person's longing for a harmonious reunification with his or her former self was always doomed to remain unfulfilled.[2]

Why are these travels of the mind, this search to discover the invented/remembered younger self such a compelling theme in contemporary Jewish women's writing? The new freedoms and choices faced by women in the wake of feminist social change have intensified the significance of the relationship between memory and current experience. Until quite recently, and in some societies even today, the shape of girls' and women's lives were largely dictated by society, custom, and the decisions of men and older women. With women's increased freedom has come a sometimes terrifying opportunity to influence one's own destiny. At the same time, women also struggle with lingering and seemingly outmoded societal expectations, which continue to impinge upon their inner world and their life choices.

Three conflicting images of women – the restricted lives of women in the past, expectations of freedom for women in the present and the actual lingering societal constraints upon women – create a triangular dynamic in which women feel pressured by and measure themselves against shifting standards. For Jewish women, the sources of constriction may be even more complicated, since they emanate from prescriptions for female behavior within both Judaic and western cultures.

This essay focuses primarily on two texts by American Jewish women writers. The first is Tillie Olsen's now classic novella, *Tell Me A Riddle* (1961); the second is Rebecca Goldstein's Jamesian, postmodernist novel, *The Dark Sister* (1991). Thirty years separate the publication of these two pieces of fiction, and the actual remembered youthful experiences depicted by these two authors could not be more different. Nevertheless, *Tell Me A Riddle*[3] and *The Dark Sister*[4] illuminate in complementary ways the intersections of gender and memory in times and societies that have often promised women more than they could easily achieve.

Both *Tell Me A Riddle* and *The Dark Sister* portray individual women trying to reclaim their past – and redeem their present selves – through remembering themselves in the context of their families. These novels provide point and counterpoint to assertions by Maurice Halbwachs that the attempt to reclaim memory almost always takes place in the context of the individual making sense of his or her relationship to social groups. Halbwachs, a student of philosopher Henri Bergson and colleague of sociologist Émile Durkheim, has become a posthumously influential theorist of memory in the past few decades. Especially important is his hypothesis, articulated in the *Social Frameworks of Memory* (1925) that 'one may say that memory depends on the social environment'. Halbwachs asserted that the family is the society that most often provides the framework, context and motivation for the individual to 'remember' incidents in the past.[5]

The self-portraits that individual women construct as they remember themselves are created not only in relationship to family, but also in response to the norms of society at large, and it is here that the ideas of contemporary cultural historians are especially useful. Michel Foucault's emphasis on the pervasive impact of culture on individual thinking and artistic expression, and Abby Warburg's exploration of 'collective memory' and 'cultural memory'[6] are each relevant to the two novels under discussion in different ways.

*Tell Me A Riddle* portrays a woman desperately journeying backward in time to her own memories of the past, in defiance of the variant memories – and deliberate forgetfulness – of family members. Olsen's novella, as we will see, provides interesting evidence on individual, collective and cultural memory, but in an intuitive and poetic, rather than deliberately philosophical or scientific mode. In contrast, philosopher and novelist Rebecca Goldstein's *The Dark Sister* incorporates philosophical and social scientific theories into the lives and thoughts of characters inhabiting the novel. Goldstein cleverly plays with intellectual trends that provide the cultural context for her characters, and weaves these ideas into the character's words and lives.

Tillie Olsen's *Tell Me A Riddle* presents a powerful evocation of the social constructedness of memory in a text that is more like poetry than a conventional fictional text in many ways. Deliberately stripped of narrative connective tissue, jumping from the consciousness and memories of one character to another, slipping between expressed and unexpressed thoughts, Olsen's novella forces the reader to participate by re-creating the often missing context for the written text. Olsen's intense, lyrical, but often disjointed text mimics the construction of memory itself. The novella progresses through the gradual revelation of the memories of several people. In the minds of one or another of her characters, the construction of memory is altered by many facts, including not only gender but also birth placement, economics, politics, culture and society. As the reader encounters each new piece of revealed memory, our understanding of the past shifts dramatically. The tapestry of what the reader had first understood to have happened unravels, and the reader is confronted with the responsibility of weaving together and constructing a new tapestry of impressions of interwoven memories.

The new tapestry of perceived 'memories' is different not only because the reader attains more information, but also because these new intricately interwoven bits of memory do not match. For most of the novella, what we understand about the past is slightly off center, like puzzle pieces that almost but do not quite fit together. Each character 'remembers' something else. The reader must resolve this 'riddle' of unmatched memories.

The subject matter of Olsen's novella deals with family relationships, especially spousal negotiations over time and intergenerational conflicts. Few readers find themselves detached from this literary detective work. Olsen's elliptical text presents a virtual minefield of painful revelations that evoke difficult memories in the minds of many readers, both those who are new to the reading of the novella, and those who have read it many times.

Eva, the protagonist of Olsen's novella, has been married to her husband for 47 years. The reader's first impression of this bickering couple, with their Yiddish-inflected banter, is that they will be the stock joke in a humorous caricature of ageing Jews, as the husband lobbies for them to sell their house and move to a Florida retirement village, the Haven, while Eva stubbornly resists even discussing such a move by turning up the vacuum cleaner and turning down her hearing aid.

Very soon, however, Eva's gendered memories reveal to us the tragic dimensions of the personal inner struggle now engaging her. She cannot move to the Haven, as her husband importunes, because she is dying and her time is running out. She needs, before it is too late, to reclaim the rhythms of her own life – rhythms that have been neglected for decades. Eva remembers years of mothering, during which her husband deliberately divested her of every opportunity to engage in reading and reflection. As a piece of feminist fiction, *Tell Me A Riddle* derives part of its power from its use of bodily imagery and memories. Olsen uses physical memories in the construction of the woman's past:

> Now, when it pleases you, you find a reading circle for me. And 40 years ago, when the children were morsels, and there was a circle, did you stay home with them once so I could go? Even once? You trained me well. I do not need others to enjoy. ...
>
> Old scar tissue ruptured, and the wounds festered anew. Chechov indeed. She thought without softness of that young wife, who in the deep night hours while she nursed the current baby, and perhaps held another in her lap, would try to stay awake for the only time there was to read. She could feel again the weather of the outside on his cheek when, coming home late from a meeting, he would find her so, and stimulated and ardent, sniffing her skin, coax: 'I'll put the baby to bed, and you – put the book away, don't read, don't read.'
>
> That had been the most beguiling of all the 'don't read, put your book away' her life had been. ... She would not exchange her solitude for anything. Never again to be forced to move to the rhythms of others. (225)

Because her body and her mind together remember so clearly the overwhelming physical and emotional flood, the miasma of feeling and doing that swept away all other activities during her mothering years, Eva refuses to embrace her daughter Vivi's new infant. The touch and smell of a baby threaten to immerse her in 'the love – the passion of tending ... [that] like a torrent drowned and immolated all else':

> And they put a baby in her lap. Immediacy to embrace, and the breath of that past: warm flesh like this that had claims and

> nuzzled away all else and with lovely mouths devoured; hot-living like an animal – intensely and now; the turning maze; the long drunkenness; the drowning into needing and being needed.

Eva's thoughts indicate to the reader that there are more pieces to her story, earlier memories and experiences, and in encountering these memories she will be able to find 'the springs' that 'were in her seeking. Somewhere an older power that beat for life. Somewhere coherence, transport, meaning' (225).

Readers often say they feel outraged and sad contemplating Eva's years of intellectual and spiritual deprivation. However, Olsen's spiraling text reveals not only Eva's earlier memories but also each of her children's and eventually her husband's memories. These conflicting memories change the reader's understanding of the past in startling ways. Taken inside the memories of Eva's children, the reader learns sequentially that each child remembers Eva as a mother very differently than Eva remembers herself. Olsen's accomplishment is not merely a Rashamon-like realization that many characters remember a similar event differently. Instead, this 1961 novella succeeds in conveying a rather postmodernist insight: even Eva, a very appealing character, suffused by the most correct feminist emotions, cannot be accepted as the one authoritative constructor of her own identity. Instead, each character's identity is illuminated by the construction provided by the conflicting and complementary memories of others.

The importance of this insight becomes clear when we unpack the dynamic interfamilial conflict expressed through these conflicting memories. On the surface it might seem that nothing is more personal than an individual person's own individual body. However, women's bodies, especially their sexual, reproductive and nurturing functions, have critical, practical and symbolic importance not only to themselves but also to family and society. From the nursing years onward, the performance of physical activities together creates collective group memories, whether in families or in larger social groups, that can form an important basis for ongoing associations. As Dorothy Noyes and Roger D. Abrahams comment, this 'mindfulness of the body, the incorporation of past experience' and the memories of many individuals of their physical activities together 'creates a unity in feeling'.[7]

Vivi assumes that her memories will evoke positive communal family feeling. In 'remembering' her nursing and nurturing mother, Vivi is invoking what she believes to be a collective memory sacred to and symbolic of the family unit. But Vivi's recollections do not strike the chord she intends, because the family's memories of these events differ from person to person. Each of the characters invent each other. To Eva's husband Eva's body signified sexual arousal and outlet; to Eva's younger children her body signified nurture and safety; to some of her grown children she is a role model for socially approved maternal behavior – or a cautionary tale of how not to behave.

Communal memories, and the social impact of the differences between individual memories within the same community, are reflected in the names Olsen gives each of Eva's children. Vivi, a middle child who is now the mother of many children, patterns herself on her mother's liveliness and engagement with physical life, because she remembers a talented, energetic, resourceful, happy and singing mother:

> ... oh, it's easy to be such a cow. I remember how beautiful my mother seemed nursing my brother, and the milk just flows. ... do I remember you sang while you sewed? That white dress with the red apples on the skirt you fixed over for me, was it Hannah's or Clara's before it was mine?
>
> Washing sweaters: Ma, I'll never forget, one of those days so nice you washed clothes outside; one of the first spring days it must have been. The bubbles just danced while you scrubbed, and we chased after, and you stopped to show us how to blow our own bubbles with green onion stalks. (227–8)

An older sister, Hannah remembers and rejects her mother's socialist atheism, and raises religious sons, arousing Eva's anger and dismay when she suggests that her mother join her in lighting Sabbath candles. And Clara, the hardened, resentful eldest daughter, remembers as clearly as Eva the years of poverty, but in Clara's memories it is she rather than Eva whose soul is stolen away by the economic struggle. Clara too is flooded by memories as she watches her mother on her deathbed, as she breaks through her brittle realism to remember the soft, singing mother of her early years:

> Pay me back. Mother, pay me back for all you took from me. Those others you crowded into your heart. The hands I needed to be for you, the heaviness, the responsibility.
>
> Is this she? Noises the dying make, the crablike hands crawling over the covers. The ethereal singing.
>
> She hears that music, that singing from childhood; forgotten sound – not heard since, since ... and the hardness breaks like a

cry: where did we lose each other, first mother, singing mother?...
I do not know you, Mother. Mother, I never knew you. (239)

As Eva remembers her own younger self she ruthlessly rejects her long attachments to family in her attempt to reclaim her life for herself before it is too late. Her refusal to hold the baby is thus not merely a physical aversion caused by her illness, but a retreat from a relationship as a way of defining herself – and not least a psychic act of heroism.

Memory links the individual not only to the small society of the family but also to larger communities. Societies beyond the family are evoked in Olsen's novella powerfully through Eva's memories of herself as the uneducated daughter of a rigidly Orthodox father in a thatched hut in Olshana, Russia, and her emancipation by her friend and mentor, a young Communist activist named Lisa. Eva remembers herself as a girl, imprisoned with her husband and Lisa as revolutionaries together in Russia. She remembers Lisa being executed in prison after ripping a traitor's jugular vein out with her teeth. 'Who knew there was that much blood in a human being', Eva mutters to her uncomprehending children. Eva's memories, deprived, as Halbwachs would have put it, of a society that can understand and contextualize their meaning, may die with her. Olsen's text presents this possibility as an incipient tragedy. When memories are connected and grounded in social context, they have meaning and value to the present and the future, as well as the past, as historian Pierre Nora reflects:

> Memory is life, borne by living societies founded in its name. It remains in permanent evolution, open to the dialectic of remembering and forgetting, unconscious of its successive deformations, vulnerable to manipulation and appropriation, susceptible to being long dormant and periodically revived. ... Memory is a perpetually actual phenomenon, a bond tying us to the eternal present.[8]

Eva's husband, who the reader has come to regard as an unwitting villain, is drawn into dialogue with Eva's memories as they emerge through her cough-studded deathbed monologue, as she sings fragments of songs remembered from her days as a young Communist revolutionary, fighting for a better, more just world, in which 'every life shall be a song'. Eva's husband at last confronts Eva's memories and life – and his own. Their children have never known their mother as a girl, or as an intellectual and a political activist, but deep in his hidden memories exists the image of Eva the girl, whom he fell in love with and married, and then prevented from continuing to be what she had been. Alone with the dying, singing, muttering Eva, the newly vulnerable husband's memories of the society-transforming activities they lived through come upon him like an ambush:

> The cards fell from his fingers. Without warning, the bereavement and betrayal he had sheltered – compounded through the years – hidden even from himself – revealed itself,
> *uncoiled,*
> *released,*
> *sprung*
> and with it the monstrous shapes of what had actually happened in the century. ... Whispered: 'Lost, how much I lost.'
> ... Still there was thirst or hunger ravening in him.
> That world of their youth – dark, ignorant, terrible with hate and disease – how was it that living in it, in the midst of corruption, filth, treachery, degradation, they had not mistrusted man nor themselves; had believed so beautifully, so ... falsely? (241–2)

Spurred by Eva's words, Eva's husband remembers their youthful idealism and their first relationship. Plunged back into those memories, he also acknowledges his personal jealousy of Eva's intellectualism, and his later role in depriving Eva of those activities, such as reading, that he feared she loved more than she loved him. This admission of his motivations couched in his memories helps the reader to put one more piece of the 'riddle' together. In these penultimate moments of Eva's journey into her past, her memories at last attain the social matrix they need in order to be contextualized. Eva's husband engages in a dialogue with her, although the dying woman probably does not hear his part of the conversation. Urged on by granddaughter Jeannie (who is fleeing from her own remembered demons), Eva's husband joins her in a confrontation of the agony and disappointments of their lives.

Finally Eva utters words that bring husband and wife both back to the body's memories, the shared memories of her as a girl and of their love and sexual union:

> 'Not look    my hair    where they cut ... .'
> (The crown of braids shorn.) And instantly he left the mute old woman poring over the Book of the Martyrs; went past the

mother treading at the sewing machine, singing with the children; past the girl in her wrinkled prison dress, hiding her hair with scarred hands, lifting to him her awkward, shamed, imploring eyes of love; and took her in his arms, dear, personal, fleshed, in all the heavy passion he had loved to rouse from her.

'Eva!' (243)

As Eva retreats from life and body, her words kindle the husband's memory of the girl and her body, linking her life once again to the present moment, and solving for the reader the riddle that gives this text its name. Who was the real Eva? Eva was the downtrodden daughter in a pious, backward European home; she was a fiery, articulate young revolutionary; she and her husband shared youthful altruism, passionate years, joy in the birth of their children; Eva was a singing, resourceful, devoted mother; Eva was also a betrayed intellectual whose inner life was systematically starved as she struggled to raise seven children in poverty; she was a deeply embittered woman whose intellectual and spiritual potential were unfairly decimated by her husband's thoughtless exploitation and emotional retreat – and by his unacknowledged jealousy of her self-reliance. Painfully complicated, yet inspiringly human, Eva and her husband huddle together as their memories mesh at story's end – and then she is gone, present only in the incomplete memories of those who live after her.

Many readers experience Olsen's novella as profoundly redemptive, as well as sad. I believe that the power of Olsen's resolution derives not only from the human, character-driven reunion of husband and wife at the last possible moment, but also in the fact that the act of memory, flickering in the last embers of their embodied physical recall, is itself redeemed in their final emotional reunion.

Utilizing very different intellectual strategies and narrative techniques, but similarly engaged by the role of gender, memory and familial context in the construction of human personality, Rebecca Goldstein's 1991 novel, *The Dark Sister*, expands the search for the remembered girl into a kaleidoscope of sly complexities. Like Olsen's, Goldstein's fiction is organized around issues of family relationships, and makes complex and profound use of the physicality of women's memories and self-perceptions. However, Goldstein, more extensively than Olsen, describes the impact of wider culture on women's understandings of who they are. While the 1961 *Tell Me A Riddle* reflects an early second wave feminist social-psychological and political understanding of the ways in which husbands and children can restrict women's intellectual work and agency, *The Dark Sister* cleverly echoes and fleshes out decades of evolving feminist literary, cultural and psychological theories.

Thus, our appreciation of Goldstein's somewhat difficult novel is enhanced by thinking about the intertextual links between her characters and plots and the ideas expressed by feminist writers such as Simone de Beauvoir, the French feminists, Adrienne Rich, Sandra Gilbert and Susan Gubar, and others. A brief three-paragraph summary of the novel's two interwoven plots will immediately begin to suggest the ways in which *The Dark Sister* renders contemporary feminist writings incarnate.

Goldstein's protagonist, Hedda, is a brilliant writer, who was once a beautiful child. During puberty, however, Hedda shot upward, becoming almost freakishly large, while her younger sister, Stella, grew round and feminine. Hedda lives alone and writes, occasionally communicating by phone with her mother and her sister, whom she dislikes and fears. Hedda remembers being ill-treated by her peers as a growing-up-girl, being called 'Jaws' because of her bony face and taunted as a witch when she dons a cloak. Moreover, Hedda finds the physical freedoms available to the modern woman terrifying and disgusting, and represses much of her own physicality. Hedda, a cerebral, hulking, reclusive, almost sexless creature, is all head.

Hedda is the author of a series of wildly successful novels, each of which have explored a stereotype of the Jewish woman. Rejecting the image of the JAP, the notorious 'Jewish American Princess', Hedda has produced a series of fictive 'JAWs', Jewish angry women. Turning stereotypes inside out, Hedda's books each feature a 'fierce but beautiful JAW' who triumphs over societal injustice; her successful books include: *Etta: The Rebbe's Daughter!*; *Hanna, The Husband's Whore!*; *Sara, The Savant's Sister!*; *Mona, The Momzer's Mother!*; *Minna, The Messiah's Mother-in-Law!*; *Clara, The Corporate Korva!*; and *Dora, The Doctor's Daughter!* (222).

Hedda is introduced to Goldstein's readers when she abandons this financially successful formula and proceeds instead to write a book that reflects the language and milieu of Henry James. Goldstein's novel and Hedda's novel within a novel mirror their own stories internally, through the Jamesian narrative structure of parallel plots. Hedda's elaborately plotted novel tells the story of two sisters, Alice and Vivianna Bonnet, who share a large home. Alice is a conventional if very tense Victorian woman who is only seen by day; Vivianna is an astronomer who is only seen by night. Alice is treated by Dr Sloper, whose unfortunate daughter is the protagonist of a famous James story, and she also encounters the ideas of the famous James brothers. Each of these men has belittling thoughts about the women in their own lives. When Hedda at last concludes her writing and ends her novel with a tragic denouement, she becomes demoralized and convinced that she has somehow betrayed her talent and her life has no meaning. She stops eating and falls deathly ill. When she is almost dead, her fat and nurturing sister Stella climbs the steps into Hedda's tower, and saves her life.

Perhaps the first aspect of this story that echoes feminist exploration is the troubled relationship between the eldest daughter and her mother and younger sister. Hedda remembers a mother of her young years who tenderly called her 'dunkele', the little dark one, but later became a feared and hypocritical adversary to her two daughters:

> The Mother always said, 'Hah!' ... And it is not in the power of the printed word to convey the sheer quality of malice that had been impacted in those three letters. There, behind the closed doors of the apartment on West End Avenue, where the public face of the Mother – righteous and forbearing, slow to anger and full of great mercy – would be taken off at the threshold. 'Putting on her face', she'd call the morning ritual of applying her makeup, a phrase the two little girls took with chilling literalism. (103)

In Goldstein's novel, both sisters want most of all not to be like The Mother, and both meanly think of each other as being like her: 'You know, you remind me of someone, Stella. You sound just like someone we both know' (103).

From Simone de Beauvoir onward, feminist writers have struggled to understand their familial memories: how and when does the beloved mother of infancy dissolve into the cruel adversary of adolescence, setting into play a drama of woman versus woman that repeats itself with each new generation. As de Beauvoir describes looking at old family photos:

> The 'Maman darling' of the days when I was ten can no longer be told from the inimical woman who oppressed my adolescence; I wept for both of them when I wept for my old mother. I thought I had made up my mind about our failure and accepted it; but its sadness comes back to my heart. ... Today I could almost be her mother and the grandmother of that sad-eyed girl. I am so sorry

for them – for me because I am so young and I understand nothing; for her because her future is closed and she has never understood anything. But I would not know how to advise them.[9]

Adrienne Rich brings another piece to the puzzle of this transformation in memories of the mother in *Of Woman Born*. She recalls the older daughter's estrangement from her mother, and a new identification with the father and intellectual work, beginning with the birth of a younger sister. Rich writes,

> I don't remember when it was that my mother's feminine sensuousness, the reality of her body, began to give way for me to the charisma of my father's assertive mind and temperament; perhaps when my sister was born, and he began teaching me to read.[10]

For both of Goldstein's sister plot dyads, Hedda and Stella, and Alice and Vivianna, Nancy Miller's reflections on Rich are suggestive: 'Before the little sister arrived on the scene. Before the expulsion from Eden that came with the sister's birth.'[11] The younger sister signifies a change of status for the older sister, and both older sisters assign a personality and meaning to the younger sister that absorbs an aspect of their own femininity that they do not wish to acknowledge – or that they are afraid of acknowledging – in themselves.

A second large pattern in Goldstein's novel that bears important intertextual connections with feminist writers is the ongoing emphasis on images of the female body. Gazing naked into a full-length mirror, for example, Hedda's troubled memories of her familial girlhood are interspersed with passages from the novel she is currently writing. Hedda ponders the mirrored image of her buttocks, and she juxtaposes imaginings about her family with the interwoven stories she places in her new novel:

> That mole she saw on the left cheek of her ass, she thought, turning around and craning her neck backward, was in actuality on the right. To get any truth at all, one had to set up a little system of two mirrors.
>
> A parallel plot! ... It was often means by which moral points were made, the two stories played off against each other, so that the import of each emerges in the crack in between, as it were. ... It came to her there in the inverted image of her sadly sunken rump. (59–60)

With dark humor, Goldstein gives Hedda's mirrored image intertextual allusions which range from the sublime to the ridiculous. We can hear echoes in these lines of Romantic literary theories suggesting literature is a mirror; of Emily Dickinson's advice that the writer ought to 'tell all the truth but tell it slant'; of the biblical injunction that one can only see God's backside, or through a dark glass.

Hedda's inspiration from looking at her naked 'rump' also echoes French feminist insistence that women's bodies must form the basis of women's writings, that women must essentially write from their bodies. One may think of Luce Irigaray: 'Woman has sex organs just about everywhere. She experiences pleasure almost everywhere ... The geography of her pleasure is much more diversified, more multiple in its differences, more complex, more subtle, and is imagined'; or Hélène Cixous: 'Oral drive, anal drive, vocal drive – all these drives are our strengths, and among them is the gestation drive – just like the desire to write: a desire to live self from within, a desire for the swollen belly, for language, for blood', or the words of Ann Rosalind Jones discussing these and other French feminist writers: 'If women are to discover and express who they are, to bring to the surface what masculine history has repressed in them, they must begin with their sexuality. And their sexuality begins with their bodies, with their genital and libidinal difference from men.'[12]

From this first picture of Hedda staring at her buttocks to determine what she shall write, throughout the novel and the novel-within-a-novel, women's artistic endeavors and psychic states of being are expressed in the imagery of female physiology. Thus, toward the end of the novel Hedda writes, William James has an epiphany that Alice and Vivianna Bonnet are in truth one and the same person. He rushes to Willow Groves and confronts Alice Bonnet, demanding to see Vivianna. Before his eyes, the brittle 'elder' sister metamorphoses into the vivid 'younger' woman. Vivianna/Alice Bonnet turns a face to William James which is intensely sexual and simultaneously spiritual in its presentation and meaning:

> Her complexion was suffused with the high color of her feeling, and her eyes were very near to spilling. The face she showed him was wonderful. If it stood for everything, never had a face had to stand for more.
>
> He had only just lifted the rare moist bloom to the level of his eye, the probing index finger placed within where he could not yet see. There remained layers upon layers upon layers to be parted. (250–1)

Confronted with a face as revealing as female genitalia, William James lacks the subtlety to meet the woman and her moment. Although he perceives that Alice and Vivianna Bonnet are two manifestations of the same person, James does not understand that both aspects are equally and intrinsically part of the same multilayered woman. He sees a dichotomy in Alice/Vivianna as a personality disorder, and persists in believing that one manifestation is the 'real' woman, while the second manifestation is an alien alteration. And so he blurts out a question which destroys the woman's momentarily unified, organic bloom: 'Which of you – I mean to say, is it you or the other who was there to begin with, so to speak? Which of you is the, as it were, rightful resident – and which the intruder?' (251). His obtuse question causes Vivianna to withdraw, leaving Alice to hiss at him, 'You are an interloper, William James, and you know nothing about it!' and then, 'We yield you nothing ... outsider' (252–3), in words which echo another New England spinster, Emily Dickinson's 'The soul selects her own society/ Then shuts the door/ On her Divine majority/ Intrude no more'.

Men impose a binary dichotomy that blights women's lives, in the world of Goldstein's novel. The culture created by men demands that women split themselves in half. The parts of themselves deemed unacceptable are reflected onto other women, in Goldstein's 'little system of two mirrors' played out through juxtaposed stories, each featuring a 'dark sister': Hedda the intellectual dark sister remembers her physical sister Stella; Hedda's novel's protagonist the withered Alice Bonnet creates a vivid younger sister, Vivianna; Hedda's novel features a parallel plot centering on William and Henry James and their historical younger sister, also named Alice, who retreats into invalidism because her intellectual and spiritual gifts have no socially-approved outlet. Each of these sisters appears to be dramatically different from other family members, and might declare, along with Alice Bonnet, 'Though we are as sisters, we are nothing alike. We are to one another as the high noon is to midnight' (29). But, in this very formulation the reader is given an early key to the symbolic doubling of experience. Although men may prefer women to be simple – either one thing or the other, women are complex, multifaceted, hidden and revealed: all of Goldstein's dark sisters are in some fashion the dark sides of each other.

Goldstein uses the novelist's mode of memory – the re-creation of past times – as a strategy to explore the violence, past and present, done to women's complexities. By writing a novel placed in the nineteenth century, Hedda – and Goldstein – can depict the real physical violence incorporated into the creation of middle- and upper-class women not so long ago. An extended metaphor involves brutally corseted women whose bodies were distorted by fashionable dictates:

> This shape was by no means easy for a woman to achieve, and the corseting it required had severe effects on its wearer's life. She couldn't take a deep breath ... It often deformed the internal organs and led to complaints of the digestive order. Even when she unlaced and unhooked herself, her ribs had been so compressed that they retained their uncomfortable positions. (As women today carry inwardly the distortions induced by previous years of cruel convention.) (55)

The family is the first agency for implementing this disfigurement, for convincing women that they cannot embrace the full extent of their own lives. Over and over again in Goldstein's *The Dark Sister*, in the intimacy of the primary family unit little girls are mutilated, and learn to internalize the precepts of that mutilation. In the age of corsets, it is mothers who fit 3-year-old girls with little training corsets, and who gradually tighten the straps as the girls grow. It is mothers who pull the whalebone stays over their adolescent daughters' ribs, occasionally breaking a daughter's bone in their enthusiasm for a tiny waist.

The distorted image of a desirable female body leads to other methods of shrinking women down as well, such as the ingestion of purgatives and to anorexia. The sickliness thus produced evidently did not seem strange in this culture, because, as Sandra Gilbert and Susan Gubar note, anorexia and agoraphobia abounded among cultivated nineteenth-century women, and 'nineteenth-century culture seems to have actually admonished women to *be* ill':

> Such diseases are caused by patriarchal socialization in several ways. Most obviously, of course, any young girl, but especially a lively or imaginative one, is likely to experience her education in docility, submissiveness, selflessness as in some sense sickening. ... In addition, each of the 'subjects' in which a young girl is educated may be sickening in a specific way. Learning to become a beautiful object, the girl learns anxiety about – perhaps even loathing of – her own flesh. Peering obsessively into the real as well as metaphoric looking glasses that surround her, she desires literally to 'reduce' her own body. In the nineteenth century, as

we noted earlier, this desire to be beautiful and 'frail' led to tight lacing and vinegar drinking. In our own era it has spawned innumerable diets and 'controlled' fasts, as well as the extraordinary phenomenon of teenage anorexia.[13]

It is not only women's bodies that are distorted in Hedda's literarily remembered universe, but even more so, their minds and imaginations are reined in and constrained. *The Dark Sister*'s plots are all about women who, as they grow up, so fully reject parts of themselves that they invent sisterly dopplegangers to house their 'monstrous' characteristics. In the nineteenth century intellectual work was viewed as being dangerous for women; women who did intellectual work were suspected of being unsexed, or monstrous. Goldstein utilizes recurring images to underscore this motif. Frequent reference is made to Adrienne Rich's powerful poem, 'Planetarium', in which a female astronomer, isolated and hiding from society, sees a sky full of female monsters. These women are monstrous because they are intellectual and perhaps even ambitious.

In the world of William and Henry James, opportunities for women are limited. Mothers might be remembered as 'insipid', or 'a vapor, a fume? Noxious or life supporting?' (3). Young women like Alice James, even when blessed with the 'Jamesian heightened consciousness', have no future. Alice is William and Henry James' dark sister, because, by virtue of her femaleness, she can only be remembered as a 'pale face in the outside darkness pressed up against the lighted window' (4). Hedda remembers a quote from Alice James' journal, in which the afflicted young woman describes the spiritual impoverishment which results from the manifest uneventfulness of her life. Even her memories are shapeless and thin:

> I have seen so little that my memory is packed with little bits which have not been wiped out by great ones, so that it all seems like a reminiscence; and as I go along the childish impressions of lights and colors come crowding back into my mind. (4)

Ultimately the purpose of memory in this novel is to illuminate the present. For an intellectual like Hedda, born into an age more receptive to talented women, options are only marginally better than they were for Alice James. Hedda too was a 'little female marvel of a creature' as a girl, who emerged, as an adult woman, into the narrow dreariness of a constricted world. Hedda discovers that 'uncommon women are natural objects of suspicion' still (20). While Hedda and Stella are not subjected to whalebone corsets, they learn about other kinds of mutilating disguises. Because of these lingering distortions of women's lives the author and intellectual Hedda becomes an anorexic living as a 'madwoman in the attic', echoing Gilbert and Gubar's memorable title, *The Madwoman in the Attic: The Woman Writer and the Nineteenth-Century Imagination*.[14]

Hedda's series of Jewish Angry Women novels are linked internally to her Jamesian creation, *The Dark Sister*. Rebecca Goldstein suggests that women, and especially Jewish women, have often come to regard large segments of their own personhood as alien, as other, as the 'dark sister' to their more politically correct, acceptable public personae. A lifetime of contact with negatively portrayed Jewish women in books and popular culture can be internalized with devastating consequences. As girls grow into women, they often learn to reject aspects of themselves they perceive as unacceptably intellectual, artistic, scientific, mystical, violent, angry, or non-maternal – any of these pieces of themselves can potentially be viewed as other, or even monstrous. Learning from their mothers how to tame their physical, intellectual and emotional wildness, girls can make themselves sick by corseting the fullness of experience into submission. Ultimately, the faces they learn to paint on can be so convincing that even they cannot see through their own disguises. Goldstein's novel uses memory to expose the dangers of binary divisions of the female self. The author illustrates with vivid detail that a woman who attempts to dichotomize and shut out whole aspects of her own being will in the end be unable to maintain the boundaries of this distorted personal identity: a vast, boundless, irrepressible universal force 'sooner or later', will 'batten us down and break us through' (268).

Olsen and Goldstein, although separated by time, experience and literary style, each argue in favor of families and societies that help women construct their memoried, gendered selves in the fullness of life, and not only in the last extremity of death. In Olsen's *Tell Me A Riddle* and Goldstein's *The Dark Sister* family relationships profoundly affect the gendered construction of memory. In both works the binary bifurcation of memoried experience cripples women by dividing them against themselves. In Olsen's novella, Eva's intellectual potential is sadly decimated during decades of marriage and childrearing. As she struggles to regain her young self, her deathbed reclamation of memories of youthful poetry and political power also divest her of equally rich memories of her love for her children and husband. The memories provided by her children and husband, however imperfectly, round out the last days of her life. The 'riddle' of Eva's life cannot be resolved without the memories of those whose lives she has shaped, and who have shaped her life as well. Similarly, in Goldstein's novel, one whole side of Hedda's personality, experience and memories remain dark and alien to her until she is able, almost at the point of death, to accept and embrace those aspects of herself that she sees reflected in the women whose relationships have provided the shaping boundaries around her life and remembered self.

Indeed, perhaps it is the very freedom – limited though it may be – that women have increasingly experienced in democratic, emancipated societies that makes relationships so important in the gendered construction of memory. Whatever the sins of fathers and mothers, siblings and husbands, women's hope for serenity and fulfillment is linked to our existence as undivided girls, to an acknowledgment of the multifacetedness of each girl's and woman's psyche, and the recognition of the ties that link us, sister to sister, beyond the tower of isolation.

NOTES

1. Lynne Sharon Schwartz, *Leaving Brooklyn* (New York: Penguin Viking, 1989), p. 146.
2. Liliane Weissberg, 'Introduction', to *Cultural Memory and the Construction of Identity*, (eds) Dan Ben-Amos and Liliane Weissberg (Detroit: Wayne State University Press, 1999), pp. 7–26, 10–11.
3. Quotes from this novella will be cited via parenthetical page numbers from Tillie Olsen, *Tell Me A Riddle* in Sylvia Barack Fishman (ed.) *Follow My Footprints: Changing Images of Women in American Jewish Fiction* (Hanover, NH: Brandeis University Press, 1992; rpt 1961), pp. 212–44.
4. Quotes from this novel will be cited via parenthetical page numbers from Rebecca Goldstein, *The Dark Sister* (New York: Penguin Viking, 1991).
5. Maurice Halbwachs, *Les Caadres sociaux de la memoire* (1925), cited in Weissberg, 'Introduction', pp. 14–15.
6. Ibid., pp. 15–16.
7. Dorothy Noyes and Roger D. Abrahams, 'From Calendar Custom to National Memory: European Commonplaces', in Ben-Amos and Weissberg, *Cultural Memory*, pp. 77–98, 79–80.
8. Pierre Nora, 'Between Memory and History: *Les Lieux de memoire*', *Representations* 26 (1989) p. 8, cited in Tamar Katriel, 'Sites of Memory: Discourses of the Past in Israeli Pioneering Settlement Museums', in Ben-Amos and Weissberg, *Cultural Memory*, pp. 99–135, 100.
9. Simone de Beauvoir, *A Very Easy Death*, trans. Patrick O'Brian (New York: Pantheon, 1965), p. 103.

10. Adrienne Rich, *Of Woman Born: Motherhood as an Experience and an Institution* (New York: W.W. Norton, 1976), p. 219.
11. Nancy K. Miller, 'Putting Ourselves in the Picture: Memoirs and Mourning', in Marianne Hirsch (ed.) *The Familial Gaze* (Hanover, NH: Dartmouth College/ University Press of New England, 1999), pp. 51–66, 61.
12. Ann Rosalind Jones, 'Writing the Body: Toward an Understanding of *l'écriture féminine*', in *Feminisms: An Anthology of Literary Theory and Criticism* (New Brunswick, NJ: Rutgers University Press, 1997) pp. 370–83, 374. On p. 372 Jones cites the passage from Luce Irigaray (*Ce Sexe qui n'en pas un*, 1977), and on p. 374 she cites the passage from Hélène Cixous ('The Laugh of the Medusa', 1975).
13. Sandra M. Gilbert and Susan Gubar, 'Infection in the Sentence: the woman writer and the anxiety of authorship', in *Feminisms*, pp. 21–32, 27.
14. Sandra M. Gilbert and Susan Gubar, *The Madwoman in the Attic: The Woman Writer and the Nineteenth-Century Imagination* (New Haven, CT: Yale University Press, 1979), includes subjects highly germain to Goldstein's imagery, including Chapter 7, 'Horror's Twin: Mary Shelly's Monstrous Eve'.

# 9

# The Impact of Gender on the Leading American Zionist Organizations

MIRA KATZBURG-YUNGMAN

INTRODUCTION

The leading Zionist organizations in the United States – the Zionist Organization of America (ZOA) and Hadassah, the Women's Zionist Organization of America – have traditionally been affected by gender differences in many respects: spheres of activity, fundamental conceptions and policies, *modus operandi*, the extent of their involvement in the Eretz Yisrael scene and their ability to sustain themselves and to function over time. In American Zionism, as in American society at large, women's organizations coexist with others that have largely male membership and leadership, the customary organizational structure of white American society at the end of the nineteenth and the beginning of the twentieth century. Such gender division is unique to the American (and later also the Canadian) Zionist movement and has no parallel in any of the European Zionist movements. From 1925 on, six organizations functioned within the American Zionist movement: The ZOA and Hadassah, as well as four small organizations also based on gender division: Poalei Zion and its feminine arm, Pioneer Women, and Mizrachi with its feminine arm, Mizrachi Women.[1]

Although the phenomenon of gender differences has been well known for years, no comprehensive historical study of the attributes of American Zionism has ever mentioned or attempted to explore its implications on the American Zionist Movement.[2] This paper aims to explore the impact of gender differences on the major American Zionist organizations in order to expand our understanding of American Zionism.

One leading force in American Zionism was the ZOA. Though theoretically the ZOA is an organization composed of households, its main activists and leaders were men. It dealt with political issues –

'masculine pursuits' at the time – and its success depended on the availability of an inspiring political challenge. The ZOA is characterized by instability. It had periods of blossoming followed by times of crisis, with a decline in its activity and membership. The 'golden age' of the ZOA was between 1943 and 1948, when, under the leadership of Abba Hillel Silver, it led American Zionists in the political and diplomatic struggle for the establishment of the State of Israel. At that time, as one observer expressed it, American Zionists were 'the strongest pressure group in American history'.[3] It was then that the ZOA reached its peak in membership and fundraising. After the establishment of the State of Israel, it sank into a severe crisis from which it has never really recovered.

The other leading force in American Zionism was Hadassah, the Women's Zionist Organization of America. Founded in New York in 1913 by a group of women of German-Jewish origin headed by Henrietta Szold, Hadassah has been the largest Zionist organization in the US during most of the period since American Zionism came into being. Hadassah has been active in two arenas: in the US, where it dealt mainly in Jewish education, and in Eretz Yisrael, where it developed medical and social-service projects. Apart from the difference in size, Hadassah differs from the ZOA, among others, in its spirit and in the continuity and stability of its activity. Hadassah is also the finest expression of the way Zionist women in America were organized.

## THE MAJOR AMERICAN ZIONIST ORGANIZATIONS AFTER THE ESTABLISHMENT OF THE STATE

From late 1948, the Zionist Organization of America (ZOA) suffered a deep crisis, evident in two major phenomena: a steep decline in membership and a search for new, meaningful fields of activity. Within four years of the establishment of Israel in 1948, ZOA membership had dwindled from 225,000 to 95,000. The most likely cause was the disappearance of its central challenge – the political effort to assure the creation of a Jewish state. Many of the ZOA's members were businessmen, very much engrossed in their private enterprises. A great challenge is necessary to bring such time-pressed people to engage in public affairs. The three years preceding the creation of Israel provided just such a challenge, unparalleled in the history of Zionism, perhaps in all of Jewish history. However, after the establishment of Israel – and despite its need for massive political and financial support – the ZOA lacked objectives challenging enough to attract new active members.[4]

The establishment of Israel also stripped the ZOA of its two traditional major roles: political-diplomatic efforts and fundraising. Diplomatic activity was now the responsibility of the new state, while raising of funds for the absorption of the masses of new immigrants encouraged other Jewish organizations to action (primarily the United Jewish Appeal which in these years raised enormous sums for Israel), thus diminishing the role of the ZOA in this field.[5]

The ZOA leadership considered possible ways to overcome the crisis that the organization was experiencing and sought new fields of endeavor both in the US and in Israel. Already at the 1949 ZOA Convention, various activities and projects for implementation in Israel were proposed.[6] In the end, only two were carried out. The first was the ZOA House in Tel Aviv which, it was hoped, would bridge the gap between Israel and American Zionists. It was established along the lines of an American community center, to enrich the cultural life of Tel Aviv. The other project was the Kfar Silver Agricultural School, near Ashkelon.[7]

In America, the ZOA adopted new initiatives in three fields: economic enterprises, public relations and education. The 1953 Convention resolved to establish an economic department which would encourage private undertakings and investments in Israel. A year later, at the 1954 Convention, resolutions were adopted calling for increased public relations and fundraising on behalf of Israel.[8]

As for the third field of activity – Jewish education in the US – the ZOA was aware of the need to enhance its efforts in this area, which had been neglected in the pre-state years due to more pressing matters. Most American Jewish youth were ignorant of their Jewish heritage and culture, and knew no Hebrew. The 1952 Convention established a department for Hebrew language and culture that created various frameworks for the study of Hebrew and supported a Hebrew radio program.[9]

Despite all these efforts in the fields of economic and cultural endeavor, in the late 1950s the ZOA 'had been rendered nearly impotent, a pale shadow of its once powerful self, with few members, little status and no purpose'.[10]

This same period was one of the most creative periods in Hadassah's history. Indeed, in Israel's early years, Hadassah was bombarded with requests for help in various areas of health. In conjunction with the Hebrew University of Jerusalem, Hadassah established the Hadassah-University Medical School. It also established a hospital in the Negev, and a hospital for immigrants from Yemen in Rosh ha-'Ayin. In view of the needs of the fledgling country, Hadassah had to decide which of its health projects it wished to retain and which it would hand over to the State authorities. Hadassah was also involved in many welfare and educational institutions and projects for children and youth. Some were its own institutions or projects; others were projects in which Hadassah was a partner with Israeli or Zionist organizations. The most prominent of these was Aliyat Hanoar.[11]

In the American arena at that time, the establishment of the State of Israel had reinvigorated Hadassah's education department. The department developed new learning materials and projects on Judaism.[12] It was then, for example, that it began to develop one of its major publications on Jewish education, *Great Ages and Ideas of the Jewish People*, written by prominent Jewish scholars of the time, in which Hadassah invested five years.[13]

The differences in the situation of these two organizations during this period were basically the direct and indirect result of gender differences. These left their imprint on both organizations during the long years in which they were active preceding the establishment of the State.

## THE INFLUENCE OF GENDER ON HADASSAH'S FUNDAMENTAL TRAITS AND CONCEPTIONS

Gender had a crucial influence on the formulation of Hadassah's conceptions. Two of these were practicality, which became one of Hadassah's main characteristics; and faith in science for the advancement of medicine.[14]

Hadassah's emphasis on practicality originated in the desire of its founders to create an organization that would respond to their perceptions of women's practical needs in view of the prevalent view of the nature of women in early-twentieth century America. One of the beliefs that prevailed at that time was that women were inclined to deal with practical issues rather than with ideology.[15] The founders thought, therefore, that Hadassah should refrain as much as possible from 'wasting energy on quarrels and political disputes', and concentrate rather on concrete targets.[16] Soon after the organization was established, therefore, Hadassah took upon itself a practical project in Eretz Yisrael which will be described below.

The other fundamental conception which left its imprint on Hadassah was that its health activity in Eretz Yisrael should be linked to science. This conception was also the basis of a central Zionist idea in Hadassah's ideology: that its contribution to *binyan ha'aretz* (a Zionist term that related to building up the country as the national home of the Jewish people) should focus on developing health services, and medical education and research, based on the finest American and professional knowledge.[17] This was also the basis for Hadassah's long-term cooperation with the Hebrew University in Jerusalem, aimed at founding and maintaining a medical school, and what gave the Rothschild Hadassah University Hospital, connected with the Hebrew University, its special character. This conception also motivated Hadassah to prefer some projects over others.

## THE INFLUENCE OF THE GENDER PERSPECTIVE ON HADASSAH'S AREAS OF ACTIVITY

The two Zionist organizations entered different fields of activity which stemmed from gender differences. These fields of activity were the major factor which in various ways influenced the differences between them. Hadassah's fields of activity are rooted in traditional Judaism and in vocations that were accepted as 'women's occupations' in American society at the turn of the twentieth century.

The Jewish roots of Hadassah's medical undertakings were the embodiment of three central *mitzvot* (religious commandments) with which women were traditionally involved: *zedaka* (charity), *gemilut hassadim* (good deeds for the benefit of others) and *bikur holim* (literally, visiting the sick; but in practice, caring for the sick). In traditional Jewish society, women did not take an active part in public prayer or in the study of religious law, nor did they participate in the management of communal affairs. They were limited to raising their children and performing acts of charity, thus enabling them to fulfill certain commandments. Even after secularization became common in much of Jewish society, women continued to be active in these fields which by then had become the responsibility of modern social welfare organizations.[18]

The American influences on Hadassah's fields of activity stemmed from various factors relating to the American women's arena at the beginning of the twentieth century. These include:

1. The emergence of professional women and the development, as a result, of new 'professions of women' that were dominated by women: nursing, social work and the teaching profession. The area of public health, a branch of the nursing profession, was especially developed and well respected.[19]
2. The American women's voluntary organizational arena. Many of the women's organizations functioned according to a set of ideas developed by 'social feminism', a central feminist stream in white American society of the time, that held that men and women differ in their traits and qualifications. Women's moral and intellectual qualities qualified them to make special contributions to social reform. Women's organizations, whose activities were directed according to social feminist principles, were active mainly in the spheres of child welfare and various social reforms, which were considered very well-suited to women's qualifications.[20]
3. Progressive movements in which women had key roles such as the 'Settlement House' movement, many of whose activists and leaders were women.[21]
4. The great emphasis on children's welfare and education, and on social movements aimed at children's welfare.[22]

Hadassah's founders, who had an immense influence on its organizational development, were influenced by all these factors and directed the organization's development accordingly.

## WELFARE PROJECTS FOR CHILDREN AND YOUTH

Activities for children and youth were the common denominator of a series of enterprises which Hadassah supported and developed. These activities aptly expressed the feminine aspect of its activity.

The factors discussed above concerning the influences of the American women's arena on Hadassah were the basis of four public health projects that it brought to Eretz Yisrael during the 1920s: mother and child stations, school lunches, a hygiene project and a playground project. All were based on American models of public health projects or movements. The American models of all these enterprises were designed for American groups in distress, mostly in the immigrant quarters of New York and other large American cities at the turn of the twentieth century. The enterprises that were brought to Eretz Yisrael by Hadassah were also connected in one way or another with the 'Settlement House' movement.[23]

The best-known of the public health projects that Hadassah brought to Eretz Yisrael were the mother and child stations, known as 'Tipot Halav' (literally, drops of milk), initiated in 1922. These were modeled on similar stations in the US, and were based on 'district nursing', an American nursing method inspired by a similar British method that stemmed from the idea that poor people should be treated in their own homes. In addition to the center, nurses also visited the mother's house.[24] The educational idea underlying this concept, which originated in American public health and the Settlement House movement, held that the mother should be educated in how to take care of her child.

Three other public health enterprises inspired by American public health projects were brought to Eretz Yisrael by Hadassah during the British Mandate. The most important of these was the School Lunch project. This was modeled on the American School Luncheon Movement initiated in New York in 1908, which aimed to provide undernourished children with good nutrition through the distribution of hot meals. The movement was established as a result of research which revealed that 60,000–70,000 children in New York City came to school hungry. The movement was also active in the educational arena in teaching about nutrition. It even succeeded in introducing nutrition as part of the high school curriculum.[25]

Hadassah established its school luncheon program in Eretz Yisrael in 1922 and, during the 1930s and 1940s, it became one of the most important welfare projects in the Yishuv (the organized Jewish community in Eretz Yisrael). Various Yishuv organizations took part in it and together they served lunches to children in most of the country's Jewish schools.[26] The school lunch project became even more important after the State of Israel was established when many new immigrants flooded the country. At that time, Hadassah turned it over to the Israeli Government.[27]

## EDUCATIONAL ACTIVITY

The teaching profession, one of the factors discussed above as formulating Hadassah's activities, left its imprint on the organization in its extensive and diversified educational activity central in both of its arenas of activity: Eretz Yisrael and the United States. In Eretz Yisrael, this took the form of a wide range of activities which were the first of their kind in that country and were meant to improve the health and quality of life of the population. Notable among these were the establishment of the first medical and nursing schools and vocational educational enterprises.

Hadassah's projects in education were totally different in nature in the United States, where its activities were 'spiritual' in nature and aimed to preserve Jewish life in America.[28] Many leaders of Hadassah throughout the organization's history were teachers who had the motivation, the aptitude and the training to foster Jewish education.

In the US, educational activity became a central focus of Hadassah leaders in order to transmit the Jewish heritage to future generations. Ideologically, therefore, Hadassah's continuing involvement in education stems from its fundamental commitment to Jewish survival, both physical and spiritual, which is the cornerstone of its ideology.[29] Thus, from the point of view of Hadassah's leaders in the 1940s and 1950s, Hadassah's educational activity was as central and as important as its health activities in Eretz Yisrael. Hadassah perceived itself at the time as one of the most important forces working for creative Jewish life in the US. Strengthening the American Jewish community spiritually and culturally was one of Hadassah's central aims and its activity in Jewish education through encouraging study groups and developing learning materials, publishing books on Jewish topics, and supporting Zionist youth movements was designed to further this aim.[30]

## HADASSAH'S EDUCATIONAL ACTIVITIES IN ERETZ YISRAEL

While Hadassah's educational endeavors in the US were in the spiritual realm, Hadassah perceived itself as an educational force and an agent of modernity in Eretz Yisrael. Its educational endeavors were partly a result of this self-perception and carried the imprint of 'practicality'.[31]

Hadassah made a considerable contribution to the Yishuv and the State in the educational realm through a series of diversified enterprises which it developed during and after the 1920s. These enterprises included, among others, higher vocational education for the medical profession: the establishment of Israel's first medical school – with the cooperation of the Hebrew University (1949); the development of the country's first nursing school (established in 1918 by the American Zionist Medical Unit); and the developing of training networks in various paramedical areas such as: nutrition, occupational therapy and audiology, to name only a few. Hadassah also established the first vocational high school for girls (1942) and made a considerable contribution to the health education of the Yishuv and later the State of Israel through the public health enterprises described above.[32] Through these medical vocational educational enterprises, established according to American institutional models, Hadassah laid the foundation for medical, nursing and paramedical education in the Yishuv and in Israel. With the exception of physicians and x-ray technicians, all these professions were 'women's professions' in the United States.

## THE NURSING PROFESSION AND THE SCHOOL OF NURSING

The first of these medical educational enterprises was the Hadassah School of Nursing, founded in 1918 by the American Zionist Medical Unit, which was organized by Hadassah and in 1921 became the Hadassah Medical Organization. About two years after its founding, Hadassah took over sponsorship of the school.[33]

Nursing as a profession did not exist in Eretz Yisrael before the establishment of the school. The nursing staff in the Jewish hospitals in Eretz Yisrael up to the First World War included non-educated men and women as well as an unknown number of Feldschers – doctors' assistants, mainly men and a few women, who had acquired their training in Europe. With the second *Aliya* (1904–14), female paramedics and midwives came to Eretz Yisrael and settled especially in the new settlements. Training of nursing staff, mostly of local women, was carried out by doctors for specific and limited activity.[34]

In the United States, nursing had developed at the end of the nineteenth century into a profession dominated by women. Nursing education was also highly developed. The American-Jewish nurses who came with the American Zionist Medical Unit established the nursing school only a few months after their arrival in Eretz Yisrael, based on American models of nursing education. The teaching methods adopted were those of the nursing schools in the US, where the unit's nurses had received their training. In Eretz Yisrael, the school's founders wished to create a model school in the spirit of the American reform nursing education of the time. The school put great emphasis on educating the nurses according to the vision of the founders' image of the good nurse.[35]

In addition to nursing, Hadassah brought a series of paramedical professions to Eretz Yisrael, and developed them. These were almost exclusively professions that had developed in the US as female professions for which women were trained in higher education institutions, mostly in universities. The women who transmitted them were trained at the best institutions in the US, and could impart what was considered the best training for these professions.

The first of the paramedical professions to be brought was nutrition. At the beginning of the 1920s, Henrietta Szold invited Julia Duskin, a young dietician who had received her training at Cornell University, to come to work in Eretz Yisrael. Until her marriage, Duskin worked on a number of kibbutzim and in Hadassah's hospital in Jerusalem.[36] After she left the profession, there was no dietician to take her place, so Hadassah sent Sara Bavly, a young Zionist woman who made *Aliya* from the Netherlands, to the United States in 1928 to study the profession in depth. Bavly, who had a Master's degree in Chemistry, studied nutrition at Columbia University (1928–29) and received a Master's degree in nutrition. When she came back to Eretz Yisrael she became involved in a series of activities connected with nutrition, which was actually the beginning of the profession in the country. Among these were the establishment of the Dietetic Department in Hadassah's five hospitals, a Nutrition Department in the Strauss Health Center in Jerusalem and a department for nutrition in the Beth Hakerem Institute of teacher training.[37]

In 1947, on the eve of the establishment of the State, Hadassah brought in another paramedical profession: occupational therapy. This feminine profession was also based on the American model using the highest American professional standards. Ethel Bloom, an American who had lived for several years in Eretz Yisrael, appealed to Hadassah to let her study for an academic degree in occupational therapy in order to introduce it into the country. She received a scholarship from Hadassah and studied rehabilitation in New York University for a BA degree and specialized in clinical work in occupational therapy. She received her degree in November 1945. Later, she studied for a second degree in management in order to become fully prepared for her expected duties in Eretz Yisrael.[38]

More experienced occupational therapists were needed in order to develop the field in Eretz Yisrael. Hadassah therefore established a professional committee for the development of occupational therapy and rehabilitation in Eretz Yisrael. The committee, one of whose members was Marjory Fish, the chairperson of the educational committee of the American Occupational Therapy Association for the teaching of occupational therapy in Columbia University, decided to open a course for training occupational therapists. Bloom, on the advice of Fish, visited the leading occupational therapy dispensaries in the United States and met with various leading professionals in the field. Together with Fish, she drafted the curriculum of the future course based on the American demands of the profession, and acquired equipment for Hadassah Hospital. The course was designed according to the professional standards determined by the American Occupational Therapists Association and the American Medical Association.[39]

The first course for occupational therapists in Eretz Yisrael was opened in 1947. Its teachers were four young American women whose training Hadassah sponsored especially to teach this course. Three of them had studied occupational therapy in Philadelphia. The second course, which was opened in 1949, was a copy of the first but its teachers were graduates of the first course.[40] The curriculum for professional training in occupational therapy as laid down by Ethel Bloom and the Hadassah committee was excellent, even when compared to that of the United States and England, and laid the foundation for the training of that profession in Israel.[41]

Hadassah's traditional conceptions of bringing the best American models of vocational education to Eretz Yisrael, and its faith in science are best reflected in its activity in the establishment of the first Israeli medical school. The Hadassah-Hebrew University Medical School was established after a lengthy process that began when the University and Hadassah concluded an agreement in 1936.[42] It was patterned after American medical schools, and this model was later followed in the establishment of other medical schools: those of Tel Aviv University (1961) and of the Ben-Gurion University of the Negev (1972).

Hadassah took an important step toward the creation of the medical school in 1945, shortly after the decision to establish it was made, by creating an advisory agency, the Medical Reference Board, in the United States. The purpose of the board was to assist in the establishment of the school by providing professional advice. Its members were prominent Jewish physicians, including some of the best in the US, medical administrators and public health experts, all of whom voluntarily served on the board.[43] The Medical Reference Board gave advice on the educational philosophy to be adopted by the medical school – an issue that had already been discussed among the bodies involved with establishing the school back in 1942.[44] The board members also drafted a curriculum for the future medical school, based on curricula of the medical schools at several leading American universities –

Harvard, Columbia and Johns Hopkins.[45] In early 1947, the committee charged with choosing the medical school's teaching method decided on a model similar to that conventional in American medical schools.[46] This decision was facilitated by the Medical Reference Board, under the influence of Hadassah, and by Dr Haim Yassky, director of the Rothschild Hospital, all of whom considered American medical practice to be the epitome of modernity and wished to see it take root in Eretz Yisrael. They made this decision even though most of the doctors of Rothschild Hospital had been trained in Central Europe, and one could not take for granted that they would accept the American doctrine.[47]

Another contribution of Hadassah to the medical school was a corollary of the decision to follow the American pattern of medical education – in-service training for the teaching staff in the US. In 1946, senior members of the Rothschild Hospital medical staff were sent to the United States, where they received research and teaching fellowships and participated in clinical programs at several of the leading American medical schools.[48] The fellowship program has since become an ongoing program.

After the medical school came into being, Hadassah contributed in two additional ways to putting it on a firm basis: by purchasing medical equipment and providing training grants for senior staff and students – an important matter, because most students were recent immigrants.[49] The funds for these grants originated in donations from Hadassah leaders and members of their families. It should be noted that the grants were not limited to doctors only, and they were made available for medical administrators, nutritionists and other specialists as well. A similar policy was followed at Hadassah's other projects in the country.[50]

## THE IMPACT OF THE SPHERES OF ACTIVITY ON THE STABILITY OF THE ORGANIZATIONS

Continuity and stability, in activity and in membership, were, as mentioned above, characteristic of Hadassah. A decisive factor that gave it these traits was the fact that Hadassah enterprises were intrinsically related to long-term ongoing activities that needed continual attention. Such activities suited the social structure of Hadassah's members – leisure-time women. Most of its members, both on the leadership level and among the rank and file, were married women who did not hold jobs. Their activities in Hadassah were a source of satisfaction and identification and provided them with a social context. For its leaders, Hadassah was also the place where they invested the professional knowledge they had acquired in college. The ZOA, on the other hand, was composed of members who were, for the most part, businessmen who were pressed for time. Thus, ad hoc activities fitted the social structure of that organization.

However, the most crucial factor in the stability, or instability, of these organizations was their rootedness, or lack of it, in the everyday life of the Yishuv. Before the State of Israel was established, Hadassah was a crucial player in Yishuv society. The development of services that are essential for any society, especially a young one, made Hadassah an integral part of the local landscape. Practically speaking, one cannot imagine the establishment of Israel's health system without Hadassah. With the establishment of the State of Israel and shortly thereafter, Hadassah was extensively active in Israel.

The ZOA, on the other hand, never developed any real connection to the everyday life of the Yishuv or the State. The political nature of ZOA activity caused it to work outside of Eretz Yisrael, concentrating its political and fundraising activities in the US. The everyday life of the Yishuv was neither dependent on nor influenced by the ZOA. It struck no roots in Yishuv society. This is the central difference between Hadassah and the ZOA. While Hadassah had firmly taken root in Israel through its health and welfare activities, the ZOA was not active in any field of endeavor in the new State. Thus, after the establishment of the State, the ZOA relinquished a major portion of its political and fundraising activities, while Hadassah found itself obligated to choose in which fields it would continue to act and in which it would devolve responsibility to the government.

Whereas the ZOA lost its central challenge, Hadassah faced new challenges in Israel, a fact that influenced its ongoing activity in the US as well. Its institutions and projects in Eretz Yisrael were the central pillar of the organization in the US and the factor that ensured the organization's continuity for so many years. The ZOA, on the other hand, had no such pillars. With the political changes and the changing historical conditions, and with no real tasks or aims, the ZOA almost vanished from the Zionist arena after completing its political role in the struggle for the founding of a Jewish state.

## HADASSAH AS A WOMEN'S ORGANIZATION

Having discussed the impact of gender on Hadassah, another question arises: Is Hadassah a women's movement that aims to improve the status of women? Feminist aims and objectives are not listed in any of the major documents that have outlined Hadassah's ideology since its inception.[51] Even the *Hadassah Handbook* practically does not touch upon the advancement of women, or issues concerning them.[52] Hadassah's leadership did not view the members as objects for social change; instead it presented them with challenges having a direct bearing on Hadassah's objectives: fundraising, recruitment of new members and efforts in the field of Jewish education.

On the basis of concepts then current concerning the nature of women, the ideas of 'social feminism' and the unique conditions in which the founders of Hadassah functioned in the Zionist arena, Hadassah's early leaders developed a set of Zionist ideas that took into account gender differences, beginning with the organization's inception in 1912 and through the 1920s. Women were then, as has already been mentioned, considered to be more practical than men and thus well-suited to carry out projects in the field of health and medicine, and especially of childcare. Men were more qualified to deal with political and ideological issues. Women had unique capabilities and special fields of interest that enabled them to contribute to the Zionist cause in these matters no less than the contribution made to Zionism by men in other – more 'masculine' – areas. On the basis of these ideas, which were also accepted by the founders of Hadassah, there developed within that movement – and in American Zionism in general – a perspective that assigned different tasks to men and women in accordance with their special attributes, and claimed that this division of labor enabled both sexes to contribute equally to efforts on behalf of Zionism and the Jewish people as a whole. The Hadassah leadership propagated these ideas within and without the organization from its establishment until the mid-1920s.[53]

The idea of unique and different roles for men and women appealed to many Jewish women in those days. Mary Mccune makes the point that concepts such as differentiation on the basis of gender, were one of the aspects that enabled Hadassah to attract non-Zionist women to its ranks and thus become an important element in the American Zionist movement of the time. Furthermore, even at that early stage, Hadassah's leadership considered medical activity to be a unique contribution of American women to the Zionist cause, and as its own special domain.[54]

This process was not limited to the realm of ideology alone; it was also characteristic of Hadassah's efforts in Eretz Yisrael, where its first actions were directly connected with the welfare of women. To implement a decision made by the young organization's founders to assume responsibility for a medical project for the welfare of women and children, early in 1913 – less than a year after it was founded – Hadassah hired two public health nurses, Rose Kaplan of New York and Rachel Landy of Cleveland. They were sent to Eretz Yisrael to establish a network of health clinics for women and children. Funding was supplied by Nathan Straus, who had generously contributed to public health projects in the US and was especially renowned for his efforts to further milk pasteurization. Straus and his wife, Lina, even accompanied the two nurses on their journey to Eretz Yisrael.[55]

Henrietta Szold, the driving force behind this initiative, intended to establish a network of community clinics that would provide the necessary services for a healthy community: health services in schools, prophylactic measures to counter tuberculosis, baby and child care and training for preventive medicine in general. Szold's model was the famous clinic in New York established by the renowned nurse Lillian D. Wald, a regional clinic that itself followed the example of such institutions in England.[56] Wald's clinic was situated on New York's Lower East Side, an area populated by Jewish immigrants, and had become a unique model for similar health centers throughout the world. Szold urged nurses Kaplan and Landy to visit the Wald clinic and study its procedures before they sailed for Eretz Yisrael.[57]

Upon their arrival, in March 1913, the nurses established a 'settlement house' among the poorer residents of the Meah She'arim quarter in Jerusalem.[58] This was in line with the policy of the Settlement House movement, which made a point of locating its institutions in poor neighborhoods in order to combat the social and physical conditions that encouraged disease.[59] They lived in a house that served both as a clinic and their home. Not long after their arrival, they were visited by Jane Adams, the well-known American social reformer and a leader of the Settlement House movement. This event is indicative of Hadassah's relationship to that movement – an important movement during the Progressive period in American history, and one that was almost entirely female in composition – and its leadership, and also of its involvement in the type of activity that was identified with women's movements in the early years of the twentieth century.[60] The First World War, however, put an abrupt end to the nurses' efforts on behalf of women in Eretz Yisrael, and they were forced to return to the US.[61]

The war also completely changed Hadassah's role in the World Zionist Organization, and more specifically – the character of its activity in Eretz Yisrael.[62] In the wake of the war, Hadassah began to develop health services for the entire population in Eretz Yisrael. Immediately after its return to the country in 1918, it established hospitals throughout the land, founded a nursing school, was active in preventive medicine and in caring for new immigrants.[63] Hadassah became a central actor in most fields of health and medical services from the final months of the First World War and throughout the entire British Mandate period.

In the 1930s, however, the nature of Hadassah's activities in Eretz Yisrael was once more transformed. It adopted a policy of devolution, gradually transferring its health and medical institutions outside Jerusalem to the Jewish municipalities and to Kupat Holim, the Health Fund of the General Federation of Jewish Labor (Histadrut).[64] Two objectives lay behind this policy: to encourage the Yishuv to provide its own services, and to enable Hadassah to undertake new projects.[65] This led to another policy change: Hadassah would now put the emphasis on developing research and university medical services rather than concentrating on public health, as in the previous decade. This decision also had geographical implications: from now on its major thrust would be in Jerusalem, centered for the most part on the Rothschild Hospital, though some other services were still provided in the city, and not throughout the country as in the 1920s. It assumed direct responsibility for the hospital which in 1939, in cooperation with the Hebrew University, had become a university hospital known as the Meir Rothschild Hadassah–University Hospital.[66]

In 1949 Hadassah devolved all of its public health institutions – those that, like the one it founded in 1913, were established primarily for women – to the Government of Israel, except for the ones in Jerusalem and the 'Jerusalem Corridor', of which it kept control to serve research and teaching functions in the School of Medicine founded in 1949 and the older School of Nursing. Since then, Hadassah's efforts in Israel have focused on medical education and its hospital in Jerusalem.[67]

What emerges from this brief survey of Hadassah's activities in Eretz Yisrael is that efforts for the welfare of women, the basis of Hadassah's first project in the country, gradually diminished over the years. In fact, they already took second place during the final months of the First World War, when Hadassah became a medical organization of the first magnitude in Eretz Yisrael. Almost from the outset, therefore, Hadassah was an organization that provided health services to the population of Eretz Yisrael at large, and it is as such that it firmly took root in the country. Almost from its establishment, involvement in ameliorating the condition of women did not characterize Hadassah. As the years passed, Hadassah's role within the Zionist movement was taken for granted, and that basic ideological concept – unique and different roles for men and women – was put aside. Thus, in the late 1940s and during the 1950s, no trace of the ideas discussed above or of feminist ideology could be found in the movement's major publications.

Paradoxically, if that is the case, Hadassah, an organization which owes its success to being a women's organization, is one whose main interest has not been, either ideologically or practically, the betterment of women's conditions or social status. The major organs through which the leadership roused members to action during the late 1940s and 1950s made, therefore, no effort to encourage a feminist identity that would militantly seek equality with men, or a sense of feminist elitism, or any other feminist ideals that went beyond the bounds of consensus. This was primarily because such ideas did not concern Hadassah, whose main objectives and activities were Zionist in nature.[68] Hadassah is, therefore, not a feminist movement aiming at the betterment of women but rather an organization to link women for Zionist activity.

## CONCLUSION

The study of how gender impacts on the leading Zionist organizations in the US illuminates their enormous differences in characteristics, development, activities and others. It suggests that gender played a crucial part in the formation of their character, spheres of activity, *modus operandi*, roots in Eretz Yisrael and longevity. Thus, gender differences can explain why the ZOA practically vanished from the Zionist scene after it fulfilled its major contribution to the Zionist enterprise: the enormous political and financial assistance in establishing the State of Israel, while Hadassah, continues to contribute, although in a much more modest way, to the Zionist cause to this day.

Gender has been an important attribute of the American Zionist movement. It was basically imported from the American environment's perceptions of gender roles, gender differences and gender divisions in spheres of activity within the family and society. It divided the roles within the American Zionist movement into political roles for men versus welfare and education for women. Thus, while the ZOA's contribution was in the 'masculine pursuits', of the political and diplomatic sphere, Hadassah made its feminist contribution in the fields of welfare and education and the importation of various American women's occupations to Eretz Yisrael. The contribution of American Zionists to the Zionist enterprise was, therefore, in a way the result of a combination of different gender traditions inherent in American society.

NOTES

This paper is based on parts of the book, *American Women Zionists: Hadassah in Israel's Formative Years*, to be published in 2005 by the Littman Library of Jewish Civilization. I am grateful to the research department of the Open University of Israel for their assistance.

1. The ZOA has been explored in many studies on the American Zionist movement as a whole. Among the major works are Melvin I. Urofsky, *American Zionism from Herzl to the Holocaust* (Garden City, NJ: Anchor, 1976) [hereafter: Urofsky, *American Zionism*]; Melvin I. Urofsky, *We Are One – American Jewry and Israel* (Garden City, NJ: Anchor, 1978) [hereafter: Urofsky, *We Are One*]; Naomi Wiener Cohen, *American Jews and the Zionist Idea* (New York: Ktav, 1975); Samuel Halperin, *The Political World of American Zionism* (Detroit: Wayne State University Press, 1961) [hereafter: Halperin, *Political World*]; Yonathan Shapiro, *Leadership of the American Zionist Organization, 1897–1930* (Urbana: University of Illinois Press, 1971); Aron Berman, *Nazism, the Jews and American Zionism, 1933–1948* (Detroit: Wayne State University Press, 1990); David Shapiro, *From Philanthropy to Activism – The Political Transformation of American Zionism in the Holocaust Years 1933–1945*, (Jerusalem: Bialik Institute, 2001, Hebrew; a shortened version was published in English).

   As for Hadassah, a considerable number of studies devoted to certain facets or periods of Hadassah, to American Zionism in general, and to the history of health and medicine in Eretz Yisrael can provide us with information on various processes in Hadassah's history. Following is a select list of the major works. Hadassah has been the subject of three PhD dissertations: D. Miller, 'A History of Hadassah, 1912–1935' (PhD dissertation, New York University, 1965) [hereafter: Miller, Hadassah]; Mira Katzburg-Yungman, 'Hadassah: Ideology and Practice, 1948–1956', (PhD dissertation, The Hebrew University of Jerusalem, 1997, Hebrew), which attempts to explore the nature of Hadassah [hereafter: Katzburg-Yungman, Hadassah]; and Carol Kutcher, 'The Early Years of Hadassah, 1912–1921' (PhD dissertation, Brandeis University, 1976) [hereafter: Kutcher, Early Years].

   Each of the major studies on American Zionism mentioned above includes a short discussion of Hadassah. See also the popular work commissioned by Hadassah that concentrates on its projects in Eretz Yisrael: Marlin Levin, *Balm in Gilead: The Story of that Hadassah* (New York: Schocken, 1976) [hereafter: Levin,

Balm]. For a recent study dealing with gender issues concerning Hadassah, see Mary Mccune, 'Social Workers in the Muskeljudentum: "Hadassah Ladies", "Manly Men" and the Significance of Gender in the American Zionist Movement, 1912–1928', *American Jewish History*, 86, 2 (June 1998), 135–65 [hereafter: Mccune, Gender]. See also Joyce Antler, *The Journey Home: Jewish Women and the American Century* (New York and London: Free Press, 1997) [hereafter: Antler, *Journey*].

2. The only study that attempted to deal with some of these issues during the early 1920s is Mccune, Gender.
3. Noach Orian (Herzog), 'The Leadership of Rabbi Abba Hillel Silver on the American-Jewish Scene 1938–1959' (PhD dissertation, Tel Aviv University, 1982, Hebrew) vol. 1, p. 5 [hereafter, Orian, Leadership].
4. For membership statistics for 1948, see Halperin, *Political World*, p. 327; for 1953, see *Proceedings [of the] 56th Annual Convention of the Zionist Organization of America* (August 26–30, 1953, New York), p. 35 [in *CZA*, call no. F38/348; hereafter: 1953 ZOA Convention]; for the social structure of the ZOA, see Orian, Leadership, p. 40; for Hadassah's social structure, see Katzburg-Yungman, Hadassah, pp. 210, 215.
5. Urofsky, *We Are One*, pp. 299–301.
6. 'The Convention in Review: A Day by Day Summary', *The New Palestine* (June 14, 1949), p. 2.
7. On the ZOA House, see 'Monossohn in Israel for Cornerstone Laying of ZOA House in Tel Aviv', *The New Palestine* (October 27, 1949), p. 2; on Kfar Silver, see 'Kfar Silver to Include College of Agriculture', *The American Zionist* (February 20, 1953), p. 2; 'Kfar Silver Gets New Water System, Dorms', *The American Zionist* (December 1954), p. 13; 'Opening of Kfar Silver', *The American Zionist* (October 1955), p. 15; 'Kfar Silver Now Has 100 Students', *The American Zionist* (December 1956), p. 17.
8. On the decision to establish an economic department and other decisions relating to economics, see 1953 ZOA Convention, p. 36; on decisions taken at the 1954 Convention, see 'ZOA Convention Sets New Standards for Israel Work', *The American Zionist* (July 1954), p. 1.
9. Resolutions 3–12: 'Zionist Educational Seminaries'; 'Yiddish Circles'; 'Hebrew Terminology'; 'Hebrew Publications'; 'Jewish Culture'; 'The American Zionist'; 'Dos Yiddishe Folk'; 'Zionist Book of the Month Club'; 'Anthology of Jewish Philosophy'; 'Radio and Television', *Proceedings [of the] Annual Convention of the Zionist Organization of America* (New York, June 12–16, 1952), pp. 422–8 [in *CZA*, call no. F38/348].
10. Urofsky, *We Are One*, p. 279.
11. On the requests for help, see Katzburg-Yungman, Hadassah, pp. 128–9, 130–2, 138–9, 146, 149–50; on the medical school, see Mira Katzburg-Yungman, 'Women and Activity in *Eretz Yisrael* – The Case of Hadassah, 1912–1958', in Shulamit Reinharz and Mark Raider (eds), *Partners to Palestine: American Jewish Women and the Zionist Enterprise* (forthcoming) [hereafter, Katzburg-Yungman, Women and Activity]; idem, Hadassah, pp. 156–61; on the hospitals, see ibid., p. 151–5; idem, Women and Activity; on the health projects, see ibid., idem, Hadassah, p. 145; on projects for children and youth, see ibid., pp. 170–205; idem, Women and Activity.
12. See, for example, Hadassah National Board Minutes, January 5, 1948, p. 8; ibid., December 12, 1948, p. 9; ibid., May 18, 1949, p. 4; Some of the publications included Naomi Ben-Asher, *Democracy's Hebrew Roots and Leader's Guide to the Book*

*of Deuteronomy*; a list of Hadassah's publications in *What to Read – Where to Find it – Survey of Pamphlets of Jewish and Zionist Interests Recommended by the Education Department of Hadassah.*

13. Katzburg-Yungman, Hadassah, pp. 40, 45–7; the book is Leo W. Schwarz (ed.) *Great Ages and Ideas of the Jewish People* (New York: Random House, 1956).
14. On practicality, see Katzburg-Yungman, Hadassah, p. 57; on faith in science for the advancement of medicine, see ibid., pp. 58–9.
15. Kutcher, Early Years, p. 330; Rosalind Rosenberg, *Beyond Separate Spheres: Intellectual Roots of Modern Feminism* (New Haven: Yale University Press, 1982), p. 76; William L. O'Neill, *Feminism in America: A History* (New Brunswick and Oxford: Transaction, 1988), p. 70 [hereafter: O'Neill, *Feminism*].
16. Kutcher, 'Early Years', p. 330.
17. *Hadassah in Eretz Yisrael, 1918–1928: Opening Address by Henrietta Szold at the Inauguration Ceremony of the Nathan and Lina Straus Health Center, on 20 Nissan 5689 [1929]* (Jerusalem, 1929, Hebrew), p. 13 [in Central Zionist Archives, Jerusalem, call no. 7250] [hereafter: *CZA*]; see also *Proceedings [of] the 33rd Annual Convention of Hadassah* (Atlantic City, NJ, October 24–27, 1947), pp. 82, 87, Hadassah Archives, New York [hereafter: *HA*]; interview with Dr Kalman J. Mann, Jerusalem, July 28, 1992.
18. 'Bikkur Holim', *Encyclopedia Talmudica*, IV (Hebrew), p. 158; Marion A. Kaplan, *The Making of Jewish Middle Class: Women, Family and Identity* (Oxford University Press, 1991), pp. 193–4.
19. O'Neill, *Feminism*, p. 142; Sheila M. Rothman, *Woman's Proper Place: A History of Changing Ideals and Practices, 1870 to the Present* (New York: Basic Books, 1978), pp. 154–6 [hereafter: Rothman, *Proper Place*]; Michael Brown, 'Henrietta Szold's Progressive American Vision of the Yishuv', in Allon Gal (ed.) *Envisioning Israel: The Changing Ideals and Images of North American Jews* (Jerusalem, The Hebrew University: Magnes Press; Detroit: Wayne State University Press, 1996), p. 75 [hereafter, Brown, Szold].
20. On social feminism see: Nancy Woloch, *Women and the American Experience* (New York: Alfred A. Knopf, 1984), pp. 326–7; Naomi Black, *Social Feminism* (Ithaca and London: Cornell University Press, 1989), pp. 53–62.
21. See, for example, footnote 23; Rivka Adams Stockler, 'The Making of Community Nursing in the Jewish Population in Eretz Yisrael', Rivka Adams Stockler, Rina Sharon (eds) *Milestones in Nursing: Historical Research on Nursing Written in Israel* (Tel Aviv University, 1995), p. 91; see also notes 23, 24.
22. See, Rothman, *Proper Place*, p. 98.
23. On the connection of Hadassah's first project in Eretz Yisrael to the Settlement House Movement, see Antler, *Journey*, p. 105.
24. Berta Landsman to Dr Blustone [director Hadassah Medical Organization], Re: District Nursing in Tel Aviv, 1.4.1927 (Lea Zwanger, personal collection); Zipora Shory-Rubin, 'Hadassah's Educational Enterprises and Health Activities During Mandatory Times', (PhD dissertation, Ben-Gurion University, 1998, Hebrew), pp. 132, 138–9 [hereafter, Rubin, Educational Enterprises]; Lea Zwanger, 'Preparation of Graduate Nurses in Israel 1918–1925', (PhD dissertation, Columbia University, 1968).
25. George Rosen, *A History of Public Health* (New York: MD Publications, 1958), pp. 299–300 [hereafter: Rosen, *Public Health*]. Although written a generation ago, the book is still considered the best in its field.

26. Akiva W. Deutsch, 'The Development of Social Work as a Profession in the Jewish Community in *Eretz Yisrael*' (PhD dissertation, The Hebrew University of Jerusalem, 1970, Hebrew), p. 209.
27. *The Government of Israel Statistical Yearbook* (1951), p. 137; ibid., 1953, p. 142.
28. For publications on Jewish topics, see footnote 12 above; on support of youth movements, see, for example, Hadassah Progress Report – Projects and Activities 1954–1955, pp. 63–7; Hadassah Annual Report 1948–1949, pp. 60–2; on study groups, see Hadassah National Board Minutes, November 5, 1952, p. 8.
29. On Hadassah's commitment to Jewish survival, see Hannah L. Goldberg, *Hadassah Handbook* (New York: National Education Committee of Hadassah, 1946–1950), p. 53.
30. Hadassah Annual Report 1948–1949; *American Jewish Year Book*, vol. 51 (1950), p. 468; ibid., vol. 53 (1952), p. 487; ibid., vol. 54 (1953), p. 503; Hadassah Constitution (1956), p. 2, *HA*.
31. On Hadassah's self-perception as an educational force in Eretz Yisrael, see a very explicit statement in Julia A. Duskin, *Hadassah's Child Welfare Program in Palestine* (New York: Hadassah, The Women's Zionist Organization of America, 1942), p. 3.
32. On the vocational school for girls, see Katzburg-Yungman, Hadassah, pp. 198–9.
33. *Twenty Years of Medical Service to Palestine, 1918–1938: Report Issued to Commemorate the Opening of the Hadassah University Medical Center, May 9, 1939, 20 Iyar 5699* (Jerusalem, 1939, Hebrew), p. 17 [hereafter: *Twenty Years*].
34. Nira Bartal, 'Theoretical and Practical Training of Jewish Nurses in Mandatory Palestine, 1918–1948, through the Prism of the Hadassah School of Nursing, Jerusalem' (PhD dissertation, Hebrew University, 2000), p. 25 [hereafter: Bartal, Nursing].
35. Ibid., pp. 29, 32, 150.
36. Julia A. Duskin, Curriculum Vitae, Hadassah Archives, New York; Interview with Avima Duskin Lombard [Julia A. Duskin's daughter], Jerusalem, December 17, 2000.
37. Sara Bavly, Introduction to List of Files to the Archives of Sara Bavly, *CZA*, A/580/7; Interview with Miriam Bavly [Sara Bavly's daughter], Jerusalem, December 16, 2000.
38. On Ethel Bloom, see Nira Sussman, 'The History of Occupational Therapy in Israel: The First Decade, 1946 to 1956' (Master's thesis, New York University, 1989), p. 63 [hereafter, Sussman, Occupational Therapy]; idem, 'The Development of Occupational Therapy in Israel during its First Decade, 1946 to 1956', *JIOT*, 2 (4) (November 1993), p. 146.
39. Ibid., pp. 147–8.
40. Sussman, Occupational Therapy, pp. 65, 90.
41. Ibid., p. 89; Interview with Nira Sussman, January 24, 2001.
42. Doron Niederland, Zohar Kaplan, 'The Establishment of the Hebrew University–Hadassah Medical School in Jerusalem', *Cathedra*, 48 (June 1988, Hebrew), pp. 145–63 [hereafter: Niederland, Medical School].
43. Ibid., p. 146.
44. Ibid., p. 156.
45. Moshe Prywes, *Prisoner of Hope* (Tel Aviv: Zmora-Bitan, 1992, Hebrew), p. 260.
46. Record of the Meeting of the Council of the Para-Faculty of Medicine, February 9, 1947, Hebrew University Archives, Jerusalem (Hebrew) [hereafter: *HUA*]; Niederland, Medical School, p. 156.

47. Ibid., loc. cit.
48. Dr Haim Yassky at the meeting of the Council of the Para-Faculty of Medicine, December 8, 1946 (Hebrew), *HUA*; Hadassah National Board Minutes, November 3, 1948, p. 6, *HA*; interview with Prof. Andre De Vries, Tel Aviv, 1992; Hadassah Biennial Report, 1949–1951, pp. 23–4, *HA*; Hadassah National Board Minutes, May 15, 1954, p. 4, *HA*.
49. Hadassah National Board Minutes, July 20, 1950, p. 4, *HA*.
50. Hadassah Biennial Report, 1949–1951, pp. 23–4, *HA*.
51. Folder: Hadassah Constitutions, *HA*.
52. *Hadassah Handbook*.
53. Mccune, Gender, pp. 137, 141, 149.
54. Ibid., p. 150.
55. Antler, *Journey*, p. 105; on the two nurses, see Dash, *Summoned*, p. 112; see also: Shvarts, *Kupat Holim*, p. 49.
56. On the Wald clinic, see Rosen, *Public Health*, pp. 380–1.
57. Antler, *Journey*, p. 105.
58. Dash, *Summoned*, p. 109; Miller, Hadassah, p. 87.
59. Antler, *Journey*, p. 105.
60. Ibid., loc. cit.
61. Dash, *Summoned*, p. 110.
62. Mccune, Gender, p. 146.
63. *Twenty Years*, pp. 17–19.
64. Niederland, Influence, p. 144.
65. *Twenty Years*, p. 24.
66. Niederland, Influence, p. 144.
67. A general memorandum sent by Hayim Shalom Halevi (Deputy Administrative Director of the Rothschild Hospital) to mayors and heads of local municipal councils; Circular by Dr Kalman Mann to city and local councils, May 16, 1952; List of 24 preventive medicine clinics in the Jerusalem Corridor operated by Hadassah on the day on which the agreement devolving its services elsewhere was signed; Kalman Mann to Chaim Shiba, Director General of the Ministry of Health, July 7, 1972; Agreement between the directors of the Hadassah Medical Organization, the Clerical Workers Union, the Nurses Union and the Hadassah Employees Union; all in Hebrew, and all found in the Israel State Archives, 2/1/4/4245 c. For the statement that Hadassah kept its medical services in Jerusalem and the Jerusalem Corridor in order to train its medical students and nurses, see: Kalman J. Mann, 'The Hadassah Medical Organization Program in the State of Israel', in Joseph Hirsh (ed.) *The Hadassah Medical Organization: An American Contribution to Medical Pioneering and Progress in Israel* (New York: Hadassah, 1965), p. 38.
68. *Hadassah Newsletter*, 1945–56; *Hadassah Headlines*, 1945–56.

# 10

# Post-Holocaust Memory: Some Gendered Reflections

## DEBRA KAUFMAN

As a sociologist, I am interested in the cultural narratives that will embed memory in tomorrow's history. What I have chosen to share with you in this chapter is part of an ongoing, larger project about post-Holocaust Jewish identity among young adults (between 20 and 30 years of age) in the United States, Great Britain and Israel.[1] The material presented here deals only with the data from the US. Specifically, my focus is on the gendered dimensions of the post-Holocaust narratives gathered during my interviews.

Feminist thinking suggests that we must undertake any scholarly pursuit in a critically self-conscious and humane fashion. The study of the Holocaust demands that we do so. Therefore, the first gendered reflection I wish to make in this chapter is that history is grounded in 'collective' memory and represents a pursuit steeped in both scholarly possibilities and ethical obligations (LaCapra, 1998). True to a feminist recounting of my project, I will begin by revealing several assumptions implicit in my work. As I have written elsewhere, until recently, what we 'know' about the Holocaust and what has been given for posterity to 'know' have been primarily understood through a master narrative developed in each scholarly discipline by and through a predominately male voice (Kaufman, 1996: 4). More importantly, I contend that contemporary collective representations of the Holocaust, particularly in the popular imagination, are gendered. For instance, in a special guest edition of *Contemporary Jewry*, Mary Lagerwey (1996) explores the sociocultural impact of text and fiction within the contemporary memory and imagination of the Holocaust. She suggests that the reception and popularity of Elie Wiesel's, *Night* and of Anne Frank's, *The Diary of a Young Girl* are differently understood in the popular imagination given the gendered nature of these works.

For Lagerwey, these two life stories have played major roles in shaping the collective memories of the Holocaust in the United States. Anne Frank's story is that of a victim of the Holocaust, a young female adolescent whose story has been rewritten by others, and who remains, contends Lagerwey, representative of the 6 million who vanished. That is, she remains in the popular imagination as representative of a sympathetic victim. In contrast, Elie Wiesel, following the western autobiographical convention that holds that one 'successful' life story can embody an entire historical event or period, writes his own story as the representative voice of the 'successful Holocaust survivor' (Lagerwey, 1996: 54). She represents passivity; he agency.

Similarly, scholars, such as Myrna Goldenberg, maintain that 'English language audiences know Holocaust literature primarily through male writers and have generalized those experiences to represent the whole' (1990: 150). Heinemann (1986) argues that apart from Anne Frank's *Diary*, texts of Holocaust memories have been primarily male. My main point here is to make clear that 'collective memory' is not only produced within a specific social and historical context, but within a gendered context as well. Importantly, such contexts affect the way in which we represent or address the past. Only recently have gender issues become explicit in both research foci and the interpretation of the Holocaust experience (see, for example, Cesarani, 2001).

## THE STUDY

In other work, I have detailed the ways in which the Holocaust is complexly woven into the identity narratives of the young adults I studied (Kaufman, 1998, 1999, 2001). While the Holocaust does play an important role in their contemporary identity narratives, those narratives are shaped by the institutional and cultural interpretations of specific regional, national and international socio-historic moments as well. Therefore, while the Holocaust represents an important political identity marker, it, as all historical reconstructions, necessarily involves judgment and selectivity based on the social context within which it is received. That judgment and selectivity is complexly linked to cultural constructions and reconstructions of the Holocaust (see Kaufman, 2001) and, for my sample, to their contemporary Jewish identities. In this chapter I will not focus on the reasons for those reconstructions, but rather on the gendered dimensions of the Jewish identity narratives I gathered. In this study, many of the identity narratives the young adults reveal are intimately linked to the Holocaust and to the way in which the Jew has been positioned historically as the 'other'. In general, the young adults in this study construct their identity narratives as Jews in relationship to other 'others'.

For many in the sample, the Holocaust is a 'defining' or 'root' experience (Fackenheim, 1987), a historical marker from which the meaning and measure of Jewish identity is taken. The 20- and 30-year-olds in my sample are not necessarily representative of all young adults of that age, but they do provide insights into the ways in which this population configures and reconfigures identity issues. For the most part, when Holocaust themes are mentioned, the young adults use those themes in their identity narratives to move them beyond particularistic concerns for their immediate communities to more universalistic concerns for other communities (for a fuller discussion, see Kaufman, 2001). In general, they define themselves as Jews through their obligations to and concerns for others, both within and outside of the Jewish community.

Yet despite this, men and women differ not only in the way they tell their identity narratives, but in the content of those narratives as well. When they appear, gender differences support findings that indicate that women both narrate and theorize from the concrete and relational ways they live their lives, while men reflect on identity in more abstract and less detailed ways. Women are more focused on their everyday lives and connections to people. Women are more concerned about the representation of the 'other' in the 'collective cultural narrative', and the consequences for interpersonal dynamics given that cultural construction, than men. Women seem more interested in identity as a means of relating to others; men seem primarily interested in identity as a way of presenting the self as an individual against all others. The women are more tentative, the men more assured, in telling their identity stories (see Kaufman, 1999).

## GENDER FINDINGS

Since earlier publications give a full description of the sample, methods of data collection and some of the gender findings (Kaufman, 1998, 1999), it is sufficient to note here that these are 70, primarily middle- to upper-middle-class, urban young adults. Most are from the eastern seaboard of the US. I interviewed them using a snowball sampling technique. Moreover, they are not necessarily, nor was I interested in, grandchildren or great grandchildren of Holocaust survivors. In this study, I have engaged my sample in what I call 'structured conversations', introducing a set of prepared questions that guide our recorded conversations. The larger themes guiding this study (of which these gender findings are a part) derive from the following question: Does the Holocaust provide themes and metaphors around which post-Holocaust Jewish identity, for 20- to 30-year-olds, is constructed and positioned? Although many hypothesize about this particular age group, few have actually studied such young adults.

Indeed, most speculation has been directed at Jews in general, rather than any specific age group. For instance, in his edited volume on contemporary Jewish identity in Europe, Jonathan Webber suggests that the keen interest in the Holocaust among Jews in Europe may reflect 'the capacity of Holocaust contemplation to provide a new basis for secular Jewish self-identification, especially in countries where there is little significant anti-Semitism' (1992: 23).[2] Secular self-identification is not only subject to time and place, but, as I will soon show, it is also colored by gender.

Initially, the themes and issues raised by the young adults in my sample did not seem to differ between men and women. However, upon repeated listening to the taped conversations, different foci emerged. For men, there was a tendency to be more abstract and less specific in responding to the questions and in their conversations in general. For instance, when speaking about the relationship between their political and Jewish identities, men more often spoke of the universal principles at stake, while women spoke specifically of the devastation to families and particularly to children. For women there was the sense that their identity was embedded in their everyday lives, both as women and as Jews. On the other hand, men never referred specifically to gender when discussing their Jewish identities. For instance, there was no parallel among men for the following answer from a 26-year-old female. In response to the question 'Why is it important, if at all, to call yourself a Jew?', she replied:

> It's extremely important ... In one way it's just so vital to who I am ... it's how I identify myself. There's always the question what are you first: Are you a woman, are you a Jew, and are you an American? I think in different scenarios it changes. Recently, I have begun to define myself as a Jew first and foremost because it's just been right there kind of at the tip of who I am and my identity. But I don't know why.

Another respondent recounted an incident in which she meant to answer by saying, 'I am a Jew' but said instead: 'I'm Sara [fictitious name]'. It was, she notes, 'as if these things were identical'. No male ever responded by saying 'I think of myself more as a male than a Jew', as did the 24-year-old who said: 'I think of myself more as a woman. I pay more attention to women's issues than Jewish issues. 'Cause I feel like ... it has not affected me, to my life, to date, being Jewish. Being a woman has.' One 30-year-old spoke of her distress at being the only female in her Sunday school class and the fact that the congregation of which she was a part would not allow her to read from the Torah. It was not surprising that when asked about how larger changes in the society have affected her identity, she responded by saying: 'Well, the whole women's movement. At some point, in the middle of junior high, it became extremely important to me, and that didn't fit with Judaism.'

I note these gender differences because they color the ways in which these young adults relate their post-Holocaust narratives, especially as they position themselves within and outside the Jewish community. In other words, while the Holocaust raises similar issues for both men and women, those issues are often explored in critically different ways. As the responses above indicate, a number of women envision themselves as the 'other' other within Judaism. Clearly, although suffering and the plight of the other is of concern in both men's and women's identity narratives, women view others with an empathy reserved for those who perceive themselves as the 'other' as well.

Jonathan Webber conjectures that the symbolism of Auschwitz may have less to do with national or nationalist representations of history and more with wider universalistic issues concerning the moral, spiritual and educational problems that affect humanity in general. In this study, in general, the men and women seem to share a similar symbolism in their identity narratives by referring to issues beyond the Jewish community when speaking of Jewish identity and the 'other'. However, the way in which they relate these narratives differs markedly. Men rarely ground their ideas in specific examples; women almost always use life examples and experiences to make their points. Rarely did men ground their thoughts in real-life examples. One 28-year-old male proclaimed:

> It is not just a matter of history, a matter of working things out historically, but the idea that we are a people of God, that we are a chosen people, and that we represent God's working in history.

> We [Jews] represent God working through history. While I don't understand nor can I really explain fascism, murder or oppression, I do know that evil exists and, it too, is a part of the working out of history. We must choose to act on the ideas and ideals that lead away from evil, but it is finally a matter of choice ... Man's choice, that too, is a part of God's working in history.

While both men and women understood the Holocaust to be an extreme version of racism, men described racism as an idea, condemned it as an idea, and believed we should fight it at an idea level more than women did. One 22-year-old male put it this way:

> We need to be ever-vigilant about racism. I think racism is very much about the way you think, the ideas you have about people, especially around differences ... you know, I think any thought that you can have equality with difference is a very mistaken idea. I don't believe in 'different but equal'. The idea of equality is critical in doing away with difference and consequently differential treatment.

Women, on the other hand, used specific life experiences to make similar points, especially about the potentially negative consequences associated with issues of distinctiveness, separateness and exclusiveness. Their concerns are with the real consequences of ideas and the way those ideas may affect the community's relationship with others. Indeed, the most interesting differences were revealed in the way in which women spoke about the consequences of difference, of separatism and of a 'distinctiveness' as Jews.

Only women seemed to connect their concerns about 'others' with their own connection to the Jewish community. One 22-year-old wondered about the lack of non-Jewish friends in her life. Another complained that the lack of diversity within her friendship circles, 'probably makes me a very narrow person'. Another woman says: 'being involved with the Jewish community has made my social life much too homogeneous and that's something that I'm trying to do a little bit more outreach on and to try to cultivate some other relationships'.

Most of those who reported that social action was crucial to their identity narratives claimed to have a sensibility and sensitivity to 'other's' suffering. This empathy was a part of their historical and collective consciousness, as a people who have suffered and who, as a people, are commanded 'to remember' and to 'report injustice'. In other areas of my work I have stated that the Holocaust was the historical marker for these young adults, against which all other atrocities were compared (1998, 1999). When the specific motto 'never again' emerges in their Holocaust narratives (borrowed from the larger cultural Holocaust narrative), these young adults are clear that it means never again to any people.[3] This is true for both men and women.

Therefore, for the majority involved in social justice causes, the impetus for such involvement stems, so they claim, from their sense of duty as Jews and because of their own history as an oppressed and once enslaved people.

## HISTORY, MEMORY AND IDENTITY POLITICS: A GENDERED ANALYSIS

The relationship of identity, memory and history to one another represents a complex interaction. I have chosen to show some of the ways in which the Holocaust as 'a' collective memory has become part of these young adults' personal identity narratives.[4] Rather than resulting in a narrow identity politics, the young people in my study seem to have moved beyond particularistic concerns to a more general concern for 'other' others. In his beautifully written book, *History and Memory after Auschwitz*, Dominick LaCapra (1998) offers some cogent comments on the way in which memory poses questions to history. It points to problems, he suggests, that are still alive or invested with emotion and value. Ideally, he claims, 'history critically tests memory and prepares for a more extensive attempt to work through a past that has not passed away' (1998: 8). Because the Holocaust 'has not passed away' and because it is so laden with emotion and cultural value, it plays an important part in the collective Jewish identity of the young adults I have studied.

These young adults formulate their identity politics within a particular socioeconomic context and at a very specific historical time. The histories these young people carry with them are both personal and cultural. Those histories are imagined differently by gender. In my earlier work, I have noted that both men and women see identity as couched in a need to be a part of a unique historical experience, a tie to a people and a past with a unique culture (see Kaufman, 1998, 1999). In addition, the post-Holocaust understanding of Jewish identity for this population has less to do with religion (see Kaufman, 1998) than it does with claims for ties to a particular cultural and historical heritage. Gender differences are clearest in the ways in which each sex narrates their understanding of identity and the consequences of being 'unique', 'separate', and 'different'. Another important difference is the way in which women consciously deal with being female in a society, in general, which still maintains stereotypical views of them and in an ethnic religious community which is still prototypically male. Perhaps this is why women are seemingly more sensitive and empathetic to other 'others'.

In conclusion, it is important to note again that the differences in the way men and women narrate their identity stories also reflect the way in which they connect or do not connect their own experiences to those narratives. As noted earlier, men are not as likely as women to ground their identities in specifics or to connect to real-life situations. Consequently, they are not as likely, as are women, to stay in touch with that experience in drawing their conclusions or reflections on identity issues.[5] For women, the experience of being grounded and embedded in one community informs the way in which they draw the more general conclusions about how to be connected to 'others' not of the same group. For men, most discussions of their relations with others remain at an abstract level, not grounded in the practical everyday relations of community life. Moreover, it appears uncomplicated for them, in ways that are apparently not true for women.

For all those under study, class, race and gender affect the way in which they present themselves as Jews. They have reached a point economically where they can 'own' their individual histories and, more important, tell their identity stories from a position of strength (Kaufman, 1999).[6] Although sexism within and outside Judaism has been decreasing, structural and social power within the Jewish community (and outside of it) are still male-dominated. Despite the fact that Jewish women, like Jewish men, now enjoy a 'white' and 'middle-class' status (see Kaufman, 1999), women are still socially and economically unequal, compared with men. Perhaps this powerlessness makes them more sensitive to the 'other', better able to assess the needs of the 'other' or, put another way, to take measure of the 'other' than are men (Kaufman, 1991; Kaufman and Richardson, 1982). Jewish women, as their non-Jewish sisters, are still chiefly responsible for mediating the everyday world of the men in their lives, of nurturing and caring for others.

The Holocaust raises identity issues for this generation in a very specific way. The collective cultural memory (i.e., 'never again') of the

Holocaust subtly infuses their identity narratives. Jewish identity is not couched within religious behavior, but rather placed within a political and social stance. The Holocaust, with its mandate to witness and to not forget, becomes then, for many, the subtle marker for both past and current reconstructions of Jewish identity. Cultural memory is tied to the perpetuation of Jewish identity. What these young people choose to remember and how they choose to interpret that memory are all part of their contemporary Jewish identities. But such inquiry goes well beyond issues of Jewish identity. For such inquiry teaches us how history and memory construct a complicated pattern of identity narrative and how that narrative is strongly conditioned by gender.

## NOTES

1. Indeed to my knowledge, at this writing, no one else has published findings about post-Holocaust narratives for this age group.
2. The implication is that countries where anti-Semitism has decreased or is at an all time low, as it is in the USA, may need the Holocaust to maintain Jewish self-identification. Others have made this point, such as Chaim Seidler-Feller (1991) and Michael Meyer (1990).
3. This was seen most clearly for those involved in what was formerly Yugoslavia. Here the most common form of activity was in the collection of food and clothing. Others felt that their work with Oxfam was another expression of their obligation to never see a population die out. Still for others, it was human rights activities, be they directed at South America, Africa or Asia (see Kaufman, 1998, 1999).
4. In the full study (Kaufman, 2001), I suggest that there is no monolithic Jewish identity or collective consciousness, for both interact with and are conditioned by time, place and personal biography.
5. Epistemologically speaking, it is tacitly assumed, although the question itself is not raised, that identity will be known in just the same way by all. But it is a serious oversimplification to take for granted that perceptions are always unproblematically 'the same'. Indeed, the process of identity acquisition and maintenance are dependent upon the cognition in which they are based, and this cognition is itself a proper object of evaluation (Kaufman, 1998, 1999). Women, as Lorraine Code writes in reference to Carol Gilligan's work on moral development, maintain contact with, and derive insights from accounts that not only arise out of experience and are firmly grounded in it, but that stay in touch with that experience in drawing their conclusions (Code, 1988: 196).
6. This is particularly true for western Jews, but presents problems where there are greater mixtures of ethnically different Jews.

# REFERENCES

Cesarani, David (2001) 'Memory, Representation and Education', in John K. Roth and Elizabeth Maxwell (eds) *Remembering For the Future: The Holocaust in an Age of Genocide*. England: Palgrave Press (pp. 231–6).

Code, L. (1988) 'Experience, Knowledge, Responsibility', in M. Griffiths and M. Whitford (eds) *Feminist Perspectives in Philosophy*. Bloomington, IN: Indiana University Press (pp. 187–204).

Fackenheim, Emil (1987) *What is Judaism? An Interpretation for the Present Age*. New York: Summit Books.

Goldenberg, Myrna (1990) 'Different Horrors, Same Hell: Women Remembering the Holocaust, in Roger S. Gottlieb (ed.) *Thinking the Unthinkable: Meanings of the Holocaust*. New York: Paulist (pp. 150–66).

Heinemann, Marelene (1986) *Gender and Destiny: Women Writers and the Holocaust*. New York: Greenwood Press.

Kaufman, Debra (1991) *Rachel's Daughters*. New Brunswick: Rutgers University Press.

Kaufman, Debra (1996) 'Introduction: Gender, Scholarship and the Holocaust', *Contemporary Jewry*, 17: 3–5.

Kaufman, Debra (1998) 'Gender and Jewish Identity among Twenty-Somethings in the United States', in M. Cousineau (ed.) *Religion in a Changing World*. New York: Greenwood Press (pp. 49–56).

Kaufman, Debra (1999) 'Embedded Categories: Identity Among Jewish Young Adults in the US', *Race Gender and Class* 6 (4): 76–87.

Kaufman, Debra (2001) 'Post-Holocaust Narratives: A Sociological Approach to Collective Consciousness, Memory and History', Invited Paper for an International Conference, funded, in part, by the American Sociological Association/National Science Foundation fund for the Advancement of the Discipline entitled: Sociological Perspectives on the Holocaust and Post-Holocaust Jewish Life, October 25–27, 2001, Rutgers, The State University of New Jersey, New Brunswick, NJ.

Kaufman, Debra and Richardson, Barbara (1982) *Achievement and Women*. New York: Free Press.

LaCapra, Dominick (1998) *History and Memory after Auschwitz*. Ithaca: Cornell University Press.

Lagerwey, Mary (1996) 'Reading Anne Frank and Elie Wiesel: Voice and Gender in Stories of the Holocaust', *Contemporary Jewry*, 17: 48–65.

Meyer, Michael (1990) *Jewish Identity in the Modern World*. Seattle: University of Washington Press.

Seidler-Feller, Chaim (1991) 'Responses', in David M. Gordis and Yav Ben Horin (eds) *Jewish Identity in America Los Angeles*. Susan and David Wilstein Institute of Jewish Policy Studies, University of Judaism (pp. 61–5).

Webber, Jonathan (1992) 'The Future of Auschwitz: Some Personal Reflections', The First Frank Green Lecture, Oxford Centre for Postgraduate Hebrew Studies, Yarnton, England.

# PART III

ZIONISM, THE YISHUV AND THE STATE OF ISRAEL

# 11

# Girls in the Zionist Youth Movements in Libya

## RACHEL SIMON

The way youth is shaped at home, in school and during extracurricular activities has a tremendous impact on the future development of society. The first two factors, home and school, are primarily, though not exclusively, dominated by adult ideas, guidance, planning, control and operation. Extracurricular activities, on the other hand, might leave much leeway, initiative and freedom to the youth. A unique phenomenon among the latter activities is the youth movement which in its essence aims to create a special and separate youth leisure environment in anticipation of a new world order, based on ideals which tend to reach utopian dimensions, most often including loyalty, friendship, equality, purity, self-sacrifice, self-fulfillment and love of nature. Jewish youth movements added their unique components of religion and Zionism, at times connected with various degrees of universal political ideologies of the Right, the Center and the Left. Much of the youth movement culture developed in Europe since the nineteenth century, while the Jewish ones drew many of their principles and modes of operation also from Israel. The operation of youth movements in Middle Eastern and North African countries was often influenced from abroad and was to a large extent part of the modernization process and a departure from traditional life.[1] Yet the society at large, including the youth, continued in most cases to keep many traditional customs and to honor the past and its representations, including leadership, behavior patterns and inter-gender relations.

While some research has been conducted on Zionist youth movements in individual Middle Eastern and North African countries, there is no comparative study dealing with the region as a whole or in comparison with Israel or Europe, and no study had been devoted to gender issues. Similarly, there are no comprehensive studies on youth movements in Libya or in the Middle East and North Africa in general, and especially no treatment of gender issues. Thus, while various studies occasionally relate to the participation of girls and gender issues, it is impossible at the current stage to make a comprehensive comparison between gender issues in the Zionist youth movements in Libya vis-à-vis other Zionist, Jewish or Middle Eastern and North African youth movements.

## DEVELOPMENTS IN LIBYA AND THEIR IMPLICATIONS ON JEWISH YOUTH

The development of the youth movements in Libya was combined with comprehensive changes in the society at large which had a significant impact on the Jewish community. The nineteenth century reforms in the Ottoman empire, under whose rule Libya was until 1911, growing European involvement, Italian rule (1911–43) and British Military Administration lasting until 1951 when Libya became an independent Arab kingdom – all these had various repercussions on the status of the Jewish community, its internal developments and its relations with the authorities, the neighboring Arab and Italian society and outside powers. Other sources of influence on Libyan Jews were developments in the Jewish world, world economy and Middle Eastern and North African politics.[2]

One segment of society to be particularly transformed as a result of changing conditions is the youth. Jewish youth in Libya encountered changes first in the field of education, when foreign schools were established. Cultural and social extracurricular activities fostered by the various educational systems initiated changes in the way youth spent their after-school time. In addition, recreational organizations of adult Jews gradually established special youth branches. The subsequent and most significant step in this development took place in the 1940s, when Zionist youth movements were established independent of educational or adult organizations, and ushered changes in the behavior and outlook of the youth.

## TRADITIONAL JEWISH YOUTH ACTIVITIES IN LIBYA

Youth oriented extracurricular activities in pre-twentieth century Libya greatly differed from the Zionist youth movements of the 1940s. The former focused on religion and were organized by traditional adult males solely for boys. The main operation of these groups was centered on the synagogue, where the boys were chanting parts of the Psalms and the liturgy, especially on the Sabbath and festivals.[3] This was an activity planned by adults and for adult purposes, and was closely related to study and learning, although it had some artistic and emotional elements involved in it. Moreover, this activity was restricted to males, young and old: females had no active part in it, except as distant listeners.

## THE EMERGENCE OF THE ZIONIST YOUTH MOVEMENTS IN LIBYA

The new Jewish youth movements of the 1940s turned from recreational in character into Zionist, and most often pioneering, organizations for both genders. The main impetus for their establishment and for the direction they followed came from Palestinian Jews: starting with soldiers who served with the British army which was stationed in Libya at the time, followed by emissaries from Palestine. Even after the Palestinian Jews had left and indigenous Jews led the youth movements, the latter continued to rely to a great extent on ideological, literary and visual materials from Zionist organizations and individuals in Palestine. The Zionist youth movements were different from the previous youth organizations not only in their goals, composition and activities, but also in their leadership: the latter was composed of people who were not of rabbinical background, were not much older than the youth they led, and even included women.

Soldiers, emissaries and youth movement leaders and regular members corresponded with organizations and individuals in Palestine, describing their activities and views, and sending them a large amount of internal documentation, such as regulations and organizational charts. In addition, local Jewish weeklies and newsletters reported on youth movement activities. Much of this information is found in archives in Israel (mainly in the Central Zionist Archives in Jerusalem and the Yad Tabenkin Archives in Ramat Ef'al), and serves as the primary source for this study. This is complemented by memoirs published by soldiers, emissaries, and youth movement members who were involved in youth movement activities in the 1940s.

## IDEOLOGY AND REALITY

The Zionist youth movements aimed at a comprehensive transformation of the Jewish community, with the goal of creating a 'New Jew', immigrating to Palestine, and preferably settling in a kibbutz, conducting a 'productive' lifestyle, namely, work in agriculture or industry. Selected older members joined a training camp introducing them to agricultural and industrial communal living. Ideologically, the youth movements advocated gender equality, in Libya as in Palestine. Realizing utopia, however, encounters numerous hurdles due to personal, social, economic and cultural factors. And because the Zionist youth movements operated in Libya in most cases for less than a decade, it is no wonder that one can observe only beginnings of the implementation of their goals, including gender equality. Nonetheless, in comparison to the past, even those steps were a great leap forward, including the recognition and advocating of these principles. Since most of the membership emigrated to Israel in 1949–52 and settled across the country in numerous urban and rural settlements, it is virtually impossible to examine wide-range and long-term implications of the youth movement experience on the graduates, except in isolated, individual cases.

## ORGANIZATIONS AND MEMBERSHIP

The main Zionist youth movements operating in Libya in the 1940s were Tenu'at ha-No'ar (the Youth Movement), which sprang out of the Ben-Yehudah Society for the study of the Hebrew language (the latter operating since the early 1930s); Tenu'at ha-Tzofim ha-Datiyim (The Jewish Boys Scouts – their official English name), which sprang out of the same organization; Makabi ha-Tza'ir (Young Maccabi), an offshoot of the World Maccabi sports organization (the latter active in Libya since the early 1920s); and the Halutz (the Pioneer), which included, at least in principle, youth 18 years and older who were graduates of the pioneering youth movements. Other organizations included Gedud Megine ha-Safah ha-'Ivrit (the Battalion of the Guardians of the Hebrew Language) and Betar.

The average annual number of members in the Zionist youth movements in Libya was around 800, about half of them girls. During the period of the mass emigration to Israel (1949–52), when the total number was 1,230,[4] the pioneering youth movements united under the umbrella organization of ha-No'ar ha-Ahid (the United Youth), officially affiliated with Bnai Akiva, the youth movement of the religious national Mizrachi party, while the Halutz became affiliated with Bahad (acronym for Berit Halutzim Datiyim, Alliance of Religious Pioneers). Until then, there was no official affiliation with Zionist youth movements outside of Libya (except for the World Maccabi Organization) and with the political parties with which they were connected, although there were strong contacts with individuals and organizations of the New Yishuv. This resulted from the understanding of the emissaries that due to the small number of activists in Libya, the general ignorance there of political life in Palestine, and the need to keep the activities of foreigners clandestine, the youth movements should not be affiliated with political organizations and be involved in party politics, but should incorporate general concepts of pioneering combined with traditional Judaism.[5]

## THE APPEAL OF THE ZIONIST YOUTH MOVEMENTS

The pioneering Zionist youth movements in Libya were established shortly after the British occupation (1942–43) by outsiders who were full of zeal to drastically change the character of the community and to turn Libyan Jews into Zionists. The youth was viewed as a major channel to reach this goal. The youth, as much of the community, was ready for as yet undefined change due to their disappointment with Italy, which for several decades served as their focus of inspiration and imitation. This frustration resulted from the events of the Second World War in Libya, when the Jews suffered under fascist anti-Jewish legislation, with many of them exiled internally and several hundreds even reached concentration camps in Europe.[6] Zionism, which had existed in Libya since the late-nineteenth century, strengthened with the arrival of Jewish Palestinian soldiers during the war. The mere presence of the soldiers was an enormous boost to Jewish morale and the rise of Zionism, which spread also as a result of initiatives of the soldiers. Thus, many Jewish children absorbed Zionist ideology as students of the new Hebrew schools which had been established by the soldiers or strongly influenced by them and were later run by teachers who received educational materials from the New Yishuv in Palestine. This made a large number of Jewish children eager to realize Zionist ideology, and the obvious course to achieve this was by joining the Zionist youth movements.

Other options of modern youth activity were very limited for Jews. While many Jews in Libya, especially in the major coastal urban centers, were Italianized to various degrees, their involvement in Italian adult and youth organizations, which was never high, greatly subsided following the Second World War. And while Jews had often had close economic and social relations with Arabs, they hardly participated in Arab and Muslim political, social and cultural organizations. Thus, Jewish youth who aspired for modern youth culture had found it almost exclusively in the Zionist youth movements.

## GENDER-BASED GRADUATED DEVELOPMENT

All founders of the Zionist youth movements in Libya were men: either Jewish Palestinian soldiers in the British army or Jewish emissaries from Palestine. Because of social and cultural conventions in Libya, it was easier for the male founders to launch their operation among boys. The first indigenous guides (madrikhim), whom the founders had trained as the primary base upon which the movements would grow, were boys in their mid-teens. Due to the local conditions, both soldiers and emissaries had to act clandestinely because of the objection of the British to external national activity among the Jews, which would be in opposition to the closely monitored national activity among the Arabs. The founders had to act swiftly, because the soldiers did not know how long their British officers would tolerate their activities within the Jewish community and when their units would be transferred to Europe. Likewise, the emissaries did not know how long they could operate before they might be forced to leave suddenly. Consequently, it was easier to start the operation among boys who were already active in the Zionist Ben-Yehudah Society and knew Hebrew.

One of the most difficult problems of the youth movement was the participation of girls, whose first steps were accompanied by apprehension from several directions. Traditionalists of the old Jewish quarter of Tripoli looked with suspicion on the 'free' and social relations that the founders of the youth movement wanted to create among male and female members. It seems that communal opposition was not the only reason that girls were slow to join the youth movement: their cultural background was another reason. Several guides and especially the emissaries, felt that one reason for the small number of girls was that their intellectual development and their level of education were lower, sometimes even to a larger extent, than those of the boys: many girls did not attend school at all, and especially not Hebrew schools where Jewish history was taught. Thus, they often lacked the ideological incentive to join the youth movement, though many eventually got it from their male relatives. Consequently, girls started to join the youth movement gradually, only after it operated for a while, following demands and explanations by an emissary, who stated that one should not view otherwise the structure of a healthy society.[7]

Once the guides' course had been concluded and its graduates could operate on their own, groups of youth were established, mostly divided into three age groups subdivided by gender: due to social conventions it was inconceivable to establish mixed groups of boys and girls. Each group met once or twice a week, and a general coeducational meeting usually took place on Saturday ('Oneg Shabbat). Even though boys and girls were members of the same organization, their activities were more often than not separate, and even in mixed-gender operations, there was in fact a virtual divide between boys and girls due to social and cultural conventions. Still, the youth movement served as a bridge between separate components of the community. Although the cultural, social and economic breakdown of the membership of the youth movements is not clear, it is evident that they included both schoolgirls and illiterate maids.[8] Thus, with its ideology of equality and promotion of manual work, the youth movement helped to develop closer inter-gender relations as well as between social classes.

After the Zionist youth movements had been operating in Libya for a while, a few females joined the guides corps, but their number was always lower than that of the males. Moreover, females guided only groups of girls while males guided groups of boys and girls alike. This resulted from the higher number of males in the youth movement and from the attitude toward leadership: it was more acceptable to have a man lead a girls' group than for a woman to head a boys' group.

The guides had a weekly meeting, chaired by a male guidance coordinator, to prepare the following week's activities. The information on these meetings and on the operation of the groups indicates that boys and girls received similar instruction. Still, the fact that girls did not acquire the same Jewish and Hebrew education that most boys received, required special adjustments in their activities. The emissaries felt that there was great ignorance regarding Judaism and Zionism, especially among girls, who lacked elementary knowledge: some could not read Hebrew and did not even understand Hebrew songs which were an important component of the youth movement culture. Consequently, it was necessary to teach them Hebrew and ancient history from the days of the Patriarchs.[9] Thus, although the overall program was similar, many girls required additional instruction of language and history.

## COMMUNAL ATTITUDE TOWARD THE YOUTH MOVEMENT AND FEMALE PARTICIPATION

The Zionist youth movements were criticized by the traditional elements in the community who realized that they aimed at a different kind of society than the existing one in every aspect, including the role of women. Female membership in the youth movement was a greater departure from tradition than joining the workforce and attending school. Becoming a wage-earner was accepted due to economic necessity, and female work was often gender segregated. Similarly, most schools were gender-based and attending them was viewed as a prerequisite for upward social and economic mobility. Joining a youth movement, on the other hand, was regarded by many as a waste of time, especially for girls, who as a result spent less time at home tending to their household chores, and this was usually in addition to the time the girls had already spent – or wasted, according to some – in school. Worse still, ideas which the girls acquired in the Zionist youth movement directed them toward a society completely different from the existing one. And even if they themselves would not be able to fulfill many of these ideas, they, as the mothers of the next generation might instill these ideas among their children of both genders.

## PROBLEMS ARISING FROM MIXED-GENDER ENVIRONMENT

A major objection against girls' participation in the Zionist youth movements was that the latter enabled meetings of non-kin boys and girls. Although the groups were gender-based, there was no total separation between boys and girls: some activities were coeducational and several girls' groups were guided by males. The fact that the founders and most guides were males could at times cause problems and suspicion. Thus, one of the Jewish Palestinian founders of the youth movement presented himself as a bachelor, and regarded it as natural that adolescent female members of the youth movement would fall in love with their guide and hope for 'shidukh' (match). Consequently, he had to be extremely careful because some female members fell in love with him.[10] In another case, an indigenous guide was apparently less careful and was suspected of behavior which was viewed as unbecoming according to local conventions regarding modesty and religiosity. He was blamed for taking the girls for hikes out of town and thus being outside of communal supervision. It was also claimed that he prevented the boys from joining what were commonly regarded as mixed-gender activities, and even worse: that he conducted these meetings in closed rooms, while the girls were lying on beds. This guide was suspended from his duties because of these accusations, which he regarded as baseless, and resulting only from the opposition of reactionary elements in the community.[11] Another activity which the youth movements, and apparently especially Maccabi, sponsored was mixed dancing on Saturday and festival evenings. Although the traditional elements in the community objected to this, they did not prevent it altogether, because this served as a safety valve, and enabled the youth to enjoy themselves in a Jewish environment, thus somewhat reducing the chances of mixing with gentiles.[12]

## INTER-GENDER RELATIONS

Traditional behavior patterns continued to be manifested even in an environment of people who regarded themselves as progressive and promoting gender equality. This was reflected in both physical and spiritual spheres. Thus, despite the talk of equality, it was female members who came every Friday morning to scrub the floors of the clubhouse (qen).[13]

The gap between boys and girls was noticed in particular during mixed-gender activities, which were conducted mainly on Saturdays and holidays. On these occasions, it became evident that girls possessed less knowledge regarding many general and Jewish subjects which were regarded as important by the leadership. Furthermore, girls were shy to participate in general discussions due to real or perceived lack of knowledge as well as customary avoidance of joining male conversations and expressing their opinion in public in mixed non-kin society. Since formal Jewish and Hebrew education for girls was a relatively new phenomenon in Libya, and contrary to boys, not all girls received it, the educational and cultural gap between boys and girls in the youth movement as regards Jewish and Hebrew culture and history was strongly felt, especially in the mixed-gender meetings.

This came on top of the traditional cultural and social separation between the genders and it made the involvement of girls in mixed-gender activities even more difficult. One of the ways to accustom boys and girls to meet and to cooperate in mutual operations was to set up couples and send them with Keren Kayemet le-Yisra'el (Jewish National Fund) collection boxes to Jewish homes to solicit donations. After a while, the ice broke and many couples were set up who eventually got married. Somewhat later, with the establishment of the Haganah (Jewish defense) cells (often drawing on youth movement membership) and the beginning of paramilitary training, girls got involved also in this mixed-gender non-traditional activity for women, though it was very difficult at first to convince girls that it was impossible to train in dresses and one had to wear trousers.[14]

## THE HALUTZ AND THE HAKHSHARAH

Jewish youth over the age of 18, and in particular graduates of the pioneering Zionist youth movements, were expected to join the Halutz which aimed to consolidate the ideological foundation of the Zionist youth and complete their adjustment to communal life and training in agriculture. The number of Halutz members, about a third of whom were women, grew from about 100 in fall 1944 to about 200 in 1948 while during the mass emigration period, the Halutz/Bahad numbered about 300.[15] In order to accomplish its intellectual objectives, the Halutz, similarly to the youth movements, conducted readings and presentations on various subjects combined with discussions once or twice a week. Yet theory in itself was not considered as sufficient for adjusting to a new lifestyle and the learning of new occupations. The main innovation of the Halutz was regarding active preparation for communal life, for which the training camp (hakhsharah) was established. Altogether, several subsequent hakhsharot were established in Libya, one ending after a short period of time (June–November 1944) because of disagreements with the owners, and two others following Arab attacks in 1945 and 1948. While the first two hakhsharot were in farms outside of Tripoli, the third was an urban hakhsharah based on crafts, industry and building, conducted at the camp and in town. Common to all hakhsharot was communal living, self-management, mutual budget and adherence to a binding, agreed upon set of regulations.

The hakhsharah was the most controversial stage in the activities of the pioneering Zionist youth movement, because it involved non-kin males and females living together at close quarters, far from family and communal supervision, and it focused on training in hitherto despised manual occupations. For most of the time, indeed, no hakhsharah managed to include female members. The first hakhsharah did not have any female members, while the second and third hakhsharot got very few female members after operating for several months. It seems that the third, the urban hakhsharah, had at the most four females out of 20 members.[16] In all cases, these women had relatives who were already members in the hakhsharah, and there was never a sole female member. Only at an interim period between two full-scale hakhsharot, when participants worked for a few hours a day and did not live in the place, a larger number of youth movement girls aged 14–15 joined the experiment: they worked in agriculture, which in itself was an innovation for Jewish urban youth of both genders, but did not participate in full communal life.[17]

The advocates of the hakhsharah felt the need to have female members for ideological reasons – but also for practical ones. Despite declarations on gender equality and emphasis on 'productive' occupations, more subtle expressions show that they felt the lack of women especially with regard to fulfilling traditional female jobs, like cooking and cleaning.[18] And indeed, once women became members of the hakhsharah, they were hardly involved in agricultural or industrial work, but performed mainly household tasks (e.g., cooking, cleaning and sewing).[19] Nonetheless, even this kind of participation was regarded as a great achievement, because families and the community at large opposed it, and the women moved physically out of traditional settings, even though they continued to perform traditional occupations. Their small number and the fact that they joined the hakhsharah later than men, were the main reasons that women did not reach leadership positions in the hakhsharah.

The hakhsharah was a model for the pioneering Zionist youth and their supporters in Tripoli, and became a frequent destination for visits, especially on the weekend, by youth and adults alike. While the youth as a whole admired the hakhsharah members for their manual work in agriculture, girls were particularly impressed by the participation of women in this experiment. Although only few women actively joined the hakhsharah, one should remember that it was difficult for men, too, to join, and their numbers were never high. Thus, there were more people – men and women alike – who supported the hakhsharah in principle, including its female component, than had actually become active members.

## CONTACTS WITH PIONEER WOMEN IN PALESTINE

As time passed, girls in the youth movement showed interest in general developments within the New Yishuv in Palestine, and especially in the status and activities of pioneer women (halutzot) and female kibbutz members (haverot). Thus, among the frequent requests of the guides for instructional materials from the various institutions in Palestine (and especially from ha-Kibbutz ha-Me'uhad and the Histadrut), one can find repeated requests for copies of publications on female issues, like *ha-Haverah ba-Kibbutz* and *Devar ha-Po'elet*, and on specific pioneer heroines, like Hanna Szenes. The requests indicated that the members, and especially the girls, were interested in these subjects, and were greatly moved by the sacrifices made by pioneer women in everyday life in the kibbutz and their participation in the war effort.[20] The unique female point of reference was also expressed by the desire of groups of girls to correspond with kibbutz girls – and not just any kibbutz child. Few of the letters[21] show the idealized views of the Tripolitan youth (girls and boys alike) regarding the life and status of kibbutz members in general and of Jewish girls and women in particular, even among the pioneers. It should be noted, that despite the fact that girls received less formal Jewish and Hebrew education than most boys, several of them were able to correspond in Hebrew with kibbutz girls.

## CONCLUSION

Several hundred Jewish boys and girls, mainly in Tripoli but also in several other Libyan towns, joined the Zionist youth movements in the 1940s. Their joining, and especially that of the girls, indicated their readiness to act in order to fulfill their desire for a different lifestyle culturally, socially, economically and politically. Fulfilling this wish was slow and full of internal and external hurdles. Although only few girls reached leadership positions in the youth movement or joined the highest level of activity – the hakhsharah – both genders underwent significant metamorphosis. Since the experience was of a short duration and the youth movement members were scattered in Israel following immigration, it is hard to tell the long-term impact of the youth movement experience upon their future life. It is clear, though, that very few Libyan Jews joined the kibbutz and no youth movement female graduate reached senior political, administrative or economic position in Israel.

Jews in Libya lived in urban and rural communities on the Mediterranean coast and in the hinterland. These communities had their socioeconomic, cultural as well as spatial characteristics, unique to their geographical settings. Yet Jewish communities in Libya as elsewhere in the Jewish Diaspora also had their 'virtual space'. Thus, for many years, trade and crafts in Libya were in Jewish hands and on the Sabbath and Jewish holidays, all work stopped in villages, towns and ports. When the Italian fascist regime wanted to force economic activity on the Sabbath, it stated that 'Tripoli is not Tel Aviv', namely, Tripolitan life should be characterized by Italian and not by Jewish customs and lifestyle. During the 1940s, the Zionist youth movements and especially the hakhsharah tried to create a 'virtual Eretz Yisrael' in Libya with songs, dance, language, discussions and 'productive work', based on the ideas they received from the Jewish Palestinian soldiers and emissaries. This 'virtual space' was idealistic, trying to leave one world yet still remain there, enter a new environment both physically and spiritually yet not forsake tradition. It was realized, however, in Libya as in other places, that it is easier to change spatial settings than sociocultural concepts and relations. Thus, although the new environment was designed to maintain gender relations based on equality, both components were not ready yet to transform the idealized concept to a reality.

## NOTES

1. On Zionist youth movements in Muslim countries see *No'ar ben Shene 'Olamot: Tenu'ot ha-No'ar be-Artsot ha-Islam* (Ramat-Ef'al: Yad Tabenkin, 1995).
2. On the Jews of Libya see Renzo de Felice, *Jews in an Arab Land: Libya, 1835–1970* (Austin: University of Texas Press, 1985).
3. On several boys' choirs in Tripoli (including photographs), see Frig'a Zu'arts, 'Amishadai Guetta, Tsuri'el Shaked, Gavri'el Arbib, Frig'a Tayar (eds) *Yahadut Luv* (Tel Aviv: Va'ad Kehilot Luv be-Yisra'el, 1982), pp. 105, 109, 116, 119, 122.
4. Yosef Mimun and Shalom Hasan, National Secretariat of Bene Akiva-Bahad, Tripoli, to the Youth and Halutz Department, Religious Section, Zionist Organization, Jerusalem, 31 July 1949 – Central Zionist Archives (henceforth: CZA), file S32/123.
5. For details see: Yishai Arnon, 'Tenu'at 'he-Haluts' bi-Tripoli u-keshareha 'im ha-Kibuts ha-Dati', *Pe'amim* 44 (Summer 1990): 132–57; Ya'ir Du'er, 'Masa' li-Tripoli', in Ben-Zion Rubin (ed.) *Luv: Hedim min ha-Yoman* (Jerusalem: ha-Agudah le-Moreshet Yahadut Luv, 1988), p. 72.
6. On the Jews of Libya during the Second World War, see R. Simon, 'It Could have Happened There: The Jews of Libya during the Second World War', *Africana Journal* 16 (1994): 391–422.
7. Du'er, p. 56.

8. Shemu'el Spiro and Mosheh Ya'ari, 'Le-Irgun 'Aliyat ha-No'ar mi-Tripoli', *Yedi'ot ha-Mahlaqah la-'Aliyat Yeladim ve-No'ar*, 11 (October, 1949), p. 22 – CZA, file S20/468.
9. Zamir (Vilo Katz) and Yariv (Ya'ir Duer), Tripoli to Ben-Yehudah and Yosifon, 2 December 1943 – CZA, file S6/1984; Y-R [Ya'ir Duer], 'he-Halutz ha-Ahid bi-Tripoli', *ha-Po'el ha-Tza'ir*, 37 (49) (1 October 1944); Avraham Adadi, Ben Yehudah Youth Movement, Tripoli, to Youth Department (Zionist Organization, Jerusalem), 14 March 1946 – CZA, file S32/1068; Duer, p. 56.
10. Duer, p. 60.
11. Elia Azaria, Tripoli (to Ya'ir Duer), 27 Tishre 706 (4 October 1945) – Yad Tabenkin Archives (henceforth: YTA), Div. 'A-25/Libya, Box 1, file 9; Yosef, Tripoli, (to Ya'ir Duer), 17 October 1945 – YTA, Div. 'A-25/Libya, Box 1, file 9. For claims on problems on religious grounds see also Yehoshu'a Mimun, Tripoli, (to Ya'ir Duer), 20 November 1945 – YTA, Div. 'A-25/Libya, Box 1, file 2; Avraham Adadi, Ben Yehudah Youth Movement, Tripoli, to Youth Department, Zionist Organization, Jerusalem, 23 April 1946 – CZA, file S32/1068.
12. *Yahadut Luv*, p. 160. On Purim, Passover and Sukkot parties, see Roberto Arbib, *The Jews of Libya at the Beginning of the Twentieth Century and their Current Condition under Arab Rule*, Report presented at the Center of the Zionist Organization, Rome on 9 February 1954 [in Hebrew] – Maccabi Archives. In 1944, the Military Police came to check that no Jewish Palestinian soldiers participated in a Purim party, because the Jewish Quarter was out of bounds for them. See Duer, pp. 74–5.
13. D. (Ya'ir Duer), 'Tenu'at ha-No'ar ha-Halutzi bi-Tripoli' (Early 705/Fall 1944) – CZA, file S32/1068; Duer, p. 71. Saulino Nahum stated that he helped them find the house; see: Saulino Nahum, Tripoli, to the Zionist Organization, Jerusalem, 26 March 1945 – CZA, file S5/787.
14. D. (Ya'ir Duer), 'Tenu'at ha-No'ar ha-Halutzi bi-Tripoli' (Early 705/Fall 1944) – CZA, file S32/1068; Duer, p. 56.
15. (Ya'ir Duer), 'Tripoli' [*Igeret?*, 1944/45?] – YTA, Div. 2/OL, Ya'ir Duer series; Yarqoni, Education, Tripoli, 14 February 1945 – YTA, Div. OL, Box 1, file 2; Yehoshu'a Mimun, Tripoli, to ha-Kibbutz ha-Me'uhad, 9 July 1946 – YTA, Div. 2/OL, Box 1, file 4.
16. Two women joined in June 1947: 'Alon Qevutzat ha-Hakhsharah, Tripoli, No. 6 (14 July 1947) – YTA, Div. 2/OL, Box 1, file 3. In 1948 there were four women: *Yoman ha-hakhsharah*, part 2 (4 January–9 June 1948) – YTA, Div. 'A/25, Ya'ir Duer Series, Box 1, file 11.
17. *34 Years of History of Maccabi Tripoli* (in Hebrew, 1954) – Maccabi Archives; Shalom Tamam, Maccabi ha-Tza'ir, Tripoli, to Youth Dept. Religious Section, Jerusalem, 7 October 1946 – CZA, file S32/121.
18. The lack of women causes difficulties in the atmosphere and the kitchen according to Yariv (Ya'ir Duer), Report on Activities in Tripoli, Summer 1944 – CZA, file S6/1984.
19. *Yoman ha-hakhsharah*, part 2 (4 January–9 June 1948) – YTA, Div. 'A/25, Ya'ir Duer Series, Box 1, file 11.
20. Avraham Adadi, Tripoli, to ha-Kibbutz ha-Me'uhad, 4 March 1946 – YTA, Div. 2/OL, Box 1, file 2.
21. The letters are kept mainly in the CZA and YTA.

# 12

# *The West in the East: Patterns of Cultural Change as a Personal Kibbutz Experience*

ESTHER MEIR-GLITZENSTEIN

European colonial rule in the Middle East and North Africa in the nineteenth and twentieth centuries had broad ramifications for all aspects of life in these regions. One of these aspects was the intercultural encounter, which is discussed extensively in the essays of the Jewish writer and thinker Jacqueline Kahanoff, a native of Egypt whose parents' families came from Iraq and Tunisia. Kahanoff, whose first name is French and whose last name is Russian-Jewish, grew up under the influence of Egyptian-Arab culture and English and French culture. She used the term 'Levantine culture' to refer to the unique culture that developed along the shores of the Mediterranean as a result of this encounter; in it, eastern elements and western influences existed side by side and one on top of another.

In one of her essays, Kahanoff describes the stages of the westernization process experienced by the inhabitants of the Islamic countries in the wake of contact with European rule and European cultures:

> In the first stage of contact between these two peoples, which are at different levels of technological development, the local elite becomes imitative, diligently picking up and digesting the ideas and techniques of the conquering culture, and thereby rejecting out of embarrassment the values of its own society. ... This elite, local in origin but western, at least to some extent, in education, little by little gains self-confidence and learns to blend the various components of its self into a fairly cohesive and harmonious whole. It then becomes more independent in judgment, more critical of western [colonial] settlers and of the ideals that they advocate but do not live by ... and moreover, it learns to have a

greater appreciation of the values of the old society. More and more this elite yearns to participate in government with the ruling group and to make use of the western techniques for the benefit and enjoyment of the local society, and not only for the benefit and enjoyment of the settlers. The settlers laugh at this elite because of the superficial, crude imitation of western mores, and the westerners are seized by an emotional idealization of the old local cultures that they essentially destroyed. In the context of the Middle East, the Levantine is someone who bought this new culture, first as something external and desirable, and then as an integral part of his own being.[1]

The first stage in the adoption of western cultural values by the Jews of Islamic countries took place in each country in accordance with the circumstances of the European powers' penetration of the region. In Iraq, which was part of the Ottoman Empire but was included in the sphere of strategic and economic interests of the British Empire, the Jewish community was influenced primarily by British culture. In the nineteenth century that culture filtered in from the British colony in India, where there was a well-established community of Jewish immigrants from Baghdad.[2] After the British took over Iraq in the First World War, there was direct British influence, both through the Mandatory government established in Iraq (1922–32) and through direct relations with institutions and companies in England. Even after Iraq achieved formal independence, the British remained a dominant factor in molding the character and administrative patterns of the country.

Throughout that period, the Jewish communities of Iraq had a modern educational system, founded in 1864 by the Paris-based Alliance Israelite Universelle as part of an overall system of philanthropic, solidarity and reform activities run by the Alliance in Jewish communities in the Middle East and North Africa. These schools strongly emphasized learning the French language, literature and culture, as well as Turkish, English and Arabic.[3] This modern education rapidly altered the social and occupational structure of Iraqi Jewry: a large middle class developed, and educated young people began to work in the civil service and liberal professions. The structural changes were accompanied by changes in all areas of life: young people abandoned the traditional attire in favor of western dress and added French or English names to their Jewish names; the middle class began to move into new, western-style neighborhoods; some middle-class Jews bought cars; and many homes even had telephones. In the old houses, too, improvements were made, including the installation of modern plumbing.[4]

One of the main goals of the Alliance was to influence the young Jewish women in Islamic countries, on the assumption that educated women would act as agents of change to build a new generation, westernized and educated. This influence was already evident among the first students in the Baghdad girls' school. A report from Baghdad in 1903, a decade after the opening of the school, notes the adoption of western dress by graduates of the school, not only for everyday use but even in conservative settings such as weddings; the demand by the educated young women for greater equality in the family; and even the adoption of western principles of cleanliness and hygiene in family life in general and in caring for small children in particular.[5]

Education spread, encountering almost no opposition from the community leadership. The community dignitaries and rabbis generally supported the existence of modern schools, despite their reservations about anti-religious teaching, and as a result middle-class society, which was sympathetic to the trend and encouraged it, gradually grew. We can get an idea of this atmosphere from a rebuke by Rabbi Shimon Agassi, apparently the only rabbi who came out vehemently against European education for young people. After bitterly denouncing modern education for boys, he also rejected the changes that had occurred in the education of girls:

> They started having the girls walk around outside completely bareheaded, with a short dress down to the knees, the rest of the legs covered only by thin stockings, and a black coat like the coats of Christian priests covering their bodies from front to back, and whoever wears some sort of ultra-audacious outfit is lauded. ... All the lowly attributes that we wrote about above regarding the boys are even more extreme among the girls, because they do not study Torah and they are also extremely arrogant and fickle. ... And the mother, instead of slapping her face when she sees her children getting such a wild education, is delighted to see her son chirping in French and her daughter chatting away in French and plucking a harp, and she says, 'I rejoice, I rejoice, when I see my children completely French, the glorious work of my hands.'[6]

This denunciation clearly depicts a community that is sympathetic to the cultural changes, with the adults expecting their children to adopt new, foreign behavioral patterns. Rabbi Agassi's protest makes it clear that there was a consensus in the community regarding the adoption of the western lifestyle – not just the superficial aspects but the essence of the lifestyle, too.

Westernization penetrated all Islamic countries in this way. With exposure to western culture moving through the socioeconomic elite to the middle and lower-middle classes. One result of the changes was that more and more young people left their home towns for the big cities. Some even left the country, traveling to the cultural centers in Egypt, Lebanon and western Europe for an education, for business or to improve their legal position and socioeconomic status. Some of these young people went to Palestine for economic, family or ideological reasons.

In this paper I wish to examine a specific case in this westernization process: the effects of immigration to Palestine on the further westernization of groups of educated, somewhat westernized teenagers with a Zionist background who moved from Iraq to Palestine shortly before the establishment of the State of Israel and spent various periods of time on kibbutzim. To this end, we will look at aspects of their exposure to the cultural values of Palestine and their reaction to them. But before we examine this intercultural encounter, let us look at the setting in which the encounter took place: the kibbutz.

## THE KIBBUTZ CONTEXT

In the 1940s and early 1950s, kibbutzim affiliated with Hakibbutz Hameuchad housed dozens of training groups for teenagers from Arab countries who were preparing to found new settlements and to absorb the waves of immigrants expected from Islamic countries. Ethnically and culturally speaking, these training groups were small islands of oriental immigrants within a society of Ashkenazim who had been in Palestine for a long time. Relations between immigrants and old-timers on the kibbutz were intense, with the old-timers being heavily involved in the integration of the newcomers, as inevitably happens in a small, intimate, demanding society like kibbutz society in the 1940s. The old-timers and immigrants were in contact in all areas of life: in the fields, in the dining room, in the clothing storeroom, at joint cultural events, and so on.

The old-timers and immigrants were separated by a cultural gap: the gap between the 'Levantine culture' as defined by Kahanoff, which drew on British and French culture, and the Yishuv culture, which drew on central and eastern European sources. In this case, the old-timers' culture was dominant: it should be kept in mind that the kibbutzim, which had adopted a radical, revolutionary value system and championed national and social revolution, were the prime force behind the conscious development of a new native-Hebrew identity before Israeli independence.[7] Because they considered it their job to impart this identity to newcomers, they insisted that the immigrants adapt to the customs and mores of kibbutz society and adopt its values, relinquishing other values and customs, which they associated with the Diaspora. Furthermore, in the name of Zionist ideology, the immigrants from Islamic countries were called upon to renounce the norms of Arab and Islamic culture that formed part of their identity: the language, the literature, the music, and all other eastern identifying marks.[8]

Due to the close-knit society and intrusive relations on kibbutzim, the immigrants there were exposed, more than in any other form of settlement, to the social, individual and intimate elements of the Ashkenazic kibbutz way of life. Being a small minority in the Ashkenazic kibbutz society also made it difficult for the oriental immigrants to cope with the overt or covert social pressure to adopt the old-timers' mores and values. Anyone who did not adopt them left and moved to the city. Those who remained took on the kibbutz value system because it was consistent with their perception of the superiority of western culture and the inferiority of their native culture, and also because it was part of the Zionist ideology.[9]

The remarks of eastern immigrants and Ashkenazic old-timers alike are indicative of this attitude. One member of the Iraqi training group at Giv'at Hashelosha wrote, 'Although the physical labor is quite hard because I'm not used to it yet, the new life and *its cultural level* give me the strength to stand firm through all these difficulties'.[10] The kibbutzniks were aware of this feeling. They, too, stated: 'The youths feel that we are European and they want to "catch up" with us, to become free of the sense of inferiority.'[11]

The Ashkenazic hosts on the kibbutzim followed the transition of the new immigrants with interest, because they were aware of the demographic significance of absorbing immigrants on kibbutzim and saw paramount importance in having as many young people as possible join kibbutzim. By then it was already clear that large numbers of Jewish immigrants would come from Islamic countries and that the further development of the kibbutzim and the preservation of their dominant status depended on attracting these immigrants to them.

Very little has been written about the absorption of the oriental immigrants on kibbutzim. Dr Shaul Sehayek's *In the Paths of Fulfillment*[12] is the only book to deal with the history of Iraqi immigrants in rural settlements. Other books on the rural settlements cover the subject of the oriental immigrants chiefly in statistical surveys, with just a few explanatory remarks on the failure of these settlements to appeal to the immigrants.[13] This paper discusses the absorption process of the oriental immigrants on kibbutzim affiliated with Hakibbutz Hameuchad shortly before Israeli independence, but it focuses not on the history of the settlements but on the adjustment process that the immigrants underwent during their transition to the kibbutz way of life. The paper is not about the ideological aspects of kibbutz life (I have written another paper on that subject) but about the cultural aspects of the transition from a post-traditional society to a modern one, from a religious society to a secular and even antireligious one, from a society in which the extended family is the basic social unit to an individualistic yet also communal society. The paper will focus on the perspective of the newcomers themselves. The main problem with this personal point of view is the paucity of available sources. The Iraqi immigrants left little documentation. Most of what exists is kept in the archives of the Babylonian Liaison Bureau[14] and consists mainly of minutes of general meetings of the training groups and the Liaison Bureau's correspondence with leading members of the training groups. Most of this material deals with administrative aspects of the settlement of the Iraqi Jews in Palestine; issues pertaining to personal and individual adjustment are not mentioned at all. The newsletters of the training groups, too, which were edited by counselors from the kibbutzim, give us a lot of information about ideological and social change but little about the individual and cultural spheres. After all, the newsletters were intended to show how well the immigrants were learning about and adjusting to kibbutz life and its ideological values.[15] Personal material would sometimes have contradicted the utopian picture that the newsletters attempted to present, and therefore it is not included in them. The few references to the personal facet of the new cultural values can be found in memoirs and journals written by some of the members, but few such documents exist and the range of topics mentioned in them is limited.

The exception is a collection of documents left by Shoshana Morad-Mu'allem, a member of one of the training groups of Iraqi immigrants. Shoshana is the nom de guerre of Hatoun-Violet, born in Basra in 1929 to Avraham and Rahel (Gorjiyeh) Morad. Shoshana was a member of the Zionist pioneering movement in Basra, and she and her friend Arella Somech-Balbul were active as counselors and members of various committees. In May 1947, concerned that the local police might have found out about Arella, the two of them left town and were moved to Baghdad. A few weeks later, they immigrated illegally to Palestine, where they joined a training group of Iraqi immigrants on Kibbutz Ashdot Ya'akov. There Shoshana met Aryeh (Albert) Mu'allem, also from Basra, who had moved to Palestine in August 1947 on an illegal flight from Baghdad.[16] In 1948 the training group joined the Iraqi seed group on Kibbutz Sede Nahum. Shoshana and Aryeh were married in September 1949, and in October of that year they and the rest of the Iraqi seed group founded Kibbutz Neve Ur in the Beit She'an Valley. Shortly thereafter, the two left the kibbutz and moved to Neve Yamin, a moshav of Iraqi immigrants near Kefar Saba.

Shoshana left a rich collection of documents, including a diary, articles that she and Aryeh had written and which had been printed in the training group's newsletter, poems, and, most of all, extensive correspondence. After moving to Palestine, Shoshana corresponded with her family in Basra – her two older brothers and her parents – and with members of the Zionist movement in the city. She also corresponded with friends in Israel and with one of her brothers, who immigrated a few months after she did. In addition, Shoshana corresponded with Aryeh when he was away from the kibbutz in the army. All these documents, covering Shoshana's first four years in Israel, are in her personal collection in the Babylonian Jewry Heritage Center archives in Or Yehuda. Because of the richness of this collection, the reader discovers numerous details about the lives of the young immigrants in their first years in Palestine, including their encounter with a new environment; arguments, crises and vacillations over various issues; the training group's experiences during the War of Independence; and the evolution of Shoshana's relationship with Aryeh. This collection is unique in that it depicts absorption from the point of view of the immigrants themselves, and most importantly, that it allows us a glimpse of their thoughts on personal, and often intimate, matters – subjects that tend not to be discussed much and about which written material is rarely found. For these reasons, the intercultural encounter will be examined primarily as portrayed in Shoshana Morad-Mu'allem's papers.

As we shall see, Shoshana's writings reflect the first stage of the westernization process, the stage of imitation and uncritical adoption of the culture, accompanied by a rejection of the traditional values of her own culture. In a letter to her brother Naji (Amnon), Shoshana tells him that she is writing her memoirs and adds, 'And I am the only girl among all my friends who is writing memoirs'. Later she asks him to send back all her letters to her so that she can 'keep them with the memoirs that I'm writing'.[17] It should be noted that the very fact of keeping a journal, writing memoirs and even holding on to the letters that she received, as well as meticulously collecting her letters and finally depositing them in the archive, is paramount evidence of the adoption of the western values and documentary tradition that characterized Zionist activity.

Shoshana also had a strong, uncompromising faith in the Zionist pioneering ideology and its social and cultural ideals, as manifested in kibbutz life. She admired the new world that had been revealed to her and tried to apply the new value system in all areas of her life. The new Jew that the Zionist movement sought to create was manifested, as we shall see below, in Shoshana's way of life, behavior and thinking throughout her early years in Israel, except in a few cases in which her individual character and the cultural values on which she was raised were decisive. The description and analysis of the cultural integration based on Shoshana Morad-Mu'allem's writings, while also paying attention to the attitudes of the other members of her training group, both male and female, give this paper its feminine perspective. Thus the paper discloses the world of the immigrant teenage girls and the issues that interested and disturbed them in the formative period in which their personality was molded and their place on the Israeli immigrant-absorption map determined.

## SOCIAL PROFILE OF THE TRAINING GROUPS FOR IRAQI IMMIGRANTS

As stated, the Jewish girls had been exposed to many aspects of western culture in their native land. The Iraqi immigrants in the training groups came from middle- and lower-middle-class urban families, and their fathers worked in petty trade, as artisans, and as clerks in the civil service and in private companies. Many of the young women in the training groups had an elementary or high school education. Almost all of them had been members of the Zionist movement or came from families that were involved in Zionist activity. Some of them had been active as counselors and served on various committees. They had been exposed to western culture by the modern schools run jointly by the Alliance and the Jewish community, which existed in all the major Jewish centers in Iraq. In the late 1940s, girls accounted for about one third of the 18,000 Jewish pupils in Iraq.[18] However, the schools did not take a feminist stance and did not seek to institute equality for women; rather, they sought to emulate the values of the bourgeois ethos of nineteenth-century western and central Europe with respect to the status of women.[19] From the time the Alliance first founded these schools, the teachers were asked to foster in the girls such qualities as 'gentleness, modesty, unpretentiousness, a desire to excel and shine in a way other than through the ludicrous display of ornaments and cheap jewelry, a belief in the equality of rich and poor, and so on'.[20] These qualities were supposed to produce educated women who were first and foremost wives and homemakers and who would raise a new educated, enlightened generation. Lower-class girls were offered a vocational education, mainly sewing and embroidery, which they could do at home to help earn a livelihood.

Despite the educational and cultural changes, the Jewish minority in Iraq was still an integral part of the majority Arab society and Islamic culture. Although this society was also changing, especially among the upper and middle classes, it maintained a traditional, conservative structure in which the patriarchal family was an essential element. The rungs in the family hierarchy were based on sex and age; the young people were subordinate to their elders and the women were subordinate to the men, especially the father, who was the head of the family. This hierarchy made the woman's inferior status an integral part of the structure of Arab society, and it was reflected in segregation, in the compartmentalization of women in individual and family life, and in the exclusion of women from public affairs.

The exclusion of women in Iraq was anchored in law, the economy and society. Women had no public or political rights,[21] it was not acceptable for middle-class women to work outside the home,[22] and the occupations that were open to them were limited and low-paying. So long as paid work for women was perceived as a stain on the family honor and as detracting from the status of the male breadwinner, girls could not gain any material benefit from their education. Consequently, middle-class Jewish families sent their daughters to the modern schools not to better their financial situation, as they did with the boys, but for prestige.[23]

A change in this respect first became perceptible in the late 1930s, when new job opportunities – teaching positions, nursing jobs and clerical jobs with private companies – began to open up to educated young women. In the 1940s some young women from the upper-middle class who had acquired a higher education began to work as doctors and pharmacists.[24] Nevertheless, education had only a limited influence on the status of women; few of the educated women went to work outside the home, and those who did usually quit their jobs after marriage. Most Jewish girls in Iraq stayed at home after graduation and waited for their intended husbands.

The newly opened window through which Iraqi Jewish girls discovered the existence of other societies and cultures that offered girls a fuller, more equal life made them aware of the inferiority of their own status. Although educated young women were often treated with more respect and esteem within the family, their status did not undergo a fundamental change so long as there was no change in the values of the surrounding society. As a result, educated young women were caught between two dichotomous worlds and their contradictory values: the western world view and the expectations that they had been given in school and the traditional values that had been imparted by the family and to which they were required to conform. These conflicting messages, along with an increased awareness of their inferior status as women, caused them to feel frustrated. Some of the young women sought to rebel against the path that their families had sketched out for them and to have a say in deciding their own fate. Some of them found a solution to their personal problems in the activities of Hehalutz, the only Zionist movement in Iraq in the 1940s.[25] They regarded the national and social platform of Zionism as the way to solve the Jewish problem in Iraq as well as the problem of their status as women. Among the members of the movement were high-school students looking for something to do in their spare time and idle high-school graduates seeking to fill their lives with content and activity. There were also illiterate young women from the lower class for whom the movement was an opportunity to take evening classes and to acquire an elementary education – in Hebrew. And there were girls who sought to escape from financial and social hardships or from family or personal problems, and who viewed their activity in the Zionist movement as a way to emigrate to Israel.

Active participation and positions of responsibility, along with exposure to egalitarian education and the special emphasis on women's equality, fostered the girls' feminist consciousness, boosted their self-confidence, and reinforced their recognition of their right to insist on their own opinion, while struggling internally against the traditional, conservative ways of thinking. The boys in the movement changed, too; they were expected to alter their patronizing, arrogant attitude toward women, regard them as equals, and thereby help them gain self-confidence and grow strong enough to face the conflicts at home.

As the girls internalized the values of equality and the various aspects of Zionist movement activity became more and more egalitarian, the gap between the two worlds in which the girls lived increased. After a few years, they had to decide between two options: to marry or to move to Palestine. Many of them chose the former option. The latter, rebellious option was chosen mainly by the more active members and those from Zionist families. It was no simple matter, especially for girls, to gain parental consent to immigrate to Palestine, and sometimes the conflict ended when the daughter ran away to Palestine. Usually, however, the girls went with or followed brothers or other relatives. Those young people who had relatives in Palestine or whose entire family wished to immigrate were shown a sympathetic attitude by their parents.

Shoshana came from a middle-class family in Basra and attended the Jewish high school in town. She joined the Zionist movement in the footsteps of her brother Naji, and she held various positions as a counselor and a member of movement committees. Shoshana's parents were vehemently opposed to her Zionist activity, belittled it, and delegitimized it. They were absolutely opposed to the idea of her emigrating to Palestine, and especially to her aspiration to join a kibbutz. But this was not an issue while Shoshana was in high school. She left for Palestine suddenly and with no preparation when, as mentioned above, her friend Arella had been discovered by the Iraqi police. The disappearance of the two girls, followed by the news of their emigration to Palestine, shocked and infuriated their families, and only threats by Zionist emissaries prevented their parents from reporting the activity of the Zionist movement to the authorities. After Shoshana arrived in Palestine, her parents refused to answer her letters; only after many entreaties did they forgive her for running away.

## TOWARD A NEW LIFE

Shoshana wrote of her enthusiasm about her first encounter with Palestine in Binetiv hahagshama (In the path of fulfillment), the newsletter of the Iraqi immigrants' training group:

> I saw the land from afar as a shining light beckoning me. I was taken out of the darkness. I saw it, the land, as a big, twinkling

star. The mountains and hills, the trees, and everything that my eye saw captivated me. ... Had I been able to lengthen my arms, I would have embraced the sight of a Jewish settlement that I saw from afar. ... I realized the vision and image that had always been with me. My feet are treading on the homeland.[26]

The reality was less poetic and grayer; the physical work arduous and the initial adjustment exhausting. But these difficulties were expected. They were perceived as part of the Zionist fulfillment process and a test that every pioneer had to undergo and overcome. Working the land was perceived as an ideal involving the return to nature, purity and joie de vivre; and through it the personality of the new Jew would be built. In a letter to her brother Naji in Basra, Shoshana described her enthusiasm on her first day of work in the fields:

We pulled weeds, and it was the first time I had held a hoe in my life. I was so happy about the work, about the enchanting view and the sunshine and the fresh air. ... I worked, singing, for at least two hours, and afterwards my back hurt and I couldn't open my fingers. I wish you could see me now, see my happy face and hear my laughter.[27]

Afterwards she worked in various jobs on the kibbutz, which she described in a letter to her father:

I work eight hours every day and I don't feel overtired. ... I have worked in a factory, in a hospital, in the fields, in the banana [orchard], in the kitchen, in the dining room, at plowing [to grow] flowers, and most of the time in the children's house, because I asked to learn to be a childcare worker in the future.[28]

This occupation was well-suited to Shoshana's expectations and vocational aspirations. She did not want to take over 'masculine' occupations because just having a job was a great achievement for her, but also because her inclination was for educational work. Shortly thereafter, she switched to the children's house, where she worked for a long time.

Shoshana's occupational route was not unusual for women on kibbutzim. Few worked in the fields, which was considered a productive occupation; few worked in the vegetable gardens or with the cows or chickens. Most were employed in the 'unproductive' services:

laundry, the clothing storeroom, the kitchen, and childcare, which even on the kibbutz remained female occupations.[29]

The kibbutz society expected the immigrants to adopt the kibbutz way of life in full. This message was conveyed directly or covertly by the counselors and through direct or indirect contact with kibbutz members. The young people were expected to make changes in all aspects of their lives, including dress, sleeping arrangements, friendships and intimate relationships, and observance of the Sabbath and festivals. These expectations caused internal dilemmas.

When they arrived at the kibbutz, the immigrants were provided with new outfits. The young women especially needed them, since the dresses that they had brought from Baghdad were not appropriate for the kibbutz. In the clothing storeroom they were offered shirts, dresses, trousers, shorts, and so on – the best kibbutz fashions of the day. The young women were disturbed and discomfited by the question of whether or not to wear shorts; on the one hand, they desperately wanted to be like the kibbutz women, but on the other hand, they shrank from such a radical divergence from the rules of modesty on which they had been raised. Naomi, a member of the training group at Gevat, wrote in her diary: 'For a moment I cringed, as if they had made me wear sha'atnez [a combination of wool and linen, forbidden by Jewish law]. "How could I dare show my legs?" I was terribly embarrassed. I asked for a skirt, and only after a long time did I dare to wear pants.'[30] Some of the young women compromised by opting for long trousers. Shoshana's vacillation was extremely short; she wore shorts the day after arriving at the kibbutz. As she described it: 'At first I was embarrassed to leave the room, but I dared myself and went out, and no one laughed at me … because all the girls dress like that and the trousers are more comfortable for working.'[31]

She felt differently about the idea of shared sleeping quarters, which was brought up by some of the members of the Ashdot Ya'akov training group. As the group members reported to the Babylonian Liaison Bureau, which was headed by Gideon Golani at Kibbutz Be'eri:

> We spoke with the young women and young men about putting the men in rooms with the women. Most of the members agreed, so we arranged to have two men and two women sleep in each room. Some of the women didn't agree, so we left them apart, because we didn't want to force them. … It was hard at first, hard both for the men and for the women. The members complained, but it's all right now.[32]

Shoshana was one of those who refused to move into joint sleeping quarters. As she explained in a letter to her brother Naji, 'Girls and boys sleep in the same room here, but I didn't agree, not because I can't stand boys, but because I want my privacy when I change my clothes. At night in the dark, sleeping together with boys isn't hard because everyone wears pajamas.'[33]

## THE ATTITUDE TOWARD RELIGION

Another problem had to do with religious observance. Most of the Iraqi immigrants came from traditional homes, where their families abided by religious precepts while adopting a forgiving attitude toward laxity in observance by the young generation. It was customary for civil servants to work on the Sabbath; some people ate non-kosher food outside their homes; and many of the young people went to the synagogue only on holidays.[34] The members of the Zionist movement were not strictly observant of religious practices and traditions; they took part in joint activities for boys and girls and activities on the Sabbath and festivals, and, of course, the subject matter that they learned in the movement was secular and even anti-religious. But the secularization process in Jewish society in Iraq did not involve any objection in principle to religious observance, and there was no anti-religious ideology. On the kibbutzim of the Hakibbutz Hameuchad, in contrast, the non-observance of religion and tradition was an integral part of the secular way of life and world view, and the Sabbath was a major arena for consolidating their national philosophy and strengthening their ideological hold on Palestine. Based on the writings of training-group members and conversations with them, it seems that the assault on religious observance did not bother the young Iraqi immigrants as a collective, and they had no complaints about the non-observance of the Jewish dietary laws, work on the Sabbath, the lack of a synagogue on the kibbutz, and so on. For example, it was reported that they chose to work on the Sabbath and used the money that they earned to establish a joint fund.[35] Shoshana personally wrote many letters on the Sabbath, traveled to visit friends, and went on trips around the country. Soon after arriving on the kibbutz, she learned to swim, and from then on swims in the Sea of Galilee were added to her Sabbath leisure pursuits.[36]

The best indication of the attitude toward tradition is Shoshana's description of the group members' behavior on the night of Tisha Be'Av (the fast of the Ninth of Av, commemorating the destruction of the First and Second Temples). In Iraq, the Jews observed the standard mourning practices: they refrained from eating meat from the beginning of the month of Av, and on Tisha Be'Av itself they would fast and lament the destruction of the Temple. But Shoshana's first Tisha Be'Av in Palestine was totally different. Her group was in Nahbir (Be'eri) in the Negev with the Iraqi group that had been among the founders of the kibbutz. As usual at such get-togethers, the settlers and their guests spent the night dancing and celebrating, whether in deliberate rejection, ignorance or disregard of the significance of the date.[37] From a letter that Shoshana wrote about this to her brother in Basra, we learn that the Zionists in Basra had done the same:

> When you wrote to me that you came home on Tisha Be'Av at ten-fifteen p.m., I was very surprised, and I said, 'Where were you all day?' Then suddenly you told me about it and I laughed a lot, because I also spent the night of Tisha Be'Av laughing and dancing. We were in Nahbir, and I'll tell you frankly that I didn't know that this week was [the week of Tisha Be'Av] and that that night was exactly that night. And while we were dancing a hora, because it was the last night [of the visit to Be'eri], and the light went out at twelve o'clock because there's no electricity there, we started to scream and laugh, and some of the comrades said it was forbidden to turn on a light because it was the night of Tisha Be'Av. It was said as a joke. When I heard this sudden news, I didn't believe it. I started to investigate and check, and it turned out that the comrade was telling the truth, and that night was the night of mourning. I spent it happily and joyfully until dawn.[38]

Shoshana's decision to continue dancing indicates full adoption, without a trace of vacillation or criticism, of the values of kibbutz society.

But not all the group members fully internalized these secular, and even anti-religious, behavior patterns. Some were disturbed by the non-observance of religion and particularly by the deliberate transgression of religious precepts. This came up especially when they were asked to do something active, such as work on the Sabbath. Some refused to work.[39] Others did their work but chastised themselves in private. One member who was required to cook on the Sabbath describes it in her memoirs: 'The decision was very difficult, because as long as I could I was careful not to desecrate the Sabbath, and here they forced me. A decision to which it was very difficult to reconcile myself.'[40]

Although most of the members accepted the secular, permissive kibbutz way of life to some extent, their parents did not. Few of their parents came to Palestine before the establishment of the State of Israel, but those who did expressed criticism and opposition. Usually they suggested, requested or demanded that their children in the training groups, and especially their daughters, abandon kibbutz life and join them in the city rather than remain in a setting that undermined the foundations of traditional life. Other relatives, too, exerted pressure. As a result of the pressure from their families and the difficulties and dilemmas of kibbutz life, more and more people, especially young women, left the kibbutzim.

### TABLE MANNERS AND HYGIENE

But this was not the case with Shoshana, at least not in her first year on the kibbutz. On the contrary, she admired the kibbutz way of life, zealously adopted the new practices, told her family in Iraq about them, and even tried to 're-educate' her parents. She was particularly impressed by the eating habits. Shoshana was amazed at the tidiness of the dining room, the table manners and the meticulous adherence to principles of hygiene. She told her family: 'The dining room is as neat and clean as a royal chamber.'[41] She also noted: 'We eat with a knife and fork here, and it's a disgrace for people to eat or pick up something in their hands without a fork.'[42]

The Jewish middle class in Iraq had been exposed to European eating habits, and knives and forks were commonly used there. But the traditional eating habits were also retained, and people continued to roll up food in pita bread and eat with their hands. Seeing the eating habits in the kibbutz dining room with her own eyes made Shoshana aware of how incomplete her westernization had been in this respect. She discovered that the exposure provided by a modern educational system and reading is not enough to impart a thorough knowledge of western culture.

Shoshana's reaction to cleanliness was similar, as we see in a few of her letters:

> The bathroom and lavatory walls are all covered with bright tiles, white as milk, up to a person's height. Everything is washed daily with water and soap even though it's clean. The cleanliness in the kitchen is amazing. ... Pots are washed twice, first with hot water

and soap and then with cold water. ... It is forbidden to drink from a cup that someone has already used. It has to be washed.[43]

She advised her brother: 'You have to keep yourself clean and get used to cleanliness, because cleanliness is something basic for a person.'[44] Elsewhere she wrote: 'I forgot to tell you that at eight o'clock every child has a shower with soap and water. Hair [is washed] only on Fridays.'[45]

These descriptions, too, tell us about specific details of western culture that Shoshana discovered when she arrived on the kibbutz. She learned that it was absolutely forbidden to eat and drink from shared dishes, and that dishes, wall tiles and the body had to be scoured fastidiously. Not to do so was perceived as a cultural flaw. Interestingly, Shoshana wrote about the shower and sink but did not mention the toilet – a place of central importance in western culture where waste is eliminated from the body and neutralized. Perhaps this was because she was uncomfortable mentioning the subject, or perhaps it was because there was no difference between the toilets in her house in Basra and those on the kibbutz.[46]

## ADOPTION OF CHILD-REARING METHODS

Shoshana's work in the children's house introduced her to child-rearing on the kibbutz, and she sought to apply the new methods in taking care of her younger brother Fuad. In a letter to her parents, she sent instructions on nutrition, sleep and clothing:

> Please pay attention to his food. If he doesn't want to eat, force him; take a spoon and put it into his mouth so that he gets used to eating. Give him fruit, even though it's expensive and scarce, as well as tomatoes. They don't have to be squeezed; he can eat them with the peel, with a little salt added. Yogurt is essential, and eggs and porridge, too. I think Uncle's wife knows how to prepare it. Ask and find out how to make it. Get him used to sleeping in the afternoon, from one o'clock until two-thirty. Give him a meal at eleven-thirty. Give him a shower and dress him in only underpants and trousers, without suspenders. And have him sleep, even if you have to force him. This is something that has to take priority even over food and drink.[47]

Later in the letter she sent instructions for her uncle Menashe's wife, too, regarding child-rearing. 'She should see to their food, even by force, because that is how the children are fed here.' She instructed Fuad himself: 'You have to listen to Father and Mother. And every day after lunch go to sleep so that you'll be handsome and Mother and Father will love you and buy you toys and nice trousers for Rosh Hashanah, white trousers.'[48]

This rigidity with respect to eating and sleeping was characteristic of the doctors, nurses and childcare workers in the Yishuv. Shoshana rejected her family's tolerant child-rearing system in favor of the new method, which was meant to force children into a rigid regime that did not necessarily suit their needs. She had no way of knowing that just a few years later objections to these child-rearing notions would be voiced within western culture itself, and that the damage caused by this method would be discussed and analyzed in research literature. Shoshana's attitude was typical of non-westerners who adopted western culture with extreme rigidity. Whereas Europeans, secure in their identity and culture, were likely to express criticism of customs and traditions by breaching them consciously, the newcomers, lacking in self-confidence, adopted the cultural patterns in full and adhered to them uncritically, in admiration of the 'higher' cultural level and disdain for or embarrassment by their own culture.[49]

This also emerges from Shoshana's subsequent letters. In one letter she adds instructions for raising her little brother:

> Answer him even when he asks questions, and don't become bored, because a 4-year-old boy asks about everything that he sees or hears. Answer him even about things that you call 'shameful'. Because it's your job to develop his thinking and encourage his mind. Never hit; it is absolutely forbidden.

Later in the letter Shoshana insists that her younger brother Faraj be involved in raising Fuad, because 'he's patient and young, and he can understand Fuad better than Mother or anyone else. Faraj, my eyes, it's your job; don't get sick of it.'[50]

Shoshana also took an interest in the education of her brother Fuad, who was 4 years old at the time. 'Are you still teaching him English?' she asked. 'I don't think you should stop; it will make his life less difficult.'[51] When she found out that her brother was not being sent to school because it was too far from home, she cried out: 'How dare you not send him to school because it's far away? Send him quickly,

*Cultural Change as a Personal Kibbutz Experience*

because he'll find happiness there. His life will be rosy and his words honey. ... You are doing him an injustice when the days pass pointlessly by.'[52]

She called on her brother Faraj to develop his artistic talents:

> I want to give you some advice now that I have seen the children here. Keep making some things out of wood, keep drawing, because you have enormous talent in both of these beautiful arts. Keep it up, provided that you clean up the work place after you finish and don't leave the place a mess and do others an injustice, while also making things unpleasant for yourself and giving yourself a headache, in which case you wouldn't be able to continue.[53]

## RELATIONS BETWEEN THE SEXES

Relations between the two sexes in the training groups were complex and delicate. It should be kept in mind that the young people came from a segregated society in which men and women were strictly separated, whereas the elimination of these dividing lines was one of the principles of the egalitarian ideology of the kibbutzim. Moreover, the Iraqi Jews tended to regard the kibbutz as a society characterized by lewdness and sexual license. Shoshana was aware of this, and in one of her first letters to her parents she explained the principles of the system:

> Don't think that there is excessive freedom here, as you imagined, and as you described the girls. ... I can tell you that there is freedom; what [freedom]! Freedom of speech, freedom of dress, freedom with food, to go and come freely, and no one oversteps the boundaries. As I have always told you, a respectable girl, wherever she may be and wherever she sits and talks, will remain respectable. I began with this discussion so that your minds would be clear and you would relax.[54]

But these boundaries were not always maintained, and problems quickly cropped up in instituting a new system of relationships that was foreign to Iraqi Jewish society. One member of the Ashdot Ya'akov training group put it as follows in a letter to his friends: 'Extremely delicate and incisive questions came up.'[55] Someone proposed a general meeting of the group to discuss the subject, in order to help group members who were wrestling with the issue or who had no idea how to treat women. But the group rejected the idea, arguing that the members were not yet ready for a public discussion of the subject and that it would therefore be better to have a private conversation with each individual who was having difficulty with the issue.[56]

Soon after describing the boundaries of sexual freedom on the kibbutz, Shoshana had to confront those very boundaries when she became close to another member of the training group, Aryeh Mu'allem. Shoshana and Aryeh had met back in Basra, where they were both members of the Zionist movement. They met again in the Ashdot Ya'akov training group after Aryeh moved to Palestine in the summer of 1947, and they quickly became close. The way their relationship developed is reflected in their correspondence, which comprised approximately 30 letters. Shoshana started off reserved, addressing a letter to 'Comrade Aryeh' and concluding it 'Yours faithfully'.[57] Aryeh, meanwhile, wrote to 'Dear comrade Shoshana Morad', referred to her as being 'far from us in distance but very, very close in terms of the heart', and also concluded with 'Yours faithfully'.[58] After being inducted into the army when the War of Independence broke out, he wrote to 'My dear Shoshana' and filled his letters with expressions of how much he missed her; Shoshana wrote to 'My dear, beloved Aryeh' and concluded with 'Looking forward to seeing you, your beloved'.[59] In a diary entry dated July 20, 1948, after having spent a long time in the shelters, she wrote: 'Aryeh, when will you come and when will they let us live our lives again and taste our pure love, which is like a brother's love for his sister?'

This relationship was nothing like what was customary in Iraq. There marriages were arranged by the parents and, even if the couple loved each other and the match had their parents' blessing, they were not supposed to be boyfriend and girlfriend – and they certainly were not supposed to act the way couples did on kibbutzim. The social and cultural revolution that this relationship entailed discomfited the couple and their fellow group members. When Aryeh sought to enlist in the army and Shoshana agreed to enlist, too, at his request (although in the end she didn't do it), she asked him not to tell the other group members about her consent lest 'they start to laugh at me, ... because the people aren't developed yet and don't yet understand'.[60] The discomfort is reflected in a letter that Aryeh received shortly thereafter from another group member, Ovadia Nazem. In his letter Ovadia recounted: 'We were working, and Avraham, who works in the vineyard, said "Send regards to Aryeh." And Ruth told him to tell

Shoshana. Then he laughed and said "Aryeh-Shoshana", and everyone laughed an awful lot. And he didn't want to say that Shoshana is your girl.'[61]

Aryeh and Shoshana were aware of the gossip about them but refused to declare their relationship openly, because Shoshana first wanted to obtain her parents' blessing. The two of them decided to wait until Shoshana's parents came to Israel. Aryeh explained this in a letter to Shoshana: 'We agreed to this not because we were afraid of what people would say and of becoming laughing stocks, as you once put it. There were other reasons.' Their decision was prompted by respect for and appreciation of their parents and the tradition of needing parental consent, as well as a desire to be 'independent' before getting married.[62] When Aryeh sought to move up the date of the marriage and not to wait for Shoshana's parents to come, an argument broke out between the two of them. It was so hard for them to discuss the subject that they expressed their opinions in notes to each other. Shoshana demanded that Aryeh comply with the traditional ritual: 'You write to my parents without letting them sense that we have a relationship, and also write to my brother Amnon, so that he'll write to my parents.'[63] Aryeh replied:

> Shoshana! What are you talking about! And where is your education? ... Woe to me ... that I should write to [your] parents or to Amnon about this rather than you. ... Why? Are we still in the Exile that the boy has to ask the parents for the girl himself. ... Shoshana, if you want to live as a free girl the way [I] know you then take my advice ... and write to them about this and we'll wait until they come and we'll get married ... or else you don't want to be the free girl that I knew, in which case wait for your parents to come and they can look for someone for you or [impose] some guy on you.

In another note he added: 'I asked you and not your parents or anyone else for your hand – If you agree, then your parents won't stand in our way – Consent you won't get from them, only from yourself.'[64]

These texts disclose their internal struggle with the attitudes of the two cultures, the western and the eastern, toward the crucial stronghold of a traditional society – the family, including the father's status and the honor of the daughter and of the family. Even in Iraq, Aryeh and Shoshana had rebelled against the values of their traditional Arab-Jewish culture. Through their kibbutz way of life they rejected even the values of westernized Jewish culture in Iraq. But deep down, they still had respect for and even venerated some of the basic family systems. It was important to them to protect Shoshana's reputation and 'her family's honor', even though in the Israeli society, and especially on the kibbutz, these values were considered unimportant and even obsolete relics of the Diaspora. The clash between western and traditional values was inevitable. What is interesting about this process is that when Aryeh changed his mind and sought to break free of the traditional family restrictions, his arguments were primarily ideological, taken from the Zionist labor movement. It was Shoshana's 'Exile mentality' that was vulnerable to attack. In the end, Aryeh won out and the two of them were married in September 1949. Shoshana's parents arrived in Israel a few months later, when illegal immigration routes were opened from Iraq to Iran, from where they continued on to Israel.

An analysis of Shoshana's attitude toward her parents reveals a dialectical relationship. Shoshana appreciated and respected her parents, and it was extremely important to her to obtain their consent for her actions and her way of life. Her respect for them emerges both in her entreaties for their forgiveness for her running away to Israel and in her insistence on obtaining their consent for her marriage. This attitude is also reflected in the style in which she addresses them in her letters – 'the light of my eyes and essence of my heart, my dear mother, the honorable Gorjiyeh', 'my dear, exalted father, the honorable Avraham' – and her reference to herself as 'your submissive daughter Shoshana'. But beyond these formalities, Shoshana was not submissive. She advised, recommended and even demanded that her parents follow in her footsteps and adopt the new values and customs that she had picked up, totally rejecting some of the customs of her parents' home. Among other things, she cast doubt on her mother's ability to understand her young son. Basically, Shoshana rejected the traditional submissiveness and obedience of sons and, especially, daughters vis-à-vis their parents and reversed the roles, making herself the guide and asking her parents to follow in her footsteps. Although Shoshana obtained her education and westernization with support and encouragement from her parents, who regarded their children's education as a lofty goal, that education led the children into an ideological rebellion that was reinforced by their activity in the Zionist movement. For Shoshana, the westernization process went far beyond what her parents had intended, especially in terms of her way of life on the kibbutz and her relationship with Aryeh.

Moreover, the shaping of her Israeli identity not only involved the adoption of western cultural values as manifested on the kibbutz and rejection and even expunging of the values of the westernized Arab-Jewish culture in which she was raised; it also drew a cultural dividing line between herself and Arabs as individuals and as bearers of a culture. In one diary entry she describes an Arab village near Hulata:

> They are still in their filth, in their ancient, disorderly hovels. I was nevertheless happy to see ... that they lived within a Jewish economy and received no education and no Jewish culture. ... First they have to have a high culture and education before they demand the homeland.

Shoshana perceived filth and disorder as evidence of primitiveness, lack of culture and therefore also national immaturity. Elsewhere in her diary she describes an Arab café that she visited and notes the miserable, disorderly conditions there. She then notes: 'And I was happy when I saw this, because I hate the Arabs and I want them to remain uneducated in their lowly culture.'[65] By excluding the Arabs and rejecting their culture, Shoshana marked out the boundaries of her new identity. Arabs and Arab culture were not part of this identity.

Despite Shoshana's strong loyalty to the western way of life and the Zionist pioneering ideology, she did not remain on the kibbutz, primarily because of pressure from Aryeh to leave. They moved to a moshav in 1950, and later to the city. Most of the Iraqi immigrants on kibbutzim did likewise. Many of them left because they felt like outsiders; others left for financial reasons. Ultimately, they had to help their families who arrived in the mass immigration of 1950–51 to get settled.

## CONCLUSION

This paper describes one young woman's encounter with Israeli society and culture. However, the encounter and her reaction were not unique. They typified many groups of immigrants who arrived in the country before and after Israeli independence. They typified groups of immigrants that had undergone rapid westernization in their countries of origin, identified the Yishuv and Israeli culture with European culture, and became even more westernized after their immigration. The phenomenon was common to immigrants from Islamic countries and from Europe. Their willingness to erase large chunks of their past and to hallow Zionist values in order to realize the dream of becoming Israeli can be seen in literature by immigrant authors and is discussed in several research studies.[66] What is unique about these westernized or Levantine immigrants is that they identified the Arab elements of their culture with outmoded traditionalism, inferiority, primitiveness and otherness, and ultimately even with the Arab enemy – under the influence of the Zionist experience and the colonial heritage. The negative image of these cultural components caused the immigrants to become alienated from them, to reject them, to expunge them rapidly, and to adopt the Ashkenazic Yishuv and Israeli culture. This behavioral pattern was not typical of other groups of immigrants from Islamic countries – most of the immigrants from Yemen and some of those from Libya, Kurdistan, Morocco, etc. – who had had a more limited encounter with western culture in their countries of origin. These immigrants did not seek to change. The pattern of the 'new Jew' was foreign to them and even ran counter to their cultural values. They went to Israel not to be pioneers but to preserve their culture and their behavioral patterns and to fulfill their religious purpose as Jews.[67] Their response to modernization and westernization requires a separate study.

## NOTES

1. Jacqueline Kahanoff, *Essais* (From the East), (Tel Aviv, 1978), pp. 49–50 (Hebrew). The essay was written in 1959.
2. Joan Roland, *Jews in British India: Identity in a Colonial Era* (Hanover and London, 1989).
3. On the Alliance schools, see Aron Rodrigue, *Education, Society and History* (Jerusalem, 1991), pp. 40–5, 49–51 (Hebrew); Maurice Sawdayee, *The Impact of Western European Education on the Jewish Millet of Baghdad, 1860–1950* (PhD diss., New York University, 1977).
4. Gideon Golani, *The Home and the Jewish Quarter in Baghdad* (Or Yehuda, 1994) (Hebrew); Aviva Muller, 'On the History of Jewish Women's Dress in Baghdad', in Shmuel Moreh (ed.) *Studies in the History and Culture of Iraqi Jewry 1* (Or Yehuda, 1980/81) (Hebrew).
5. Rodrigue, *Education*, pp. 91–3. A report by an Alliance teacher in Baghdad in 1913 describes the way of life before the Alliance had its influence: 'Sloppy dress, coarse language, prevalent drunkenness, sly tricks. ... All this was among the men. And as for the women – early marriage ... a life of asceticism and physical degeneration. ... Child-rearing runs completely counter to all rules of hygiene and cleanliness' (ibid., p. 177).
6. From a 1913 sermon by Rabbi Shimon Agassi, published in 1964, p. 54.
7. Maoz Azaryahu, *State Cults* (Sde Boker Campus, 1995), p. 49 (Hebrew). On the

*Cultural Change as a Personal Kibbutz Experience* 237

    traits of the 'new Jew' according to Zionist socialism, see Anita Shapira, *New Jews, Old Jews* (Am Oved, 1997), pp. 168–9 (Hebrew).
8. Amnon Raz-Krakotzkin, 'Exile within Sovereignty', *Theory and Criticism* 5 (1994), pp. 8, 125–8 (Hebrew).
9. For the influence of western culture on the personality, outlooks and mentality of local residents subject to European colonial rule, see Frantz Fanon, *Black Skin, White Masks* (New York, 1968). Although Fanon is talking about blacks, the syndrome that he uncovers and analyzes applies in many ways to the personalities of the Jews in these countries.
10. Yehoshua, 'The Babylonian Immigrants Speak Out', from *Alon Ha-Giv'a* (the newsletter of Giv'at Hashelosha), no. 1105 (Hebrew). Emphasis mine.
11. Report by Tzivya, a counselor at Kevutzat Caesarea, 'With Immigrant Youth from Babylonia', *Devar Hapo'elet* (Sivan, 1949/50), no. 5, p. 142 (Hebrew).
12. Shaul Sehayek, *In the Paths of Fulfillment: Zionist Pioneering Youth from Iraq Settling the Land* (Or Yehuda, 1997) (Hebrew).
13. Ze'ev Tzur, *Hakibbutz Hameuchad Settling the Land*, Vol. 3 (Tel Aviv, 1984) (Hebrew).
14. The Babylonian Liaison Bureau was founded in Hakibbutz Hameuchad and was run by Iraqi immigrants. Its job was to maintain contact between the immigrants and the Zionist movement in Iraq.
15. See Esther Meir-Glitzenstein, 'Ethnic and Gender Identity of Iraqi Women Immigrants in the Kibbutz in the 1940s', in Margalit Shilo, Ruth Kark and Galit Hasan-Rokem (eds) *Jewish Women in the Yishuv and Zionism* (Yad Ben-Zui, Jerusalem, 2001), pp. 109–30.
16. On the immigration operation known as Operation Michaelberg, see Shlomo Hillel, *East Wind* (Operation Babylon), (Tel Aviv, 1985), pp. 18–54 (Hebrew).
17. 'Dear brother, far in body but close in soul and love, the honorable Naji', July 13, 1947, personal file of Shoshana Mu'allem, archives of the Babylonian Jewry Heritage Center (hereafter: BJHC).
18. Haim Cohen, *The Jews in the Contemporary Middle East* (Jerusalem, 1972/73).
19. On the role of women in the gender ethos of the European middle class, see Billy Melman, 'Freedom behind the Veil: A Look at the "Other" in the 18th and 19th Centuries: Western Women on Mediterranean Women', in Yael Atzmon (ed.) *Window to the World of Jewish Women* (Jerusalem, 1994/95), p. 237 (Hebrew).
20. Rodrigue, 'The Alliance's Instructions to Its Teachers, 1903', p. 87. The traits of educated women are discussed in 'Regina's Marriage', in Rodrigue, *Education*, pp. 91–3. On vocational education for poor girls, see Yosef Meir, *The Sociocultural Development of Iraqi Jewry* (Tel Aviv, 1989), pp. 223–7 (Hebrew).
21. The status of women in Iraq did not change until 1959, after the overthrow of the monarchy, when amendments were made to personal-status legislation, including restriction of the right to polygamy. The amendments encountered vehement opposition. On this subject, see Phebe Marr, *The Modern History of Iraq* (Boulder, CO, 1985), p. 172.
22. This idea that women's work was humiliating to the husband and family was characteristic not only of Iraq but of the bourgeoisie in general, including university-educated women in Palestine, 'most of whom did not work because they could afford not to' (Chana Herzog, *'Women's Organizations in Civilian Circles: A Forgotten Chapter in Yishuv Historiography'*, *Cathedra* 70 [1993/94], p. 128 [Hebrew]).

23. It should be noted that in Iraq there was no opposition in principle to modern education, unlike in the Jewish communities of eastern Europe. See Paula Hyman, *Gender and Assimilation in Modern Jewish History* (Washington, 1995).
24. Among the Iraqi immigrants in Israel were about 60 women with a university education, including 12 lawyers, 17 physicians, 9 pharmacists and 20 teachers. Those who worked were doctors and teachers. Lower-middle-class women could work as domestic servants, washerwomen, seamstresses, or embroiderers or even prostitutes. Middle-class women tended not to go out to work even if they were professionals, e.g., teachers, nurses or clerks. Those who had to work stopped working after marriage. However, in the 1940s there were also some women, especially teachers, who worked by choice. Of the 35,000 female immigrants aged 15 and above who arrived in Israel in 1949–51, 2,300 (6.5 per cent) worked, 60 per cent of them as seamstresses and 20 per cent as clerks, teachers and doctors (Haim Cohen, *The Jews in the Contemporary Middle East* [Jerusalem, 1972/73], p. 166 [Hebrew]).
25. About the Zionist teenagers see: Esther Meir-Glitzenstein, 'The Struggle of Zionist Women for Equality and Immigration to Eretz Yisrael', in Yael Azmon (ed.) *Will You Listen to My Voice? Representations of Women in Israeli Culture* (Tel Aviv, 2001), pp. 365–90.
26. *Binetiv Hahagshama*, Elul 1947. Division 2 Foreign, Container 3, Yad Tabenkin Archives.
27. Shoshana to Amnon, July 4, 1947.
28. Letter to 'my dear father, the honorable Avraham Yehezkel', July 19, 1947.
29. Sylvie Fogiel-Bijaoui, 'From Revolution to Motherhood: The Case of Women in the Kibbutz, 1910–1948', in Deborah Bernstein (ed.) *Pioneers and Homemakers: Jewish Women in Pre-State Israel* (New York, 1992), pp. 223–8.
30. Naomi Kashi (Nissim), 'From Iraq to Israel', mss, p. 40 (Hebrew).
31. Shoshana to her brother Amnon in Basra, June 20, 1947, Shoshana Mu'allem file, BJHC. All the other letters from and to Shoshana are also in this file.
32. Letter from Yoel at Ashdot Ya'akov to Gideon [Golani] at Be'eri, June 20, 1947, Hehalutz archives, BJHC.
33. Shoshana to her brother Naji, July 13, 1947.
34. See Cohen (note 24 above), pp. 153–4.
35. Aryeh to Shoshana, December 9, 1947.
36. Shoshana to her brother Naji (Amnon), August 17, 1947.
37. Shoshana to her brother Naji, August 4, 1947. On the complexity of the attitude toward religion in the labor movement, see Anita Shapira, 'The Religious Motifs of the Labor Movement', *New Jews Old Jews* (Tel Aviv, 1997) (Hebrew). On the deliberate disdain for mourning on Tisha Be'Av, see pp. 269–70. It should be noted that the Iraqi immigrants, as foreigners and newcomers, could not have been aware of the complexity of the attitude toward religion and related only to the practical aspects of the issue.
38. 'To the light of my eyes, far in body but close in mind, the honorable Naji', August 4, 1947.
39. Decisions of the labor committee, January 12, 1948, Hehalutz archives, BJHC.
40. Kashi (see note 30 above), p. 36. In the second meeting of the central committee of the Zionist movement in Iraq, September 8–9, 1945, it was reported that people on Kibbutz Maoz had been forced to light fires on the Sabbath. The speaker warned that reports of anti-religious education in Palestine were liable to destroy the movement. Division 2 foreign, container 2, file 5, Yad Tabenkin Archives.

*Cultural Change as a Personal Kibbutz Experience* 239

41. 'Good evening, light of the eyes', Shoshana to Naji, August 18, 1947.
42. Shoshana to Naji, August 4, 1947.
43. Shoshana to her mother Gorjiyeh, August 18, 1947.
44. Shoshana to her father Avraham, July 6, 1947.
45. To 'the noble light of my eyes, my mother, the honorable Gorjiyeh', August 18, 1947.
46. See Mary Douglas, *Purity and Danger* (London, 1966).
47. 'To my dear, exalted father, the honorable Avraham', July 19, 1947.
48. 'To the light of my eyes and essence of my heart, my dear mother, the honorable Gorjiyeh', August 26, 1947.
49. Gadi Elgazi, 'Body Manners and Organizing Society: "The Civilization Process" of Norbert Elias', *Zemmanim*, 70, Spring 2000; see also Fanon (note 9 above), pp. 17–40.
50. 'To my dear, exalted ... father ... my dear, gracious mother', from 'your submissive daughter Shoshana', July 6, 1947.
51. 'To my dear, exalted father, the honorable Avraham', July 19, 1947.
52. Ibid.
53. 'To my dear, exalted, honorable father', July 6, 1947.
54. 'To my dear parents, the honorable Gorjiyeh and Avraham', August 4, 1947.
55. S. Shimshon, 'Upon Our Arrival at Sede Nahum', The Newsletter in Bet-Hashita, p. 15 (Hebrew). Division 2 Foreign, Yad Tabenkin.
56. Aryeh to Shoshana, November 13, 1947; Sehayek (see note 12 above), p. 114.
57. November 8, 1947.
58. December 11, 1947.
59. July 11, 1948.
60. December 4, 1947.
61. 'To our dear comrade Aryeh', from Ovadia Nazem, February 13, 1948, Shoshana Mu'allem file, BJHC.
62. Aryeh to Shoshana, undated.
63. Shoshana to Aryeh, undated.
64. Diary, July 20, 1947 (Hulata), Shoshana Mu'allem file, BJHC.
65. Diary, July 11, 1947.
66. Examples can be found in books by Aharon Appelfeld, Eli Amir, and Sammy Michael. The subject is discussed in research studies by Chana Yablonka (*Foreign Brothers* [Jerusalem: Yad Ben-Zvi, 1994] [Hebrew]) and Oz Almog (*Sabra: A Portrait* [Tel Aviv: Am Oved, 1997] [Hebrew]).
67. Nitza Druyan, 'Yemenite Jewish Women: Between Tradition and Change', in Bernstein (ed.) (see note 29 above).

# 13

# Women's Names and Place(s): Exploring the Map of Israel

## SHULAMIT REINHARZ

Nations, cities, towns, counties, organizations, villages and people all have names. Their name provides an identity, a label that points to an individual character. Nations are not called nation 1, 2 or 3, nor are cities or people assigned mere numbers or letters other than by bureaucracies that wish to extract taxes, send them to war or homogenize people in some other way. Nazi Germany stripped Jews of their names, labeling each man Abraham and each woman Sarah. And then they stripped them of names altogether and gave Jews brief numbers tattooed on their forearms.

Names connote meaning within a culture, evoke history or are descriptive. Naming sustains memory, or the possibility of remembering. That is why it is so challenging to explore the history of women – their names change so frequently.[1] Their names are so frequently overlooked or forgotten. What were the names of the wives of great men, the men that perhaps were made great by the wives? Who was Noah's wife? Few names of women in the Bible, in contrast with men, are theophoric, that is, a name based on a verb, as in Nathanel or Asiel. Women's names are more likely to be secular and descriptive 'based on the time of birth, or the origin of the bearer of the name, on a characteristic physical or spiritual quality, or the relationship of the parents'.[2]

Naming is the right of parents or guardians, and it is the public and political function of government. Governmental bodies allocate names to geographical parts, thereby bringing them into meaningful existence. A name is selected typically for its positive, rather than negative, value. Thus, looking at place names of an unfamiliar area may reveal what is valued or essential in that society.

How are names bestowed on places or buildings or people? The name may be granted as a gift to reward a group or person. A name can be used as a payment for a donation (i.e., naming opportunities). A name can be used to honor a fallen soldier; to commemorate a military hero or a political leader; or to enshrine in memory an important occasion. *A name is a formal strategy for sustaining memory*. To study the names given to towns and places is to understand what is honored in that society.

After a while, the name becomes a mere word, no longer reminding people of the individual or occasion it is intended to signify. For example, when people hear the name 'New York', they are more likely to think of the place itself than to think of York, or what was new about the site. Nevertheless, the *potential* to be re-remembered or to re-invoke memory is always there. People can stop and draw attention, in other words, to the meaning behind the name.

The topic of 'memory' and official naming raises the question of what is remembered and how things are remembered. What is socially constructed as worthy of being remembered? Who should be remembered, why, and how? Some things are remembered consciously, or are easily brought into consciousness through photographs, written records, or conversations. We can remember a place in which we grew up, in which we fell in love, in which we lived for a while, or in which we experienced a trauma. But other memories are deeply repressed, and only accessible through special means such as therapy or dreams.

Sigmund Freud's *The Interpretation of Dreams* (1913/1931) gives some guidance about the interpretation of places and spaces in dreams. He helps us understand memories of place by suggesting that the spaces in dreams are sometimes symbolic representations of sexual organs or sexual longings. Places have erotic overtones. Because, according to psychoanalytic theory, dreams are opportunities in which to fulfill our wishes, spaces and places in dreams are environments we long for. We remember where we have been and where we want to be through the dreams we remember, as much as through the memories of the actual experience. Names can play the same function – the mere sound of the name can evoke pleasure, fear, disgust and other strong emotions.

In the case of pre-State Israel, there was no official body within the Jewish community (the Yishuv) during the second half of the nineteenth century that had the authority to assign names to settlements, nor did the British or Ottoman authorities take part in this activity.[3] Rather, the people who established the settlements or who lived in them conferred the names on the places themselves. The inhabitants themselves named their villages.

In the 1920s, with the creation of the British mandate for Palestine, a Names Committee was created by the Jewish National Fund (JNF) to bestow names on the new agricultural settlements created on JNF land and funded by the national fund. This committee continued to operate until 1951, when it was replaced by the Government of Israel Names Committee, 'the authorized, official, and exclusive body for bestowing names on Israeli settlements'.[4] Between 1922 and 1941, Menachem Ussishkin headed the directorate, which established the Names Committee. The following individuals were members of the Names Committee prior to 1948: Menachem Ussishkin, Professor Yitzhak Vilkansky, Akiva Ettinger, Yosef Weitz, Professor Nachum Slushat, Professor Avraham Brawer, Yosef Meyuchas, Avraham Elmaliach, Yitzhak Ben-Zvi, Zeev Vilnay, Yosef Sprinzak, Professor Yosef Klausner, Professor Shmuel Klein, Yeshahyahu Peres and Dr Binyamin Maisler (Mazar). Yaakov Aricha was the secretary who arranged all the affairs and managed the correspondence. The Names Committee had no women.

The decisions of the Names Committee were challenged frequently but usually unsuccessfully. The Committee operated according to numerous principles, none of which seemed to consider gender. The Zionist Executive occasionally pressured the Names Committee to assign to a settlement the name of a person 'to honor or commemorate a certain individual, either to fulfill promises made to various bodies in recompense for a contribution that had been donated to the JNF, or to promote fundraising activities'.[5] Some examples are the following:

- Kfar Yehoshua named for Yehoshua Hankin on his 60th birthday.
- Ramat David, 1931, chosen to honor British Prime Minister David Lloyd George.
- A request was made to create a settlement named for Chaim Arlosoroff the year he was murdered (1933).
- Kfar Ussishkin was named for Menachem Ussishkin on his 70th birthday, as was a group of six settlements called Metzudat Menachem Ussishkin.
- Moshe Glickson received a town, Kfar Glickson.
- Dr Efraim (Fishel) Rottenstreich was honored with his name being applied to the first urban neighborhood established by the Names Committee.
- Kibbutz Beerot Yitzhak in the Negev memorialized Rav Yitzchak Nissenboim.
- Moshav Bitan Aaron in the Sharon Plain was named for Canadian Zionist Aaron Frieman at the request of the Zionist Organization in Canada.

- Kfar Yehezkel was the first name to be given as a reward for a contribution, named for Yehezkel Sassoon of Baghdad, the brother of an 'anonymous' donor.
- In 1947, the Names Committee authorized the name Neoth Mordechai for one of the kibbutzim in the Hula Valley to commemorate Mordechai Rozovsky, the leader of the Zionist movement in Argentina and chairman of the Argentine JNF.[6]

People did complain about one aspect of the naming process – that the names were not Hebrew. At the time, Jews were adopting Hebrew names as they cast off their old selves and adopted their new identities. David Green became David Ben Gurion and expected others to follow suit. So too with the names of towns, the past of the galut was supposed to be denied. In April 1946 the following town names were criticized, among others: Metzudat Ussishkin, Shekhunat Borochov, Kiryat Bialik, Kfar Blum, Kfar Brandeis, Givat Brenner, Kfar Glickson, Kfar Hess, Sdeh Warburg, Kfar Felix Warburg, Kfar Vitkin, Ramat Tyomkin, Kfar Natan Lansky, Tel Mond, Kiryat Motzkin, Kfar Massaryk, Kfar Marmoreck, Kfar Pines, Kfar Ruppin.[7] Apparently, women were not yet on the radar screen as naming options. And yet, there was a close tie between actual women and the actual land.

The land itself, the geographic spaces, and the emerging places were of extreme significance to the women and men who came to settle in Palestine. Jewish *women*, along with men, came to the land of Israel throughout the 1880s and particularly from the 1880s on. Some older widows came to die and be buried *in* the land, particularly in the land of Jerusalem. Others came to live *on* the land. The actual land, not the land of fantasy and yearning, was inhospitable in many ways. It was difficult to eke a living, a life, out of it. Unless the person lived in one of the small 'holy' cities, the immigrant had to reconcile him or herself with the land, just to survive.

Before they even arrived, the women had a broad array of attitudes to the land itself developed from religious texts or socialist fantasies. Nevertheless, although the women made a mark through their efforts at farming and guarding and rearing children, they were very unlikely to name the place they helped establish. For example, the collective named Sejera established by Manya Wilbushewitz on a hill in the Galilee did not change its name to Tel Manya. Rather, Sejera was renamed Ilaniyah, the Hebrew translation of the Arabic Sejera, meaning tree. The name of the town does not suggest the rich history of its early days.

Although some places were named for individuals who died in the attempt to establish a settlement (e.g., Kibbutz Kfar Giladi for Yisrael Giladi), many places adopted names from Biblical phrases or presumed Biblical locations (e.g. Merchavia) rather than from contemporary pioneers. The giving of Biblical names was also a political act that provided added legitimization for reclaiming and repossessing the land the Jews had lived on 2000 years ago.

The paucity of women's names for places, however, may seem to imply that women lacked deep attachment to the land, that they did not endure considerable sacrifice in settling it, or that they were not present. This is completely unfounded. Women did record their 'experience of place' in essays, poems and letters. The map of Israel, from the deserts to the beaches to the swamps to the foothills of the mountains, is described in letters, poems and essays suffused with their longings, strivings and sensations. Essays, letters and poems makes it clear that the landscape of Palestine is something people fell in love with. Women's experience of the openness of the landscape was as both a harsh uncooperative stage, and a sense of new possibilities, new beginnings, rebirth from a mother's body, a coming home. For example, one woman of the First Aliyah wrote in 1890 to her sister-in-law and friend:

> Eventually, we hope that the face of the land will be renewed. In areas where jackals run, railroads will run full of passengers instead of desolate rocks – there will be hotels for tourists; in places where man does not set foot, people will work and engage in all sorts of handicrafts, day and night. My heart pounds inside to think of all these pleasant hopes. If God has revived our previous land and turned the desolate desert into populated town, we pray that God will also turn all of the scorched and ravaged areas into homes for people, into vineyards and grapevines.[8]

The experience of working the land was sensual, although frequently described in masculine terms. For example, Esther Becker, from the generation of the Shomer, wrote:

> That new district, the great, open space of the Emek, the Valley of Jezreel, awoke a deep and permanent love in me. More than once I longed to leave the kitchen and join the line of the comrades who were driving the first Jewish plow through the Emek; for it seemed to me that there was no greater happiness than this in all the world.[9]

The beauty of the land was usually contrasted, in their writings, with the wretchedness of their living quarters. The indoors is cramped, inadequate, female; the outdoors is vast, limitless and available to the men. The chafing that so many women expressed at being confined to the kitchen was not simply an expression of annoyance at being held down by traditional sex roles, but also at being denied the opportunity to touch the land. The erotic thrill of the land was continuously experienced through accumulated layers of memory. Once again, Esther Becker:

> Beyond Jenin, the Emek, the Valley of Jezreel, was absolutely unrecognizable. A host of memories awoke in me as I looked on the Jewish settlements – many of them unknown to me even by name – which were now scattered through the great valley. And closing my eyes, I could conjure up the Emek as it once had been, with its solitary Jewish settlement of Merchaviah in the center. ... To the new settlement that we started in Fuleh, the Jews gave the name of Merchaviah, from the Hebrew for 'broadness of God', for the road acres of the valley stretched far and wide on every side of the settlement.

The land also was symbolically 'Jewish' although difficult, in contrast with the cities of Europe which were anti-Jewish, unhealthy, profane. Deborah Dayan wrote:

> It seems to me that only yesterday I was a thing torn by doubts and hesitations. In the noisy city, in the great library, in the museum, in the classes, the question would suddenly confront me: Why are you doing these things? Who needs you? Can't they do without you and people like you? And in such moments a paralyzing apathy would creep over me; I wanted to see no one, speak with no one. But now? My comrades are out in the field, mowing the harvest that we have sown. Close by, I hear the mill grinding out grain. And the flour from the mill comes straight to me, and I bake the bread for all of us.[10]

Given that there is ample evidence that the women became deeply attached to the land, did the settlements that they built sustain the memory of their labor? Did the settlements bear their names? Did any places receive a woman's name? And if so, what are the names? The answer to this question is not surprising.

Before 1967, there were 1,187 named places in Israel,[11] in toto, of which 19 (or 0.01 per cent) were named for women. In the remainder of this paper, I will provide some information about those names,[12] focusing on the identity of the person. The names are as follows:[13]

- seven are Biblical women
- one was a pioneer
- four are members of the vast Rothschild family
- three are women Zionist leaders from North America
- four fought in the Second World War
- three towns bear a woman's name, but the reference is to an organization – Hadassah.

Many of these 19 women had such extraordinary attributes that they were deemed worthy of being remembered by the naming of a town. Some received this recognition in part because they were married to great philanthropists. Surely, many more than 19 women deserve to be remembered? Insufficient naming then imposes a gender bias on memory and the learning of history.

The seven women of the Bible are:

- the prophetesses, Devorah and Chulda
- the daring warrior Yael
- a daughter who argued for female rights of inheritance, Hoglah
- the kind-hearted Naomi, daughter-in-law of the Moabite, Ruth
- one of the matriarchs, Rachel.

The places named after the women of the Bible are the following:

1. Devorah (Devorat HaTabor), founded in 1956, is a settlement near Afula. In this region Devorah, the prophetess, won her victory over the Canaanites and thus the settlement is named for her.
2. Chulda is a kibbutz founded in 1931, named for the prophetess who was one of the 'indoor prophetesses', whom people consulted in her home, as opposed to in the street or synagogue. She prophesied disaster, but also showed compassion. Chulda is located close to Mazkeret Batya, due east of Ashdod.
3. Yael, a kibbutz founded in 1960, is in the northeast section of the country and is named for the Canaanite's wife. In the Bible Yael is called 'blessed above all women' because she was brave and killed Sisera, the enemy of the Jews.

4. Hoglah is a moshav established in 1933. Hoglah is one of the daughters of Zelophehad, son of Hepher, descendant of Manasseh. Zelophehad died in the wilderness without having sired any sons (Numbers, 26:33, 27:1). His five daughters (Mahlah, Noah, Hoglah, Milcha and Tirzah) requested of Moses that they be recognized as female heirs and granted their father's inheritance of land. Their petition was granted. The Biblical people lived in the Hefer Plain which is in the area where the moshav is located.
5. Naami, a settlement founded in 1982, is located just north of Jericho in an area to which Naomi and Ruth returned.
6. Kfar Rut is located near Macabim.
7. Ramat Rachel, a kibbutz founded in 1927 by members of the Gedud Ha'avodah, an organized named for Yosef Trumpeldor. The tomb of Rachel is close by and for all intents and purposes, the kibbutz has become part of the city of Jerusalem. The kibbutz was destroyed in 1929 and rebuilt in 1930.

The sole pioneer settler for whom a place is named is Olga Hankin. Givat Olga is a neighborhood in the western section of Hadera, established in 1950 and named for Olga Hankin, the wife of the much younger Yehoshua Hankin, who came to Palestine with his father in 1882. Olga was a midwife who served both Jewish and Arab families. Yehoshua Hankin purchased from the Arabs the land on which Hadera was developed. Olga and Yehoshua are buried in Ma'ayan Harod in the foothills of Mount Gilboa.

The four women of the extended Rothschild family are:

- Dorothy (Devorah) Rothschild, wife of James Rothschild
- Hannah, Countess of Rosebery, daughter of Baron Meyer Nathan Rothschild
- Batya, mother of Edmond James de Rothschild
- Adelaide, wife of Edmond James de Rothschild.

Shdemot Devorah is located on Har Tabor and established on PICA land with funds from the Baron Edmund de Rothschild. It is named for Devorah (Dorothy) (1895–1988), the wife of James Rothschild, President of PICA (The Palestine Jewish Colonization Association). Shdemot Deborah (Omer) is a moshav founded on May 23, 1939 by members of the organization Moledet who seceded from the federation of moshavim because they wanted to build an individualistic moshav ovdim and not a collective.

Pardess Chana is a town in the northern Sharon Plain, north of Hadera, near the Mediterranean Sea, founded in 1929, bought with funds from the Baron Edmund de Rothschild through PICA. Pardess Chana is named for an extraordinarily wealthy woman, Hannah Rothschild, who at the age of 26 inherited the fortune of her father, the Baron Meyer Nathan Rothschild of London. Shortly thereafter in 1878, she married Archibald Primrose, fifth Earl of Rosebery, not a Jew and somewhat less wealthy than she. Rosebery 'was a leading Liberal peer, an outstanding orator' and a highly regarded individual. The couple devoted their energies and much of their resources to improving conditions for the poor in England. In 1890, Hannah died of typhoid fever, after which Lord Rosebery became Foreign Secretary of England. Their son, Neil Primrose, was an officer in the British army and was killed in Palestine during the First World War on November 15, 1917.

Mazkeret Batya and Givat Ada are named for women who were the wife (Ada) and mother (Batya) of the Parisian born Baron Edmond James de Rothschild (1845–1934), a philanthropist, patron of Jewish settlement in Eretz Yisrael, and art collector. In 1877 Edmond de Rothschild married Adelaide, the daughter of Wilhelm Karl Rothschild, who was known for his extreme religiosity and his unwillingness to become involved with matters concerning Eretz Yisrael. In 1882, following the pogroms in Russia, the Baron became interested in the Palestine settlement work done by the Hovevei Zion movement. He started his Palestine-based philanthropy by saving the settlement of Rishon LeZion from economic collapse. In 1883, he purchased land for the founding of a model agricultural settlement named Ekron, which he set up at his own expense. Ekron was the name of an ancient city believed to be in the area. In 1887, the Baron changed the name of the town to Mazkeret Batya, his mother's name, because she had died that year. The Baron continued to support Rishon LeZion and Ekron/Mazkeret Batya and subsequently Rosh Pina and Zamarin, which was later named Zikhron Ya'akov in memory of his father. In 1903, the Baron founded a town (Givat Ada) in the Hadera area that he named for his wife, Ada.

The three women Zionist leaders from North America are:

- Lillian Freiman, President of Hadassah-WIZO Canada
- Batya (Bessie) Gotsfeld, President of Mizrachi Women, United States
- Henrietta Szold, Founder of Hadassah.

Lillian Freiman (1885–1940) was born in Mattawa, Ontario, married into the longstanding Freiman family and was a Zionist her entire life. From 1919 to 1940 she was president of Canadian WIZO-Hadassah. In 1920–21 she brought 150 Jewish children to Canada who had been orphaned by pogroms. Touring Canada, she raised funds for their support and recruited foster parents. Lillian Freiman was acknowledged by many as a major leader in secular and Jewish causes in Canada. Because of the major responsibilities given to her by the Canadian government, and the exemplary manner in which she executed them, Lillian Freiman received the honorary citation OBE from King George V, for her public and philanthropic activities. The town named for her, Havatzelet Hasharon, established in 1943, is located in the Hefer Valley. The Hefer Valley was bought for $10 million, a sum that was collected starting in 1927 by the Zionist Federation of Canada.

Kfar Batya is a youth village on the border of Ranana, founded in 1959 by the Federation of Mizrachi Women of the United States. The village is named for Bessie Goldstein Gotsfeld (1888–1962) who founded and became president of the Federation of Mizrachi Women, a religious Zionist fundraising group, and later conceived of the founding of the youth village. Gotsfeld was a Zionist and social worker, born in Poland and resident then of Seattle. Her first visit to Palestine occurred in 1930, leading to her establishing a girls' vocational training school. She stayed in Palestine for 25 years and established many childcare centers and training programs.

Kfar Szold, east of Kiryat Shmonah, is a kibbutz founded in 1942 and named for Henrietta Szold (1860–1945), founder of Hadassah in 1912. Henrietta Szold was the first woman elected to the Zionist Executive. Born in the United States, she lived in Palestine during the second half of her life. In 1933, she led Aliyat HaNoar, an organization created to save Jewish children in Nazi Europe and bring them to safety in Palestine.

Three settlements were named for the following paratroopers or fighters in the Second World War:

- Havivah (Emma) Reik
- Hanna Szenes
- Zviah Lubetkin.

Givat Havivah is an educational and cultural institution and seminar of the Kibbutz Artzi movement, Hashomer Hatzair, located near the road that joins Hadera and Afula. The seminar is named for Havivah Reik (1914–44), one of four Haganah envoys from Palestine who was parachuted into Europe during the Second World War. Havivah Reik was sent to the area where she had grown up – Slovakia – only five years after she had arrived in Palestine. A member of Kibbutz Ma'anit, her mission was partially successful, but ultimately she was captured by the Germans. Kibbutz Lahavot Havivah in the Hefer Valley east of Hadera, and Givat Havivah were named for her.

Yad Chana is a kibbutz located near Tulkarem (West Bank) that was founded in 1950 in memory of Hannah Senesh, a paratrooper who left Palestine on a mission into Hungary, was caught by the Germans, and subsequently tortured and executed. While in Palestine, Hanna Szenes had studied agriculture at Nahalal and was a member of Kibbutz Sedot Yam, near Caesaria, and also wrote poetry. A museum/memorial exists for her, called Beit Hana.

Maaleh Zviah, or Zviah, is southeast of Carmiel. Zviah Lubetkin, born in 1914, was a fighter in the Warsaw Ghetto uprising who survived by escaping through the sewage system. In the summer of 1939, Zviah attended the Zionist Congress in Basel and after being forced into the ghetto, she fought the Nazis during the revolt. Zviah was a member of the Zionist labor youth movement, Dror, and married Yizhak Cukierman, a leader of the revolt. Yizhak and Zviah founded Kibbutz Lohamei Hagetaot.

This brief list of 19 places is a first attempt to draw together towns and neighborhoods named for women so as to analyze their commonalities. All of these places and their connection to the individual women for whom they are named deserve to be explored in far greater depth for the purpose of uncovering important nuances and details. Some places may even have been unwittingly overlooked in this overview. But two things are clear: first, the very existence of a town named for a woman creates the opportunity to link gender, memory and place, an opportunity that might not otherwise exist. And second, the list of names is very small. Even a cursory glance at an index of a map of Israel lists town after town named for a man. The same is true for streets in towns and cities.

This imbalance can be corrected in the future as new places require naming. Then, perhaps, responsible people can ask: Are women involved in the naming process? For whom should a town be named? What characteristics do we value in people? And how can we utilize 'place' to remember women and to create a gender balanced past?

## EPILOGUE

Harvest

Our people are working the black soil,
Their arms reap the gold sheaves,
And now when the last ear its stalk leaves
Our faces glitter as with gilded oil.

From where comes the new light and voice,
From where the resounding song at hand?
From where the fighting spirit and new faith?
From you, fertile Emek, from you, my land.[14]

## NOTES

This paper was prepared for the conference held at Bar-Ilan University, January 2–4, 2001, 'Gender, Place and Memory in the Modern Jewish Experience'. This paper benefited from financial support by Rachel and Haron Dahan of Baltimore, MD, to whom I wish to express gratitude.

1. See Mary Jo Deegan, 'Mary Elizabeth Burroughs Roberts Smith Coolidge, 1860–1945', in Mary Jo Deegan (ed.) *Women in Sociology: A Bio-bibliographical Sourcebook* (New York: Greenwood Press, 1991).
2. 'Names', *Encyclopedia Judaica*, v. 12, p. 806.
3. See Yossi Katz, 'Reclaiming the Land: Factors in Naming the Jewish Settlements in Palestine during the Era of the British Mandate', in Aaron Demsky (ed.) *These are the Names: Studies in Jewish Onomastics*, vol. 2 (Bar-Ilan University Press, Ramat-Gan), p. 63.
4. Ibid., p. 64.
5. Ibid., p. 81.
6. Ibid., p. 88.
7. Ibid., pp. 88–9.
8. Ran Aaronsohn, 'Through the Eyes of a Settler's Wife: Letters from the Moshava', in Deborah S. Bernstein (ed.) *Pioneers and Homemakers: Jewish Women in Pre-State Israel* (Albany, NY: SUNY Press, 1992), pp. 29–47, 40–1.
9. *The Plough Woman* (1932/1975), p. 42.
10. Ibid., p. 55.
11. This list of names does not include names of Arab towns named for women, a subject matter about which I have no knowledge.
12. What is the ratio of towns with women's names to towns named for men?
13. I received assistance in this study from Esther Carmel-Hakim, an instructor at the University of Haifa and a partner in the project 'Putting Women on the Map of Israel', sponsored by the Hadassah International Research Institute on Jewish Women.
14. Hannah Senesh, Nahalal 1940; translated from the Hungarian by Peter Hay. See also *Hannah Senesh: Her Life and Diary* (New York: Schocken, 1966), p. 246.

# 14

# A Tale of Two Monuments

## MAOZ AZARYAHU

Commemorative monuments represent the past in terms of sacred history. They render the past visual and concretize abstract ideas in terms of location and architecture. Significantly, monuments are designed to tell a story, but actually they interweave two stories that together create the tale of any particular monument. One is the history they depict in the landscape: a version of the past that often assumes mythical significance. The other, which is usually concealed, is the history of the monument itself, namely, the story of its construction. From this perspective, monuments represent the intersection of the history of memory and the biography of their creators.

The tale of two monuments is about two monuments that were created by women and cast in monumental mold the heroic sacrifice of women. The two monuments examined are the 'Work and Defense' monument at Hulda, designed and built by Batya Lichansky and inaugurated in 1937 and 'Motherhood', designed and built by Chana Orloff at kibbutz Ein Gev and unveiled in 1951.

## PRELIMINARY NOTES:
## THE ZIONIST COMMEMORATION PROJECT

The Zionist memorial belonged to the emergent Hebrew-Native culture in Jewish Palestine.[1] By articulating the linkage between history and territory in a dramatic fashion, their appearance in the landscape of Zionist settlement articulated the renewal of the connection between the Jewish people and the ancient homeland. Monuments to victory – the Galedim (witnesses) – were erected by the Israelites to commemorate military victories or extraordinary events at the place where they took place. The 'missing link' in the reappearance of the monument in the Jewish landscape was a tombstone in the form of a monumental sculpture. The prominent example was the Roaring Lion that was erected on the grave of Trumpeldor and his seven comrades in Tel Hai. The Last Stand of Tel Hai, which took place in 1920, was invested with mythical meanings, and the monument, inaugurated in 1934, was the quintessential Zionist monument to heroic sacrifice. The Roaring Lion permeated the Zionist imagination. It also reinforced the notion of the monument as a canonical form of symbolic expression laden with patriotic meanings. After 1948, the monumental commemoration of fallen soldiers of Israel's War of Independence in cities, villages and battlefields associated the myth of heroic sacrifice with the Israeli landscape and integrated the memory of the war into the symbolic structures of Israeli patriotism.

According to the Zionist, strongly secular pioneering ethos, heroism was defined in terms of a total dedication to and sacrifice for the ultimate Zionist goal, namely, the Jewish resettlement of the ancient homeland. The pioneering ethos defined heroism as selfless and absolute service. The pioneering ethos did not distinguish between men and women. Strongly influenced by socialist notions of gender equality, men and women were considered as equal partners in the Zionist project of national redemption. The emphasis on the equal contribution of men and women to the toll of heroic sacrifice was a central element in the myth of heroism. It was especially strong in the ethos of the Palmach, the elite units of the Hagana in the period before Independence. The participation of women in military operations during the War of Independence was mainly evident in cooperative settlements. The symbolic equality between men and women was reproduced in the myth of heroic sacrifice, where men and women were accorded equal membership. The cultic rhetoric referred to the fallen as 'heroes' and 'sons', but that was according to the rules of the Hebrew language. In general, the myth of heroic sacrifice did not extol manhood. The main theme was the ultimate unity of settlers defending their homes. The equal role accorded to men and women found its strongest expression in Nathan Altermans' poem 'The Silver Platter'. This was a major text of the myth of heroic sacrifice. In this canonical text of patriotic culture, the sacrifice of the nation was represented by the figures of a young man and a woman as a metaphor for the silver platter on which independence was served. In terms of numbers, it is worth noting that 9 per cent of those killed in Israel's War of Independence were women; 1 per cent of the women serving in the army during the war were killed.

## TWO SCULPTRESSES: A BIOGRAPHICAL OUTLINE

*Batya Lichansky*[2]

Batya Lichansky was born in the Ukraine in 1900 to a Zionist family and came with her mother to Palestine in 1910 to visit her sister Rachel. They stayed, and were followed in 1912 by her father and the other two sisters. Rachel, an ardent Zionist, was married to Yitzhak Ben-Zvi, a Zionist leader, and the second President of the State of Israel. In 1919 Batya Lichansky was admitted to the Bezalel Art School in Jerusalem, where she studied sculpture. A year later she left for Rome to study art at the academy. In 1921 she returned to Palestine and became a member of the Labor Battalion. She was a founding member of Kibbutz Ein Harod, but left in 1923 for Berlin to continue her studies. Berlin was at that time a hub of artistic activity. In order to be able to support herself she began studying carpentry, yet gravitated again to study sculpture. She remained three years in Berlin, and moved for another three years to Paris, where she attended the Beaux Arts Academy. In 1929 she returned to Palestine permanently.

The creative work of Batya Lichansky included numerous sculptural works, among them a dozen public monuments. Committed to labor Zionism, her works depicted leading figures and heroes of the Labor movement. In 1944 and in 1957 she received the Dizengoff Prize awarded by the municipality of Tel Aviv. In 1986 she was awarded the Israel Prize for

> [H]er contribution to the state and society, for her life work, the fruits of her untiring labors, executed in extremely difficult conditions and carried out with a modesty of spirit that has no parallel. Batya's exemplary conduct, which comes to expression in her artistic sculptural creations eternalizing Jewish and Israeli human and moral values, is synonymous with the pioneering spirit and deeds of those who built the Land of Israel.

Batya Lichansky belonged to the labor establishment; being the sister of Rachel Yanait-Ben-Zvi and the sister-in-law of Yitzhak Ben-Zvi were also significant. With the decline of the pioneering ethos, Batya Lichansky was virtually forgotten, her style deemed anachronistic and old-fashioned, and her artistic achievements ignored by those in charge of artistic distinctions within the art community in Israel. Batya Lichansky never married. Her lesbian orientation was never mentioned openly, which was not surprising in light of the dominant values of the era when she was artistically active.

*Chana Orloff* [3]

'One thing matters to me: to realize a living work.'

Chana Orloff was born in 1887 and emigrated to Palestine with her family in 1905. Soon afterwards she decided to study cutting and dressmaking in Paris. On her arrival in Paris, then a hub of artistic creativity, she decided to become an artist, and in the following years she matured as a sculptor. In this period she displayed her works in Amsterdam, Paris and New York. In 1916 she married and bore a son. Her husband died during the influenza epidemic of 1918. Though embedded into the Parisian art scene, Chana Orloff maintained close links with Jewish Palestine. Her home in Paris was a meeting point for artists who came from Palestine. Distinguished figures of the small Jewish community, most notably Bialik, the Hebrew national poet, and Dizengoff, the mayor of Tel Aviv, visited her. According to conventional wisdom, the idea to found Tel Aviv's museum of art was raised when Dizengoff visited her. The museum was founded in 1932 at the mayor's private residence. In the spring of 1935 the first exhibition of Orloff's work at the Tel Aviv museum was held.

After the Nazis occupied Paris Chana Orloff and her son found refuge in Switzerland. She returned to Paris in 1945. After a three-year stay in the USA she returned to Paris in 1948. In later years she visited Israel, founded in 1948, more and more. On April 17, 1949, the Tel Aviv museum opened a retrospective exhibition of Orloff's works. The reviews hailed Orloff as 'an artist in the full meaning of the term'.[4] This exhibition reintroduced the artist to the Israeli public, and the question of her resettling in Israel was also raised. The assumption of one reviewer was that if it indeed happened, this would be a substantial contribution to the quality of Israeli art. In 1951 two monographs on Chana Orloff were published in Israel, which enhanced her reputation as an important artist. In the 1950s she traveled often between Paris and Israel, also because of commissions for public monuments. In 1961 a 'traveling exhibition' of Orloff's works was organized. In 1968 she arrived in Israel to organize a comprehensive retrospective exhibition at the Tel Aviv museum. She died in Tel Aviv before the exhibition was opened.

## TWO MONUMENTS

### Hulda

In August 1929 Arab forces attacked Hulda, an isolated Jewish settlement east of Rehovot. After a day of fighting, British forces arrived and evacuated the defenders. Among those killed was Ephraim Chizik, the deputy commander, whose sister, Sara, was killed nine years earlier in Tel Hai. As was the case with Tel Hai, the battle for Hulda became a Zionist myth and a symbol of the heroic stand of the few against the many. However, the myth of Hulda was secondary in its importance to that of Tel Hai, which until Israel's War of Independence was the quintessential Zionist myth of heroic sacrifice.

The official effort to cast the heroic myth of Hulda in stone began immediately after the battle. In 1930 a committee under the patronage of the Vaad Leumi and the Histadrut was formed. The committee commissioned Batya Lichansky, then newly back from her studies in Europe, to create a memorial at Ephraim Chizik's burial site. The monument was praised as 'the first effort in the Land of Israel to erect a public monument, not as a present by an individual but by the shared means of the public according to the decision of the Histadrut [the left-wing federation of labor] and the national institutions'.[5] The public character of the monument was evident in the constitution of the public committee in charge of the work. Its members included also Rachel Yanait-Ben-Zvi, the artist's sister, the wife of Yitzhak Ben-Zvi, a prominent figure in the Zionist leadership and a member of the Vaad Leumi (the National Committee), and a prominent figure in her own right in the Zionist leadership.

As publicly proclaimed, the underlying idea of the monument was 'work and defense, an eternal memory to men of work and defense who have to get out from time to time from the regular framework of their work and substitute their tools with their weapons of defense'. The commemorative and ideological functions of the monument were concretized in the form of a monumental statue. The work process lasted seven years and was trouble-laden. The 40-ton stone was quarried near Jerusalem, where it was roughly processed according to the model. Transferring the stone to Hulda proved to be problematic too, and the stone mass had to be cleft into two. The artist lived in Hulda to complete the sculpture. In an effort to raise funds the public was asked to make contributions. In February 1935 it was announced that 100 Palestine pounds were needed to complete the sculpture. In later narratives of the monument, the dedication of the artist and the hardships she had to endure while working on the statue provided a secondary heroic tale – secondary to the primary one, namely, the heroic defense of Hulda and the martyrdom of those who had sacrificed their lives for the pioneering cause.

The inscription at the base of the stone reads: 'Here Ephraim Chizik fell while defending Hulda. Eternal memory to the defenders of Hulda Tarpat (5,629 according to the Jewish calendar).' The memorial depicts three human figures whose heads jut forth from the massive stone: Ephraim Chizik, his sister Sara Chizik and the 'unknown guardsman' or 'unknown defender'. Ephraim Chizik, who is buried underneath, is the main figure in the monumental configuration. He is holding a grenade behind his back, with his arm stretching to protect his sister Sara and the unspecified, third figure. In a later appraisal of the monument, the critic Haim Gamzu evaluated the sculpture:

> Jutting out of the rock in the upper part of the monument are three heads. They would appear to be lacking in proportion. Apparently, this is the intention. They are also proof of her [Lichansky's] sublime achievement in controlling the hard Jerusalem stone. In particular the head of Ephraim Chizik is evidence of a work of great perfection.[6]

The base of the sculpture displayed work implements in a wheat field. The juxtaposition of the heroes and the symbolism of toiling the land reinforced the ideological function of the monument: to cast the pioneering ethos, the basic tenets of which were work and defense, in stone. At her speech during the inauguration ceremony, held on August 26, 1937, Rachel Yanait, the artist's sister and a member of the memorial's committee, reasserted the ideological message of the monument:

> Not just a memorial to the unknown soldier sent by the rulers to the battlefield and killed somewhere, but a monument to people of work, living people who are motivated by an internal need and aware of the collective vocation, they dedicate themselves to working and building, and while working they are ready to defend themselves.[7]

This theme was repeated in other speeches delivered on the occasion. One speaker appealed directly to Ephraim and Sara Chizik: 'Blessed you are Ephraim, blessed you are Sara, that you gave the most sacred.'[8]

FIGURE 14.1

Batya Lichansky working on top of the Work and Defense monument, 1937. *Source*: A Epstein (ed.), *Batia Lichansky* (Tel Aviv: Ministry of Defense, 1988).

# A Tale of Two Monuments

FIGURE 14.2

Chana Orloff, on top of the ladder, while the Ein Gev monument is being put in place. In the background, the Sea of Galilee. (Courtesy of the Ein Gev archive.)

The statue marked the gravesite of Ephraim Chizik, but the depiction of Sara, his sister, buried at the Kfar Giladi cemetery, at the northern tip of the country, together with her comrades established a thematic link between Hulda and Tel Hai as nodal points of the Zionist myth of heroic sacrifice. This point was explicitly made in Ben-Zvi's speech at the inauguration ceremony: 'What happened in Hulda became a moral property of the entire Yishuv and the entire nation ... Hulda in the south and Tel Hai in the north are two links in one chain.'[9] The allusion to Tel Hai also compelled a comparison between the two monuments, which, until the foundation of the State of Israel in 1948, were the most distinguished Zionist monuments. Whereas Melnikov's Roaring Lion – the most prominent Zionist monument in the pre-state era – echoed ancient images of heroism and was allegorical, Batya Lichansky's monument commemorated the protagonists of the heroic drama (notwithstanding the mystery about the identity of the third figure, namely, the 'unknown guard').

Unlike Melnikov's monument, the major theme of Lichansky's work was pioneering. The sacrifice of Sara and Ephraim Chizik referred to the 'defense' aspect of labor pioneering. This aspect, albeit central to the monument, was augmented by further allusions to pioneering which were specifically mentioned during the dedication ceremony. One speaker maintained that 'besides the stone monument there exists in Hulda a living memorial, namely, the Gordonia group', referring to members of the pioneering movement who resided at that settlement at the time. From another perspective, Hanna Chizik, the sister of Sara and Ephraim, while thanking the sculptress for her work, maintained that 'her work is also a pioneering work, which deserves cordial appreciation'.[10]

The ideological meanings of the monument were affirmed during memorial ceremonies conducted at the site. In August 1949 a memorial ceremony commemorated the 20th anniversary of the battle of Hulda.[11] Members of the Chizik family were present at the ceremony. Ephraim Chizik's sister, an officer in the Israeli defense forces, gave veterans of the battle a model of the statue. This act demonstrated the symbolic association of the statue to the heroic myth of Hulda. In 1989 a public ceremony at the gravesite commemorated the 60th anniversary of the battle.[12] Among the guests were veterans of the Hagana and the 89-year-old sculptress. Most of those who attended were personally related to the period or to the people who took part in the events commemorated there. Ironically, the commemorative act and the fact that only *Davar*, the daily newspaper of the Histadrut reported on it, indicated the extent to which the heroic story of Hulda and the statue that marked the gravesite had been virtually forgotten by the Israeli public.

*Ein Gev*

The monumental commemoration of Israel's War of Independence began shortly after the war ended. A significant aspect of the commemorative project included the memorials built by individual settlements to commemorate residents and members who fell in battle. This type of memorial work was initiated by cities, towns and cooperative settlements, such as kibbutzim and moshavim. According to the cooperative ethos, residents were members who shared not only a place of residence but also were members of a close-knit community sharing the same ideological convictions. The fact that the population of most Jewish settlements was relatively small made the commemorative effort into a communal project that involved personal acquaintance with those commemorated. The building of such local memorials became a cultural norm. This was evinced in the rapid spread of this commemorative mechanism throughout the entire country, which resulted in a situation where in the early 1950s virtually all existing Jewish settlements either inaugurated their memorials or were engaged in the construction of such a memorial. Batya Lichansky, for instance, was commissioned with the design and building of the memorial built in Kfar Yehoshua, a moshav in the Valley of Jezreel. Significantly, some of these memorials also commemorated the heroic stand of the settlement during the war. This dual narrative function conflated the memory of victory with the memory of those who died during the battle. Triumph and heroic sacrifice were thus entwined in the form of a memorial.

Located at the eastern shore of the Lake of Galilee, Ein Gev was an isolated Jewish kibbutz that withstood repeated Syrian attacks in May and June 1948. Six members of the kibbutz – five men and one woman – were killed during the battle. Representing the perspective of the defenders, the account of the battle was simple and powerful: 'A few, not young women and men, members of the kibbutz, who built a flourishing kibbutz in hard work, people of work and defense, stood in this place with their back to the sea, confronting a huge and well equipped enemy.'[13]

In 1949, the kibbutz decided to commemorate both the victory in battle and the fallen members of the kibbutz. In 1950, the book *The*

*Fortress on the Eastern Shore of Lake Kinneret* published testimonies and detailed the course of battle on Ein Gev. One kibbutz member wrote:

> If one day a great artist will arise, who will have the power to give expression to the war of the Jews – I think that he will have to choose one figure: a Jewish woman, a mother in Israel, defending with her weapon her children and homeland.[14]

These sentences did not refer to the kibbutz in particular, but to Israel's War of Independence in general. Nevertheless, as it later became evident, his idea was concretized in the form and theme of the memorial statue built at the kibbutz.

The designer of the memorial space was the architect Benyamin Chelnov, who had also designed the mausoleum of the Zionist leader Max Nordau at the Trumpeldor Cemetery in Tel Aviv.[15] According to his design, the memorial space included a memorial room, an archive, a memorial wall with a Biblical inscription from the book of Nechehmia and a plastered yard, designated *Azara*, a name that referred to the Temple's court, which indicated the sacred character of the place. Chelnov had the idea to approach Chana Orloff, who lived in Paris, to design a monument to the defenders of the kibbutz. It may be assumed that Orloff's exhibition at the Tel Aviv museum in 1949 and the enthusiastic reviews published in the Israeli press also contributed to the decision to approach Chana Orloff with the request to design a commemorative statue. Teddy Kollek, then a member of the kibbutz and the future mayor of Jerusalem, established the connection with the artist and she was given a book depicting the siege of and battle for Ein Gev. According to a later report, 'She was deeply impressed by the book, and especially by the fact that female members fought shoulder to shoulder with the male members in repelling Syrian attacks on the settlement'.[16] After realizing that among the fallen members of the kibbutz was Chana Tuchman, a mother who was aged 31 when killed in battle, she decided that the theme of the statue should be 'motherhood'. The statue she designed reproduced a photo of Chana Tuchman holding up her baby son, both smiling, he to the viewer, she to him. The figurative statue depicting a woman holding up a son was alternately entitled 'motherhood' or 'mother and son'.

The sculptress volunteered her skill, reputation and time, with the kibbutz paying only for the material. The funds for the statue were allocated from the sum paid by the government to the families of fallen soldiers. A member of the kibbutz was entrusted with the task of raising funds and discussing issues pertaining to the statue with the artist who lived in Paris. The costs amounted to a few thousand dollars. The statue was cast in Paris and then transferred to Israel. On May 28, 1952, three years after the project began, the statue designed by Chana Orloff was unveiled at its designated place – overlooking the blue water of the Sea of Galilee. The inauguration ceremony was modest: it was a local event, with members of the kibbutz only attending – except for one guest of honor: the sculptress, Chana Orloff.

The pride of the kibbutz was reflected in what was written in the kibbutz's bulletin a few weeks after the inauguration ceremony:

> It is not our job now to give an artistic appraisal of this creation by Chana Orloff. People of taste and knowledge have already done that and will surely do in the future. Early echoes of the impression this statue made reached us after it left the atelier of the artist and was exhibited in Paris. It is enough to note what a respectable art magazine has written, expressing sorrow that this piece of art would leave France! If this is the case, we are glad that this creation of the artist was positioned at the memorial yard of our kibbutz.

The statue designed by Chana Orloff is the figurative reference to 'motherhood' in Israel's commemorative landscape. In the 1950s, most memorials did not contain figurative elements, due mainly to the Jewish prohibition of iconic representation. A few monuments in kibbutzim, where secularist ideology predominated, cast the theme of heroic sacrifice in figurative mold. Among those, only two monuments depicted women. The more famous example was Natan Rapoport's heroic monument in Negba that depicted three figures: two men and a woman, that as a group represented the defenders of the kibbutz against the repeated attacks of the Egyptian army. These three monumental figures remind one of communist statues common in eastern Europe. The combination of two men and a woman was intended to give a figurative expression to the pioneering ethos and its emphasis on equality between men and women as members of a pioneering community committed to cultivating the land and defending the settlement.

The monument in Ein Gev was the only one in Israel that was dedicated to and depicted 'motherhood'. The distinct character of this theme in Israeli iconography should be juxtaposed with its popularity in western iconographic tradition. The virgin carrying her baby son in her arms is a recurrent theme in Christian iconography. In the era of nationalism this symbolism was secularized, and the figure of the mother became a metaphor for the motherland, while the child represented the people's future and in particular the younger generation whose freedom was gained in battle. This theme also appeared in Soviet memorials that commemorated the Great Patriotic war (1941–45). In this respect, the combination of a woman carrying a baby was permeated with iconographic allusions and thematic associations that were foreign to Jewish tradition and exceptional in the thematic landscape of Zionist commemoration.

For the kibbutz, the statue represented 'A farmer woman, rooted in the soil, raising up her baby-child and protecting it from any enemy and danger. In this symbol the artist wants to embody the stand of all Jewish settlements and that of Ein Gev in particular in the War of Liberation.'[17] According to another interpretation, 'this two meters high monument describes the image of a mother who holds in her strong arms a healthy baby – the symbol of our young state, a symbol of the young generation, which is entrusted with the task to continue the construction and creation project begun by the pioneer father'.[18] From another perspective, the statue celebrated the role of women in the campaign in particular and the Jewish mother defending her child in general:

> [This statue] articulates the awareness that became prevalent among us during the war regarding the role of the female-member (or comrade) in the battle ... there was not any precedent similar to our War of Liberation, where relatively so many women actively participated and played such a decisive role in all stages of the war. In her statue the artist commemorates the Jewish mother defending her child.[19]

This issue was raised in a speech delivered during the dedication ceremony. In this speech, the role of women in defending the settlements was a source of pride: 'In the history of peoples and wars, revolutions and struggles for national liberation there were also cases where a woman played an important role, but these were few only.'[20] According to the speaker, and in accordance with the emerging heroic myth, the role of women in the fighting, as well as the heroic stand of the few against the many, distinguished Israel's War of Independence from other wars: 'And therefore it seems to me that with the exception of the stand of the few against the many, the active participation of the woman is the thing that symbolizes the special character of the War of Liberation.'

These interpretations articulated the perspective of the kibbutz. Anchored in the ethos of Zionist pioneering, these interpretations conflated pioneering and patriotic meanings. The idea that the commemoration of 'the spirit of those great days' should express the role of women in the battle was already formulated by a member of the kibbutz before the details of the commemoration project were elaborated upon. From his perspective, the fact that Chana Orloff chose 'this idea: the mother who defends her child' was a lucky coincidence that implied that his original idea was indeed appropriate.

From another perspective, the statue expressed the concerns and sensitivities of the artist. Chana Orloff had been preoccupied with giving a figurative expression to motherhood. This theme had persisted in Orloff's work. Earlier in 1914 she had sculpted a woman holding a child in her arms. This small wooden piece was entitled 'Motherhood'.[21] In 1916 she sculpted 'Pregnant Woman'; 'The Family' in 1916; 'Pregnant Woman and Child' in 1920. It seems not too far-fetched to suggest that this preoccupation pertained to her biography: a mother raising her son alone. In this regard, the extreme experience of the Nazi occupation of Paris and the flight to Switzerland with her son was also significant. The experience of motherhood and the special relationship between herself and her son provided her with an emotional access to the story of the battle on Ein Gev. In 1947 she sculpted 'Mother and Child;[22] in 1948 she sculpted another version of the same theme, also entitled 'Mother and Child': a woman holding a child in her arms.[23] In this biographical context it is understandable why she identified with and was inspired by Chana Tuchman, and more specifically, the photo showing her smiling while carrying her smiling child. With mother and child being a recurrent theme of her artistic work, this photo facilitated access to the dramatic events she was asked to commemorate. For Chana Orloff, this particular photo and the tragedy behind was a metonym for the heroic story of Ein Gev. In a way, the statue she designed translated the photo and through it her biographical attachment to the experience it conveyed into a monumental idiom.

## CONCLUDING REMARKS

When Chana Orloff designed the commemorative sculpture at Ein Gev, Batya Lichansky built the commemorative monument in Kfar Yehushua in memory of the residents of the moshav who had fallen in Israel's War of Independence. Throughout 1956–58 she built the memorial at Kibbutz Bet Keshet, which also commemorated her nephew who fell in the war. In 1953 Chana Orloff built the monument in Ramat-Gan in memory of Dov Gruner, a member of the Irgun Zvai Le'umi (IZL) who had been executed by the British in 1947. In 1955 Orloff was commissioned by the Histadrut to design a monument to the 'Hebrew working woman'. As a commemorative measure, the monument was meant to celebrate the part of women in the pioneering project in monumental form. The intention of the artist was 'to extol the basic feminine virtues' and their contribution to the nation.[24] Orloff prepared four plaster versions depicting different types of female pioneers. However, this monument was never cast in bronze.

The cultic association of women with motherhood has been a major theme of the Roman-Catholic worship of the Madonna. Notwithstanding the pagan background of the Christian cult, the visual image of Mary carrying the infant Christ in her arms has been embedded into western culture. Following the French revolution, and in the framework of enlightenment and secularization, the female figure was transformed from a particular woman, albeit endowed with supra-natural capacity, to an allegory that personified abstract ideas, such as freedom or the nation. The Statue of Liberty – donated by the French and set up at the entrance to New York – cast the idea of liberty in the bronze image of a young woman. The female figures of Marianne, Britannia ('rule Britannia') and Germania personified the French, British and the German nations respectively. These female figures exuded a sense of esthetic perfection. The figure of Germania, for instance, was displayed on postage stamps issued by the German Reichspost in 1900.[25] 'Germania with the emperor's crown' conflated the idea of the nation with imperial ideology; this particular image of Germania was that of a famous actress. Though less conspicuous, this neo-classical imagery persists, though mainly as a theme appearing on special coins. In 1986 the federal mint of the USA struck gold coins featuring Liberty. In 1988 the Royal Mint of Great Britain issued gold coins featuring Britannia on the reverse side of the coin; the obverse side featured the head of the queen.[26] The notion of the woman as a personification of the motherland was a prominent theme of Soviet monuments built to commemorate the Great Patriotic War (1941–45). The woman holding a child propagated an overt Christian imagery, albeit in a patriotic and secular, even anti-religious, framework of interpretation.

In a cultural context where figurative statues were the exception rather than the rule because of the constraints imposed by Jewish tradition, casting heroic sacrifice in a figurative mold was mainly limited to the commemorative landscapes associated and permeated with the pioneering ethos. The ideological commitment to the principle of gender equality was fundamental to labor-oriented pioneering. The rhetoric of equality was also articulated in the monumental representation of the heroic sacrifice of women as partners in the pioneering project.

Built in the early 1950s, the commemorative monument built by Natan Rapoport at Kibbutz Negba in memory of the stand of the kibbutz against Egyptian attacks in 1948 cast heroic sacrifice in the form of three representative figures, one of which is of a young kibbutz member. Laden with heroism and iconographic allusions to Soviet-type socialist realism, Rapoport's monument celebrated the heroic pioneering with supra-human figures. All three figures – the soldier and two members of the kibbutz, a man and a woman – had a representative function. They were anonymous, as becoming of their symbolic function as representative members of a group.

The tale of two monuments is about how two women cast the contribution of two other women to the Zionist narrative of heroic sacrifice in a commemorative mold. The monuments Batya Lichansky and Chana Orloff built in Hulda and Ein Gev respectively were different in many respects. The monument at Hulda was a sculptured tombstone, whereas the monument at Ein Gev was a commemorative sculpture, the location of which was determined by the artist according to esthetic considerations. Both creations conflated the local story with the national narrative. The Hulda monument was commissioned by the national leadership of the Yishuv and was permeated with supra-local motives. The Ein Gev monument represented a local variation on a national theme.

Their differences notwithstanding, it is worth noting that the women these two monuments commemorated were specific, with names, biographies – and a familial context, which the artists integrated into the narrative fabric of the commemorative monuments they designed and constructed. The Hulda monument is about the relationship between brother and sister. The Ein Gev monument is about a mother and her son. These two configurations are significant in the manner in which they depict specific women in a family context that seems to reflect the different perspectives of the artists, perspectives that were strongly evocative of their particular biographies.

## NOTES

1. On monumental commemoration of fallen soldiers in Israel see M. Azaryahu, *State Cults: Celebrating Independence and Commemorating the Fallen* (Sde-Boker, 1995), pp. 186–213 (Hebrew); I. Shamir, *Commemoration and Remembrance: Israel's Way of Molding its Collective Memory Patterns* (Tel Aviv, 1996).
2. The biographical details are according to: A. Epstein, *Batya Lichansky* (Tel Aviv, 1988).
3. The biographical outline presented here is based on: Ch. Kofler, 'To the Land of Israel and Away 1905–1968', *Chana Orloff – line and material*, exhibition catalogue, 1984, Tefen Open Museum.
4. L. Levy, 'A meeting with Chana Orloff', *Dvar HaShavua* 14, April 12, 1949, p. 17. See also B. A., 'Chana Orloff', *Dvar HaShavua* 15, April 19, 1949, p. 12.
5. An appeal to the public, *Haltaretz*, February 7, 1935, p. 5.
6. *Davar*, December 12, 1939.
7. Shamir, *Commemoration and Remembrance*, p. 25.
8. *Davar*, August 27, 1937, p. 1.
9. Ibid.
10. Ibid.
11. *Dvar HaShavua* 34, September 1, 1949, p. 3.
12. *Davar*, October 17, 1989.
13. 'The dedication of the Azara', *Ein Gev* (the kibbutz bulletin), June 23, 1952.
14. Efra, *Ein Gev in Battle* (Tel Aviv, 1950), p. 213; quoted in *Igeret*, June 11, 1952 (Ein Gev Archive).
15. *Haboker*, August 20, 1937, p. 12.
16. *Ein Gev* (the kibbutz bulletin), May 1980, p. 13.
17. *Igeret*, June 11, 1952 (Ein Gev archive).
18. *Ein Gev* (the kibbutz bulletin), May 1952.
19. *Ein Gev* (the kibbutz bulletin), June 1952.
20. 'With the dedication of the statue' (Ein Gev archive).
21. *Chana Orloff*, exhibition catalogue, p. 117.
22. Ibid., p. 123.
23. Ibid., p. 131.
24. Kofler, *To the Land of Israel*, p. 183.
25. Michel, *Briefmarken-Katalog Deutschland 1982* (Munich, 1981), p. 60.
26. *Yediot Ahronot*, August 13, 1988.

# 15

# Time, Place, Gender and Memory: From the Perspective of an Israeli Psychologist

## AMIA LIEBLICH

While this Conference gathers mainly scholars of history and culture, I will talk from the perspective of a psychologist, looking at the major concepts in the Conference's title. Rather than a coherent paper, I see my presentation as a matrix of several dimensions, which cross, intersect and create challenging interactions. While talking about several such intersections, I will use poems of the Israeli poet Lea Goldberg to demonstrate some of my ideas.

In my approach to the concepts of time, place and gender, I would start from the issue of identity. What does 'identity' mean? Identity may be viewed as the individual's answer to the question: Who are you? What are you? What is important for you in your life? Where are you heading? Furthermore, identity is the reflexive view of the person on herself, as well as the internalization of how I believe others are viewing me. Identity is deeply connected to words, to the language whereby I can talk to others and to myself. Last but not least, identity is defined within a culture, as cultures construct the dimensions along which I can experience and think.

Time, space and gender are three basic dimensions of identity in most cultures. They enable the person to locate herself in the world. The first awareness of the person awakening each morning relates to place orientation: Where am I? In my bed? In a hotel? In a friend's house? And more: In what country? Am I on a trip somewhere? Israeli children are familiar with the verses of Lea Goldberg which describe the 'absent minded man from Azar Village' (Goldberg, 1968). He is never sure where he is, and what the time is, and ends up lost in a train going back and forth between Jerusalem and Tel Aviv. While children find this story amusing, as an adult reciting it to children, I have always felt it slightly anxiety provoking. The absent-minded hero does not only lose his way, but he is lost to himself – in other words he loses his identity as well.

Place is not just an address on a map. When Virginia Woolf talked about 'a room of one's own' (1929), what she had in mind was a space to allow for personal development and autonomy. Lea Goldberg, who described herself in her poems as a woman who loved 'the great loneliness of foreign and despised cities' (Goldberg, 1979, vol. 3: 109; translated by Rachel T. Back) was very clear in evoking the state of mind of a displaced person. In her poem 'A journey with no name', originally published in 1960, she says:

> Where am I? How can I explain where am I?
> My eyes don't gaze out of any window.
> My face is not reflected in any mirror.
> All the many streetcars in the city travel without me.

And later in the same poem:

> Already it has been weeks since someone addressed me
> by name, and it's so simple:
> The parrots in my kitchen
> haven't yet learned it.
> People in all corners of the city
> don't know it.
> It exists only on paper, in writing
> and it has no voice, no sound or note.
>
> For days I walk nameless
> in the street whose name I know.
> For hours I sit nameless
> facing a tree whose name I know.
> Sometimes, nameless, I think
> of someone whose name I don't know.
> (1979, vol. 3: 31–4, translated by Rachel T. Back)

Time is another dimension needed for immediate orientation and the construction of identity. Am I late? Too early? Did I oversleep for school? And also: What is in the news? Who is the prime minister now? And last year? When Virginia Woolf created the fictitious hero/heroine Orlando (Woolf, 1928), she gave him/her more than 300 years of life, and with tongue-in-cheek named her work 'a biography'. Within such a context, it is almost expected that the protagonist will start as a male and be somehow transformed into a female at a later stage of life!

There are several interesting differences in the constancy of the dimensions of time and place, and in our ability to control them. In normal situations, a person, even a child, can give his/her name and tell whether he/she is male or female. This is called 'gender constancy', which is also doubted today in the generation of drag-queens and trans-sexual operations. Most of us – but not all – are free to change places, to travel, to choose the country we want to live in, while time flows, or is 'passing' as Lea Goldberg put it, without our control. Our names as well as gender, which are in most cases stable, travel with us across time and space.

We could have discussed other dimensions, such as belonging to certain national, ethnic, religious or social groups as part and parcel of one's individual identity, with the immense repercussions of these dimensions in history all over the world. More than once, people's religion or nationality have determined life and death issues, as we all know – but I will keep these subjects out of the present paper.

Identity is an elusive concept, as much as it is central to psychological understanding. It is elusive because it is internal, subjective and intimate and extremely hard to 'operationalize', namely to measure or view. Moreover, identity resides within as well as outside, it is on the border of the inner world of the individual and the cultural, historical and political worlds she resides in (Erikson, 1950, 1968). Identity is not a body with physical dimensions. Presently, some even doubt that the physical body exists, and see it, rather, as a social construction (Butler, 1993). It is not surprising, therefore, that some scholars question the whole conceptualization of identity, and see it as another simplification or illusion whose function is to make human reality look somewhat simpler, more stable and less threatening (see, for example, Gergen, 1991).

It is perhaps wiser to speak about 'identities' rather than 'identity', as many psychologists agree today. The classic theory of Erikson (1968) presented identity as the major developmental task of adolescence. Once it is 'acquired', after a period of trial and error and experimentation during the 'moratorium' of adolescence, it remains fixed like an identity number, or social security number, and rarely changes for the rest of one's life. Postmodern thinkers, who deny the existence of a harmonious, coherent, inner unity titled 'identity', have rejected this view. According to the postmodern view, identity develops and undergoes many changes in life, it consists of various fragments, which often contradict or conflict with each other, and rarely form a complete whole. In different contexts, we may appear as having different identities or personalities, without being taken for a 'multiple personality' or being blamed of deceit or fraud.

Another fascinating issue arises from a critical outlook on the concept of identity. Is there really such an entity as a separate 'me' within the boundaries of my skin, of my body? Maybe this is another fiction regarding human identity, while in fact, every moment, every human picture has more than a single actor, but rather a self-in-relation. That the self cannot and should not be divided from its network of relationships, is an innovation of the feminist psychologists, headed by Jean B. Miller (1976) and Carol Gilligan (1982). It is one step further than the contributions of the Object-Relations theorists, headed by Melanie Klein (1983). According to this theory, one's identity, or the self, is like an internal 'stage', a theatre, and the 'actors' are representations of all the significant others (e.g. parents, siblings), or parts of them, which we have encountered throughout our lives, particularly in our childhood. These representations are naturally not realistic, but based on distorted, often childish, perceptions and memories, mixed with idealizations, projections and so on, so that the 'real people' who form the internal matrix of our beings may be quite different from their internalized objects.

Jean B. Miller (1976, 1991) and Carol Gillgan (1982) claim, however, that this rich, complex picture of human identity misses the main point, which is revealed by studying women, namely that a human being is never fully separated and individuated. We must conceptualize identity always in a context of relationship. Real relationships should be taken into account when studying identity, and not just internalized relationships. Moreover, all experience is relational. All our lives evolve around love, hate, the wish to nourish, the wish to destroy, to educate, to influence, to come closer, to create distance, to understand, to be understood, to contain, to be contained, to know who I am in the eyes of another, to know that the other is there for me, and many more such relational experiences. The boundaries between the 'I' and the 'you' are false or artificial. In actuality we always deal with contacts, dyads and groups.

Family therapists contribute to these arguments by conceiving of a 'disturbed identity' or pathology of the individual, such as the anorexia nervosa of an adolescent girl, as an indicator of the imbalance, stress or maladjustment of the entire system, namely the family. The so-called sick girl is probably the weakest segment of the family, which manifests the defects of the system as a whole. Or, she may be the 'alarm signal', calling for help for the entire family in its crisis (see, for example, Minuchin, 1974).

All these observations grow richer when placed in conjunction with the gender distinction, which like eyeglasses, once you are used to it you can't do without it. Starting from the end of the former section, it was the discovery of feminist scholarship that the dimension of relatedness vs. autonomy has a profound impact in psychological theory and practice. Gilligan (1982) discovered that boys and girls have entirely different approaches to moral dilemmas. Boys use the principle of justice, and girls use the principle of care. Boys judge morality according to a logical and hierarchical value system, which underlies objective justice, while girls' morality attempts to minimize hurt for everyone, to take responsibility over the other's lot and to care for his or her wellbeing. Thus, toward the end of the twentieth century, identity was often conceived on the dimension marked by two opposing modalities: of separateness vs. relationship, autonomy vs. intimacy, as contained within the boundaries of the individual, or being a coordinate within a fabric of human contacts (see also Bakan, 1966).

While in the first steps of this theory, women's identity was regarded as relational, in contradistinction from men's individualistic identity, currently it is usually argued that the relational networking is simply easier to see in the psychology of women (Chodorow, 1978), but in fact it is true for all human beings (see Josselson, 1992). Each of us has masculine and feminine components, and the two modalities, in different proportions. Furthermore, our life cycle development produces a different balance of the two modalities for each gender, in different life stages. During mid-life, for example, men become more sensitive to and caring for the people around them (sometimes too late … ), while women become more assertive, ambitious and individualistic (Gutmann, 1987). One should be very careful with such sweeping generalizations, however, which lead to essentialistic thinking. It is possible that the major distinction is not by gender, but by social status, power and wealth (Tavris, 1992). Men are usually stronger and more dominant in society, but when women reach the top, they may behave like men toward the weaker segments of their society, be they female or male. I will come back to this argument later.

I have mentioned before the idea about the fragmented identity, which is perhaps characteristic of the postmodern individual. This, however, may have been the nature of women's identity since women took on roles outside of their private domain. Many of us remember clearly the time we were mothers of young children, and at the same time students or young academicians. Remember the wild ride to bring a child to the babysitter and be prompt on time in the lecture hall. Remember the hurried phone calls to the babysitter during the breaks. (And these were the times before cellular phones yet!) Or, leaving a faculty meeting before it ends to rush a child to the doctor, to attend a school performance where she had the dancer's role ... Career women of my generation used to notice how our male partners, who worked as many hours as we did, walked out of the door and forgot home and family completely, until they returned in the evening, expecting a meal. At the same time, we women were always divided, our minds keeping track of the home front, of the children's whereabouts, even as we were lecturing or doing another academic task. Like a juggler keeping five balls in the air, so do women divide their attention between their various tasks and responsibilities. In her book *Composing a Life* (1989), Catherine Bateson, the famous daughter of two distinguished scholars, Margaret Mead and Gregory Bateson, talked about women's multiple lives and multiple identities. When she was the president of a famous American college, she formed the unforgettable saying (which used to hang above my desk when I was a Dean at the Hebrew University) 'Being a mommy is part of being a good president'. Her thesis was that the variety of roles and identities women wear and shed in the course of a normal day should not be conceived as conflicting but rather as enriching. The social and inner division experienced by women, especially if they work also outside their homes, is not destructive, as many suggested, but on the contrary – it fertilizes, refreshes and contributes to each of the woman's identities. It prevents burn-out in either home or workplace, and it nurtures the woman's creativity and originality both in daily life and in her work. We should not complain about the hectic schedule many of us women maintain, but be proud of our rich, multi-faces lives.

Is women's identity really more divided than men's? This is very difficult to prove in research, and in any case, again, it may sound like another dichotomizing essentialistic claim. The divided identity may be more prevalent among the weak and the powerless people in society. Can it be really turned into an asset?

Going back to the subjects of time and space, from what was said before it may be concluded that women, who are more relational, are more aware of their historical time and national-geographical place.

Men, on the other hand, whose identity is more individualistic, are autonomous to create an independent self, little affected by time and space as limiting factors in life. This claim is much too simple as we will see later. Let me turn then to attempts to define feminine time as compared with masculine time.

In a classic paper of Julia Kristeva (published in French in 1979 and in English in 1986) she termed the concept of 'feminine time' and characterized it as 'cyclical' and 'monumental', to be distinguished from the canonical masculine time which is 'linear'. It should be remarked that anthropologists (e.g. Dorothy Lee, 1950), used a very similar distinction to describe time of western (linear) vs. non-western (cyclical) civilizations. Kristeva's arguments about feminine time can be added to the popular theories among sociologists, claiming that women's lives are taking place in the private domain, in their homes and families, while men's lives evolve in the public domain, in fields of fighting and hunting, in government, economy or institutionalized religion. Furthermore, scholars have argued that woman's existence is highly connected to nature, whereas men's is to culture. While Lakan later added language as a central aspect of masculinity, feminist scholars talked about women's existence as manifested in silence, or the absence of voice/language (Belenky *et al.*, 1986). All these distinctions are evidently interrelated.

(For example, recently, when I took the dog for a walk, caring for the natural needs of another creature, my partner sat down for his daily meditation, a cultural practice to elevate his own mind. I could see this as a demonstration of the differences outlined above. But we all know many men who walk dogs, and women who meditate, and essentialism is again something to beware of.)

To elaborate these distinctions, a woman is conceived as spending most of her time at home, with her infants and children, taking care of the livestock and a small vegetable garden in the courtyard. All of these create cycles of repetitive schedules and demands, of hunger and satiation, birth and death, dirt and cleanliness, flowering and withering, and so on and on. The change of seasons is interwoven with the recurrence of the menstrual cycle, of pregnancy and lactation, all of which form the cycles of women's time, within her limited and secure home space. Furthermore, the feminine time dimension leaves very little control to the woman herself. Natural forces rather than the woman's free will dictate it. Thus, a woman's identity, more than a man's, is connected to her mother, her children, her spouse and her friends. She creates couples, triangles (see Chodorow, 1978) and complicated social networks (see Gilligan, 1982). Her identity is defined by her inner space, meaning both the home sphere as well as the feminine uterus who 'wishes' to be filled (Erikson 1968/1974). Man's identity is anchored in the public sphere and his cultural setting – for example, his belonging to a community, nationality, religion, his economic status and his contribution to the collective. According to Kristeva, a woman ignores the past and current political world events with their dramatic turbulence, and lives more in the framework of small, local, familial and seasonal changes. Her time is a-historical, eternal, or monumental, it is the time of a mother who lives on forever in the lives of her sons and daughters.

If we want to summarize these polarities brought up in our discussion so far in a simplistic manner, we could put under Man: linear, historical, cultural, expressed-in-language and public, and under Woman: cyclical, monumental, a-historic, natural, silent and private.

Looking in Hebrew literature, I find an excellent example for the above in the story 'Exile' by the female author Dvora Baron (see Lieblich, 1997; Lubin, 1995). From the perspective of women, housewives and cooks, in the simple language of daily conversation, the reader learns about major and dramatic events which are happening at the time: war, exile and redemption in the context of the First World War. It is a wonderful expression of feminine time, which moves forever in circles and waves, from one meal to the next, through domestic dramas of birth, marriage, illness and death in the small community of exiles. The kitchen, which is in the story at center-stage rather than its margin, as usual, threatens the national-Zionist narrative of desperation and redemption. It is indeed a very constricted field to contain such immense events. At the same time, however, it is certainly universal, and epitomizes the human condition, since all of us are born of women, in need of food and love, and doomed to die.

Lea Goldberg used to call herself 'meshorer' (male poet) and not 'meshoreret' (poetess) (Lieblich, 1995). In her poetry I find manifestations of both the linear and the cyclical time, as can be demonstrated in some short examples. I think that the following poem may represent cyclical time:

> I strode into this night
> which is endless
> and suddenly it was morning
> the sun lit up
> the faces of the living
> who envied the dead.
>
> (1978: 61; translated by Rachel T. Back)

The following poem is, in my reading, a mixture of linear and cyclical time:

> How the passing Time tries me,
> its double reckoning my duty and my right:
> Every day it constructs and ruins me
> at once shaping both my death and my life.
> (1979, vol. 2: 151; translated by Rachel T. Back)

From the point of view of the topic of the present conference, taking into account the former discussion, it may sound as if I imply that women of our generation would be less affected by, and concerned about, questions of Jewish existence and future, as if they are removed from history and its repercussions. I certainly do not think so. Indeed, a woman has an open heart and ear to her children and other significant people around her, but this does not mean that she will have no more energy, need or will to care for the external world. As proposed by Bateson, the opposite is true. While still deeply involved in motherhood, women of our generation have made significant steps into the world of business, politics and religion, they have gained recognition in academia and the arts, and produced gradual changes regarding gender equality in our society. The gender gap has not vanished, but I hope that the present Conference will contribute to a better understanding of women's place in the 'Modern Jewish Experience'.

I would like to insert here a word of criticism focusing on the representation of reality, rather than reality itself. As long as men were the sole leaders of recording and representing the 'Modern Jewish Experience', whether in writing about Zionism, the settlement of Eretz Israel or the Holocaust, women's voice in these and other events was silenced, and the stories of women who did act, and had their share in the events, have been omitted from history. Moreover, because of the absence or poverty of a language or narratives for the description of women's experiences (Heilbrun, 1988), since language/culture is male-dominated, woman's place in history has not been preserved, recorded and communicated as something that really took place. We need 'herstory' scholarship to balance 'history', as many feminists have claimed before me.

Last but not least let me turn to the place of memory in the matrix of topics which forms this paper. The current academic psychology of memory is deeply engaged in proposing complicated, computer-like, models for the cognitive functioning of the mind, how information is stored, how is it retrieved, and what we know about the brain to allow such processes. There is little there about a whole person thinking and recalling. On the other end, clinical psychology is entangled in problems of repressed memories and their sudden return, foreign memories which are 'planted' in one's mind by suggestion, and the extreme distortions one may find in the personal narratives of the mentally disturbed.

From my own point of view, identity is but a slice, a cross-section, in the continuum of memory flow, representing the here-and-now moment. But my identity includes also who was I yesterday night, who was I last year, or during my childhood. Like several other psychologists (see Bruner, 1990; McAdams, 1993), in my research I approach the study of identity and memory simultaneously through the life stories men and women tell me about their lives. In an open-ended interview, giving only a very general introduction, I have asked people to give me an oral narrative presentation of their autobiography. They do it, of course, from their perspective of the present moment in time and place, and as an outcome of the particular context or interaction which form the 'research setting'. Looking at these resulting texts (after transcribing recorded conversations), the set of memories people choose to bring up, their content, form and order, is, in my view, the best avenue to study identity. But this kind of study negates the line or the distinction between memory and identity. It subsumes memory, not an 'objective' or 'historical' memory, but the cultural and individual construction given at the moment, which is highly subjective, relational and contextual. It is not 'historical truth' but 'narrative truth' (Sarbin, 1986) we are dealing with. Moreover, personal memory feeds on national or collective myths, in the same manner that personal identity contains the ideas and values of the period and culture in which our lives are embedded. A person who gives up his or her memory is a person who gives up his or her identity and relationships – a stage we sometimes witness in people who are about to die. As formulated by Lea Goldberg, again:

> Our loves are not many.
> Passing by,
> we tried to smile at the pine trunks,
> at the hills' green stone;
> and without waiting for their reply
> went on
> happy with all

> things that are not ours,
> that are not with us,
> and that cannot forget
> because they cannot recall.
>
> (1978: 34; translated by Robert Friend)

In the next section of this paper I turn to two recent Israeli life-stories studies, which indicate how women and men structure their identity, express their memories, and particularly how they refer to time and space in their narratives. The first study was conducted by me in Kibbutz Gilgal during 1994–98 (see Lieblich, 2000a), focusing on the stories narrated by kibbutz members about their individual history within their community. The second study was carried out by Tuval-Mashiach as part of her doctoral dissertation on gender, status and life stories (Tuval-Mashiach, 2000).

In my own study I found, as expected from the literature review, that when telling the history of their kibbutz, the narratives of women included reference to many more people than the stories of men. All the female members mentioned when and how they started their family, and told me about each one of their children, as part of the kibbutz story, without me having to inquire about this. Men could complete a long interview without any mentioning of their families. They talked in general about historical or political events, which took place in Israel, the region, and/or in the kibbutz. They spoke much less about individuals, and much more about the economic development of the collective, about various difficulties and crises in the different branches of the kibbutz, about committees and functions in which they themselves had often played a major role. They analyzed processes of development in a highly abstract manner, and described possible scripts for the future in the same impersonal style. When people were mentioned in the men's narratives, it was often with a critical tone, even anger, regarding their performance as devoted kibbutz members. To me, these masculine narratives were often quite boring.

Narratives provided by the female members were much more 'human'. The story was often structured or anchored around personal events, which had happened to individuals, children, women or men, particularly from the teller's family. Sadness and laughter, anger, complaints and gossip colored these stories. Women rarely analyzed the economy of the collective, but they did tell long stories to illuminate for me issues related to the situation in the dining hall, the central laundry or the educational system. One of the women elaborated in great detail on the process of abandoning the communal sleeping arrangement and bringing the children from their dormitories back home. In another interview, the same woman also told me with obvious pain about the recent changes in the way Friday night dinner was served to the members. These were in fact highly important collective processes, but the fact remains that this female informant chose to demonstrate these processes by means of their private, universal, 'natural' aspects.

An additional demonstration can be provided from the way male and female members of Gilgal referred to 'The Crisis', which happened ten years prior to our conversation and tore the community into two sectors, one of which – almost half of the kibbutz membership – had finally left. Almost all the male interviewees referred to the Crisis as one of the major events in the history of Gilgal. When Rami attempted to explain this, he gave me an abstract sociological explanation about two groups and the tension between them. He said:

> As a group, there was something about the Kibbutz-born members which threatened the members who had come from the cities. I don't think that the Kibbutz-born were aware of this, they were really good people. They implicitly oppressed the city-born members, however, they behaved as if they were superior somehow. They walked around in the kibbutz as if it belonged to them. I, myself am from the city, but personally I was closer to the kibbutz-born sector. (72)[1]

Another man, Ami, gave another general theory. He gave his account in a clear and confident style, explaining the situation as follows:

> People had left the kibbutz because there was simply nothing for them to do here. They felt that they were wasting away in very simple jobs. They were talented people and could achieve much more. Going to the fields every spring and fall, bending down to pick vegetables, could not satisfy them. Moreover, at the end of the day they felt their hurting backs, and they realized they could not go on like this for a long time. It was not interesting either. This frustration led to the quarrel, which produced the crisis. Then they left. (77)

Women, on the other hand, could hardly relate to the crisis and its reasons. Most of the women did not bring it up until I asked them directly about it. When I did ask, many said simply that they could not fathom the reason for the event, that it was arbitrary or stupid. This, for example, is the way in which Zippi told me about the Crisis. Note that her story does include first person statements, and evaluative, emotional expressions. It also emphasizes the sudden, as if surprising, nature of the occurrence:

> We were neutral. We were in the middle. We had no opinion about this faction or the other. Suddenly I found myself in a situation that if I talked to someone about what was happening, I would later discover that the other half of the members stopped talking to me. You have to decide to what camp you belong. Why should I decide all of a sudden? ... It was horrible. (82)

But for Zippi this major event left only few traces beside its negative emotional aspects. This can be drawn from the following quoted dialogue between us:

> Zippi: We went to people and tried to understand what did they want, why did they wish to stay or to leave. We sat very seriously with each camp and selected our side.
>
> I: What side was it?
>
> Zippi: I don't remember anymore ... I think it was the side of the kibbutz-born. But I am not sure about that. (83)

In another conversation, this one with Ada, I tried again to receive an account of the Crisis. She said sadly: 'Look, we actually didn't understand what was happening around us. But it was a terrible period. If you talked to one, you were banned by the other' (85). When I asked her to elaborate a little more, she said that she did not remember. It was a rough time for her, she explained, her father had died a year earlier, and right during the Crisis her first baby was born, so these were the real things that had filled her world then.

In Beit Hashita, a kibbutz I studied 22 years ago, there had also been a rupture in the community in 1952, named 'The Division', when almost half of the kibbutz had left to go to another kibbutz (see Lieblich, 1981). As in Gilgal, the men were much more coherent than the women in giving an account of this historical event. Only men, and none of the women, were able to depict the political, even international, process, which had underlain this event (that had taken place in many kibbutzim at the time).

In the study conducted by Tuval-Mashiach, mid-life men and women were interviewed and provided their life stories. To clarify the influence of social status vs. the variable of gender, occupational standing of the interviewees was also considered. Half of the group were middle-class people, and the other half, high class, namely top managers and directors, highly placed physicians or lawyers, and so on (Tuval-Mashiach, 2000). While this thesis is very rich in its findings, and it is beyond the scope of the present paper, several conclusions are relevant to the ideas developed here. The variety among women's stories was wider, and their emerging identities indeed more fragmented. Women's stories included a number of interwoven plots, and as claimed by the theories, they were less linear than the stories provided by men. Men's life stories, especially the high status men, were organized around a single theme or plot – the narrative of their work, or their success story. The major messages emerging from the Israeli men's stories concerned ambitiousness and the drive toward outstanding achievements or excellence. They conveyed the ability to overcome obstacles and were characterized by emotional restraint. Although they were all married, and most of them fathers, they almost neglected to mention these parts of their life, nor did they refer to other meaningful relationships. Middle-class women emphasized their families and relationships as a major aspect of their identities, as expected. High-class women however, manifested a new kind of feminine identity, more androgynous, perhaps, like in Bateson's examples in her study in the USA.

A closer analysis of the stories revealed that men and women have, indeed, different time concepts as the basis for their narratives. Men convey a sense of control, they 'master' time and bend it to their wishes. In other words, the various circumstances encountered in their lives did not deter them from their goals, did not deflect them. On the contrary, they made these circumstances serve their narrative. They experienced deterrence as a challenge, and the need to cope with it – a source of empowerment. Women's narratives frequently conveyed that they 'served' time, they were at the mercy of circumstances and other people's priorities. Their story-lines were often deflected, and if they reached their goals, it was by a roundabout and interrupted course.

Finally, we may add again to the matrix of this paper the Israeli perspective. It seems to me that as Israelis, both women and men, we are keenly aware of our time and space, our siege position (real or imagined, this does not matter in the world of narratives) in the geo-political world and environment which surrounds us. This awareness is certainly higher than in more secure societies, be it the Swiss or the American. To prove this point one need only to take account of the time an average Israeli listens to or watches the news. The time-place we live in, and the fact we are Jewish, one or two generations after the Holocaust, plays a major part in our identities. My accumulated studies reveal that for many Israelis, but more so for men than for women, the various wars in the region serve as markers or anchors for the construction of a life story. Women, however, are no less tuned to our time/place, although they manifest it in somewhat more subdued voice. Being wives or mothers of soldiers, for example, is a focal element in Israeli women's identity (see Lieblich, 1978, 2000b), and the emotions attached to this element vary as an outcome of the changing times and events, and even as an outcome of the place one resides in in Israel. Whether we live here because of Zionism or Post-Zionism, or if due to the forced immigration of our parents or grandparents, all these are time-place concepts, evidently, and they deeply affect our identities.

If I go back to my study of Gilgal, the importance of the place in the identity of Gilgal's members was striking, and led to a separate analysis (Marten, 1999). In people's narratives, they kept relating to the site of their kibbutz, various landscapes, the Jordan Valley, the desert, the mountains, the neighbors – Jewish and Arab villages, nomads – and the kibbutz as a home, its gardens, the houses, the paths, the trees. All these seem to be an important part of the narrators' identity, perhaps even more so because they saw the place as being under the threat of evacuation, and experienced their life there as under siege. It is perhaps a generalization one can make, namely that the more a place struggles with its survival, or the more uncertain its existence, the larger will be the significance or place of its localization in its individual residents' identities.

Let me close this paper with another poem by Lea Goldberg, a poem about a modern Jewish experience, according to my reading – about the Holocaust. It speaks about one moment when time stopped, expressing the wish to stop linear time from its progress toward calamity, or the wish to bring back the good times of the past. Furthermore, it is written from a woman's perspective, focusing on nature and home, using the private images of the table and the meal set on it, such a-historic notions, to lament the loss experienced by the Jewish people as a whole.

From 'Ending' (3)

I imagined that time had stood still
that apple trees are still standing as old
in full bloom, or the autumn gardens
are spreading again a carpet of their gold

As though our world has not been shattered
as though we've not seen all we've seen
as though our house and place are still standing
within a white table set for feast.

(1979, vol. 1: 246; translated by Rachel T. Back)

NOTE

1. The following quotes are translated from the Hebrew original. Page numbers are from the Hebrew source (Lieblich, 1995). An English version of the book, with all the quoted poems, is forthcoming (*Learning about Lea*. London: Athena Press, 2003).

REFERENCES

Bakan, D. (1966) *The Duality of Human Existence: Isolation and Communion in Western Man*. Boston: Beacon.
Baron, Dvora (1970) *Exile*. Tel Aviv: Am Oved (Hebrew).
Bateson, M.C. (1989) *Composing a Life*. New York: The Atlantic Monthly Press.
Belenky, M.F., Clinchy, B.M., Goldberger, N.R. and Tarule, J.M. (1986) *Women's Ways of Knowing*. New York: Basic Books.
Bruner, J. (1990) *Acts of Meaning*. Cambridge, MA: Harvard University Press.
Butler, J. (1993) *Bodies that Matter: On the Discursive Limits of Sex*. New York: Routledge.
Chodorow, N. (1978) *The Reproduction of Mothering: Psychoanalysis and the Sociology of Gender*. Berkeley: University of California Press.
Erikson, E.H. (1950) *Childhood and Society*. New York: Norton.
Erikson, E.H. (1968) *Identity: Youth and Crisis*. New York: Norton.
Erikson, E.H. (1968/1974) 'Womanhood and the Inner Space', in J. Strouse (ed.) *Women Analysis. Dialogues on Psychoanalytic Views of Femininity*. New York: Grossman Publishers (pp. 291–319).
Gergen, K.J. (1991) *The Saturated Self: Dilemmas of Identity in Modern Life*. New York: Basic Books.
Gilligan, C. (1982) *In a Different Voice*. Cambridge, MA: Harvard University Press.
Goldberg, Lea (1968) *Ha-mefuzar mi-kfar Azar*. Tel Aviv: Sifriat Ha-Poalim (Hebrew).
Goldberg, Lea (1978) *Remnants of Life*. Tel Aviv: Sifriat Ha-Poalim (Hebrew).
Goldberg, Lea (1979) *Collected Poems*, Volumes 1, 2, 3. Tel Aviv: Sifriat Ha-Poalim (Hebrew).

Gutmann, D.L. (1987) *Reclaimed Powers: Toward a New Psychology of Men and Women in Later Life*. New York: Basic Books.
Heilbrun, G. Carolyn (1988) *Writing a Woman's Life*. New York: Norton.
Josselson, R. (1992) *The Space Between Us: Exploring the Dimensions of Human Relationships*. San Francisco: Jossey-Bass.
Klein, M. (1983) *Hidden Selves: Between Theory and Practice in Psychoanalysis*. London: Hogarth.
Kristeva, J. (1986) 'Women's Time', in *The Kristeva Reader*, ed. Toril Moi. New York: Columbia University Press.
Lee, D. (1950) 'Codifications of Reality: Linear and Nonlinear', *Psychosomatic Medicine*, May 1950, No. 12.
Lieblich, A. (1978) *Tin Soldiers on Jerusalem Beach*. New York: Pantheon.
Lieblich, A. (1981) *Kibbutz Makom*. New York: Pantheon.
Lieblich, A. (1995) *El Lea*. Tel Aviv: Kibbutz Hameuchad (Hebrew).
Lieblich, A. (1997) *Conversations with Dvora Baron*. Berkeley: California University Press.
Lieblich, A. (2000a) *Gilgulo shel Makom*. Tel Aviv: Schoken (Hebrew).
Lieblich, A. (2000b) 'On Mourning for Soldier-sons in Israel', in R.J. Siegel, E. Cole and S. Steinberg-Oren (eds) *Jewish Mothers Tell Their Stories*. New York: The Uaworth Press (pp. 75–86).
Lubin, O. (1995) 'Trifles from Nachama's Kitchen: An Alternative Nationalism in "Exile" by Dvora Baron', *Theory and Criticism*, 7: 159–75 (Hebrew).
Marten, N. (1999) *Place-identity among Gilgal Members in View of the Changes in the Community and the Threat of Evacuation*. MA Thesis, Jerusalem: The Hebrew University (Hebrew).
McAdams, D. (1993) *The Stories we Live by: Personal Myths and the Making of the Self*. New York: William Morrow.
Miller, J.B. (1976) *Towards a New Psychology of Women*. Boston: Beacon Press.
Miller, J.B. (1991) 'The Development of Women's Sense of Self', in J.V. Jordan, A.G. Kaplan, J.B. Miller, I.P. Stiver and J.L. Surrey (eds) *Women's Growth in Connection*. New York: Guilford Press (pp. 11–26).
Minuchin, S. (1974) *Families and Family Therapy*. Cambridge, MA: Harvard University Press.
Sarbin, T.R. (ed.) (1986) *Narraive Psychology: The Storied Nature of Human Conduct*. New York: Praeger.
Tavris, C. (1992) *The Mismeasure of Women*. New York: Simon and Schuster.
Tuval-Mashiach, R. (2000) *Identity, Gender and Status in the Life Stories of Israeli Women and Men*. Doctoral dissertation, Jerusalem: The Hebrew University (Hebrew).
Woolf, Virginia (1928) *Orlando*. London: Hogarth Press.
Woolf, Virginia. (1929) *A Room of One's Own*. London: Hogarth Press.

# *Index*

Note: page numbers in *italics* refer to information contained in tables.
Page numbers underlined refer to illustrations.

10th Infantry Regiment (Finnish) 118
24th Infantry Regiment (Finnish) 118
Abrahams, Roger D. 150
activism 48
Adams, Jane 179
Afghanistan 51
Agassi, Shimon 215–16
agoraphobia 160
Agudat Yisrael 11
Akiba 72
Alechem, Scholem 71
Alexander II, Tsar of Russia 52, 110
Alexander III, Tsar of Russia 110
Aliyat Hanoar 168, 249
allegory 130, 138, 266–7
Alliance Israelite Universelle 214, 215, 221
Allies 78, 79, 80, 81, 82, 85, 96, 98
Alterman, Nathan 253
Altmann, Tosia 59–60, 61, 63
American Joint Distribution Committee 87, 94
American Medical Association 175
American Occupational Therapy Association 174, 175
American School Luncheon Movement 171
American Zionist Medical Unit 172, 173
American Zionist Movement xxi, 165–82; *see also specific organizations*
annihilation of the Jews 33, 74–5, 108, 134; *see also* Final Solution; genocide; Holocaust
anorexia 160–1, 162
*anschluss* 121
anti-Jewish legislation, Libyan 203
anti-Semitism 119, 120, 133, 195; Finnish 108–9, 110–11, 117, 124; as instrument of the capitalist classes 134; Polish 3, 12, 14–15, 17, 56, 68; Russian 110; *see also* annihilation of the Jews; Final Solution; genocide; Holocaust
antifascists, memorials to 133, 135, 139
*Apua hakevat kädet* memorial 122–3, <u>123</u>
Arabs/Arabic culture 204, 217, 221, 235, 236
Aricha, Yaakov 242
Arlosoroff, Chaim 242
Armand, Inessa 53
Armée Juive 75
Ashdot Ya'akov training group 225, 231–2
Ashkenazic kibbutz 216, 217, 236
Augustine, St 18
Auschwitz 92–3, 124, 191
Austria 81, 121
autobiographies *see* diaries; memoirs; Yivo (Jewish Scientific Institute), Vilna, autobiography collection
Axis countries 120; *see also specific countries*

baby boom, amongst Jewish survivors 79, 83, 86–90, 96, 97; as form of revenge 90, 91, 93, 98–9
Babylonian Jewry Heritage Center archives 219
Babylonian Liaison Bureau 218, 225
Back, Rachel T. 270, 277, 284
Baghdad girls' school 215
Bahad 203
Bakan, D. 273
Baltic States 112
Bar-Ilan University conference, January 2001 xix
Baron, Dvora 276
Barthes, Roland 128
Bartov, Hanoch 82
Basevitz, Lilia 62
Basok, Ido 5
Bat-Dori, Shulamit 57
Bateson, Catherine 274, 277, 282
Bateson, Gregory 274
Baumel, Judy 128
Bavly, Sara 174
Becker, Esther 244, 245
Beit Hana 250
Belenky, M.F. 275
Belgium 68, 70, 73
Ben Gurion, David 96–7, 243
Ben-Gurion University 175
Ben-Yehudah Society for the study of Hebrew language 202, 204
Ben-Zvi, Yitzhak 242, 254, 256, 260
Bergson, Henri 147
Berlin 78, 130; *see also* West Berlin
Betar 14, 16–17, 72, 202
Beth Hakerem Institute of teacher training 174
Bezalel Art School 254
Bialik, Haim Nachman 255
Bialystok ghetto uprising 74
Bible: Christian 111; Hebrew 24
Bielicka-Bornstein, Chasia 71, 73
*binyan ha'aretz* 169
Birenau death camp 122
birth rates: amongst Polish Jewry 70; *see also* baby boom
Bistritski, Nathan 22–3
Bloom, Ethel 174, 175
Bnai Akiva 203
Bnot Agudat Yisrael youth movement 9, 10, 13, 24–5
bodily constructions of memory 149, 153–4
body, female 150–1, 157–9, 160–1
Bohr, Niels 121
Bolshevik revolution 51–2, 53, 54
Bolshevism 53–5, 111

Borowska, Hina  60
Brawer, Avraham  242
Brecht, Bertolt  130
Breshko-Breshkovskaya, Yekaterina  52
Brison, Susan  98
Britain  78, 80, 241, 256, 266
Britannia  266
British Empire  214
British Military Administration, Libya  200, 203
Broder, Pierre  74–5
Bruner, J.  278
Brussels  72
Brzozowski, Stanislaw  55
BT, Ms (woman from the Warsaw ghetto)  47
Buber-Neumann, Margarete  135
Buchenwald Memorial (Cremer)  128, *129*, 137
Bund  72
Bunkers, Suzanne  7
Burgauer, Erica  134
Butler, J.  271
Byrne, Secretary of State  85

Cala, Alina  5
Cambodia  51
Canada  249
capitalist classes  134; *see also* elite; upper classes
cemeteries, for the fallen (Finnish)  114–16, *115*
censuses: Palestinian 1940 mobilization  61–3; Polish 1921  3; Polish 1931  3, 68
CENTOS (refugee aid committee)  43–4, 45, 46
Central Committee of Liberated Jews  83, 93
Central Historical Commission, Munich  94
Central Memorial for the Victims of War and Tyranny, Berlin  130, *132*
Central Zionist Archives, Jerusalem  201
Cesarani, David  188
charity  169
Cheigham, Rachel  75
Chelnov, Benyamin  262
child-rearing  229–31, 274, 283
children's welfare  170–1, 179
Chizik, Ephraim  256, 257–60
Chizik, Hanna  260
Chizik, Sara  256, 257–60
Chodorow, N.  273
choice  48
Christianity  130, 132, 135, 137, 138–9, 266, 267
Chulda  246
Chulda (kibbutz)  246
Cixous, Hélène  158
Code, Lorraine  195
Cohen, Virginia  71
Cold War  79, 84–5
collective memory  150–1, 188, 192, 193, 194–5
Collingwood, Robin George  46
colonialism, European  213–15, 236
Columbia University  176
*Commentary* (journal)  85
Communism: and gender equality  52–3; and Holocaust memorials  134–5; interwar Polish  6, 8, 13–14, 15, 21
Communist Party  134; and female resistance fighters  72, 73, 75; and gender equality  53, 53
Communist Youth League  60, 135, *136*
comradeship  117
concentration camps: Gross-Rosen 128; for Jewish Displaced Persons  79, 80–1, 82–4, 85–6, 87, 88, 89, 94; memorials to  xx, 126–39, *127*, *129*; Ravensbrueck  xx, 126, 137; Weisswasser  128; *see also* Auschwitz; death camps
Congress Poland  56
Continuation War  113, 117, 118, 121
contraception  88
counter-memory  126, 139
countercultures  51, 54, 61, 64–5
Cremer, Fritz  126–8, 130
Crum, Bartley  85, 87
Cukierman, Yizhak  250
cultural historians  146, 147

daily life: of Jewish immigrants in the interwar period  69; and Jewish women's identity  189, 190, 192, 194; of Polish interwar Jewry 68; of women in the Warsaw ghetto  30–46, 47–9
*Dark Sister, The* (Goldstein)  147–8, 154–62
*Davar* (newspaper)  261
Dayan, Deborah  245
de Beauvoir, Simone  155, 156–7
death camps  121, 122; *see also* concentration camps
demonization, of Zionism  134
Denmark  121
Devar ha-Po'elet  210
Devorah  246
Devorah (Devorat Ha Tabor)  246
diaries  146
Diaspora  211, 217, 234
Dickinson, Emily  158, 159
Dietic Departments  174
difference  192
disease  31, 36
disnaming  128
displaced persons: state of mind of  270; *see also* Jewish Displaced Persons
district nursing  171
Dizengoff, Meir  255
Draenger, Gusta  75
dream analysis  241
Dresden  124
Dror  72, 250
Durkheim, Émile  147
Duskin, Julia  174

East Germany  138; *see also* German Democratic Republic
eastern Europe  79, 80
economic enterprises, of the Zionist Organization of America  167
education: accounts of in the Yivo autobiographies  11–13, 17; of female resistance fighters  67, 71, 72; Hadassah's involvement in  166, 168, 171–6, 178, 180, 182; of Iraqi Jewry  214, 215, 220–2, 229–30, 234; Libyan  200, 204–6, 207, 210; training grants 176; Zionist Organization of America's involvement in  167
Ehrenburg, Ilya  91
Eichmann, Adolf  120
Ein Gev  xxi, 252, *259*, 261–5, 266, 267–8
Eisenhower, Dwight D.  81
Ekron  248
elites: colonialized Muslim  213–14; *see also* capitalist classes; upper classes
Elmaliach, Avraham  242
emigration  37, 68–9
Engels, Friedrich  52–3

# Index

Epstein, Mira 59
equality *see* gender equality
Eretz Yisrael 248; Hadassah in 165, 166, 168–9, 170–6, 177, 179–80, 182; *see also* Israel, State of
Erikson, E.H. 271–2, 276
Esther (pseudonym of a young woman from Grójec) 6, 9–10, 11, 12, 13, 14, 17, 19, 24–5
Estonia 121, 122
Ettinger, Akiva 242
Europe, post-Second World War, and Jewish Displaced Persons 78–99
Europe, pre-/during the Second World War: and female Jewish identity in interwar Poland xx, 3–26; and female resistance fighters xx, 67–75; and women leaders in left-wing organizations xx, 51–65; and women in the Warsaw ghetto xx, 29–49
European colonialism 213–15, 236
ex-nominating 128

Fackenheim, Emil 189
families: Arabic 221; context of and memory 147, 150–4, 156–7, 160, 162–3; of female resistance fighters xx, 67–72; women's concerns regarding 190
family therapy 272–3
fashion, kibbutzim 225
fathers: amongst interwar Polish Jewry 8, 9, 19–20, 23; of female resistance fighters 69–70, 71, 72; image of 19–20; representation in fiction 157
Federation of Mizrachi Women of the United States 248, 249
feminism: and American post-Holocaust memory 187; Bolshevik 54; and female leadership in left-wing organizations 54, 56, 57; fiction 154–5, 156–8; and Hadassah 178, 181, 182; kibbutz 62–3; social 170, 178
fiction, construction of memory in xxi, 145–63
Final Solution 33; and female resistance fighters 74, 75; lack of Finish involvement 108, 120; survivors of 80; *see also* annihilation of the Jews; genocide; Holocaust
Finland: and the Continuation War 113, 117, 118, 121; and the deportation of Jews to Germany 109, 122–3, 124, 125; Jewish refugees in 121–2; and the Lapland War 113, 117; memory of the Holocaust and Second World War xx, 108–25; sacrifice of 113–18; unity of 113, 116–18; victory of 113, 118; and the Winter War 112, 113, 114, 116, 117, 118
Finnish army: comradeship 117; Jewish soldiers in 108, 109, 110–11, 112–13, 114, 116, 117–18; Second World War losses 113, 114
Finnish Civil War 1918 116
Finnish Independence Day, Dec 6, 1944 116
Finnish Jewish Veterans' Organisation 108
Finnish school system 111
First World War 55, 57, 179–80, 214, 248, 276
Fish, Marjory 174–5
forgetting, strategies of, monuments as 128
Foucault, Michel 147
France: female resistance fighters 68, 69–70, 72–3; Jewish immigrants 69–70
Frank, Anne 187, 188
Frank, Hans 63
Frank, Leonhard 12
freedom, women's 146, 155, 163

Freiman, Lillian 248, 249
Freud, Sigmund 82, 241
Frieman, Aaron 242
Friend, Robert 279
fundraising 167, 176, 179, 181

Gagnier, Regenia 7
Galicia 56, 57
Gamzu, Haim 257
GDR-USA Friendship Committee 137
Gedud Megine ha-Safah ha-'Ivrit (the Battalion of the Guardians of the Hebrew Language) 202
gender xix, xx, xxi; and American post-Holocaust memory 187–95; and the construction of memory in fiction by American Jewish women xxi, 145–63; and female Jewish identity in interwar Poland xx, 3–26; and female resistance fighters xx, 67–75; and Hadassah xxi, 165–82; influence on Hadassah's areas of activity 169–70; influence on Hadassah's traits and conceptions 168–9; and identity xxii, 271, 273–7, 279–83; and Israeli monuments xxi, 252–68; and Israeli settlements named for women xxi, 240–51; and Jewish Displaced Persons xxi, 78–99; and war memorials xxi, 126, 128–33, 134–5, 138–9, 252–68; and women leaders in left-wing organizations xx, 51–65; and women in the Warsaw ghetto xx, 29–49; and Zionist Youth Movements in Libya xxi, 199–211
gender constancy 271
gender equality: amongst the Iraqi Jewry 215, 222–3, 234; representation in Israeli monuments 253, 267; lack of Arabic 221; and women leaders in left-wing organizations 52–5, 57–8, 62–3, 64; and the Zionist Youth Movements in Libya 202, 207–8
genocide: Finish knowledge of 121; *see also* annihilation of the Jews; Final Solution; Holocaust
George V, King of England 249
Gergen, K.J. 271
German Democratic Republic (GDR): as guard against anti-Semitism 133–4; war memorials of 126, 128, 130, 132, 133–4, 135, 137, 139; *see also* East Germany
German government xx
German-Israeli Foundation 138
German–Polish War 1939 57, 58–61, 63–4
Germania 266
Germany: and the Final Solution 74; and Finland in the Second World War 108–9, 112–13, 116, 117, 120, 121–2, 124–5; guilt forgotten 84; and the Holocaust 119, 121–2; and Jewish Displaced Persons in occupied post-war 78–99; and the Molotov-Ribbentrop non-aggression pact 116; and the numbering of Jews 240; post-Second World War Jewish relations 90–1, 98; *see also* East Germany; German Democratic Republic; Nazis; West Germany
Gestapo 39, 121, 122, 125
ghettos 25; Bialystok 74; female leadership in 59–60, 61, 63, 64; and female resistance fighters 73, 74; *see also* Warsaw ghetto
Giladi, Yisrael 144
Gilbert, Sandra 155, 160–1, 162
Gilligan, Carol 195, 272, 276
Gillis, John R. 133

girlhood, distortions of the memories of  145, 146, 147, 152–4, 162, 163
girls: education of Libyan Jewish  204–6, 207, 210; and moral issues  273; and the Zionist Youth Movements  204–10
Givat Ada  248
Givat Brenner  243
Giv'at Hashelosha  217, 225
Givat Havivah  249–50
Givat Olga  247
Glickson, Moshe  242
God  23, 24, 111, 191–2
Golani, Gideon  225
Goldberg, Lea  269–70, 271, 276–7, 278–9, 283–4
Goldberg, R. (pseudonym Rega)  8, 12, 13–14, 15–16, 17, 19, 21, 23
Goldberg, Sarah  72
Goldenberg, Myrna  188
Goldman, Wendy  54
Goldstein, Rebecca  xxi, 145; *Dark Sister, The* 147–8, 154–62
Gotsfeld, Batya  248, 249
Government of Israel Names Committee  242, 243
Great Patriotic War  264, 267
Gringauz, Samuel  85, 95
Gross-Rosen concentration camp  128
Grossman, Chaika  73, 74
Grossman, Hajka  58–9, 60, 61, 63
Gruner, Dov  266
Gubar, Susan  155, 160–1, 162
guides corps  205
Guta (woman from the Warsaw ghetto)  38–43
Gutman, Israel  74
Guttmann, D.L.  273

ha-Haverah ba-Kibbutz  210
ha-No'ar ha-Ahid (the United Youth)  203
Ha'avodah, Gedud  247
Hacohen, Yisrael Meir  24
Hadassah Medical Organization  173
Hadassah School of Nursing  173
Hadassah (Women's Zionist Organization of America)  xxi, 165–82, 246, 248; children's welfare  170–1, 179; and education  166, 168, 171–6, 178, 180, 182; and Eretz Yisrael 165, 166, 168–9, 170–6, 177, 179–80, 182; and feminism  178, 181, 182; and Israel 167–8, 171, 173, 177, 180; medical projects of  166, 167–8, 169–71, 172–6, 177, 178–9, 180–1; practicality of  168, 172; commitment to science  168, 169; stability of  176–7; as women's organization  178–81; and the Yishuv  172, 173, 177, 180
Hadassah-Hebrew University Medical School 168, 175
Hadera  247
Haendler, Werner  135–7
Haganah cells  208
Hager, Kurt  134
Hakhsharah (training camps)  208–9, 210, 211
Hakibbutz Hameuchad  216, 218, 226
Halbwachs, Maurice  147, 152
Halutz (the Pioneer)  202, 203, 208–10
Hankin, Olga  247
Hankin, Yehoshua  242, 247
Harrison, Earl G.  80–1
Harrison Report  80–1, 84, 85
Hartman, Geoffrey H.  126, 139

Harvard University  176
Harviainen, Tapani  109, 110, 111, 116, 118, 121
Hashomer Hatzair movement  16–17, 249–50; female resistance fighters of  72–4; gender policies 55; and the German–Polish War 1939  57, 58–61, 63–4; morals of  73; and the Palestinian 1940 mobilization census  61–3; and the Russo–Polish War  55–7; and the Vrutsky discussion on the role of women in 57–8; women leaders at times of crisis  xx, 51, 52, 55–65
Haukeland, Niels  122
Havatzelet Hasharon  249
Hebrew Bible  24
Hebrew language  167
Hebrew names  243
Hebrew University, Jerusalem  167–8, 169, 172, 180
Hechalutz organization  59, 60
Hefer Valley  249
Hehalutz  222
Heilbrun, G. Carolyn  26, 277
Heinemann, Marelene  188
Heller, Celia  5
*Helsingin Sanomat* (Finnish newspaper)  124
Helsinki cemetery  114–16, **115**, 118
Hepher  247
Herf, Jeffrey  34
heritage, Jewish, transmission of  172
heroic sacrifice: of the Finnish Jews  113–18; monuments to 252, 253, 256, 257–60, <u>258</u>, <u>259</u>, 261, 262–5, 267; of women  252, 253, 256, 257–60, 261, 262–5, 267; *see also* heroines; martyrdom
heroines  132–3, 139, 252, 253, 256, 257–60, 261, 262–5, 267
Heymont, Irving  84, 87–8
Himler, Heinrich  112–13
Hiroshima  124
Hirschmann, Ira  85, 98
Histadrut  256, 266
historical empathy  46
history, as the 'other'  46
Hitler, Adolf  93, 120
Hoffmann-Curtius, Kathrin  126
Hoglah  246, 247
Hoglah (mostav)  247
Holland  71
Holocaust  25, 283–4; communist memorials to  134–5; and female resistance fighters  xx, 67–75; Finnish knowledge of  120–1; Finnish memories of  xx, 108–9, 119–25; GDR memorials to  xx, 126–39, <u>127</u>, <u>129</u>; memoirs composed following 6; nationalistic narratives regarding  119, 124–5; and the Polish Jews  3, 25; and women leaders in left-wing organizations  51, 58–65; and women in the Warsaw ghetto  xx, 29–49; *see also* annihilation of the Jews; Final Solution; genocide; post-Holocaust memory
Holocaust survivors: in the Displaced Persons camps  80, 81–2, 86, 87, 88, 89, 90, 91–2, 94–5, 97–8, 99; as rapists  91–2; remembering  94–5; in the Soviet Zone  134
Honecker, General Secretary  137
hope  37, 96
Horowitz, Sarah  130–2
housing  245
Hovevei Zion movement  248
Hulda  xxi, 252, 256–61, 267
Hulme, Kathryn  82–3, 84

# Index

hunger 10, 36–7, 40, 46
hygiene, kibbutzim 228–9
Hyman, Abraham S. 88
Hyman, Paula 4

identification papers, false 74
identity xxii, 269–84; binary divisions of 162; complex nature of Jewish xix; construction in fiction xxi, 150, 154–5, 159–62; contemporary/secular Jewish 188–9, 190–5; defining 269; difficulties with the concept of 271; discovery of female through autobiography 18; disturbed 272–3; Erikson's views of 271–2; and the father–child relationship 19–20; fragmented/postmodern conceptions of 272, 273–4, 282; and gender xxii, 271, 273–7, 279–83; as 'identities' 271–2; impact of society on 154–5, 159–62; Israeli 282–3; amongst Jewish women in interwar Poland xx, 3–26; and the kibbutzim 217, 235; and memory xxii, 277–9; in Object-Relations theory 272; over-simplified nature of 271; and place xxii, 269–70, 271, 274–6, 282–3; and post-Holocaust memory 188–9, 190–5; and relationship 272, 275–6, 279; and time xxi, 269, 270–1, 274–7, 282–4
identity narratives 188–9, 190–5, 279–83
ideological awakening 18–19
illness, encouragement of female 160–1
imagery 149
Imperial Army 109–10
income, in the Warsaw ghetto 35–6, 37, 38
individuals, responsibility to the community 47–8
intellect, restraint on women's 149, 150, 152–3, 154, 161–2
intercultural encounters 213–36
International Women's Day 53
Iraqi Jewry: immigration to the Palestinian kibbutz 216, 217, 218–36; westernization of 214–16, 217, 219–22, 228–9, 230, 233–5
Irgun Zvai Le'umi (IZL) 266
Irigaray, Luce 158
Islamic countries: cultural influence on the Jewish populations of 217, 221, 235, 236; westernization 213–14; *see also* Muslims
Israel, State of xx, xxi, 135, 137; commemoration of the Holocaust 119; establishment, and the Zionist Organization of America 166, 166–7, 177, 181; and the GDR 133–4; and Hadassah 167–8, 171, 173, 177, 180; Iraqi Jewry's immigration to 222, 234, 236; Israeli identity 282–3; monuments of xxi, 128, 252–68; patriotism 253, 265; proclamation 89; settlements named for women xxi, 240–51; War of Independence 219, 253, 256, 261–2, 264–5, 266; and Zionist Youth Movements in Libya 201, 202, 210; *see also* Eretz Yisrael
Israeli Government 171
Italy 81, 200, 203, 204, 211

Jablonia camp 56
Jakobson, Max 111, 113, 117, 118, 120, 121, 122
James, Henry 155, 156, 159, 161
James, William 158–9, 161
Jehovah's Witnesses 139
Jesus Christ 111
Jewish American Princess (JAP) 155
Jewish Angry Women (JAWs) 155, 162

Jewish Brigade soldiers 82
Jewish Children's Relief (OSE) 73
Jewish Displaced Persons xx, 78–99; demographics 80; search for normality 99; self-perceptions of 79–86, 90; stigmatization 81–2; as survivors 79, 99; as victims 79, 95, 99; as villains 79, 84–5, 97–8, 99
Jewish Displaced Persons' Conference, St Ottilien 1945 93, 94
Jewish National Fund (JNF) 241–2; Argentine 243
Jewish Problem 4
Jewish Question 120
Jewish School (Finnish) 111
Jewish Scouts 73–4
Jewish State: dreams of 95–6, 98; *see also* Eretz Yisrael; Israel, State of
Johns Hopkins University 176
Jones, Ann Rosalind 158
Josselson, R. 273

Kahanoff, Jacqueline 213, 216
Kaila, Eino 121
Kalish 58
Kaplan, Israel 94
Kaplan, Marion 70–1
Kaplan, Rose 179
Kaufman, Debra 187, 188, 189, 193, 194, 195
Keren Kayemet le-Yisra'el (Jewish National Fund) 208
Kfar Batya 249
Kfar Blum 243
Kfar Brandeis 243
Kfar Felix Warburg 243
Kfar Glickson 242, 243
Kfar Hess 243
Kfar Marmoreck 243
Kfar Massaryk 243
Kfar Natan Lansky 243
Kfar Pines 243
Kfar Ruppin 243
Kfar Rut 247
Kfar Silver Agricultural School, Ashkelon 167
Kfar Szold 249
Kfar Ussishkin 242
Kfar Vitkin 243
Kfar Yehezkel 243
Kfar Yehoshua 242, 261, 266
Khmer Rouge 51
Kibbutz Artzi movement 249–50
Kibbutz Ashdot Ya'akov 219
Kibbutz Be'eri 225
Kibbutz Beerot Yitzhak 242
Kibbutz Beit Hashita 281–2
Kibbutz Bet Keshet 266
Kibbutz Buchenwald 97
Kibbutz Ein Harod 254
Kibbutz Gilgal 279, 280–1, 283
Kibbutz Kfar Giladi 244
Kibbutz Lahavot Havivah 250
Kibbutz Lohamei Hagetaot 250
Kibbutz Ma'anit 250
Kibbutz Negba 267
Kibbutz Neve Ur 219
Kibbutz Sede Nahum 219
kibbutzim: absorption of Jewish immigrants from Islamic countries xxi, 216–23, 223–36; attitude to religion 226–8; child-rearing methods

229–31; fashions for women 225; relations between the sexes 231–5; sleeping quarters 225–6; table manners and hygiene 228–9; women in xxi, 57–8, 61–3, 64, 210, 216–23, 223–36
Kielce pogrom 81
Kiryat Bialik 243
Kiryat Motzkin 243
Klass, Salomon 108
Klausner, Abraham 94
Klausner, Yosef 242
Klein, Melanie 272
Klein, Shmuel 242
Kligsberg, Moshe 10–11, 20–1
Kolleck, Teddy 262
Kollman, Georg 122
Kollwitz, Kaethe 130
Koonz, Claudia 128
KR, Ms (woman from the Warsaw ghetto) 33–8, 41
*Kristallnacht* pogrom 120
Kristeva, Julia 275, 276
Kupat Holim 180

Łódź 56
La Guardia, Fiorella 85, 98
Labor Battalion 254
LaCapra, Dominick 89–90, 187, 193
Lagerwey, Mary 187, 188
Laitinen, E. 113
Lakan, J. 275
Lammert, Will 126, 139
land/landscape 244, 245
Landsberg Displaced Persons camp 84
Landy, Rachel 179
*Lang ist der Weg* (Displaced Persons film) 95–6
language 167, 275, 277
Lapland War 113, 117
League for International Understanding 135
Lee, Dorothy 275
left-wing organizations: women leaders at times of crisis xx, 51–65; *see also specific organizations*
leftism 6
Leipzig Synagogue Choir 137
Lenin, Vladimir Ilyich 53
Levantine culture 213, 214, 216–17, 236
Levi, Primo 135
Levin, Meyer 87, 92
Lévy, Denise 74
liberation, dangers/disappointments of 89
Liberty 266
Libya: virtual Jewish space in 211; Zionist youth movements in xxi, 199–211
Lichansky, Batya xxi, 252, 254–5, 256–61, *258*, 266, 267
Lieblich, A. 276, 279, 281, 283
Lilienblum, Moshe Leib 24
Livson, Aron 108
Lloyd George, David 242
love: amongst interwar Polish Jewry 8, 9, 20–3; fictional portrayals of 152–4; Jewish-ethnic German 39–40, 42, 43, 90–1; in the kibbutzim 231–5; parental 67; of the women of the Warsaw ghetto 39–41, 42
Lubetkin, Tzivia/Zvi 59, 60, 63, 249, 250
Lubin, O. 276
Luostarinen, Heikki 111
Lutheran Church 111, 116

Luxemburg, Rosa 52
Lwow pogrom 56

Maaleh Zviah 250
Ma'ayan Harod 247
McAdams, D. 278
Mccune, Mary 178
McNarney, General 83
Madajsker, Sonya 60–1
Maisler, Binyamin 242
Makabi ha-Tza'ir (Young Maccabi) 202, 207
Manasseh 247
Mannerheim, Marshall 116
marriages: amongst Jewish Displaced Persons 86, 87, 88–9, 91; marital age amongst interwar Polish Jewry 7
Marten, N. 283
martyrdom 130; *see also* heroic sacrifice
Marx, Karl 52–3
*Maschiachskinder* (children of the Messiah) 90
Mason, Mary 18
masturbation 20–1
maternalism *see* motherhood
Mauthausen memorial site 130, **131**
Mazkeret Batya 248
Mead, Margaret 274
medical projects, Hadassah's involvement in 166, 167–8, 169–71, 172–6, 177, 178–9, 180–1
Medical Reference Board 175–6
Meir Rothschild Hadassah-University Hospital 180
Melnikov, Aaron 260
memoirs 146; of Iraqi Jewish migrants 218–20, 223–35
'memorial stone', Ravensbrueck Memorial site 137, **138**
memorials 94; *Apua hakevat kädet* 122–3, <u>123</u>; Buchenwald Memorial 128, <u>129</u>, 137; Central Memorial for the Victims of War and Tyranny, Berlin 130, <u>132</u>; Finnish xx, 114–16, <u>115</u>, 122, <u>123</u>, 125; Mauthausen memorial site 130, <u>131</u>; Neubrandenburg memorial site 128, <u>129</u>; Ravensbrueck Memorial xx, 126–39, <u>127</u>, <u>136</u>, <u>138</u>; Sachsenhausen Memorial 137; *see also* monuments
memory xix, xx, xxi; American post-Holocaust xxi, 187–95; and autobiography xx, 4–26; bodily constructions of 149, 153–4; collective 150–1, 188, 192, 193, 194–5; construction in fiction by American Jewish women xxi, 145–63; and familial context 147, 150–4, 156–7, 160, 162–3; Finnish recollections of the Holocaust and Second World War xx, 108–25; and identity xxii, 277–9; and Jewish Displaced Persons xx, 79, 94–7; and naming 240, 241, 242, 245, 250; slippery nature/distortions of 30, 46, 145–6, 147, 152, 278; social constructedness of 147, 148, 152; as tainted by today's culture 30, 46; in terms of sexuality and reproduction 79, 94–7; *see also* counter-memory; memorials; monuments
Mendelsohn, Ezra 5
Merchaviah 245
Merkin, Daphne 145
Metzudat Menachem Ussishkin 242, 243
Meyer, Michael 195
Meyuchas, Yosef 242
middle classes: female resistance fighters amongst

# Index

69–71; and identity 282; amongst the Iraqi Jewry 214–15, 228
Mila 18th hideout 50
Miller, Jean B. 272
Miller, Nancy 157
Minuchin, S. 273
Mire, Gola 58, 61
Mizrachi 165
Mizrachi Women 165
Mizrachi party 203
Moledet 247
Molotov-Ribbentrop non-aggression pact 116
monuments: Israeli, and gender xxi, 252–68; *see also* memorials
Morad, Avraham 218, 234
Morad, Faraj 230, 231
Morad, Fuad 229, 230–1
Morad, Naji 220, 223, 224, 226
Morad, Rahel (Gorjiyeh) 218, 234
Morad-Mu'allem, Shoshana 218–20, 223–35; on child-rearing practice in the kibbutz 229–31; family conflict of 223; on kibbutzim fashion 225; on kibbutzim sleeping quarters 225–6; on kibbutzim table manners and hygiene 228–9; on relations between the sexes in the kibbutz 231–5; on religious observance in the kibbutz 226–8
moral issues: gender differences in the approach to 273; of the Hashomer Hatzair movement 73; of women in the Warsaw ghetto 42–3
Moseley, Marcus 5
Moses 247
Moshav Bitan Aaron 242
'Mother with dead son' (Kollwitz) 130, 132
'Mother, The' (Wittig) 128, 129
'Mother' (Thieme) 130, 131
motherhood: fictional constructions of 149–52, 156–7, 160, 161; images of in memorials xxi, 126, 127, 128–32, 129, 131, 133, 138–9, 252, 259, 261–5, 266
'Motherhood', Ein Gev (Orloff) xxi, 252, 259, 261–5, 266, 267–8
mothers, of female resistance fighters 69, 70, 71–2, 73
Mu'allem, Aryeh 219, 232–4, 235
Muslims 204; *see also* Islamic countries

Naami settlement 247
names: Hebrew 243; *see also* disnaming; place names
Names Committee 241–2
Naomi 246, 247
national continuity, representation in war memorials 130, 138, 139
National People's Army 134–5, 136
national personification 266–7
Nazem, Ovadia 232–3
Nazis 99, 249, 250, 255, 265; baby boom following the atrocities of 86, 87; extermination policies of 135; and Finland 108–9, 112, 124–5; and the German–Polish War 1939 58–61; and the Holocaust 119, 120; and Jewish Displaced Persons 78, 80–1; and the numbering of Jews 240; policies towards Polish Jews 30, 33, 34, 39, 43, 44, 45; war memorials regarding the atrocities of 139; on women's ability to survive 63; *see also* Third Reich

Nemilov, Anton Vitalievich 12
Neoth Mordechai 243
Neubrandenburg memorial site 128, 129
Neve Yamin 219
'new Jew' 236
New Yishuv, and Zionist Youth Movements in Libya 203, 210
Niederland, William 81
Niewyk, Donald L. 87
night killings 33
Nissenboim, Rav Yizchak 242
Nora, Pierre 152
Nordau, Max 262
norms 128, 147
Noyes, Dorothy 150
numbering of the Jews 240
nursing 171, 173–6, 179
nutritional therapy 174

'O Deutschland, bleiche Mutter' ('Germany, pale Mother') (Cremer) 130, 131
Object-Relations theory 272
occupational therapy 174–5
Ohringer, Mirjam 71
Olsen, Tillie xxi, 145, 147; *Tell Me a Riddle* 147, 148–54, 162–3
*Oneg Shabbat* underground documentation project xx
Orbach, Larry 92–3
Orloff, Chana xxi, 252, 255, 259, 261–5, 266, 267–8
other: and female identity 18; Jewish women's interest in 192, 193, 194, 195; Jewish women's position as in Judaism 191, 197; Jews position as in history 189; Polish Jewry as 14; study of history as 46; 'unacceptable' female attributes as 162
Ottoman empire 200, 214, 241
Ozick, Cynthia 145

Padower, Saul 80, 86
Palestine 57, 59, 64, 79, 82, 241, 248, 249, 250; and the 1940 mobilization census 61–3; and the establishment of a national Jewish state 79, 81; immigration of Iraqi Jewry to 216–17, 218, 219, 223–35; and Jewish Displaced Persons 83, 85, 87, 91, 93, 95, 96–7, 98; Jewish monuments in 252, 254, 255; and Zionist Youth Movements in Libya 201, 202, 203, 204, 206–7, 210, 211
Palestine Jewish Colonization Association (PICA) 247, 248
Paley, Grace 145
Palmach 253
Pardess Chana 248
parents: of female resistance fighters 69, 70–2, 73; *see also* fathers; mothers
patriarchy: amongst Polish interwar Jewry 19, 25; Arabic 221
patriotism, Israeli 253, 265
Peres, Yeshahyahu 242
Peretz 67
Perovskaya, Sofia 52
personality, of young Jewish women in interwar Poland 23–5
Pieta 130
Pinson, Koppel S. 94
Pioneer Women 165
piousness 71–2

place   xix–xx, xxi; and female Jewish identity in interwar Poland   xx, 3–26; and identity   xxii, 269–70, 271, 274–6, 282–3; inner   276; and women in the Warsaw ghetto   xx, 29–49
place names, Israeli   240–51; after men   242–3, 244; after women   xxi, 245–50; Biblical   244, 246–7; Hebrew   243
Plotnicka, Frumka   60
Poalei Zion   75, 165
pogroms   110; 50th anniversary of the November 1938 pogrom   137; Kielce   81; *Kristallnacht*   120; Lwow   56
Poland   110; census 1921   3; census 1931   3, 68; commemoration of the Holocaust   119; female resistance fighters in   67, 68, 73, 74, 75; and the German–Polish War 1939   57, 58–61, 63–4; ghettos   xx, 25, 29–49, 59–60, 61, 119, 250; interwar female Jewish identity in   xx, 3–26; interwar Jewish relations   14–15; and Jewish Displaced Persons   80; and the Russo–Polish War   55–7
Polish Commonwealth   55
Polish public school   3
Politburo   135
political diplomatic efforts, of the Zionist Organization of America   167
political motivation, of female resistance fighters xx, 72–5
post-Holocaust memory, American   xxi, 187–95
post-traumatic stress disorder (PTSD)   81
postmodernism   150, 272, 273–4
poverty   10–11, 67, 68; *see also* hunger
power   273
practicality   168, 172
*Pravda* (newspaper)   53
press, Finnish   120
Primrose, Archibald, fifth Earl of Rosebery   248
Primrose, Neil   248
professions for women   169–70, 221–2, 227; absence in Arabic culture   221; in the kibbutz 224–5, 227; nursing   171, 173–6, 179; *see also* work
prostitution   39, 40, 41–2, 43
Psalms   23
psychoanalysis   241
public relations, and the Zionist Organization of America   167

Rabinowicz (pseudonym Hanzi)   8–9, 12–13, 14, 15, 16–17, 20, 21–4
Rachel (matriarch)   246, 247
racism   192
Raivo, Petri   113, 114, 115, 118
Ramat David   242
Ramat Gan   266
Ramat Rachel   247
Ramat Tyomkin   243
Rangell, Johan Wilhelm   112–13
rape   89, 91–3
Rapoport, Natan   263, 267
Rautkallio, Hannu   110–11, 112, 113, 114, 117, 118, 120, 121, 122, 124
Ravensbrueck concentration camp   xx, 126, 137
'Ravensbrueck group of mothers' (Cremer) 126–8, 127
Ravensbrueck Memorial   xx, 126–39, 127, 136, 138; 50th anniversary of the camp's liberation 137; marginalization of the Jewish prisoners of   133, 134, 137, 138
Red Army   89, 91, 92, 116, 118, 121, 126
Reik, Haviva   63, 249–50
Reitala, A.   114
religious beliefs: of young Jewish women in interwar Poland   23–4; *see also* secularization
resistance fighters   61, 119; family origins   xx, 67–72; female   xx, 67–75, 96–7, 250; Israeli places named after   250; political motivation xx, 72–5
resistance to the Holocaust   25, 32, 72; broadening of the concept   91
revenge: and female resistance fighters   74–5; of Jewish Displaced Persons   xx, 79, 90–4, 95, 98–9; in terms of sexuality and reproduction 79, 90–4
Rich, Adrienne   155, 157, 161
Richardson, Barbara   194
Ringelblum, Emmanuel   43, 60
Rishon LeZion   248
'Roaring Lion' monument (Melnikov)   252–3, 260
Roma   137, 139
Roman Catholicism   266
Roosevelt, Eleanor   83
Rosh Pina   248
Rothschild, Adelaide   247, 248
Rothschild, Batya   247, 248
Rothschild, Dorothy   247
Rothschild, Baron Edmond de   248
Rothschild, Baron Edmond James de   247, 248
Rothschild Hadassah University Hospital   169, 175, 176, 180
Rothschild, Hannah   247, 248
Rothschild, James   247
Rothschild, Baron Meyer Nathan   247, 248
Rothschild, Wilhelm Karl   248
Rottenstreich, Efraim   242
Rousseau, Jean Jacques   18
Rozencwajg, Fanny   73
Rozencwajg, Guta   67
Rozovsky, Mordechai   243
Rubinstein, Ida   72, 73
Russia   52–5; *see also* Soviet Union
Russian Empire   109–10
Russo–Polish War   55–7
Ruth   246, 247

Sabbath   211, 226
Sachsenhausen Memorial   137
sacrifice, heroic: of the Finnish Jews   113–18; monuments to   252, 253, 256, 257–60, 258, 259, 261, 262–5, 267; of women   252, 253, 256, 257–60, 261, 262–5, 267
Salminen, Johannes   124
Salsitz, Norman   17
salvation   130
Sarbin, T.R.   278
Sawicka, Hanka   60
School Lunch project, Eretz Yisrael   171
Schwartz, Lynne Sharon   145
science, Hadassah's commitment to   168, 169
Sdeh Warburg   243
Second World War   203, 204, 249–50; Finnish memories   xx, 108–9, 112–25
secularization   226–8
Segev, Tom   97
Sehayek, Shaul   218

# Index

Seidler Feller, Chaim 195
Seitz, Gustav 128
Sejera (renamed Ilaniyah) 243
self-expression, of young Jewish women in interwar Poland 18–20
self-image, of Polish Jewish women 68–9, 70
self-in-relation 272
self-perceptions, of Jewish Displaced Persons 79–86, 90
Settlement House Movements 170, 171, 179
sex 158; amongst interwar Polish Jewry 20–3; in the kibbutzim 231–5
Shandler, Jeffrey 26
Shdemot Devorah 247
Shekhunat Borochov 243
silence 95, 275, 277
Silver, Abba Hillel 166
Sinti 137, 139
Sisera 246
SKIF (Jewish socialist children's association) 13, 14
Slepak, Cecilia xx, 29–49
Slushat, Nahum 242
smuggling, in the Warsaw ghetto 36–7, 40
social class: capitalist classes 134; middle classes 69–71, 214–15, 228, 282; Muslim elites 213–14; amongst Polish interwar Jewry 7, 8, 15–17; upper classes 282; working classes 7, 8
social feminism 170, 178
social justice 192–3
Social Revolutionary Party 52
social status 7, 8, 15–17, 273, 282
social-service projects 166
socialism 62; amongst interwar Polish Jewry 16–17, 24; and the Hashomer Hatzair movement 52
society, impact on women's identity 154–5, 159–62
solidarity, depiction in war memorials 130, 133, 139
Somech-Balbul, Arella 219, 223
Soviet Union 54; and the Continuation War 113; and Finland 112, 113, 114, 116–17, 118; German invasion of, 1941 112; and Jewish Displaced Persons 79, 80; and the Molotov-Ribbentrop non-aggression pact 116; monuments of 264, 266–7; and the Winter War 112, 113, 114; *see also* Russia; Russian Empire
Soviet Zone 134
Spanish Civil War 72
Spiegel, Sam 56
Sprinzak, Yosef 242
Stalin, Joseph 116
Stampfer, Shaul 7
starvation 36
State Police (Finnish) 121–2
stereotypes, of Jewish women 155
Stone, I.F. 82
Straus, Lina 179
Straus, Nathan 179
Strauss Health Center, Jerusalem 174
*Streicherhof* 93
style: of female autobiographies 18–19; of male autobiographies 18
Suomen Juutalaisten Sotaveteraanien Veljespiiri (Jewish war veterans in Finland organisation) 118
survivor syndrome 81
Sweden 112
Syria 261

Szenes, Hanna 210
Szold, Henrietta 166, 174, 179, 248, 249

Taliban 51
Tavris, C. 273
teachers, influence of 12
Tel Aviv museum 255
Tel Aviv University 175
Tel Hai, last stand of 253, 256, 260
Tel Mond 243
*Tell Me a Riddle* (Olsen) 147, 148–54, 162–3; construction of memory in 148, 149–54; subject matter 148–9
Temkin, Bathia 43–6, 47
Tennenbaum, Mordechai 74
Tenu'at ha-No'ar (the Youth Movement) 202
Tenu'at ha-Tzofim ha-Datiyim (The Jewish Boy Scouts) 202
Thieme, Gerhard 130
Third Reich 108, 120, 121, 124
time: feminine/cyclical 275–6, 276–7, 282, 283–4; and identity xxi, 269, 270–1, 274–7, 282–4; masculine/linear 275–7, 282
Tipot Halav (mother and child stations) 171
Tisha Be'Av 226–7
TOPOROL (society for agricultural training) 47
Torah 191
Tosia's land (Palestine) 59
'Tragende' ('Woman, carrying') memorial (Lammert) 126, <u>127</u>, 130, 134–5, 139
Treblinka, mass deportations to 30, 33, 37
triumph 261, 262
Truman, Harry S. 80
Trumpeldor, Yosef 247, 253
Tuchman, Chana 262, 265
Tuomisto, A. 114
Tuval-Mashiach, R. 279, 282
Tzivia's land (Palestine) 59

Ukraine 110
Union of the Polish Patriots in USSR 60
United Jewish Appeal 167
United Nations Relief and Rehabilitation Administration (UNRRA) 81, 82, 84, 85, 98
United Nations (UN) 79
United Partisan Organization 60–1
United States xx, 135; and American post-Holocaust memory xxi, 187–95; commemoration of the Holocaust 119; construction of memory in fiction by American Jewish women xxi, 145–63; and the German Democratic Republic 135–7; and Hadassah 165–82; immigration laws 89, 98; and Jewish Displaced Persons 78, 79, 80–1, 85, 94, 98; and the nursing professions 173–6
unity, of the Finnish Jews 113, 116–18
unknown soldier, monuments to 257, <u>258</u>, 260
*Unzer Wort* (newspaper) 74–5
upper classes: identity 282; *see also* capitalist classes; elites
US Army 94
US Congress 137
Ussishkin, Menachem 242

Vaad Leumi (National Committee) 256
victory, of the Finnish Jews 113, 118
Vilkansky, Yitzhak 242

Vilna concentration  59
Vilnay, Zeev  242
violence, and women  159–60
voluntary organizations, American women's  170

Wahrhaftig, Zorach  84
Waksman, Hélène  71
Wald, Lilian D.  179
Wannsee meeting  120
War of Independence (Israeli)  219, 253, 256, 261–2, 264–5, 266
Warburg, Abby  147
Wardi, Rafael  122
Warsaw, and the Hashomer Hatzair movement  56, 57, 58–9, 63
Warsaw ghetto 250; choice in  48; daily life in  30–46, 47–9; disease in  31, 36; income in  35–6, 37, 38; love in  39–41, 42; moral issues  42–3; night killings  33; prostitution in  39, 40, 41–2, 43; resistance fighting in 119; women in  xx, 29–49; and women's leadership in the Hashomer Hatzair movement  59–60, 61
Wasilewska, Wanda  60
Waxman, Hélène  70
wealth  273
Webber, Jonathan  190, 191
Weimar Republic  134
Weinburg, Sam  46
Weinreich, Max  4
Weissberg, Liliane  146
Weisswasser concentration camp  128
Weitz, Yosef  242
Wenk, Silke  128
West Berlin  134
West Germany  79, 138–9
Westerlund, Aarne  117
westernization  213–16, 217, 219–22, 228–9, 230, 233–5
Wiesel, Elie  92, 187, 188
Wilbushewitz, Manya  243
Winter War  112, 113, 114, 116, 117, 118
Wittenberg, Itzik  60–1
Wittig, Arndt  128
WIZO-Hadassah  248, 249
women: American Zionist organizations for (Hadassah)  xxi, 165–82; anger of  26; and the baby boom amongst Jewish survivors  88; bodies of  150–1, 157–9, 160–1; concentration camps for  xx; construction of memory in fiction by American Jewish  xxi, 145–63; position in the Displaced Persons camps 96–7; education of Iraqi Jewish  215, 220–2, 234; exclusion from prayer in Jewish society 169; exclusion in Iraq  221; issues of freedom  146, 146–7, 155, 161–2, 163; gendered nature of the post-Holocaust memories of  187, 188, 189, 190–1, 192–4, 195; identity  xx, xxi, 3–26, 150, 154–5, 159–62, 189–95, 273–7, 279–83; in inter-war Poland  17–18; Iraqi Jewish immigrants in the kibbutz  xxi, 218–35; Israeli settlements named for  xxi, 245–50; and the land/landscape  244, 245; as leaders in left-wing organizations  xx, 51–65; modern day constraints on  146–7, 161–2; monuments to the heroic sacrifice of  252, 253, 256, 257–60, <u>258</u>, <u>259</u>, 261, 262–5, 267; names 240; professions for  169–70, 173–6, 221–2, 227; resistance fighters  xx, 67–75;

restraints on the intellects of  149, 150, 152–3, 154, 161–2; sculptors  xxi, 252–68; use in sculpture 266–7; silence of  275, 277; social standing in Judaism  191, 194; and war memorials  126, <u>127</u>, 128–33, <u>129</u>, <u>131</u>, 134–5, 138–9, 252, 253, 256, 257–60, <u>258</u>, <u>259</u>, 261, 262–5, 267; in the Warsaw ghetto xx, 29–49; work of  30–46, 47–9, 62, 63, 68, 72, 73; *see also* girlhood; girls
Woolf, Virginia  6, 270–1
work: of female resistance fighters  73; female rights to  62, 63; of Polish interwar Jewry  68, 72; of women in the Warsaw ghetto 30–46, 47–9; *see also* professions for women
'Work and Defense', Hulda (Lichansky)  xxi, 252, 256–61, <u>258</u>, 267
working classes, autobiographies  7, 8
World Jewish Congress  123–4, 137
World Maccabi Organization  203
World Zionist Organization  180

Yaari, Meir  57
Yad Chana  250
Yad Tabenkin Archives, Ramat Ef'al  201
Yael  246
Yael (kibbutz)  246
Yanait-Ben-Zvi, Rachel  254, 256, 257
YASK (Worker's Sports Club)  72
Yassky, Haim  176
Yehezkel Sassoon of Baghdad  243
Yesodei ha'Torah schools  11
Yishuv xx, xxi, 61, 260, 267; and Hadassah  172, 173, 177, 180; and Iraqi Jewish immigrants  217, 230, 235, 236; New  203, 210; organizations of  171; and the Zionist Organization of America  177
Yivo (Jewish Scientific Institute), Vilna, autobiography collection  xx, 4–26; advantages/methodological challenges of 5–7; recurrent themes 10–25; sample auto-biographies  8–10
Young, James E.  119
Youth Association of the Communist Party  72
youth, Jewish female: distortions of the memories of  145, 146, 147, 152–4, 162, 163; in interwar Poland  xx, 3–26; *see also* girlhood; girls
Youth League  137
youth movements  xx, 51; and female resistance fighters  72; Polish interwar  9, 10, 13–14, 21, 24–5; traditional Jewish in Libya 200–1; *see also specific movements*; Zionist Youth Movements
Yugoslavia  195

Zamarin  248
Zasulitch, Vera  52
Zeilsheim Displaced Persons camp  83, 88
Zelophehad  247
Zertal, Idith  82
*Zhenotdel*  54
Zikhron Ya'akov  248
Zionism  xx, xxi, 62, 219, 283; American  xxi, 165–82; Betar  16–17; and demands for a national Jewish state in Palestine  79, 81; demonization of 134; female leaders of  60; and female resistance fighters  72, 74, 75; and gender equality  57; Hadassah  xxi, 165–82; and Iraqi Jewish migrants  217, 220, 222, 223, 224, 226, 232, 234, 236; and Jewish Displaced

# Index

Persons 82, 84, 85, 90, 94, 96, 97, 98; monuments of 252–3, 254; myths of heroic sacrifice 256, 260
Zionist Executive 242, 249
Zionist Federation of Canada 249
Zionist Organization of America (ZOA) 165; Conventions 167; crisis 166–7, 181; fundraising 167; golden age 166; major roles 167; male domination of 165–6, 182; political diplomatic efforts 167; stability 177
Zionist Organization of America (ZOA) House, Tel Aviv 167

Zionist Organisation of Canada 242
Zionist Youth Movements: appeal 203–4; communal attitudes to mixed-sex membership 206, 208–9; gender-based graduated development 204–6; ideology and reality 202; inter-gender relations 207–8; Libyan xxi, 199–211; male founders 204; mixed-sex xxi, 199, 201, 202, 204–9; organizations and membership 202–3; problems arising from the mix-sexed environment 206–7; *see also specific organizations*